P9-ECV-437

89.95
6/3/10

Red, White & Black

RED, WHITE & BLACK

Cinema and the Structure
of U.S. Antagonisms

FRANK B. WILDERSON III

DUKE UNIVERSITY PRESS
Durham & London 2010

CHABOT COLLEGE LIBRARY

© 2010 Duke University Press
All rights reserved

Printed in the United States of America on acid-free paper ∞
Designed by Jennifer Hill
Typeset in Adobe Warnock Pro by Achorn International, Inc.

Library of Congress Cataloging-in-Publication Data
appear on the last printed page of this book.

CHABOT COLLEGE LIBRARY

For my parents, Drs. Frank and Ida-Lorraine
Wilderson, who taught me how to think.
And for Anita Wilkins, who shared this journey
with me.

CONTENTS

ACKNOWLEDGMENTS

STRANGE AS it might seem, this book project began in South Africa. During the last years of apartheid I worked for revolutionary change in both an underground and above-ground capacity, for the Charterist Movement in general and the ANC in particular. During this period, I began to see how essential an unflinching paradigmatic analysis is to a movement dedicated to the complete overthrow of an existing order. The neoliberal compromises that the radical elements of the Chartist Movement made with the moderate elements were due, in large part, to our inability or unwillingness to hold the moderates' feet to the fire of a political agenda predicated on an unflinching paradigmatic analysis. Instead, we allowed our energies and points of attention to be displaced by and onto pragmatic considerations. Simply put, we abdicated the power to pose the question—and the power to pose the question is the greatest power of all. Elsewhere, I have written about this unfortunate turn of events (*Incognegro: A Memoir of Exile and Apartheid*), so I'll not rehearse the details here. Suffice it to say, this book germinated in the many political and academic discussions and debates that I was fortunate enough to be a part of at a historic moment and in a place where the word *revolution* was spoken in earnest, free of qualifiers and irony. For their past and ongoing ideas and interventions, I extend solidarity and appreciation to comrades Amanda Alexander, Franco Barchiesi, Teresa Barnes, Patrick Bond, Ashwin Desai, Nigel Gibson, Steven Greenberg, Allan Horowitz, Bushy Kelebonye (deceased), Tefu Kelebonye, Ulrike Kistner, Kamogelo Lekubu, Andile Mngxitama, Prishani Naidoo, John Shai, and S'bu Zulu.

I returned to the United States in the latter part of 1996 and was fortunate enough to pick up the thread of these debates—but in a U.S. context—with political activists who despite their lengthy incarceration, or maybe because of it, had remained true to a vision of comprehensive change. I am speaking of U.S. political prisoners and political exiles living in Cuba. The political prisoners and exiles who have had the greatest impact on my thinking and, subsequently, on the zeitgeist of this book are Nehanda Abiodun, Mumia Abu Jamal, Sundiata Acoli, Charles Sims Africa, Debbie Sims Africa, Janet Holloway Africa, Merle Africa (deceased), Ramona Africa, Safiya Bakhari-Alston (deceased), Herman Bell, Marilyn Buck, Marshall Eddie Conway, Linda Evans, Ruchell Cinque Magee, Jalil Muntaqim, Sekou Odinga, Mutulu Shakur, and Russell Maroon Shoats. They have given generously of their time by way of correspondence with both me and my students. Their perspectives have strengthened our resolve to imbue our research questions with a level of political integrity that is often looked down upon in the academy. Thank you!

My engagement with and critique of Marxism, White feminism, psychoanalysis, postcolonial studies, and film studies would not have evolved into a book were it not for years of challenging exchanges with provocative intellectuals in these fields. Namely, Stephen Barker, Chris Berry, Julia Bryan-Wilson, Thomas Elsaesser, Harun Farocki, Ruth Wilson Gilmore, Renate Holub, Anton Kaes, Steve Martinot, Janet Neary, Joel Olson, Dylan Rodriguez, Mark Sandberg, Donovan Sherman, Kaja Silverman, Charles Sugnet, Gary Whitmer, and Linda Williams.

My three years as a member of a University of California think tank, the Multicampus Research Group on International Performance and Culture, have been a tremendous boon to this project. I have presented chapters and ideas from the book at annual MRG research retreats, as well as to individual group members, and received priceless feedback and editing suggestions. Thank you, Moradewun Adejunmobi, Patrick Anderson, Sue-Ellen Case, Catherine Cole, Susan Foster, Marcela Fuentes, Leo Cabranes Grant, Lynette Hunter, Shannon Jackson, Suk-Young Kim, Daphne Lei, Peter Lichtenfels, Bryan Reynolds, Jon Rossini, John Rouse, Emily Roxworthy, Carol Sorgenfrei, Priya Srinivasan, Shannon Steen, Ngugi wa Thiong'O, and Simon Williams!

J. Reynolds Smith, executive editor at Duke University Press and friend, facilitated the swiftest submission-to-initial-acceptance of a book that I have ever experienced or am likely to experience. Though the subsequent peer-review process ran its normal course, the energy and enthusiasm that Reynolds Smith showed for the original manuscript (within two short weeks of receiving it over the transom!) kept my spirits high as the wheels of the peer-review process turned. In addition, I want to acknowledge how kind and helpful the Duke University Press editorial associate Sharon Parks Torian was at every step along the way.

What is a Black? A subject? An object? A former slave? A slave? The relational status, or lack thereof, of Black subjectivity (subjectivity under erasure) haunts Black studies as a field just at it haunts the socius. Since my return from South Africa, I have had the good fortune to be involved in an extended dialogue about our relational status, with Black intellectuals whose work is both formidable and humbling. They include Lindon Barrett (deceased), Jocelyn Burrell, Gregory L. Caldwell, Barbara Christian (deceased), Huey Copeland, Zakiyyah Iman Jackson, Ronald Judy, Sara Kaplan, Kara Keeling, Claude-Rheal Malary, David Marriott, Fred Moten, Matt Richardson, Omar Ricks, Akinyele Umoja, João C. Vargas, and Jaye Austin Williams.

Adrian Bankhead and Saidiya Hartman read the manuscript and made many helpful suggestions for revisions, but this does not begin to explain my gratitude to them for how they read: as two Black people who looked unflinchingly at the void of our subjectivity, thus helping the manuscript to stay in the hold of the ship, despite my fantasies of flight. And to Raudemar Hernandez Abreu and Alexis Vaubel, a special thanks for reconnecting me with those ancestors who were not afraid to stay with us in the hold of the ship.

The embarrassment of riches of Heinrich Böhmke, Joy James, Amanda Lashaw, and Jared Sexton! What I have said of everyone above I could say of these four and still not have said enough. Heinrich taught me how, in struggle, to embody strategic rigidity but remain tactically flexible. Joy showed me how to maintain one's credentials as an academic without sacrificing one's principles as a revolutionary. In a Gramsci reading group, Amanda was alive to bending Gramsci toward the Black position, and she helped me change my research question from "What does it mean to be free?" to "What does it mean to suffer?" Jared taught me that the truth of the paradigm (though not the totality) is not capital and not Oedipus, but anti-Blackness.

Finally, I extend my appreciation to my partner Anita Wilkins, who encouraged me to "make the problem my topic" during those frustrating moments when seemingly insurmountable problems in theorization threatened to sabotage the forward momentum of the writing. More than that, she shared this intellectual journey with me, for instance, by staying up late many a night to discuss the issues with me, and by incorporating the "problems" of the book into her own teaching, and then generously sharing her pedagogic experiences with me. And she watched the same four films with me over and over again—and never complained. With love and gratitude, thank you.

Unspeakable Ethics

WHEN I WAS a young student at Columbia University in New York there was a Black woman who used to stand outside the gate and yell at Whites, Latinos, and East and South Asian students, staff, and faculty as they entered the university. She accused them of having stolen her sofa and of selling her into slavery. She always winked at the Blacks, though we didn't wink back. Some of us thought her outbursts bigoted and out of step with the burgeoning ethos of multiculturalism and "rainbow coalitions." But others did not wink back because we were too fearful of the possibility that her isolation would become our isolation, and we had come to Columbia for the precise, though largely assumed and unspoken, purpose of foreclosing on that peril. Besides, people said she was crazy. Later, when I attended the University of California at Berkeley, I saw a Native American man sitting on the sidewalk of Telegraph Avenue. On the ground in front of him was an upside-down hat and a sign informing pedestrians that here they could settle the "Land Lease Accounts" that they had neglected to settle all of their lives. He, too, was "crazy."

Leaving aside for the moment their state of mind, it would seem that the structure, that is to say the rebar, or better still the grammar of their demands—and, by extension, the grammar of their suffering—was indeed an ethical grammar. Perhaps it is the only ethical grammar available to modern politics and modernity writ large, for it draws our attention not to how space and time are used and abused by enfranchised and violently powerful interests, but to the violence that underwrites the modern world's capacity to think, act, and exist spatially and temporally. The violence that robbed her of her body and him of his land provided the stage on which other violent and consensual dramas could be enacted. Thus, they would have to be crazy, crazy enough to call not merely the actions of the world but the world itself to account, and to account for *them* no less! The woman at Columbia was not demanding to be a participant in an unethical network of distribution: she was not demanding a place within capital, a piece of the pie (the demand for her sofa notwithstanding). Rather, she was articulating a triangulation between two things. On the one hand was the loss of her body, the very dereliction of her corporeal integrity, what Hortense Spillers charts as the transition from being a being to becoming a "*being* for the captor,"[1] the drama of value (the stage on which surplus value is extracted from labor power through commodity production and sale). On the other was the corporeal integrity that, once ripped from her body, fortified and extended the corporeal integrity of everyone else on the street. She gave birth to the commodity and to the Human, yet she had neither subjectivity nor a sofa to show for it. In her eyes, the world—not its myriad discriminatory practices, but the world itself—was unethical. And yet, the world passes by her without the slightest inclination to stop and disabuse her of her claim. Instead, it calls her "crazy." And to what does the world attribute the Native American man's insanity? "He's crazy if he thinks he's getting any money out of us"? Surely, that doesn't make him crazy. Rather it is simply an indication that he does not have a big enough gun.

What are we to make of a world that responds to the most lucid enunciation of ethics with violence? What are the foundational questions of the ethico-political? Why are these questions so scandalous that they are rarely posed politically, intellectually, and cinematically—unless they are posed obliquely and unconsciously, as if by accident? Give Turtle Island back to the "Savage." Give life itself back to the Slave. Two simple sentences, fourteen simple words, and the structure of U.S. (and perhaps global) antagonisms would be dismantled. An "ethical modernity" would no longer sound like an oxymoron. From there we could busy ourselves with important conflicts that have been promoted to the level of antagonisms, such as class struggle, gender conflict, and immigrants' rights.

One cannot but wonder why questions that go to the heart of the ethico-political, questions of political ontology, are so unspeakable in intellectual meditations, political broadsides, and even socially and politically engaged feature films. Clearly they *can* be spoken, even a child could speak those lines, so they would pose no problem for a scholar, an activist, or a filmmaker. And yet, what is also clear—if the filmographies of socially and politically engaged directors, the archive of progressive scholars, and the plethora of left-wing broadsides are anything to go by—is that what can so easily be spoken is now (500 years and 250 million Settlers/Masters on) so ubiquitously unspoken that these two simple sentences, these fourteen words not only render their speaker "crazy" but become themselves impossible to imagine.

Soon it will be forty years since radical politics, left-leaning scholarship, and socially engaged feature films began to speak the unspeakable.[2] In the 1960s and early 1970s the questions asked by radical politics and scholarship were not *Should the United States be overthrown?* or even *Would it be overthrown?* but when and how—and, for some, what would come in its wake. Those steadfast in their conviction that there remained a discernable quantum of ethics in the United States writ large (and here I am speaking of everyone from Martin Luther King Jr. prior to his 1968 shift, to the Tom Hayden wing of Students for Democratic Society, to the Julian Bond and Marion Barry faction of the Student Nonviolent Coordinating Committee, to Bobby Kennedy Democrats) were accountable, in their rhetorical machinations, to the paradigmatic zeitgeist of the Black Panthers, the American Indian Movement, and the Weather Underground. Radicals and progressives could deride, reject, or chastise armed struggle mercilessly and cavalierly with respect to tactics and the possibility of "success," but they could not dismiss revolution-as-ethic because they could not make a convincing case—by way of a paradigmatic analysis—that the United States was an ethical formation and still hope to maintain credibility as radicals and progressives. Even Bobby Kennedy (as a U.S. attorney general) mused that the law and its enforcers had no

ethical standing in the presence of Blacks.[3] One could (and many did) acknowledge America's strength and power. This seldom rose to the level of
an ethical assessment, however, remaining instead an assessment of the
"balance of forces." The political discourse of Blacks, and to a lesser extent
Indians, circulated too widely to wed the United States and ethics cred-
ibly. The raw force of COINTELPRO put an end to this trajectory toward a
possible hegemony of ethical accountability. Consequently, the power of
Blackness and Redness to pose the question—and the power to pose the
question is the greatest power of all—retreated as did White radicals and
progressives who "retired" from the struggle. The question lies buried in
the graves of young Black Panthers, AIM warriors, and Black Liberation
Army soldiers, or in prison cells where so many of them have been rot-
ting (some in solitary confinement) for ten, twenty, or thirty years, and
at the gates of the academy where the "crazies" shout at passersby. Gone
are not only the young and vibrant voices that effected a seismic shift
on the political landscape, but also the intellectual protocols of inquiry,
and with them a spate of feature films that became authorized, if not by
an unabashed revolutionary polemic, then certainly by a revolutionary
zeitgeist.

Is it still possible for a dream of unfettered ethics, a dream of the Settlement and the Slave estate's[4] destruction, to manifest itself at the ethical
core of cinematic discourse when this dream is no longer a constituent
element of political discourse in the streets or of intellectual discourse in
the academy? The answer is "no" in the sense that, as history has shown,
what cannot be articulated as political discourse in the streets is doubly foreclosed on in screenplays and in scholarly prose, but "yes" in the
sense that in even the most taciturn historical moments, such as ours,
the grammar of Black and Red suffering breaks in on this foreclosure,
albeit like the somatic compliance of hysterical symptoms—it registers in
both cinema and scholarship as a symptom of awareness of the structural
antagonisms. The election of President Barack Obama does not mitigate
the claim that this is a taciturn historical moment. Neoliberalism with a
Black face is neither the index of a revolutionary advance nor the end of
anti-Blackness as a constituent element of U.S. antagonisms. If anything,
the election of Obama enables a plethora of shaming discourses in response to revolutionary politics and "legitimates" widespread disavowal
of any notion that the United States itself, and not merely its policies and

practices, is unethical. Between 1967 and 1980, we could think cinematically and intellectually of Blackness and Redness as having the coherence
of full-blown discourses. From 1980 to the present, however, Blackness
and Redness manifest only in the rebar of cinematic and intellectual (political) discourse, that is, as unspoken grammars.

This grammar can be discerned in the cinematic strategies (lighting,
camera angles, image composition, and acoustic design), even when the
script labors for the spectator to imagine social turmoil through the rubric of conflict (i.e., a rubric of problems that can be posed and conceptually solved) as opposed to the rubric of antagonism (an irreconcilable
struggle between entities, or positions, the resolution of which is not
dialectical but entails the obliteration of one of the positions). In other
words, even when films narrate a story in which Blacks or Indians are
beleaguered with problems that the script insists are conceptually coherent (usually having to do with poverty or the absence of "family values"),
the nonnarrative, or cinematic, strategies of the film often disrupt this
coherence by posing the irreconcilable questions of Red and Black political ontology—or nonontology. The grammar of antagonism breaks in on
the mendacity of conflict.

Semiotics and linguistics teach us that when we speak, our grammar
goes unspoken. Our grammar is assumed. It is the structure through which
the labor of speech is possible.[5] Likewise, the grammar of political ethics—
the grammar of assumptions regarding the ontology of suffering—which
underwrites film theory and political discourse (in this book, discourse
elaborated in direct relation to radical action), and which underwrites
cinematic speech (in this book, Red, White, and Black films from the
mid-1960s to the present) is also unspoken. This notwithstanding, film
theory, political discourse, and cinema assume an ontological grammar,
a structure of suffering. And this structure of suffering crowds out others,
regardless of the sentiment of the film or the spirit of unity mobilized by
the political discourse in question. To put a finer point on it, structures of
ontological suffering stand in antagonistic, rather then conflictual, relation to one another (despite the fact that antagonists themselves may not
be aware of the ontological position from which they speak). Though this
is perhaps the most controversial and out-of-step claim of this book, it
is, nonetheless, the foundation of the close reading of feature films and
political theory that follows.

The difficulty of writing a book which seeks to uncover Red, Black, and White socially engaged feature films as aesthetic accompaniments to grammars of suffering, predicated on the subject positions of the "Savage" and the Slave, is that today's intellectual protocols are not informed by Fanon's insistence that "ontology—once it is finally admitted as leaving existence by the wayside—does not permit us to understand the being of the black man."[6] In sharp contrast to the late 1960s and early 1970s, we now live in a political, academic, and cinematic milieu which stresses "diversity," "unity," "civic participation," "hybridity," "access," and "contribution." The radical fringe of political discourse amounts to little more than a passionate dream of civic reform and social stability. The distance between the protester and the police has narrowed considerably. The effect of this on the academy is that intellectual protocols tend to privilege two of the three domains of subjectivity, namely preconscious interests (as evidenced in the work of social science around "political unity," "social attitudes," "civic participation," and "diversity,") and unconscious identification (as evidenced in the humanities' postmodern regimes of "diversity," "hybridity," and "relative [rather than "master"] narratives"). Since the 1980s, intellectual protocols aligned with structural positionality (except in the work of die-hard Marxists) have been kicked to the curb. That is to say, it is hardly fashionable anymore to think the vagaries of power through the generic positions within a structure of power relations—such as man/woman, worker/boss. Instead, the academy's ensembles of questions are fixated on specific and "unique" experiences of the myriad identities that make up those structural positions. This would be fine if the work led us back to a critique of the paradigm; but most of it does not. Again, the upshot of this is that the intellectual protocols now in play, and the composite effect of cinematic and political discourse since the 1980s, tend to hide rather than make explicit the grammar of suffering which underwrites the United States and its foundational antagonisms. This state of affairs exacerbates—or, more precisely, mystifies and veils—the ontological death of the Slave and the "Savage" because (as in the 1950s) the cinematic, political, and intellectual discourse of the current milieu resists being sanctioned and authorized by the irreconcilable demands of Indigenism and Blackness—academic enquiry is thus no more effective in pursuing a revolutionary critique than the legislative antics of the loyal opposition. This is how left-leaning scholars help civil society recuperate and maintain stability. But this stability is a state of emergency for Indians and Blacks.

The aim of this book is to embark on a paradigmatic analysis of how dispossession is imagined at the intersection of (a) the most unflinching meditations (metacommentaries) on political economy and libidinal economy, (e.g., Marxism, as in the work of Antonio Negri, and psychoanalysis, as in the work of Kaja Silverman), (b) the discourse of political common sense, and (c) the narrative and formal strategies of socially or politically engaged films. In other words, a paradigmatic analysis asks, *What are the constituent elements of, and the assumptive logic regarding, dispossession which underwrite theoretical claims about political and libidinal economy; and how are those elements and assumptions manifest in both political common sense and in political cinema?*

Charles S. Maier argues that a metacommentary on political economy can be thought of as an "interrogation of economic doctrines to disclose their sociological and political premises.... in sum, [it] regards economic ideas and behavior not as frameworks for analysis, but as beliefs and actions that must themselves be explained."[7]

Jared Sexton describes libidinal economy as "the economy, or distribution and arrangement, of desire and identification (their condensation and displacement), and the complex relationship between sexuality and the unconscious." Needless to say, libidinal economy functions variously across scales and is as "objective" as political economy. It is linked not only to forms of attraction, affection, and alliance, but also to aggression, destruction, and the violence of lethal consumption. Sexton emphasizes that it is "the whole structure of psychic and emotional life," something more than, but inclusive of or traversed by, what Antonio Gramsci and other Marxists call a "structure of feeling"; it is "a dispensation of energies, concerns, points of attention, anxieties, pleasures, appetites, revulsions, and phobias capable of both great mobility and tenacious fixation."[8]

This book interrogates the assumptive logic of metacommentaries on political and libidinal economy, and their articulations in film, through a subject whose structure of dispossession (the constituent elements of his or her loss and suffering) they cannot theorize: the Black, a subject who is always already positioned as Slave. The implications of my interrogation reach far beyond film studies, for these metacommentaries not only have the status of paradigmatic analyses, but their reasoning and assumptions permeate the private and quotidian of political common sense and buttress organizing and activism on the left.

In leftist metacommentaries on ontology (and in the political common sense and the radical cinema in fee, however unintentionally, to such metacommentaries), subjects' paradigmatic location, the structure of their relationality, is organized around their capacities: powers subjects have or lack, the constituent elements of subjects' structural position with which they are imbued or lack prior to the subjects' performance. Just as prior to a game of chess, the board and the pieces on it live in a network of antagonisms. The spatial and temporal capacities of the queen (where she is located and where she can move, as well as how she can move) articulate an irreconcilable asymmetry of power between her and a rook or a pawn for example. Vest the rook with the powers of the queen (before the game begins, of course) and it is not the outcome of the game that is in jeopardy so much as the integrity of the paradigm itself—it is no longer chess but something else. And it goes without saying that no piece may leave the board if it is to stand in any relation whatsoever to its contemporaries (asymmetry aside); this would be tantamount to leaving the world, to death. Power relations are extant in the sinews of capacity. For Marxists, the revolutionary objective is not to play the game but to destroy it, to end exploitation and alienation. They see the capacity to accumulate surplus value embodied in one piece, the capitalist, and the embodiment of dispossession as being manifest in the worker. But the worker's essential incapacity (powers which cannot accrue to the worker, suffering as exploitation and alienation) is the essence of capacity, life itself, when looked at through the eyes of the Slave.

Socially or politically engaged films pride themselves on their proclivity to embrace what the Left views as the essence of dispossession: the plight of the exploited and alienated worker. Throughout this book, I argue that as radical and iconoclastic as so many socially or politically engaged films are (and they are indeed a breath of fresh air compared to standard Hollywood fare), in their putative embrace of working-class incapacity there is also, from the standpoint of the Slave, a devastating embrace of Human capacity—that which the Slave lacks. In other words, the narrative strategies of films that articulate the suffering of the worker are shot through with obstinate refusals to surrender their cinematic embrace to the structure of the Slave's domination, something infinitely more severe than exploitation and alienation.

I have little interest in assailing political conservatives. Nor is my argument wedded to the disciplinary needs of political science, or even sociology, where injury must be established, first, as White supremacist event, from which one then embarks on a demonstration of intent, or racism; and, if one is lucky, or foolish, enough, a solution is proposed. If the position of the Black is, as I argue, a paradigmatic impossibility in the Western Hemisphere, indeed, in the world, in other words, if a Black is the very antithesis of a Human subject, as imagined by Marxism and psychoanalysis, then his or her paradigmatic exile is not simply a function of repressive practices on the part of institutions (as political science and sociology would have it). This banishment from the Human fold is to be found most profoundly in the emancipatory meditations of Black people's staunchest "allies," and in some of the most "radical" films. Here—not in restrictive policy, unjust legislation, police brutality, or conservative scholarship—is where the Settler/Master's sinews are most resilient.

The polemic animating this research stems from (1) my reading of Native and Black American metacommentaries on Indian and Black subject positions written over the past twenty-three years and (2) a sense of how much that work appears out of joint with intellectual protocols and political ethics which underwrite political praxis and socially engaged popular cinema in this epoch of multiculturalism and globalization. The sense of abandonment I experience when I read the metacommentaries on Red positionality (by theorists such as Leslie Silko, Ward Churchill, Taiaiake Alfred, Vine Deloria Jr., and Haunani-Kay Trask) and the metacommentaries on Black positionality (by theorists such as David Marriott, Saidiya Hartman, Ronald Judy, Hortense Spillers, Orlando Patterson, and Achille Mbembe) against the deluge of multicultural positivity is overwhelming. One suddenly realizes that, though the semantic field on which subjectivity is imagined has expanded phenomenally through the protocols of multiculturalism and globalization theory, Blackness and an unflinching articulation of Redness are more unimaginable and illegible within this expanded semantic field than they were during the height of the FBI's repressive Counterintelligence Program (COINTELPRO). On the semantic field on which the new protocols are possible, Indigenism can indeed become partially legible through a programmatics of structural adjustment (as fits our globalized era). In other words, for the Indians' subject position to be legible, their *positive* registers of lost or threatened cultural identity must be foregrounded, when in point of fact the antagonistic register of dispossession that Indians "possess" is a position in relation to a socius structured by genocide. As Churchill points out, everyone from Armenians to Jews have been subjected to genocide, but the Indigenous position is one for which genocide is a constitutive element, not merely an historical event, without which Indians would not, paradoxically, "exist."[9]

Regarding the Black position, some might ask why, after claims successfully made on the state by the Civil Rights Movement, do I insist on positing an operational analytic for cinema, film studies, and political theory that appears to be a dichotomous and essentialist pairing of Masters and Slaves? In other words, why should we think of today's Blacks in the United States as Slaves and everyone else (with the exception of Indians) as Masters? One could answer these questions by demonstrating how nothing remotely approaching claims successfully made on the state has come to pass. In other words, the election of a Black president aside, police brutality, mass incarceration, segregated and substandard schools and housing, astronomical rates of HIV infection, and the threat of being turned away en masse at the polls still constitute the lived experience of Black life. But such empirically based rejoinders would lead us in the wrong direction; we would find ourselves on "solid" ground, which would only mystify, rather than clarify, the question. We would be forced to appeal to "facts," the "historical record," and empirical markers of stasis and change, all of which could be turned on their head with more of the same. Underlying such a downward spiral into sociology, political science, history, and public policy debates would be the very rubric that I am calling into question: the grammar of suffering known as exploitation and alienation, the assumptive logic whereby subjective dispossession is arrived at in the calculations between those who sell labor power and those who acquire it. The Black qua the worker. Orlando Patterson has already dispelled this faulty ontological grammar in *Slavery and Social Death*, where he demonstrates how and why work, or forced labor, is not a constituent element of slavery. Once the "solid" plank of "work" is removed from slavery, then the conceptually coherent notion of "claims against the state"—the proposition that the state and civil society are elastic enough to even contemplate the possibility of an emancipatory project for the Black position—disintegrates into thin air. The imaginary of the state and civil society is parasitic on the Middle Passage. Put another way, No slave, no world. And, in addition, as Patterson argues, no slave is *in* the world.

If, as an ontological position, that is, as a grammar of suffering, the Slave is not a laborer but an anti-Human, a position against which Humanity establishes, maintains, and renews its coherence, its corporeal integrity; if the Slave is, to borrow from Patterson, generally dishonored, perpetually open to gratuitous violence, and void of kinship structure, that is, having no relations that need be recognized, a being outside of relationality, then our analysis cannot be approached through the rubric of gains or reversals in struggles with the state and civil society, not unless and until the interlocutor first explains how the Slave is of the world. The onus is not on one who posits the Master/Slave dichotomy but on the one who argues there is a distinction between Slaveness and Blackness. How, when, and where did such a split occur? The woman at the gates of Columbia University awaits an answer.

In "The Black Boy Looks at the White Boy," James Baldwin wrote about "the terrible gap between [Norman Mailer's] life and my own." It is a painful essay in which Baldwin explains how he experienced, through beginning and ending his "friendship" with Mailer, those moments when Blackness inspires White emancipatory dreams and how it feels to suddenly realize the impossibility of the inverse: "The really ghastly thing about trying to convey to a white man the reality of the Negro experience has nothing whatever to do with the fact of color, but has to do with this man's relationship to his own life. He will face in your life only what he is willing to face in his." His long Paris nights with Mailer bore fruit only to the extent that Mailer was able to say, "Me, too." Beyond that was the void which Baldwin carried with him into and, subsequently, out of the "friendship." Baldwin's condemnation of discourses that utilize exploitation and alienation's grammar of suffering is unflinching: "I am afraid that most of the white people I have ever known impressed me as being in the grip of a weird nostalgia, dreaming of a vanished state of security and order, against which dream, unfailingly and unconsciously, they tested and very often lost their lives."[10] He is writing about the encounters between

Blacks and Whites in Paris and New York in the 1950s, but he may as well be writing about the eighteenth-century encounters between Slaves and the rhetoric of new republics like revolutionary France and America.[11]

Early in the essay, Baldwin puts his finger on the nature of the impasse which allows the Black to catalyze White-to-White thought, without risking a White-to-Black encounter: "There is a difference," he writes, "between Norman and myself in that I think he still imagines that he has something to save, whereas I have never had anything to lose."[12] It is not a lack of goodwill or the practice of rhetorical discrimination, nor is it *essentially* the imperatives of the profit motive that prevent the hyperbolic circulation of Blackness from cracking and destabilizing civil society's ontological structure of empathy—even as it cracks and destabilizes "previously accepted categories of thought about politics."[13] The key to this structural prohibition barring Blackness from the conceptual framework of Human empathy can be located in the symbolic value of that "something to save" which Baldwin saw in Mailer. It was not until 1967–68, with such books as *Tell Me How Long the Train's Been Gone*—after he had exhausted himself with *The Fire Next Time*—that Baldwin permitted himself to give up hope and face squarely that the Master/Slave relation itself was the essence of that "something to save."

Toward the end of the first volume of *Capital*—after informing us "that conquest, enslavement, robbery, murder, in short, force, play the greatest part in the methods of primitive accumulation" (e.g., methods which produce the Slave)—Karl Marx makes a humorous but revealing observation about the psychic disposition of the proletariat. In drawing a distinction between the worker and the Slave, Marx points out that the Slave has no wage, no symbolic stand-in for an exchange of labor power. The worker, in contrast, has cash, though not much of it. Here Marx does not comment so much on the not-much-of-it-ness of the worker's chump change, but on the enormous ensemble of cathected investments that such a little bit of change provides: "[It] remains in his mind as something more than a particular use-value. . . . [For] it is the worker himself who converts the money into whatever use-values he desires; it is he who buys commodities as he wishes and, as the *owner of money*, as the buyer of goods, *he stands in precisely the same relationship to the sellers of goods as any other buyer.*"[14]

Marx goes on to tell us that whether the worker saves, hoards, or squanders his money on drink, he "acts as a free agent" and so "learns to control himself, in contrast to the slave, who needs a master."[15] It is sad, in a funny sort of way, to think of a worker standing in the same relationship to the sellers of goods as any other buyer, simply because his use-values can buy a loaf of bread just like the capitalist's capital can. But it is frightening to take this "same relationship" in a direction that Marx does not take it: If workers can buy a loaf of bread, they can also buy a slave. It seems to me that the psychic dimension of a proletariat who "stands in precisely the same relationship" to other members of civil society due to their intramural exchange in mutual, possessive possibilities, the ability to own either a piece of Black flesh or a loaf of white bread or both, is where we must begin to understand the founding antagonism between the something Mailer has to save and the nothing Baldwin has to lose.

David Eltis is emphatic in his assertion that European civil society's decision *not* to hunt for slaves along the banks of the Thames or other rivers in the lands of White people or in prisons or poor houses was a bad business decision that slowed the pace of economic development in both Europe and the "New World." Eltis writes: "No Western European power after the Middle Ages crosses the basic divide separating European workers from full chattel slavery. And while serfdom fell and rose in different parts of early modern Europe and shared characteristics with slavery, serfs were not outsiders either before or after enserfment. The phrase 'long distance serf trade' is an oxymoron."[16]

He goes on to show how population growth patterns in Europe during the 1300s, 1400s, and 1500s far outpaced population growth patterns in Africa. He makes this point not only to demonstrate how devastating chattel slavery was on African population growth patterns—in other words, to highlight its genocidal impact—but also to make an equally profound but commonly overlooked point: Europe was so heavily populated that had the Europeans been more invested in the economic value of chattel slavery than they were in the symbolic value of Black slavery and hence had instituted "a properly exploited system drawing on convicts, prisoners and vagrants. . . . [they] could easily have provided 50,000 [White slaves] a year [to the New World] without serious disruption to either international peace or the existing social institutions that generated and supervised these potential European victims."[17]

I raise Eltis's counterposing of the symbolic value of slavery to the economic value of slavery in order to debunk two gross misunderstandings: One is that work—or alienation and exploitation—is a constituent element of slavery. Slavery, writes Orlando Patterson, "*is the permanent, violent domination of natally alienated and generally dishonored persons.*"[18] Patterson goes to great lengths to delink his three "constituent elements of slavery" from the labor that one is typically forced to perform when one is enslaved. Forced labor is not constitutive of enslavement because whereas it explains a common practice, it does not define the structure of the power relation between those who are slaves and those who are not. In pursuit of his "constituent elements" of slavery, a line of inquiry that helps us separate experience (events) from ontology (the capacities of power—or lack thereof—lodged in distinct and irreconcilable subject positions, e.g., Humans and Slaves), Patterson helps us denaturalize the link between force and labor so that we can theorize the former as a phenomenon that positions a body, ontologically (paradigmatically), and the latter as a possible but not inevitable experience of someone who is socially dead.[19]

The other misunderstanding I am attempting to correct is the notion that the profit motive is the consideration in the slaveocracy that trumps all others. David Marriott, Saidiya Hartman, Ronald Judy, Hortense Spillers, Orlando Patterson, and Achille Mbembe have gone to considerable lengths to show that, in point of fact, slavery is and connotes an ontological status for Blackness; and that the constituent elements of slavery are not exploitation and alienation but accumulation and fungibility (as Hartman puts it):[20] the condition of being owned and traded. Patterson reminds us that though professional athletes and brides in traditional cultures can be said to be bought and sold (when the former is traded among teams and the latter is exchanged for a bride price), they are not slaves because (1) they are not "generally dishonored," meaning they are not stigmatized in their being *prior to any transgressive act or behavior*; (2) they are not "natally alienated," meaning their claims to ascending and descending generations are not denied them; and (3) they have some choice in the relationship, meaning they are not the objects of "naked violence." The relational status of the athlete and the traditional bride is always already recognized and incorporated into relationality writ large. Unlike the Slave, the professional athlete and traditional bride are subjected to accumulation and fungibility as one experience among many experiences, and not as their ontological foundation.

Eltis meticulously explains how the costs of enslavement would have been driven down exponentially had Europeans taken White slaves directly to America rather than sailing from Europe to Africa to take Black slaves to America. He notes that "shipping costs . . . comprised by far the greater part of the price of any form of imported bonded labor in the Americas. If we take into account the time spent collecting a slave cargo on the African coast as well, then the case for sailing directly from Europe with a cargo of [Whites] appears stronger again." Eltis sums up his data by concluding that if European merchants, planters, and statesmen imposed chattel slavery on some members of their own society—say, only 50,000 White slaves per year—then not only would European civil society have been able to absorb the social consequences of these losses (i.e., class warfare would have been unlikely even at this rate of enslavement), but civil society "would [also] have enjoyed lower labor costs, a faster development of the Americas, and higher exports and income levels on both sides of the Atlantic."[21]

But what Whites would have gained in economic value, they would have lost in symbolic value; and it is the latter which structures the libidinal economy of civil society. White chattel slavery would have meant that the aura of the social contract had been completely stripped from the body of the convict, vagrant, beggar, indentured servant, or child. This is a subtle point but one vital to our understanding of the relationship between the world of Blacks and the world of Humans. Even under the most extreme forms of coercion in the late Middle Ages and in the early modern period—for example, the provisional and selective enslavement of English vagrants from the early to mid-1500s to the mid-1700s—"the power of the state over [convicts in the Old World] and the power of the master over [convicts in the New World] was more circumscribed than that of the slave owner over the slave."[22]

Marx himself takes note of the preconscious political—and, by implication, unconscious libidinal—costs to civil society, had European elites been willing to enslave Whites.[23] In fact, the antivagabond laws of King Edward VI (1547) proclaimed,

If anyone refuses to work, he shall be condemned as a slave to the person who has denounced him as an idler. The master shall feed his slave
on bread and water, weak broth and such refuse meat as he thinks fit.
He has the right to force him to do any work, no matter how disgust-
ing, with whip and chains. If the slave is absent for a fortnight, he is
condemned to slavery for life and is to be branded on the forehead or
back with the letter S. . . . The master can sell him, bequeath him, let
him out on hire as a slave, *just as he can any other personal chattel or
cattle.* . . . All persons have the right to take away the children of the
vagabonds and keep them as apprentices, the young men until they
are 24, the girls until they are 20.[24]

These laws were so controversial, even among elites, that they could
never take hold as widespread social and economic phenomena. But I am
more interested in the symbolic value of Whiteness (and the absence of
Blackness's value), gleaned from a close reading of the laws themselves
than I am in a historical account of the lived experience of the White
poor's resistance to, or the White elite's ambivalence toward, such ordinances. The actual ordinance manifests the symptoms of its own internal
resistance long before either parliament or the poor themselves mount
external challenges to it.

Symptomatic of civil society's libidinal safety net is the above ordinance's repeated use of the word *if*: "If anyone refuses to work . . ." "If the
slave is absent for a fortnight . . ." The violence of slavery is repeatedly
checked, subdued into becoming a contingent violence for that entity
which is beginning to call itself "White" at the very same moment that
it is being ratcheted up to a gratuitous violence for that entity which is
being called (by Whites) "Black." All the ordinances of the sixteenth, seventeenth, and eighteenth centuries which Marx either quotes at length or
discusses are ordinances which seem, on their face, to debunk my claim
that slavery for Whites was and is experiential and that for Blacks it was
and is ontological. And yet all of these ordinances are riddled with con-
tingencies, of which frequent and unfettered deployment of the conjunction *if* is emblematic.

Spillers and Eltis remind us that the archive of African slavery shows
no internal recognition of the libidinal costs of turning human bodies into
sentient flesh. From Marx's reports on proposed vagabond-into-slave

legislation, it becomes clear that the libidinal economy of such European legislation is far too unconsciously invested in "saving" the symbolic value of the very vagabonds such laws consciously seek to enslave. In other words, the law would rather shoot itself in the foot (i.e., sacrifice the economic development of the New World) than step into a subjective void where idlers and vagabonds might find themselves without contemporaries, with no relational status to save.

In this way, White-on-White violence is put in check (a) before it becomes gratuitous, or structural, before it can shred the fabric of civil society beyond mending; and (b) before conscious, predictable, and sometimes costly challenges are mounted against the legislation despite its dissembling lack of resolve. This is accomplished by the imposition of the numerous *on condition that* and *supposing that* clauses bound up in the word *if* and also by claims bound up in the language around the enslavement of European children: a White child may be enslaved *on condition that* she or he is the child of a vagabond, and then, only until the age of twenty or twenty four.

Spillers searched the archives for a similar kind of stop-gap language with respect to the African—some indication of the African's human value in the libidinal economy of Little Baby Civil Society. She came up empty-handed: "Expecting to find direct and amplified reference to African women during the opening years of the Trade, the observer is disappointed time and again that this cultural subject is concealed beneath the overwhelming debris of the itemized account, between the lines of the massive logs of commercial enterprise [e.g., a ship's cargo record] that overrun the sense of clarity we believed we had gained concerning this collective humiliation."[25]

It would be reassuring to say that Europeans rigorously debated the ethical implications of forcing the social death of slavery on Africans before they went ahead with it; but, as Marx, Eltis, and Spillers make abundantly clear, it would be more accurate simply to say that African slavery did not present an ethical dilemma for global civil society. The ethical dilemmas were unthought.

During the emergence of new ontological relations in the modern world, from the late Middle Ages through the 1500s, many different kinds of people experienced slavery. In other words, there have been times when natal alienation, general dishonor, and gratuitous violence have turned individuals of myriad ethnicities and races into beings who are socially dead. But *African*, or more precisely *Blackness*, refers to an individual who is by definition always already void of relationality. Thus modernity marks the emergence of a new ontology because it is an era in which an entire race appears, people who, a priori, that is prior to the contingency of the "transgressive act" (such as losing a war or being convicted of a crime), stand as socially dead in relation to the rest of the world. This, I will argue, is as true for those who were herded onto the slave ships as it is for those who had no knowledge whatsoever of the coffles. In this period, chattel slavery, as a condition of ontology and not just as an event of experience, stuck to the African like Velcro. To the extent that we can think the essence of Whiteness and the essence of Blackness, we must think their essences through the structure of the Master/Slave relation. It should be clear by now that I am not only drawing a distinction between what is commonly thought of as the Master/Slave relation and the constituent elements of the Master/Slave relation,[26] but I am also drawing a distinction between the experience of slavery (which anyone can be subjected to) and the ontology of slavery, which in modernity (the years 1300 to the present) becomes the singular purview of the Black. In this period, slavery is *cathedralized*. It "advances" from a word which describes a condition that anyone can be subjected to, to a word which reconfigures the African body into Black flesh. Far from being merely the experience of the African, slavery is now the African's access to (or, more correctly, banishment from) ontology.

In their own ways, Spillers, a Black woman and cultural historian, and Eltis, a White historian of the transatlantic slave trade, make the similar points. First, they claim that the pre-Columbian period, or the late Middle Ages (1300–1500), was a moment in which Europe, the Arab world, and Asia found themselves at an ontological crossroads in society's ability to meditate on its own existence. Second, Spillers and Eltis ask whether the poor, convicts, vagrants, and beggars of any given society (French, German, Dutch, Arab, East Asian) should be condemned to a life of natal alienation. Should they have social death forced on them in lieu of real death (i.e., executions)? Should this form of chattel slavery be imposed on the internal poor, en masse—that is, should the scale of White slavery (to the extent that any one nation carried it out at all) become industrial?

And, most important, should the progeny of the White slave be enslaved as well?

It took some time for this argument to unfold. Eltis suggests the argument ensued—depending on the country—from 1200 to the mid-1400s (1413–23), and that, whereas it was easily and forthrightly settled in places like England and the Netherlands, in other countries like Portugal, parts of southern France, and parts of the Arab world, the question waxed and waned.

Again, what is important for us to glean from these historians is that the pre-Columbian period, the late Middle Ages, reveals no archive of debate on these three questions as they might be related to that massive group of black-skinned people south of the Sahara. Eltis suggests that there was indeed massive debate which ultimately led to Britain taking the lead in the abolition of slavery, but he reminds us that that debate did not have its roots in the late Middle Ages, the post-Columbian period of the 1500s or the Virginia colony period of the 1600s. It was, he asserts, an outgrowth of the mid- to late eighteenth-century emancipatory thrust—intra-Human disputes such as the French and American revolutions—that swept through Europe. But Eltis does not take his analysis further than this. Therefore, it is important that we not be swayed by his optimism about the Enlightenment and its subsequent abolitionist discourses. It is highly conceivable that the discourse that elaborates the justification for freeing the slave is not the product of the Human being having suddenly and miraculously recognized the slave. Rather, as Saidiya Hartman argues, emancipatory discourses present themselves to us as further evidence of the Slave's fungibility: "The figurative capacities of blackness enable white flights of fancy while increasing the likelihood of the captive's disappearance."[27] First, the questions of Humanism were elaborated in contradistinction to the human void, to the African qua chattel (the 1200s to the end of the 1600s). Second, as the presence of Black chattel in the midst of exploited and unexploited Humans (workers and bosses, respectively) became a fact of the world, exploited Humans (in the throes of class conflict with unexploited Humans) seized the image of the Slave as an enabling vehicle that animated the evolving discourses of their own emancipation, just as unexploited Humans had seized the flesh of the Slave to increase their profits.

Without this gratuitous violence, a violence that marks everyone experientially until the late Middle Ages when it starts to mark the Black ontologically, the so-called great emancipatory discourses of modernity—Marxism, feminism, postcolonialism, sexual liberation, and the ecology movement—political discourses predicated on grammars of suffering and whose constituent elements are exploitation and alienation, might not have developed.[28] Chattel slavery did not simply reterritorialize the ontology of the African. It also created the Human out of culturally disparate entities from Europe to the East.

I am not suggesting that across the globe Humanism developed in the same way regardless of region or culture; what I am saying is that the late Middle Ages gave rise to an ontological category—an ensemble of common existential concerns—which made and continues to make possible both war and peace, conflict and resolution, between the disparate members of the human race, East and West. Senator Thomas Hart Benton intuited this notion of the existential commons when he wrote that though the "Yellow race" and its culture had been "torpid and stationary for thousands of years . . . [Whites and Asians] must talk together, and trade together, and marry together. Commerce is a great civilizer—social intercourse as great—and marriage greater."[29] Eltis points out that as late as the seventeenth century, "prisoners taken in the course of European military action . . . could expect death if they were leaders, or banishment if they were deemed followers, but never enslavement. . . . Detention followed by prisoner exchanges or ransoming was common." "By the seventeenth century, enslavement of fellow Europeans was beyond the limits" of Humanism's existential commons, even in times of war.[30] Slave status "was reserved for non-Christians. Even the latter group however . . . had some prospect of release in exchange for Christians held by rulers of Algiers, Tunis, and other Mediterranean Muslim powers."[31] But though the practice of enslaving the vanquished was beyond the limit of wars among Western peoples and only practiced provisionally in East-West conflicts, the baseness of the option was not debated when it came to the African. The race of Humanism (White, Asian, South Asian, and Arab) could not have produced itself without the simultaneous production of that walking destruction which became known as the Black. Put another way, through chattel slavery the world gave birth and coherence to both its joys of domesticity and to its struggles of political discontent; and

with these joys and struggles the Human was born, but not before it murdered the Black, forging a symbiosis between the political ontology of
Humanity and the social death of Blacks.

In his essay "To 'Corroborate Our Claims': Public Positioning and the
Slavery Metaphor in Revolutionary America," Peter Dorsey (in his con-
currence with the cultural historians F. Nwabueze Okoye and Patricia
Bradley) suggests that in mid- to late eighteenth-century America Blackness was such a fungible commodity that it was traded as freely between
the exploited (workers who did not "own" slaves) as it was between the
unexploited (planters who did). This was due to the effective uses to which
Whites could put the Slave as both flesh and metaphor. For the revolutionaries, "slavery represented a 'nightmare' that white Americans were
trying to avoid."[32] Dorsey's claim is provocative, but not unsupported: he
maintains that had Blacks-as-Slaves not been in the White field of vision
on a daily basis that it would have been virtually impossible for Whites to
transform themselves from colonial subjects into revolutionaries:

> Especially prominent in the rhetoric and reality of the [revolutionary]
> era, the concepts of freedom and slavery were applied to a wide vari-
> ety of events and values and were constantly being defined and rede-
> fined. . . . Early understandings of American freedom were in many
> ways dependent on the existence of chattel slavery. . . . [We should]
> see slavery in revolutionary discourse, not merely as a hyperbolic rhe-
> torical device but as a crucial and fluid [fungible] concept that had a
> major impact on the way early Americans thought about their politi-
> cal future. . . . The slavery metaphor destabilized previously accepted
> categories of thought about politics, race, and the early republic.[33]

Though the idea of "taxation without representation" may have spoken
concretely to the idiom of power that marked the British/American relation as being structurally unethical, it did not provide metaphors powerful
and fungible enough for Whites to meditate and move on when resisting
the structure of their own subordination at the hands of "unchecked political power."[34]

The most salient feature of Dorsey's findings is not his understanding
of the way Blackness, as a crucial and fungible conceptual possession of
civil society, impacts and destabilizes previously accepted categories of
intra-White thought. Most important, instead, is his contribution to the

evidence that, even when Blackness is deployed to stretch the elasticity of civil society to the point of civil war, that expansion is never elastic enough to embrace the very Black who catalyzed the expansion. In fact, Dorsey, building on Bradley's historical research, asserts that just the opposite is true. The more the political imagination of civil society is enabled by the fungibility of the slave metaphor, the less legible the condition of the slave becomes: "Focusing primarily on colonial newspapers . . . Bradley finds that the slavery metaphor 'served to distance the patriot agenda from the antislavery movement.' If anything, Bradley states, widespread use of the metaphor 'gave first evidence that the issue of real slavery was not to have a part in the revolutionary messages.' "[35] And Eltis believes that this philosophical incongruity between the image of the Slave and freedom for the Slave begins in Europe and predates the American Revolution by at least one hundred years: "The [European] countries least likely to enslave their own had the harshest and most sophisticated system of exploiting enslaved non-Europeans. Overall, the English and Dutch conception of the role of the individual in metropolitan society ensured the accelerated development of African chattel slavery in the Americas . . . because their own subjects could not become chattel slaves or even convicts for life."[36]

Furthermore, the circulation of Blackness as metaphor and image at the most politically volatile and progressive moments in history (e.g., the French, English, and American revolutions) produces dreams of liberation which are more inessential to and more parasitic on the Black, and more emphatic in their guarantee of Black suffering, than any dream of human liberation in any era heretofore.

Black slavery is foundational to modern Humanism's ontics because "freedom" is the hub of Humanism's infinite conceptual trajectories. But these trajectories only appear to be infinite. They are finite in the sense that they are predicated on the idea of freedom from some contingency that can be named, or at least conceptualized. The contingent rider could be freedom from patriarchy, freedom from economic exploitation, freedom from political tyranny (e.g., taxation without representation), freedom from heteronormativity, and so on. What I am suggesting is that first political discourse recognizes freedom as a structuring ontologic and then it works to disavow this recognition by imagining freedom not through political ontology—where it rightfully began—but through political experience (and practice); whereupon it immediately loses its ontological foundations. Why would anyone do this? Why would anyone start off with, quite literally, an earth-shattering ontologic and, in the process of meditating on it and acting through it, reduce it to an earth-reforming experience? Why do Humans take such pride in self-adjustment, in diminishing, rather than intensifying, the project of liberation (how did we get from 1968 to the present)? Because, I contend, in allowing the notion of freedom to attain the ethical purity of its ontological status, one would have to lose one's Human coordinates and become Black. Which is to say one would have to die.

For the Black, freedom is an ontological, rather than experiential, question. There is no philosophically credible way to attach an experiential, a contingent, rider onto the notion of freedom when one considers the Black—such as freedom from gender or economic oppression, the kind of contingent riders rightfully placed on the non-Black when thinking freedom. Rather, the riders that one could place on Black freedom would be hyperbolic—though no less true—and ultimately untenable: freedom from the world, freedom from Humanity, freedom from everyone (including one's Black self). Given the reigning episteme, what are the chances of elaborating a comprehensive, much less translatable and communicable, political project out of the necessity of freedom as an absolute? Gratuitous freedom has never been a trajectory of Humanist thought, which is why the infinite trajectories of freedom that emanate from Humanism's hub are anything but infinite—for they have no line of flight leading to the Slave.

A Note on Method

Throughout this book I use *White*, *Human*, *Master*, *Settler*, and sometimes *non-Black* interchangeably to connote a paradigmatic entity that exists ontologically as a position of life in relation to the Black or Slave position, one of death. The Red, Indigenous, or "Savage" position exists liminally as half-death and half-life between the Slave (Black) and the Human (White, or non-Black). I capitalize the words *Red*, *White*, *Black*, *Slave*, *Savage*, and *Human* in order to assert their importance as ontological positions and to stress the value of theorizing power politically rather than culturally. I want to move from a politics of culture to a culture of politics (as I argue in chapter 2). Capitalizing these words is consistent with my argument that the array of identities that they contain is important but inessential to an analysis of the paradigm of power in which they are positioned. Readers wedded to cultural diversity and historical specificity may find such shorthand wanting. But those who may be put off by my pressing historical and cultural particularities—culled from history, sociology, and cultural studies, yet neither historical, sociological, nor, oddly enough, cultural—should bear in mind that there are precedents for such methods, two of which make cultural studies and much of social science possible: the methods of Karl Marx and Jacques Lacan. Marx pressed the microcosm of the English manufacturer into the service of a project that sought to explain economic relationality on a global scale. Lacan's exemplary cartography was even smaller: a tiny room with not much more than a sofa and a chair, the room of the psychoanalytic encounter. As Jonathan Lee reminds us, at stake in Lacan's account of the psychoanalytic encounter is the realization of subjectivity itself, "the very being of the subject."[37] I argue that "Savage," Human, and Slave should be theorized in the way we theorize worker and capitalist as positions first and as identities second, or as we theorize capitalism as a paradigm rather than as an experience—that is, before they take on national origin or gendered specificity. Throughout the course of this book I argue that "Savage," Human, and Slave are more essential to our understanding of the truth of institutionality than the positions from political or libidinal economy. For in this trio we find the key to our world's creation as well as to its undoing. This argument, as it relates to political economy, continues in chapter 1, "The Ruse of Analogy." In chapter 2, "The Narcissistic Slave," I shift focus from political economy to libidinal economy before undertaking more concrete analyses of films in parts 2, 3, and 4.

No one makes films and declares their own films "Human" while simultaneously asserting that other films (Red and Black) are not Human cinema. Civil society represents itself to itself as being infinitely inclusive, and its technologies of hegemony (including cinema) are mobilized to manufacture this assertion, not to dissent from it. In my quest to interrogate the bad faith of the civic "invitation," I have chosen White cinema as the sine qua non of Human cinema. Films can be thought of as one of an ensemble of discursive practices mobilized by civil society to "invite," or interpellate, Blacks to the same variety of social identities that other races are able to embody without contradiction, identities such as worker, soldier, immigrant, brother, sister, father, mother, and citizen. The bad faith of this invitation, this faux interpellation, can be discerned by deconstructing the way cinema's narrative strategies displace our consideration and understanding of the ontological status of Blacks (social death) onto a series of fanciful stories that are organized around conflicts which are the purview only of those who are not natally alienated, generally dishonored, or open to gratuitous violence, in other words, people who are White or colored but who are not Black. (I leave aside, for the moment, the liminality of the Native American position—oscillating as it does between the living and the dead.)

Immigrant cinema of those who are not White would have sufficed as well; but, due to its exceptional capacity to escape racial markers, Whiteness is the most impeccable embodiment of what it means to be Human. As Richard Dyer writes, "Having no content, we [White people] can't see that we have anything that accounts for our position of privilege and power. . . . The equation of being white with being human secures a position of power." He goes on to explain how "the privilege of being white . . . is not to be subjected to stereotyping in relation to one's whiteness. White people are stereotyped in terms of gender, nation, class, sexuality, ability and so on, but the overt point of such typification is gender, nation, etc. Whiteness generally colonises the stereotypical definition of all social categories other than those of race."[38]

Unlike Dyer, I do not meditate on the representational power of Whiteness, "that it be made strange," divested of its imperial capacity, and thus make way for representational practices in cinema and beyond that serve as aesthetic accompaniments for a more egalitarian civil society in which Whites and non-Whites could live in harmony. Laudable as that dream is, I do not share Dyer's assumption that we are all Human. Some of us are only part Human ("Savage") and some of us are Black (Slave). I find his argument that Whiteness possesses the easiest claim to Humanness to be productive. But whereas Dyer offers this argument as a lament for a social ill that needs to be corrected, I borrow it merely for its explanatory power—as a way into a paradigmatic analysis that clarifies structural relations of global antagonisms and not as a step toward healing the wounds of social relations in civil society. Hence this book's interchangeable deployment of *White*, *Settler*, and *Master* with—and to signify—Human. Again, like Lacan, who mobilizes the psychoanalytic encounter to make

claims about the structure of relations writ large, and like Marx, who mobilizes the English manufacturer to make claims about the structure of
economic relations writ large, I am mobilizing three races, four films, and
one subcontinent to make equally generalizable claims and argue that
the antagonism between Black and Human supercedes the "antagonism"
between worker and capitalist in political economy, as well as the gendered "antagonism" in libidinal economy. To this end, this book takes
stock of how socially engaged popular cinema participates in the systemic
violence that constructs America as a "settler society" (Churchill) and
"slave estate" (Spillers). Rather than privilege a politics of culture(s)—that
is, rather than examine and accept the cultural gestures and declarations
which the three groups under examination make about themselves—I
privilege a culture of politics: in other words, what I am concerned with
is how White film, Black film, and Red film articulate and disavow the
matrix of violence which constructs the three essential positions which
in turn structure U.S. antagonisms.

Part 2, "*Antwone Fisher* and *Bush Mama*" considers pitfalls of em-
plotting the Slave in cinematic narratives. Through an analysis of Denzel
Washington's *Antwone Fisher* and Haile Gerima's *Bush Mama*, I illustrate
what happens when sentient objects perform as sentient subjects. This is
the problem of the Slave film—that is, a film where the director is Black.
In addition, to qualify as a Slave film the narrative strategies of the film
must intend for the film's ethical dilemma(s) to be shouldered by a central
figure (or figures if the film is an ensemble piece) who is Black. The aim of
part 2 is to explore how films labeled Slave by the position of their director and their diegetic figures labor imaginatively in ways which accompany the discursive labor of Slave ethics, ethics manifest in the ontology
of captivity and death or accumulation and fungibility. Furthermore, part
2 seeks to explore those cinematic moments (in the synchronicity of the
story on celluloid and in the diachronicity of the film's historical context)
when the Slave film is unable to embrace ethical dilemmas predicated
on the destruction of civil society and instead makes a structural adjustment, as it were, that embraces the ethical scaffolding of the Settler/
Master's ensemble of questions concerning institutional integrity.

The narrative progression of most films moves from equilibrium to
disequilibrium to equilibrium (restored, renewed, or reorganized). This
is also the narrative spine of most political theory (e.g., Antonio Negri's

and Michael Hardt's writings on the fate of the commons under capitalism). This is true whether or not the film is edited chronologically or associationally. *Antwone Fisher* (2002) is a perfect example of how this three-point progression of classical narrative works and why it cannot emplot the Slave. The film begins with Antwone's dream of a large family gathering at which he is the center of attention (equilibrium). But Antwone soon awakes to the disequilibrium of his life as a Navy seaman with anger management issues, juxtaposed with the disequilibrium of his memories as a foster child, abused and terrorized by Black women. The film ends with the opening dream blossoming in his waking life, as he is reunited with his long-lost blood relations. The assertion of the film is that Antwone's period of disequilibrium is not to be found in the structure of his ontological condition, but rather in the performance of his actions (his anger problem) and the actions of those around him (the abuse he suffered in the foster home).

Thus the film is able to emplot a Black person (invite him into the fold of civic relations) by telling the story of his life episodically and not paradigmatically. It narrates events while mystifying relations between capacity and the absence of capacity. This allows cinema to disavow the quintessential problem of the oxymoron *slave narrative*. The three-point progression of a drama for the living cannot be applied to a being that is socially dead (natally alienated, open to gratuitous violence, and generally dishonored). To "fix" the oxymoron, cinema must either disavow it (cast Blacks as other than Black) or tell the story in such a way that equilibrium is imagined as a period before enslavement. Disequilibrium then becomes the period of enslavement, and the restoration or reorganization of equilibrium is the end of slavery and a life beyond it. The second approach is rare because it is best suited for a straightforward historical drama, such as *Roots*, and because deep within civil society's collective unconscious is the knowledge that the Black position is indeed a position, not an identity, and that its constituent elements are coterminous with and inextricably bound to the constituent elements of social death—which is to say that for Blackness there is no narrative moment prior to slavery. Furthermore, a hypothetical moment after slavery would entail the emergence of new ontological relations (the end of both Blackness and Humanness) and a new episteme. It is impossible for narrative to enunciate from beyond the episteme in which it stands, not knowingly, at least. At the heart of my deliberations on Slave cinema is the question *How does a film tell the story of a being that has no story?*

By Red or "Savage" film I mean, of course, a film where the director is a North American Indian and where the film's narrative strategies intend for its ethical dilemma (or dilemmas) to be shouldered by a central figure (or ensemble cast) that is Indian. Unlike Settler/Master or Slave film, however, there is no risk in reifying a definition of "Savage" cinema through dubious and unnecessary canon formation because the filmography is just emerging. The first component of my argument, which exists throughout part 3, "*Skins*," is that sovereignty or sovereign loss, as a modality of the "Savage" grammar of suffering, articulates itself quite well within the two modalities of the Settler/Master's grammar of suffering, exploitation, and alienation. The second component of my argument is that, whereas the genocidal modality of the "Savage" grammar of suffering articulates itself quite well within the two modalities of the Slave's grammar of suffering, accumulation and fungibility, Native American film, political texts, and ontological meditations fail to recognize, much less pursue, this articulation. The small corpus of socially engaged films directed by Native Americans privilege the ensemble of questions animated by the imaginary of sovereign loss. However, the libidinal economy of cinema is so powerful that the ensemble of questions catalyzed by the genocide grammar of suffering often force their way into the narrative of these films, with a vengeance that exceeds their modest treatment in the screenplay. Chris Eyre's *Skins* is exemplary of these pitfalls and possibilities.

Part 4, "*Monster's Ball*," explores the relationship between (a) Settler/Master (Human) cinema that self-consciously engages political ethics, (b) radical political discourse (what does it mean to be free?) in the era of the film's release, and (c) the Settler/Master's most unflinching metacommentary on the ontology of suffering. By "Settler/Master film," I mean a film whose director is White.[39] In addition, to qualify as a Settler/Master film the narrative strategies of the film must intend for the film's ethical dilemma(s) to be shouldered by a central figure (or ensemble cast) that is White. Again, a film founded on the ethical dilemmas of any of the junior partners of civil society (colored immigrants) would work just as well. My goal is not to establish the canonical boundaries of Settler/Master cinema but to explore how a film labeled White by the position of its director and diegetic figures labors imaginatively in ways which accompany the discursive labor of ethics for the Settler/Master relationship and for civil society. I also seek to explore those cinematic moments—in the synchronicity of the story on celluloid and in the diachronicity of the film's historical context—when the Settler/Master film tries (is perhaps compelled) to embrace ethical dilemmas predicated on the destruction of civil society—the ethical dilemmas of the "Savage" and the Slave.

I do not claim to have cornered the market on a definition of socially engaged feature film. Ultimately, the power of a film like *Mary Poppins* to help reposition a subject politically or explain paradigmatic power relations cannot be adjudicated, definitively, against a film like *The Battle of Algiers*. While my own interests and pleasures lead me more toward the end of the spectrum where *The Battle of Algiers* resides, I have selected films which have consciously attempted some sort of dialogue with the pressing issues and social forces that mobilize America's most active political formations. *Bush Mama* (1978), *Antwone Fisher* (2002), *Monster's Ball* (2001), and *Skins* (2002) are examples of Slave, Settler/Master, and "Savage" films which, at the level of intentionality, attempt cinematic dialogues with issues such as homelessness, the "crisis" of Black and Red families, and the social force of incarceration. Though I have spent years screening, analyzing, and writing about a large number of films that fall into these categories, for the purpose of demonstrating the importance of such films in our unconscious and unspoken knowledge of grammars of suffering, I have found it more effective to perform a close reading of four such films rather than write a book that surveys the field. Given the gesture of sincerity with which such films announce themselves to be socially engaged, I seek to determine how unflinchingly they analyze the structure of U.S. antagonisms.

The three structuring positions of the United States (Whites, Indians, Blacks) are elaborated by a rubric of three demands: the (White) demand for expansion, the (Indian) demand for return of the land, and the (Black) demand for "flesh" reparation (Spillers). The relation between these positions demarcates antagonisms and not conflicts because, as I have argued, they are the embodiments of opposing and irreconcilable principles or forces that hold out no hope for dialectical synthesis, and because they are relations that form the foundation on which all subsequent conflicts in the Western Hemisphere are possible. In other words, the originary, or ontological, violence that elaborates the Settler/Master, the "Savage," and the Slave positions is foundational to the violence of class warfare, ethnic conflicts, immigrant battles, and the women's liberation struggles of Settler/Masters. These antagonisms—whether acknowledged through the conscious and empirical machinations of political economy or painstakingly disavowed through what Jared Sexton terms the "imaginative labor" of libidinal economy—render all other disputes as conflicts, or what Haunani-Kay Trask calls "intra-settler discussions."[40]

As I stated above, in the 1960s and 1970s, as White radicalism's discourse and political common sense found authorization in the ethical dilemmas of embodied incapacity (the ontological status of Blacks as accumulated and fungible objects), White cinema's proclivity to embrace dispossession through the vectors of capacity (the ontological status of the Human as an exploited and alienated subject) became profoundly disturbed. While many socially and politically engaged film scripts and cinematic strategies did not surrender completely to incapacity (i.e., to the authority of the Slave's grammar of suffering), many failed to assert the legitimacy of White ethical dilemmas (the supremacy of exploitation and alienation as a grammar of suffering) with which cinema had been historically preoccupied.[41] The period during which COINTELPRO crushed the Black Panthers and the Black Liberation Army also witnessed the flowering of Blackness's political power—not so much as institutional capacity but as a zeitgeist, a demand that authorized White radicalism. But by 1980 White radicalism had comfortably re-embraced capacity without the threat of disturbance—it returned to the discontents of civil society with the same formal tenacity as it had from 1532[42] to 1967, only now that formal tenacity was emboldened by a wider range of alibis than simply free speech or the antiwar movement; it had, for example, the women's, gay, antinuclear, environmental, and immigrants' rights movements as lines of flight from the absolute ethics of Redness and Blackness. It was able to reform (reorganize) an unethical world and still sleep at night. Today, such intrasettler discussions are the foundation of the "radical" agenda.

At the beginning of the twenty-first century, the irreconcilable demands embodied in the "Savage" and the Slave are being smashed by the two stone-crushers of sheer force and liberal Humanist discourses such as "access to institutionality," "meritocracy," "multiculturalism," and "diversity"—discourses that proliferate exponentially across the political, academic, and cinematic landscapes. Given the violent state repression of Red, White, and Black political movements in the 1960s and 1970s, and the forces of multiculturalism and neoliberalism in the 1980s and 1990s, my project asks whether it is or ever was possible for the feature film, as institution and as text, to articulate a political ethics that acknowledges the structure of U.S. antagonisms. Unlike radically unsettled settler societies, such as Israel and pre-1994 South Africa, the structure of antagonisms is too submerged in the United States to become a full-fledged discourse readily bandied about in civil society—the way a grammar is submerged in speech. Film studies and socially engaged popular films constitute important terrains which, like other institutions in the United States, work to disavow the structure of antagonisms; but they also provide interesting sites for what is known in psychoanalysis as repetition compulsion and the return of the repressed.

My analysis of socially engaged feature films insists on an intellectual protocol through which the scholarship of preconscious interests and unconscious identifications are held accountable to grammars of suffering—accountable, that is, to protocols of structural positionality. In this way, the ontological differences between Red, White, and Black grammars of suffering are best examined in relation to one another. To this end, this book explains the rhetorical structure of Settler/Master (i.e., Gramsci, Lacan, Negri, Fortunati), "Savage" (Trask, Alfred, Churchill, Deloria), and Slave (Fanon, Spillers, Mbembe, Hartman, Judy, Marriott, Orlando Patterson) grammars of ontological suffering; and it shows how these three grammars are predicated on fundamental, though fundamentally different, relationships to violence. Poststructuralism makes the case that language (Lacan) and more broadly discourse (Foucault) are the modalities which, in the first ontological instance, position the subject structurally. I have no qualms with poststructuralism's toolbox per se. What I am arguing for is a radical return to Fanon, to an apprehension of how gratuitous violence positions the "Savage" and the Slave, and how the freedom from violence's gratuitousness, not violence itself, positions the Settler/Master.

Another aim of this book is to show how these different relationships to violence are structurally irreconcilable between the Master and the Slave and only partially reconcilable between the Settler and the "Savage."

A rhetorical analysis of Settler, "Savage," and Slave metacommentaries on suffering that runs alongside my analysis of film will show these meditations to spring from the irreconcilability between, on the one hand, a "Savage" object of genocide or a Slave object of captivity and fungibility and, on the other, a Settler subject of exploitation and alienation. This leads us back to the perplexing question of the "Savage"/Slave relation. Whether violence between the "Savage" and the Slave is essentially structural or performative is not a question that has been addressed at the level of the paradigm by those who meditate on positional ontology (Ronald Judy notwithstanding). It is a question we turn to now in chapter 1, "The Ruse of Analogy."

1

The Structure of
Antagonisms

ONE

The Ruse of Analogy

THIRTY TO FORTY years before the current milieu of multiculturalism, immigrants rights activism, White women's liberation, and sweatshop struggles, Frantz Fanon found himself writing in a post World War II era fixated on the Jewish Holocaust as the affective destination that made legible the ensemble of questions animating the political common sense of oppression. The Holocaust provided a "natural" metaphor through which ontologists in Fanon's time, such as Jean-Paul Sartre, worked out a grammar through which one can ask the question, *What does it mean to suffer?* The Jewish Holocaust as "natural" metaphor continues to anchor many of today's metacommentaries. Giorgio Agamben's meditations on the *Muselmann*, for example, allow him to claim Auschwitz as "something so unprecedented that one tries to make it comprehensible by bringing it back to categories that are both extreme and absolutely familiar: life and death, dignity and indignity. Among these categories, the rue cipher of Auschwitz—the *Muselmann*, the 'core of the camp,' he whom 'no one wants to see,' and who is inscribed in every testimony as lacuna—wavers without finding a definite position."

Agamben is not wrong so much as he is late. Auschwitz is not "so un-precedented" to one whose frame of reference is the Middle Passage, followed by Native American genocide. In this way, Auschwitz would rank third or fourth in a normative, as opposed to "unprecedented," pattern. Agamben goes on to sketch out the ensemble of questions that Churchill and Spillers have asked, but he does so by deploying the Jewish Muselmann as the template of such questions, instead of the Red "Savage" or the Black Slave: "In one case, [the Muselmann] appears as the non-living, as the being whose life is not truly life; in the other, as he whose death cannot be called death, but only the production of a corpse—as the inscription of life in a dead area and, in death, of a living area. In both cases, what is called into question is the very humanity of man, since man observes the fragmentation of his privileged tie to what constitutes him as human, that is, the sacredness of death and life. The *Muselmann* is the non-human who obstinately appears as human; he is the human that cannot be told apart from the inhuman."[1] In the historiography of intellectual thought, Agamben's widely cited template of the Muselmann is an elaboration of Sartre's work. As philosophers, they work both to fortify and extend the interlocutory life of widely accepted political common sense which positions the German/Jewish relation as the sine qua non of a structural antagonism, thus allowing political philosophy to attribute ontological—and not just social—significance to the Jewish Holocaust.

Fanon has no truck with all of this. He dismisses the presumed antagonism between Germans and Jews by calling the Holocaust "little family quarrels," recasting with this single stroke the German/Jewish encounter as a conflict rather than an antagonism.[2] Fanon returns the Jew to his or her rightful position—a position *within* civil society animated by an ensemble of Human discontents. The Muselmann, then, can be seen as a provisional moment within existential Whiteness, when Jews were subjected to Blackness and Redness—and the explanatory power of the Muselmann can find its way back to sociology, history, or political science, where it more rightfully belongs.

This is one of several moments in *Black Skin, White Masks* when Fanon splits the hair between social oppression and structural suffering, making it possible to theorize the impossibility of a Black ontology (thus allowing us to meditate on how the Black suffers) without being chained to the philosophical and rhetorical demands of analogy, demands which the evidentiary register of social oppression (i.e., how many Jews died in the ovens, how many Blacks were lost in the Middle Passage) normally imposes on such meditations. The ruse of analogy erroneously locates Blacks in the world—a place where they have not been since the dawning of Blackness. This attempt to position the Black in the world by way of analogy is not only a mystification, and often erasure, of Blackness's grammar of suffering (accumulation and fungibility or the status of being non-Human) but simultaneously also a provision for civil society, promising an enabling modality for Human ethical dilemmas. It is a mystification and an erasure because, whereas Masters may share the same fantasies as Slaves, and Slaves can speak as though they have the same interests as Masters, their grammars of suffering are irreconcilable.

In dragging his interlocutors kicking and screaming through "Tact of Blackness," or what Ronald Judy has translated more pointedly as "The Lived Experience of the Black," Fanon is not attempting to play "oppression Olympics" and thus draw conclusions that Blacks are at the top of every empirical hierarchy of social discrimination, though that case has also been made.[3] Having established that, yes, the Jew is oppressed (and, yes, the Black is oppressed), Fanon refuses to let the lived experience of oppression dictate the terms of his meditations on suffering. "The Jew," he writes, "belongs to the race of those [who] since the beginning of time have never known cannibalism. What an idea, to eat one's father! Simple enough one has only not to be a nigger. . . . in my case everything takes on a new guise. I am the *slave* not of an *idea* others have of me but of my own appearance."[4]

Two tensions are at work here. One operates under the labor of ethical dilemmas—"simple enough one has only not to be a nigger."[5] This, I submit, is the essence of *being* for the White and non-Black position: ontology scaled down to a global common denominator. The other tension is found in the impossibility of ethical dilemmas for the Black: "I am," Fanon writes, "a *slave* not of an *idea* others have of me but of my own appearance." Being can thus be thought of, in the first ontological instance, as non-niggerness, and slavery then as niggerness. The visual field, "my own appearance," is the cut, the mechanism that elaborates the division between the nonniggerness and slavery, the difference between the living and the dead.

Whereas Humans exist on some plane of being and thus can become existentially present through some struggle for, of, or through recognition, Blacks cannot reach this plane.[6] Spillers, Fanon, and Hartman maintain that the violence that continually repositions the Black as a void of historical movement is without analog in the suffering dynamics of the ontologically alive. The violence that turns the African into a thing is without analog because it does not simply oppress the Black through tactile and empirical technologies of oppression, like the "little family quarrels" which for Fanon the Jewish Holocaust exemplifies. Rather, the gratuitous violence of the Black's first ontological instance, the Middle Passage, "wiped out [his or her] metaphysics . . . his [or her] customs and sources on which they are based."[7] Jews went into Auschwitz and came out as Jews. Africans went into the ships and came out as Blacks. The former is a Human holocaust; the latter is a Human *and* a metaphysical holocaust. That is why it makes little sense to attempt analogy: the Jews have the Dead (the *Muselmann*) among them; the Dead have the Blacks among them.

This violence which turns a body into flesh, ripped apart literally and imaginatively, destroys the possibility of ontology because it positions the Black in an infinite and indeterminately horrifying and open vulnerability, an object made available (which is to say fungible) for any subject. As such, "the black has no ontological resistance in the eyes of the white man" or, more precisely, in the eyes of Humanity.[8]

How is it that the Black *appears* to partner with the senior and junior partners of civil society (Whites and colored immigrants, respectively), when in point of fact the Black is not in the world? The answer lies in the ruse of analogy. By acting *as if* the Black is present, coherent, and above all human, Black film theorists are "allowed" to meditate on cinema only after "consenting" to a structural adjustment.[9] Such an adjustment, required for the "privilege" of participating in the political economy of academe, is not unlike the structural adjustment debtor nations must adhere to for the privilege of securing a loan: signing on the dotted line means feigning ontological capacity regardless of the fact that Blackness is incapacity in its most pure and unadulterated form. It means theorizing Blackness as "borrowed institutionality."[10]

Ronald Judy's book *(Dis)Forming the American Canon: African-Arabic Slave Narratives and the Vernacular* and his essay "On the Question of Nigga Authenticity" critique the Black intelligentsia for building aesthetic canons out of slave narratives and hardcore rap on the belief that Blacks can "write [themselves] into being."[11] Judy acknowledges that in such projects one finds genuine and rigorous attention to the issue that concerns Blacks as a social formation, namely, resistance. But he is less than sanguine about the power of resistance which so many Black scholars impute to the slave narrative in particular and, by extension, to the "canon" of Black literature, Black music, and Black film:

> In writing the death of the African body, Equiano['s eighteenth-century slave narrative] gains voice and emerges from the abject muteness of objectivity into productive subjectivity. It should not be forgotten that the abject muteness of the body is not to not exist, to be without effect. The abject body is the very stuff, the material, of experiential effect. Writing the death of the African body is an enforced abstraction. It is an interdiction of the African, a censorship to be inarticulate, to not compel, *to have no capacity to move, to be without effect, without agency, without thought.* The muted African body is overwritten by the Negro, and the Negro that emerges in the ink flow of Equiano's pen is that which has overwritten itself and so becomes the representation of the very body it sits on.[12]

Judy is an Afro-pessimist, not an Afrocentrist. For him the Negro is a symbol that cannot "enable the representation of meaning [because] it has no referent."[13] Such is the gratuitousness of the violence that made the Negro. But it is precisely to this illusive symbolic resistance (an aspiration to "productive subjectivity"), as opposed to the Negro's "abject muteness," and certainly not to the Slave's gratuitous violence, that many Black scholars in general, and Black film theorists in particular, aspire when interpreting their cultural objects.

My claim regarding Black film theory, modeled on Judy's claim concerning Black studies more broadly, is that it tries to chart a project of resistance with an ensemble of questions that fortify and extend the interlocutory life of what might be called a Black film canon. But herein lies the rub, in the form of a structural adjustment imposed on Black film scholars themselves. "Resistance through canon formation," Judy writes, must be "legitimated on the grounds of conservation, the conservation of authenticity's integrity."[14] A tenet that threads through Judy's work is that throughout modernity and postmodernity (or postindustrial society, as Judy's echoing of Antonio Negri prefers) "Black authenticity" is an oxymoron, a notion as absurd as "rebellious property,"[15] for it requires the kind of ontological integrity which the Slave cannot claim. The structural adjustment imposed on Black academics is, however, vital to the well-being of civil society. It provides the political economy of academia with a stable "collegial" atmosphere in which the selection of topics, the distribution of concerns, esprit de corps, emphasis, and the bounding of debate within acceptable limits appear to be "shared" by all because all admit to sharing them. But Judy suggests that the mere presence of the Black and his or her project, albeit adjusted structurally, threatens the fabric of this "stable" economy by threatening its structure of exchange: "Not only are the conjunctive operations of discourses of knowledge and power that so define the way in which academic fields get authenticated implicated in the academic instituting of Afro-American studies, but so is the instability entailed in the nature of academic work. That instability is discernable even in the university's function as conservator."[16]

This academy-wide instability, predicated on the mere presence of the Black and his or her object, has three crisis-prone elements which Blackness, should it ever become unadjusted, could unleash. First, African American studies cannot delimit "a unique object field" (i.e., a set of literary texts, or a Black film canon) which threatens the nature of academic work, for Black studies itself is indexical of the fact that "the object field—that is, the texts—has no ontological status, but issues from specific historical discursive practices and aesthetics." Second, these "specific historical discursive practices and aesthetics," heterogeneous as they might be at the level of content, are homogeneous to the extent that their genealogies cannot recognize and incorporate the figure of the Slave. As a result, "interjecting the slave narrative into the privileged site of literary expression achieves, in effect, a (dis)formation of the field of American literary history" and, by extension, the field of Black film studies. "The slave narrative as a process by which a textual economy is constituted—as a *topography* through which the African American achieves an emancipatory subversion of the propriety of slavery—jeopardizes the genealogy of Reason."[17] Once Reason's very genealogy is jeopardized then its content, for example, the idea of "dominium," has no ground to stand on. We will see, below, how and why "dominion" is recognized as a constituent element of the Indian's subjectivity and how this recognition enables partial incorporation.

A third point, however, proves just as unsettling, if not more so, than a crisis in the genealogy of Reason. For if Slave narratives as an object field have "no ontological status," such that the field's insertion into the field of literary history can disform not just the field of literary studies but the field of knowledge itself (the paradigm of exchange within the political economy of academia), and (dis)form the hegemony of Reason's genealogy, then what does this tell us about the ontological status of narrating Slave themselves? This question awaits both the Black filmmaker and the Black film theorist. It is menacing and unbearable. The intensity of its ethicality is so terrifying that, as a space to be inhabited and terror to be embraced, it can be seized by a significant number of Black artists and theorists only at those moments when a critical mass of Slaves have embraced this terror in the streets.

Normally, in moments such as the present (with no such mass movement in the streets), the "effect of delineating a peculiar African American historiography" seems menacing and unbearable to the lone Black scholar; and so the Black scholar labors—unwittingly, Judy implies—to adjust the structure of his or her own "nonrecuperable negativity" in order to tell "a story of an emerging subjectivity's triumphant struggle to discover its identity" and thereby ascend "from the abject muteness of objectivity into productive subjectivity."[18] The dread under which such aspirations to Human capacity labor (a labor of disavowal) is catalyzed by the knowledge, however unconscious, that civil society is held together by a structural prohibition against recognizing and incorporating a being that is dead, despite the fact that this being is sentient and so appears to be very much alive. Civil society cannot embrace what Saidiya Hartman calls "the abject status of the will-less object."[19] Explicating the rhetorical and philosophical impossibility of such an embrace, Judy writes:

> The assumption of the Negro's transcendent worth as a human presupposes the Negro's being comprehensible in Western modernity's terms. Put somewhat more crudely, but nonetheless to the point, the humanization in writing achieved in the slave narrative require[s] the conversion of the incomprehensible African into the comprehensible Negro. The historical mode of conversion was the linguistic

representation of slavery: the slave narrative [or Black film and Black film theory]. By providing heuristic evidence of the Negro's humanity the slave narrative begins to write the history of Negro culture in terms of the history of an extra-African self-reflective consciousness.[20]

But this exercise is as liberating, as "productive of subjectivity," as a dog chasing its tail. For "precisely at the point at which this intervention appears to succeed in its determination of a black agent, however, it is subject to appropriation by a rather homeostatic thought: the Negro."[21] And the Negro, as Fanon illustrates throughout *Black Skin, White Masks*, "is comparison," nothing more and certainly nothing less, for what is less than comparison? Fanon strikes at the heart of this tail-chasing and the dread it catalyzes when he writes: "No one knows yet who [the Negro] is, but he knows that fear will fill the world when the world finds out. And when the world knows the world always expects something of the Negro. He is afraid lest the world know, he is afraid of the fear that the world would feel if the world knew."[22] By aspiring to the very ontological capacity which modernity foreclosed to them—in other words, by attempting to "write themselves into being"—Black film theorists and many Black films experience as unbearable a tenet shared by Judy and other Afro-pessimists that "humanity recognizes itself in the Other that it is not."[23] This makes the labor of disavowal in Black scholarly and aesthetic production doubly burdensome, for it is triggered by a dread of both being "discovered," and of discovering oneself, as ontological incapacity. Thus, through borrowed institutionality—the feigned capacity to be essentially exploited and alienated (rather than accumulated and fungible) in the first ontological instance (in other words, a fantasy to be just like everyone else, which is a fantasy to *be*)—the work of Black film theory operates through a myriad of compensatory gestures in which the Black theorist assumes subjective capacity to be universal and thus "finds" it everywhere. *We all got it bad, don't we, Massa.*

We can say that White film theory is hobbled in much the same *style* as Black film theory, but it is burdened by a completely different set of stakes, or more precisely with nothing at all at stake ontologically. In chapter 2 I will show how dependent the explanatory power of White film theory is on the Lacanian insistence that the Subject (Lacan's analysand) is a universal entity who exists, a priori, within a community of what Lacan calls "contemporaries" (what I dub civil society) and does not reside on what Hortense Spillers calls "the slave estate."[24] Bound up in the notion of prior existing contemporaries is the assumption that relationality itself is not in question (which is always *the* question for the Slave). What is in question instead is the status of those prior existing relations—whether, in Lacan's vernacular, the relation is sutured by "empty speech," the monumentalization of the ego, or "full speech," an encounter between beings who live either under the neurotic yoke of the *moi* (ego) or in a liberated or deconstructive relation to the ego. Other touchstones of cohesion that bound and elaborate these theoretical analyses of film include a sense of the universality of a domestic scene (again, I would note, slaves have quarters but not homes), and of subjective positioning by way of the symbolic order, an understanding of positioning in which violence plays a contingent as opposed to originary or gratuitous role, in the ontological schema of the subject.

Due to the presence of prior existing relations in a world of contemporaries, no "fear of the fear of the world" is at stake when White theorists meditate ontologically (whether through a cultural object such as film or on a set of intellectual protocols) and find—as do their Black colleagues—capacity everywhere. It would be more accurate to say not that they find capacity everywhere, since they do not look everywhere, but that they find it where they are, among their "contemporaries," and assume its ubiquity. Unlike the Negro, there is nothing homeostatic about the White (or other Humans). If the Black is death personified, the White is the personification of diversity, of life itself. As Richard Dyer reminds us, "The invisibility of whiteness as a racial position in white . . . discourse is of a piece with its ubiquity. When I said above that this book wasn't merely seeking to fill a gap in the analysis of racial imagery, I reproduced the idea that there is no discussion of white people. In fact for most of the time white people speak about nothing but white people, it's just that we couch it in terms of 'people' in general. . . . Yet precisely because of this and their placing as norm [Whites] seem not to be represented to themselves *as* whites but as people who are variously gendered, classed, sexualised and abled."[25] Thus the threat of discovering oneself in one's own scholarly or artistic endeavors as "comparison" is not a fate that awaits White academics. White academics' disavowal of Black death as modernity's condition of possibility (their inability to imagine their productive

subjectivity as an effect of the Negro)[26] stems not from the unbearable
terror of that (non)self-discovery always already awaiting the Black, but
from the fact that, save brief and infrequent conjunctures of large-scale
Black violence (eighteenth- and nineteenth-century slave revolts and
twentieth-century "urban unrest"), the socius provides no catalyst for
White avowal. In short, thought—essential, ontological thought—is all
but impossible in White cultural and political theory—but it is not (as
we will see with *Monster's Ball* in part 4) impossible in the unconscious
of the White film itself. This state of affairs, the unbearable hydraulics of
Black disavowal and the sweetness and light of White disavowal, is best
encapsulated in the shorthand expression "social stability," for it guarantees the civility of civil society. Put anecdotally, but nonetheless to the
point, when pulled individually by the button, both inmate and guard
might be in favor of "criminal rehabilitation," both might even believe
that the warden is a "swell guy,"[27] and in their enthusiasm they both might
even take for granted that by "criminal" they are speaking of the inmates
and not the guards, or for that matter the warden. However, while the
shared experiences in the political economy of the prison—a common
policy agenda, that is, rehabilitation—or the shared identifications in the
libidinal economy of prison—the unconscious captation of both inmate
and guard by the image of the warden—may certainly be important to any
meditation on either prison economy, they are certainly not essential to
such reflection. This means that they cannot break in on the mutually exclusive constituent elements that make the positions of inmate and guard
irreconcilable, at least, not with such a force as to rupture that positional
exclusivity and bring about the end of the (prison) world. This holds true
regardless of the fact that the mobility of symbolic material, that is, the
idea of "criminal rehabilitation" and the agreement on who constitutes
a criminal, and the mobility of imaginary captation, that is, the *image* of
the warden, are both without limit in their capacity for transgression.

The libidinal economy of modernity and its attendant cartography (the
Western Hemisphere, the United States, or civil society as a construct)
achieves its structure of unconscious exchange by way of a "thanatology"
in which Blackness overdetermines the embodiment of impossibility, incoherence, and incapacity. Furthermore, political economy achieves its
symbolic (political or economic) capacity and structure of preconscious
exchange by way of a similar thanatology. Judy goes so far as to say that

at the crux of modernity's crisis is the dilemma "how to represent the Negro as being demonstrably human within the terms of the law."[28] Here, of course, he does not mean "law" in a juridical sense but rather "law" as a portal of intelligibility through which one can be said to have the capacity to access "Reason" and thus be recognized and incorporated as a bona fide subject.

Through Judy's analysis of the Negro (the slave) as modernity's necessity (the Other that Humanity is not: "Simple enough one has only not to be a nigger"), that which kick-starts and sustains the production of the Western Hemisphere, we can begin to make the transition from the parasitic necessity of Whiteness in libidinal economy to its parasitic necessity in political economy. Whiteness is parasitic because it monumentalizes its subjective capacity, its lush cartography, in direct proportion to the wasteland of Black incapacity. By "capacity" I have meant something more comprehensive than "the event" and its causal elements and something more indeterminate than "agency." We should think of it as a kind of facility or matrix through which possibility itself—whether tragic or triumphant—can be elaborated: the ebb and flow between, on the one hand, "empty speech," racist actions, repressive laws, and institutional coherence and, on the other hand, "full speech," armed insurrection, and the institutional ennui. This is what I mean by capacity. It is a far cry from Spillers's state of "being for the captor" and Judy's "muted African body," a far cry from pure abject- or objectness: without thought, without agency, "with no capacity to move."[29] In short, White (Human) capacity, in advance of the event of discrimination or oppression, is parasitic on Black incapacity:[30] Without the Negro, capacity itself is incoherent, uncertain at best.

Where in all of this is the Indian? The "Savage" has been glaringly absent in my preceding meditations on the Master and the Slave, for the same reason that Asians and Latinos are omitted from my study altogether. Latinos and Asians stand in *conflictual relation* to the Settler/Master, that is, to the hemisphere and the United States writ large—they invoke a politics of culture, not a culture of politics. They do not register as antagonists. But this is only partially true of "Savage" position.

Granted, the "Savage" relation to the Settler by way of libidinal economy's structure of exchange is far from isomorphic, at the level of content, what Fanon calls "existence."[31] For example, there is indeed important and resounding dissonance between the Indian's spiritual or divine imagining of the subject in libidinal economy and the Settler/Master's secular, or psychoanalytic, or even religious imaginings.[32] But these differences do not cancel each other out. That is, they are not differences with an antagonistic structure, but differences with a conflictual structure, because articulation, rather than a void, makes the differences legible. In other words, "Savage" capacity is not obliterated by these differences. In fact, its interlocutory life is often fortified and extended by such differences. The modern or postmodern subject alienated in language, on the one hand, and the Great Spirit devotee, or child of Mother Earth, on the other, may in fact be elaborated by different cosmologies,[33] predicated on what Vine Deloria Jr. has noted as conflictual visions, but Lacan's analysand (meaning a subjective capacity for full or empty speech) does not require the Indian as its parasitic host, despite the Indian's forcible removal to clear a space for the analyst's office. This is because alienation is essential to both the "Savage" and the Settler's way of imagining structural positionality, to the way Native American metacommentaries think ontology. Thus, the analysand's essential capacity for alienation from being (alienation that takes place in language) is not parasitic on the "Savage's" capacity to be alienated from the spirit world or the land (which for Indians are cosmologically inseparable). Whereas historically, the secular imperialism which made psychoanalytic imaginings possible wreaked havoc on the "Savage" at the level of Fanonian existence, that contact did not wipe out his or her libidinal capacity—or Native metaphysics. This is true not in some empirical sense, for as a Black I have no access to the Indian's spirit world. I am also barred from subjectivity in even the most revolutionary schemata of White secularism (Lacanian psychoanalysis and Negri's Marxism). Rather, it is true because the most profound and unflinching metacommentators on the "Savage" and libidinal economy (although Indians would probably replace "libidinal economy" with "spirit world" and "the subject" with "the soul") and the most unflinching metacommentators on the Settler and libidinal economy *say* it is true. Having communed around their shared capacity for subjective alienation since the dawn of modernity (what Indians call "contact"), they formed a community of interpretation. Even as Settlers began to wipe Indians out, they were building an interpretive community with "Savages" the likes of which Masters were not building with Slaves.

In the 1530s the Thomist ecclesiastics of the School of Salamanca agreed that Indians possessed subjective dominion in a way that slaves did not. Judy maintains that this claim was made possible on the basis of ethnographic evidence with which Hernán Cortés and others had returned from the "New" World to Spain. For the Thomists and the Spanish explorers,

> Indians are humans and not animals. . . . they possessed a certain rational order in their affairs. . . . Cortes's ethnographic data . . . described a culture with extensive evidence of rationality and civility: a material culture capable of constructing cities of stone, urbanization (society based on the *polis*), sophisticated and hierarchical social organization, commerce, juridical institutions, and above all highly ritualized religious practice. . . . Forfeiture of the natural right of *dominium*, then, would require that the Indian was truly irrational and so in violation of the law of nature. In the face of overwhelming evidence of the Indians' rationality and civility, even the two most frequently cited acts of abomination held against Indians, cannibalism . . . and sacrifice[,] . . . were viewed . . . as no more than singular temporary aberrations of reason and so not evidence of true irrationality, which made them insufficient grounds for denying the Indians possession of *dominium*.[34]

It should be noted that when cannibalism is blackened it is considered to be a genetic predisposition rather than a "temporary aberration of reason." However compelling the "overwhelming" ethnographic evidence was for the Thomists, the evidence itself is beached on the shore of "existence." It has no ontological buoyancy. It is not the mechanism through which the Settler—at least in libidinal economy—is freed from performing his necrophilia on the "Savage." In short, it does not explain the *how* of this relation. Again, they could have "found" such "overwhelming" ethnographic evidence in Africa, but did not. Judy reminds us that even "Hegel [three hundred years after the School of Salamanca] explicitly exclude[d] Africa from the dialectic, on the grounds of the primitiveness of the Negro." Judy's statement in itself is a non sequitur because the Negro is Hegel's, meaning modernity's, creation: there is no way to Africa through the Black. What precisely and specifically prompted the communal imaginings in libidinal economy between Settler and "Savage"— but not between Master and Slave, given that modernity's Settler and

Master are one and the same (the Human)—is a question of origins that does not concern me, for it might clarify the historical record at the expense of mystifying paradigmatic relations of power. To know the precise origin of power does not ensure an understanding of its arrangements. What concerns me is a certain will to analogy which the Settler insists on, when thinking the Aztec, but which is lacking in the absolute (by not even being raised to be rejected) when his mind strays to Africa. Such questions as to the *why* of Carib cannibalism and Aztec sacrifice present epistemological dilemmas, the ecclesiastics, the intellectuals of early modern civil society, had to answer in order for conquest of the Indians to continue: "Vitoria [a leading Salamancan Thomist] based his answer to this question on analogy: the Indians are like children. As *dominium* is a natural right independent of objective property, children can be said to have *dominium*, although they may not exercise it properly. In this state of improper use, children are not irrational, but they are unrational, their reason is potential. Instead of being natural slaves, the Indians are a class of natural children, much like the European peasantry." Analogy, then, is more than a rhetorical device. To be sure, its communal power cannot stop war or stave off conquest and imperialism; in fact, it often evinces generative agency where such transgressions are concerned. But it brokers a community of interpretation between Settler/Master and "Savage" as well as—and this is key—cradles that relation in the swaddling of conflictual harmony and shields the relation from the cold incoherence of antagonism. Analogy delivers the Indian from the wound of irrationality (in favor of unrationality); his or her subjectivity is questioned, and it is this calling into question—the semiotic play, the conflictual harmony— more than the content of that ensemble of questions which enables "productive subjectivity."[35] For though the Indian exists liminally in relation to the Settler, as do the Settler's children and "his" Old World peasants, he or she remains ontologically possible. That is to say, the "Savage," unlike the Slave, is half-alive.

The archive of Native American literature which successfully articulates between Native Americans touchstones of spiritual cohesion and the tenets of psychoanalysis, and between Red and White tenets of kinship and domesticity (i.e., lineage vs. marriage), is symptomatic of what I am calling *conflictual harmony*, emerging as it does through an absence of structural antagonism between the Settler and the "Savage," at least in the libidinal economy. However, this conflictual harmony is disturbed, possibly ruptured, when the "Savage" is produced in the realm of political economy. Here the "Savage" attains the status of an antagonism: in other words, if the analysand does not require the Indian as the embodiment of Thanatos (death personified) for her or his coherence, then perhaps the proletariat does. This requires apprehension of genocide, as opposed to sovereignty, as the second of the "Savage's" two positioning modalities.

Again, if accumulation and fungibility are the modalities through which embodied Blackness is positioned as incapacity, then genocide is that modality through which embodied Redness is positioned as incapacity. Ontological incapacity, I have inferred and here state forthright, is *the* constituent element of ethics. Put another way, one cannot embody capacity and be, simultaneously, ethical. Where there are Slaves it is unethical to be free. The Settler/Master's capacity, I have argued, is a function of exploitation and alienation; and the Slave's incapacity is elaborated by accumulation and fungibility. But the "Savage" is positioned, structurally, by subjective capacity and objective incapacity, by sovereignty and genocide, respectively. The Indian's liminal status in political economy, how her or his position shuttles between the incapacity of a genocided object and the capacity of a sovereign subject, coupled with the fact that Redness does not overdetermine the thanatology of libidinal economy (this liminal capacity within political economy and complete freedom from incapacity within libidinal economy) raises serious doubts about the status of "Savage" ethicality vis-à-vis the triangulated structure (Red, White, and Black) of antagonisms. Clearly, the coherence of Whiteness as a structural position in modernity depends on the capacity to be free from genocide, perhaps not as a historical experience, but at least as a positioning modality. This embodied capacity (genocidal immunity) of Whiteness jettisons the White/Red relation from that of a conflict and marks it as an antagonism: it stains it with irreconcilability. Here, the Indian comes into being and is positioned by an a priori violence of genocide.

Whiteness can also experience this kind of violence but only a fortiori: genocide may be one of a thousand contingent experiences of Whiteness but it is not a constituent element, it does not make Whites White (or Humans Human). Whiteness can grasp its own capacity, be present to itself, coherent, by its unavailability to the a priori violence of Red genocide, as well as by its unavailability to the a priori violence of Black accumulation and fungibility. If it experiences accumulation and fungibility, or genocide, those experiences must be named, qualified, that is, "White slavery," or the Armenian massacre, the Jewish Holocaust, Bosnian interment, so that such contingent experience is not confused with ontological necessity. In such a position one can always say, "I'm not a 'Savage'" or "I'm being treated like a nigger." One can reassert one's Humanity by refusing the ruse of analogy. Regardless of Whites' historical, and brief, encounters with the modalities of the "Savage" and the Slave, these modalities do not break in on the position of Whiteness with such a force as to replace exploitation and alienation as the Settler/Master's constituent elements. We might think of exploitation and alienation as modalities of suffering which inoculate Whiteness from death. If this is indeed the case, then perhaps Whiteness has no constituent elements other than the immanent status of immunity. Still, this immunity is no small matter, for it is the sine qua non of Human capacity.

Indians perpetually shuttle between death and civil society: at one moment they are isolated from Human community (civil society or "contemporaries") in their genocidal effect (much like Slaves); at another moment, the moment of the sovereign effect, Indians are wedged back into the Human fold. For Slaves, this shuttling between death and civil society is simply not allowed. Still, what is not allowed can be disavowed—which accounts for the anxious need to imagine Black slavery as a historical rather than ontological phenomenon.

The Indian is not the pure embodiment of thanatology in either libidinal or political economy. Furthermore, the relation of negation between White and Black is absolute in that sentient beings positioned by exploitation and alienation are immune to accumulation and fungibility. For example, it is true that labor power is exploited and that the worker is alienated in it. But workers labor *on* the commodity, they are not the commodity itself, their labor power is. Tragic as alienation in labor power is, it does not resemble "the peculiar character of violence and the natal alienation of the slave." "The slave had no socially recognized existence outside of his master, he became a social nonperson. . . . the definition of the slave, however recruited, [is] a socially dead person. Alienated from all 'rights' or claims of birth, he ceased to belong in his own right to any legitimate social order. All slaves experienced, at the very least, a secular excommunication. . . . [The slave is] truly a genealogical isolate. Formally isolated in his social relations with those who live, he also was culturally isolated from the social heritage of his ancestors. He had a past, to be sure. But a past is not a heritage."[36]

The "Savage" on the other hand, though a genocided object, is not "a genealogical isolate." The modality of genocide which positions the "Savage" coexists with the modality of sovereignty which also positions him or her. The genocided object cannot sustain a heritage; like the accumulated and fungible object it had a past, not a heritage. Sovereignty, on the other hand, rescues the "Savage" from the genealogical isolation of the Slave. Sovereignty has the capacity to embrace the ethical dilemmas of both the "social heritage of . . . ancestors" and "social relations with those who live." Sovereignty, however battered or marginalized, is not a form of "borrowed institutionality," it requires no structural adjustment. Therefore, the relation of negation between Red and White cannot be sustained as an absolute. While White exploitation and alienation can no more secure structural articulation between their modalities and those of Red genocide than they can with accumulation and fungibility, they can (and historically do) secure such articulation with Red sovereignty. This push and pull of positional tension between Settler and "Savage" is as much a marker of modernity as is the slave coffle. From Father Vicente Valverde's late sixteenth-century invocation of papal bulls before Atahualpa, "attempting to convince the Great Inca . . . that Pope Alexander had the authority to grant dominion over Peru to the Spanish monarchy" and Atahualpa's rejoinder that "he could not conceive how a foreign priest should pretend to dispose of territories which did not belong to him"; to the School of Salamanca's meditations on "Savage" dominium; to the late eighteenth-century tracing of the U.S. constitution along the contours of Iroquois governance; to the emergence of new formations of engendered White masculinity by way of early nineteenth-century marriages to Choctaw and Cherokee "princesses"; all the way up to Deloria's meditations on the myriad articulations between Indigenous cosmology and the tenets of Jung, modernity is laced with this network of connections, transfers, and displacements between the ontological capacity of the "Savage" and the ontological capacity of the Settler. Herein, for most metacommentators on "Savage" ontology there lies the possibility of ascendancy from genocide's ontological isolation.[37]

But the Slave can hold out no such ascendant hope to the "Savage." To put a finer point on it: What prevents the Indian from slipping into Blackness? Redness regains the coherence that the a priori violence of modernity ripped from her or him by way of its capacity to be free from, or at least partially immune to, accumulation and fungibility. Simple enough one has only not to be . . . Again, the Indian's immunity is not from historical experience—thousands of Indians were enslaved—but rather from accumulation and fungibility as positioning modalities. Indians and Whites can be caught in the grip of slavery without transforming and reracializing the institution itself. But Blackness cannot disentangle itself from slaveness.

"The moment in Western history when the recognition of alternative worlds becomes possible—in the Spanish encounter with the Aztecs—is also the moment when humanism achieves hegemony."[38] Let us bear in mind a lesson from Antonio Gramsci: Hegemony is not the imposition of decrees. Hegemony is influence, leadership, and consent; it is the influence of a ruling social group, the leadership of ideas, of an ensemble of questions such as "meritocracy" and "individualism"; and it is the subalterns' spontaneous consent to be lead by the ruling group's ensemble of questions.[39] Antonio Gramsci is simply wrong when he asserts, like Marx and Lenin before him and like Antonio Negri and Michael Hardt after him, that relationality between subalterns and rulers who form a historic bloc by way of subaltern consent to the leadership of ruling class questions is an antagonistic relationality. The "Savage"/Settler historic bloc formed by Humanism's hegemony over the "Savage's" "alternative world"[40] would form the basis of an antagonism if the bloc's capacity were not both barred to and vouchsafed by the Slave. The bloc does not recognize the Slave's world as an alternative or competing world because the violence that produces the Slave makes it impossible to think "Slave" and "world" together. As such, the Slave's consent is immaterial to modernity's "Savage"/Human bloc because Slave consent cannot be recognized and incorporated. Therefore, the moment in Western history in which Humanism becomes hegemonic (and detrimental to the Indian's way of life) is not a moment in which the Slave achieves relationality (even as a subaltern) except in that his or her negativity stands now in relation not only to the Settler/Master, but to the "Savage" as well, and so becomes all the more nonrecuperable and all the more isolated.

This state of affairs is more than a little disturbing, for it suggests that the relativity of the Indian's relative isolation and relative humanity, the push and pull of Indians' positional tension, is imbricated with—if not dependent on—the absolute isolation of the Slave. Central to the triangulation of antagonisms is a structural antagonism between the "Savage" and the Settler, as well as structural solidarity, or capacity for articulation (conflictual harmony), between the "Savage" and the Master. This solidarity or antagonism totters on that fulcrum called the Slave.

TWO

The Narcissistic Slave

IN THE INTRODUCTION and chapter 1, we saw how the aporia between Black *being* and political ontology has existed since Arab and European enslavement of Africans. The crafting of questions through which one might arrive at an unflinching paradigmatic analysis of political ontology, a language that could express the structural and performative violence of *Slave-making*, is repeatedly thwarted. Humanist discourse, whose epistemological machinations provide our conceptual frameworks for thinking political ontology, is diverse and contrary. But for all its diversity and contrariness it is sutured by an implicit rhetorical consensus that violence accrues to the Human body as a result of transgressions, whether real or imagined, within the symbolic order. That is to say, Humanist discourse can only think a subject's relation to violence as a contingency and not as a matrix that positions the subject. Put another way, Humanism has no theory of the Slave because it imagines a subject who has been either alienated in language or alienated from his or her cartographic and temporal capacities.[1] It cannot imagine an object who has been positioned by gratuitous violence and who has no cartographic and temporal capacities to lose—a sentient being for whom recognition and incorporation is impossible. In short, political ontology, as imagined through Humanism, can only produce discourse that has as its foundation alienation and exploitation as a grammar of suffering, when what is needed (for the Black, who is always already a Slave) is an ensemble of ontological questions that has as its foundation accumulation and fungibility as a grammar of suffering.[2]

A Culture of Politics

The violence of the Middle Passage and the Slave estate,[3] technologies of accumulation and fungibility, recompose and reenact their horrors on each succeeding generation of Blacks. This violence is both gratuitous (not contingent on transgressions against the hegemony of civil society) and structural (positioning Blacks ontologically outside of Humanity and civil society). Simultaneously, it renders the ontological status of Humanity (life itself) wholly dependent on civil society's repetition compulsion: the frenzied and fragmented machinations through which civil society reenacts gratuitous violence on the Black—that civil society might know itself as the domain of Humans—generation after generation.

Again, we need a new language of abstraction to explain this horror. The explanatory power of Humanist discourse is bankrupt in the face of the Black. It is inadequate and inessential to, as well as parasitic on, the ensemble of questions which the dead but sentient thing, the Black, struggles to articulate in a world of living subjects. My work on film, cultural theory, and political ontology is my attempt to contribute to this often fragmented and constantly assaulted quest to forge a language of abstraction with explanatory powers emphatic enough to embrace the Black, an accumulated and fungible object, in a Human world of exploited and alienated subjects.

The imposition of Humanism's assumptive logic has encumbered Black film studies to the extent that it is underwritten by the assumptive logic of White or non-Black film studies. This is a problem of cultural studies writ large. In this chapter, I want to illustrate briefly how we might break the theoretical impasse between, on the one hand, the assumptive logic of cultural studies and, on the other, the theoretical aphasia to which cultural studies is reduced when it encounters the (non)ontological status of the Black. I will do so not by launching a frontal attack against White film theory, in particular, or even cultural studies broadly speaking, but by interrogating Jacques Lacan—because Lacanian psychoanalysis is one of the twin pillars buttressing film theory and cultural studies.[4]

Unfortunately, cultural studies that theorizes the interface between Blacks and Humans is hobbled in its attempts to (a) expose power relationships and (b) examine how relations of power influence and shape cultural practice. Cultural studies insists on a grammar of suffering which assumes that we are all positioned essentially by way of the symbolic order, what Lacan calls the wall of language—and as such our potential for stasis or change (our capacity for being oppressed or free) is overdetermined by our "universal" ability or inability to seize and wield discursive weapons. This idea corrupts the explanatory power of most socially engaged films and even the most radical line of political action because it produces a cinema and a politics that cannot account for the grammar of suffering of the Black—the Slave. To put it bluntly, the imaginative labor[5] of cinema, political action, and cultural studies are all afflicted with the same theoretical aphasia. They are speechless in the face of gratuitous violence.

This theoretical aphasia is symptomatic of a debilitated ensemble of questions regarding political ontology. At its heart are two registers of imaginative labor. The first register is that of description, the rhetorical labor aimed at explaining the way relations of power are named, categorized, and explored. The second register can be characterized as prescription, the rhetorical labor predicated on the notion that everyone can be emancipated through some form of discursive, or symbolic, intervention.

But emancipation through some form of discursive or symbolic intervention is wanting in the face of a subject position that is not a subject position—what Marx calls "a speaking implement" or what Ronald Judy calls "an interdiction against subjectivity." In other words, the Black has sentient capacity but no relational capacity. As an accumulated and fungible object, rather than an exploited and alienated subject, the Black is openly vulnerable to the whims of the world, and so is his or her cultural "production." What does it mean—what are the stakes—when the world can whimsically transpose one's cultural gestures, the stuff of symbolic intervention, onto another worldly good, a commodity of style?

Frantz Fanon echoes this question when he writes, "I came into the world imbued with the will to find a meaning in things, my spirit filled with the desire to attain to the source of the world, and then I found that I was an object in the midst of other objects." He clarifies this assertion and alerts us to the stakes which the optimistic assumptions of film studies and cultural studies, the counterhegemonic promise of alternative cinema, and the emancipatory project of coalition politics cannot account for, when he writes: "Ontology—once it is finally admitted as leaving existence by the wayside—does not permit us to understand the being of the black."[6]

This presents a challenge to film production and to film studies given their cultivation and elaboration by the imaginative labor of cultural studies, underwritten by the assumptive logic of Humanism; because if everyone does not possess the DNA of culture, that is, (a) time and space transformative capacity, (b) a relational status with other Humans through which one's time- and space-transformative capacity is recognized and incorporated, and (c) a relation to violence that is contingent and not gratuitous, then how do we theorize a sentient being who is positioned not by the DNA of culture but by the structure of gratuitous violence? How do we think outside of the conceptual framework of subalternity—that is, outside of the explanatory power of cultural studies—and think beyond the pale of emancipatory agency by way of symbolic intervention?

I am calling for a different conceptual framework, predicated not on the subject-effect of cultural performance but on the structure of political ontology, a framework that allows us to substitute a culture of politics for a politics of culture. The value in this rests not simply in the way it would help us rethink cinema and performance, but in the way it can help us theorize what is at present only intuitive and anecdotal: the unbridgeable gap between Black being and Human life. To put a finer point on it, such a framework might enhance the explanatory power of theory, art, and politics by destroying and perhaps restructuring the ethical range of our current ensemble of questions. This has profound implications for non-Black film studies, Black film studies, and African American studies writ large because they are currently entangled in a multicultural paradigm that takes an interest in an insufficiently critical comparative analysis— that is, a comparative analysis in pursuit of a coalition politics (if not in practice then at least as a theorizing metaphor) which, by its very nature, crowds out and forecloses the Slave's grammar of suffering.

The Dilemmas of Black Film Studies

As the backlash to the Civil Rights and Black Power movements has set in, a small but growing coterie of Black theorists are returning to Fanon's astonishing claim that "ontology—once it is finally admitted as leaving existence by the wayside—does not permit us to understand the being of the black man. For not only must the black man be black; but he must be black in relation to the white man."[7] Though they do not form anything as ostentatious as a school of thought, and though their attitudes toward and acknowledgments of Fanon vary, the moniker *Afro-pessimists* neither infringes on their individual differences nor exaggerates their fidelity to a shared set of assumptions. It should be noted that of the Afro-pessimists—Hortense Spillers, Ronald Judy, David Marriott, Saidiya Hartman, Achille Mbembe, Frantz Fanon, Kara Keeling, Jared Sexton, Joy James, Lewis Gordon, George Yancey, and Orlando Patterson—only James and Patterson are social scientists. The rest come out of the Humanities. Fanon, of course, was a doctor of psychiatry. Reading them, and connecting the dots at the level of shared assumptions, rather than the content of their work or their prescriptive gestures (if any), it becomes clear that though their work holds the intellectual protocols of unconscious identification accountable to structural positionality, it does so in a way that enriches, rather than impoverishes, how we are able to theorize unconscious identification. That is to say that though meditations on unconscious identifications and preconscious interests may be their starting point (i.e., how to cure "hallucinatory whitening," and how to think about the Black/non-Black divide that is rapidly replacing the Black/White divide),[8] they are, in the first instance, theorists of structural positionality.[9]

The Afro-pessimists are theorists of Black positionality who share Fanon's insistence that, though Blacks are indeed sentient beings, the structure of the entire world's semantic field—regardless of cultural and national discrepancies—"leaving" as Fanon would say, "existence by the wayside"—is sutured by anti-Black solidarity. Unlike the solution-oriented, interest-based, or hybridity-dependent scholarship so fashionable today, Afro-pessimism explores the meaning of Blackness not—in the first instance—as a variously and unconsciously interpellated identity or as a conscious social actor, but as a structural position of noncommunicability in the face of all other positions; this meaning is noncommunicable because, again, as a position, Blackness is predicated on modalities of accumulation and fungibility, not exploitation and alienation. Unfortunately, neither Black nor White film theory seems to have made this shift from exploitation and alienation as that which positions film theory's "universal" cinematic subject to genocide, accumulation, and fungibility as modalities of gratuitous violence which positions the Slave. In this respect, film theory mystifies structural antagonisms and abets social and political stability. Even the bulk of Black film theory is predicated on an assumptive logic of exploitation and alienation, rather than accumulation and fungibility, when regarding the ontological status of the Black.

Film theory, as concerns Black American cinema from 1967 to the present, is marked by several characteristics. Nearly all of the books and articles are underwritten by a sense of urgency regarding the tragic history and bleak future of a group of people marked by slavery in the Western Hemisphere; this, they would all agree, is the constitutive element of the word *Black*. To this end, most are concerned with how cinematic representation hastens that bleak future or intervenes against it. Cinema then, has pedagogic value, or, perhaps more precisely, pedagogic potential. Broadly speaking, Black film theory hinges on these questions: What does cinema teach Blacks about Blacks? What does cinema teach Whites (and others) about Blacks? Are those lessons dialogic with Black liberation or with our further, and rapidly repetitive, demise?

Given the period under consideration, the writing of Black film theorists tends to share a common anxiety about the status of the filmic text and the nature of its coherence. But let's keep in mind a point that I will expand on below: the ground of that anxiety has to do with the film's hegemonic value—as though there are representations that will make Black people safe, representations which will put us in danger, representations which will make us ideologically aware, and those which will give us false consciousness. For many, a good deal of emphasis is put on the interpellative power of the film itself.

In *Representing Blackness: Issues in Film and Video*, Valerie Smith notes two dominant trends: the first impulse reads "authentic" as synonymous with "positive" and seeks to supplant representations of Black lasciviousness and "irresponsibility" with "respectable" ones. To this end, she notes Gordon Parks's *The Learning Tree* (1968) and Michael Schulz's *Cooley High* (1975). But she adds that one can also find this impulse manifest in the films of certain White directors: Stanley Kramer's *Home of the Brave* (1949) and *Guess Who's Coming to Dinner* (1967), Norman Jewison's *In the Heat of the Night* (1967), and John Sayles's *Passion Fish* (1992). The second impulse is unconcerned with demonstrating the extent to which Black characters can conform to received, class-coded notions of respectability. Rather, it equates authenticity either with the freedom to seize and reanimate types previously coded as "negative" (i.e., the criminal or the buffoon) or with the presence of cultural practices rooted in Black vernacular experience (jazz, gospel, rootworking, religion, etc.). Duke Ellington's *Black and Tan* (1929) is an early example; it has been followed—after the two great migrations—by the urban-as-authentic Blaxploitation films of the late 1960s and the 1970s and finally the "new jack" pictures of the 1990s: *New Jack City* (1991) and *Menace II Society* (1993).

Smith claims that not only has Black filmmaking been preoccupied with a response to negative visual representation, but this preoccupation also has overdetermined criticism of Black film: that is, identifying and critiquing the recurrence of stereotyped representations in Hollywood films, Donald Bogle's *Toms, Coons, Mulattoes, Mammies, & Bucks* and Thomas Cripps's *Black Film as Genre* "inventoried the reproduction of certain types of Black characters in visual media." Smith finds that these "groundbreaking" texts "also legitimated a binarism in the discourse around strategies of Black representation that has outlived its usefulness." Furthermore, she elaborates, "despite their constructedness, media representations of members of historically disenfranchised communities reflect and, in turn, affect the lived circumstances of real people. But the relationship between media representations and 'real life' is nothing if not complex and discontinuous; to posit a one-to-one correspondence between the inescapability of certain images and the uneven distribution of recourse within culture is to deny the elaborate ways in which power is maintained and deployed."[10]

The problem with the positive/negative debate, as Smith and a second wave (my shorthand) of Black film theorists like bell hooks, James Snead, and Manthia Diawara see it, is threefold. First, the debate focuses critical scrutiny on how Blacks have been represented in Hollywood films at the expense of analytical, theoretical, and historical work on the history of Black-directed cinema. Second, it presupposes consensus about what a positive or negative (or authentic) image actually is. Hardworking, middle-class, heterosexual Blacks may be positive to some Black viewers but reprehensible (if only because they are totalizing) to Black gays and lesbians. Third, "it focuses viewer attention on the existence of certain types and not on the more significant questions around what kind of narrative or ideological work that type is meant to perform."[11]

Bogle's *Toms, Coons, Mulattoes, Mammies, & Bucks* reveals how the image of Blacks in American movies has changed and also the (he would say "shocking") way in which it has remained the same. In 1973, Bogle's study was the first history of Black performers in U.S. film. Bogle notes that only one other "formal piece of work" had been written before his, the Englishman Peter Noble's *The Negro in Films* (1948). Bogle dismisses Noble's book as exemplifying "the typical, unintentionally patronizing, white liberal 'tasteful' approach."[12] By his own admission *Toms, Coons* is as much a history of the contributions of Black performers to U.S. film as it is a statement of his own evolving aesthetic and perspective.

Bogle's book is called by many a classic and definitive study of Black images in Hollywood. I would prefer "classic and exhaustive"—leaving the adjective *definitive* for James Snead's three-times-shorter *White Screens, Black Images*. Bogle's tome is more of a historical inventory (and we're all grateful to him for it) than a history or a historiography. If there was a Black person who had a speaking role in a Hollywood film, she or he is more than likely inventoried in Bogle's book. Prior to this inventory, not only was there not a published cinematic record of so many of the Black stars in the first seventy years of the twentieth century, but for many of them, as Bogle points out in the first half of his book, there was no public record of them as *people*: "The lives of early Black performers . . . usually ended up so tragically, or so desperately unfulfilled, with Hollywood often contributing to their tragedies. . . . One important Black actor ended his days as a redcap. Another became a notorious Harlem pool-shark. Some became hustlers of all sorts. At least two vivacious leading ladies ended up as domestic workers. Other Black luminaries drifted into alcoholism, drugs, suicide, or bitter self-recrimination."[13]

Bogle's *Toms, Coons, Mulattoes, Mammies, & Bucks*, Cripps's well-known *Black Film as Genre*, and Gladstone L. Yearwood's *Black Film as a Signifying Practice* are three early examples of what I call First Wave Black film theory (with the notable exception of Yearwood, who began writing almost thirty years after Bogle and Cripps) and decidedly emphatic voices that theorize the emancipatory and pedagogic value of Black cinema from the text to the spectator. They "stress the need for more positive roles, types, and portrayals, while pointing out the intractable presence of 'negative stereotypes' in the film industry's depiction" of Blacks.[14] Here, however (again with the notable exception of Yearwood) semiotic, poststructuralist, feminist, and psychoanalytic tools of the political modernists were neglected in their hunt for the "negative" or "positive" image. Yearwood's work is exceptional for its use of the antiessentialist tools of semiotics and poststructuralism in a call for an Afrocentric, essentialist aesthetic.

Yearwood argues that Black film criticism is best understood as a twentieth-century development in the history of Black aesthetic thought. He maintains that Black filmmakers use expressive forms and systems of signification that reflect the cultural and historical priorities of the Black experience. In this way, the book resonates with much of what is advanced in Diawara's volume of edited essays *Black American Cinema*. However, the Afrocentrism of Yearwood's book, at times, seems to try to isolate the Black film's narrational processes from Black filmmakers' position under White supremacy.

Part 1 of Yearwood's book presents an overview of Black film and an introduction to Black film culture. It surveys the emergence of the Black independent film movement from the perspective of the Black cultural tradition. This marks a shift away from much of what takes place in Diawara's *Black American Cinema*, which locates the emergence of Black independent film in relation to certain political texts (like Fanon's *The Wretched of the Earth*) and domestic and international struggles for liberation and self-determination. Yearwood's book gives a close reading of films at the level of the diegesis, but it also betrays a kind of conceptual anxiety with respect to the historical object of study—in other words, it clings, anxiously, to the film-as-text-as-legitimate-object of Black cinema. Yearwood writes:

> The term Black cinema describes a specific body of films produced in the African Diaspora which shares a common problematic. . . . A primary assumption is that Black culture is syncretic in nature and reflects hybridized forms that are unique to the Americas. This process

of creolization, which is evident in African American classical music (Jazz), represents the forging of a new ontology and epistemology. It is the product of cultural practices that have developed from the experience of slavery, the struggle for freedom from oppression and the recognition that interdependence is the key to our survival.[15]

Later he notes: "As an expression that emanates from the heart of the African American community, good Black film can represent that which is most unique and best in Black culture. A good Black film can provide an intellectual challenge and engage our cognitive faculties. It can often present incisive commentary on social realities."[16] These two quotes are emblematic of just how vague the aesthetic foundation of Yearwood's attempt to construct a canon can be. In contrast, the book excels in its synthesis of so much of the literature on Black film which precedes it (including Diawara's work). But in trying to show how Black filmmakers differ from White filmmakers and that the Black film as text is a stand-alone object, Yearwood reverts to conclusions general enough to apply to almost any filmography; furthermore, his claims are underwritten by the philosophical, and semiotic, treatises of European (not African) theoreticians.

James Snead, Jacqueline Bobo, bell hooks, Valerie Smith, and Manthia Diawara belong to what I call the second wave of Black film theorists, who complicated the field by using methodologies which (a) examine the film as a text and a discourse and (b) bring into this examination an exploration of cinema's subject-effects on implied spectators. The emphasis here should be on *implied*, for, in most cases, these books and articles are not grounded in overt theories and methodologies of spectatorship. The advance, if you will, of this body of work over that of Cripps and Bogle is twofold. First, these works challenged the binarism of good/bad, positive/negative images of cinema. Thus, they opened the space for the iconography of third positions like unwed Black women, gangsters, gays, and lesbians to enter into the Black cinematic "family." Second, by way of sophisticated textual analyses, they were able to show how Black images can be degraded and White images can be monumentalized and made mythic, rather than simply making proclamations (good/bad) based on uninterrogated values (i.e., nuclear family values, upward mobility values, heterosexual values) already in the room. To put it plainly, they replaced social values as the basis of cinematic interpretation with semiotic codes, and in so doing made central the question of ideology—much as White political modernists were doing on the heels of Lacan.

In "A No-Theory Theory of Contemporary Black Cinema," Tommy Lott reflects on the paradoxes inherent in the very category of "Black film." His claim: the essentialist criteria by which a "Black" film is understood to be one directed by a person of African American descent too frequently allows biological categories to stand in for ideological ones. Conversely, aesthetically grounded definitions of Black film risk privileging independent productions uncritically. With this direct political challenge to both Yearwood and Bogle, he suggests that the notion of Third Cinema could be appropriated for Blacks. (Such appropriation resembles how White film theorists developed the concept of countercinema through their translations of Lacan's writings on the psychoanalytic cure of "full speech.") Here is Lott's appropriation of Third Cinema for Black Americans—his response to the identity politics of Bogle and Yearwood: "What makes Third Cinema third (i.e., a viable alternative to Western cinema) is not exclusively the racial makeup of a filmmaker, a film's aesthetic character, or a film's intended audience, but rather a film's political orientation within the hegemonic structures of postcolonialism. When a film contributes ideologically to the advancement of Black people, within a context of systematic denial, the achievement of this political objective ought to count as a criterion of evaluation on a par with any essentialist criterion."[17]

Second wave Black film theorists such as Snead, Lott, Smith, Diawara, and hooks were able to bring a dimension to Black film theory that stemmed from their willingness to interrogate not just the narrative in relation to time-worn tropes of Black upward mobility, but also from their desire to interrogate cinematic formalism (i.e., mise-en-scène, acoustics, editing strategies, lighting), in other words, cinema as an apparatus or institution in relation to the derelict institutional status of Black people. But these writers fell short in perceiving Blackness as having either some institutional status or the potential for institutional status. They were not inclined to meditate on the archaic persistence of two key ontological qualities of the legacy of slavery, namely, the condition of absolute captivity and the state of virtual noncommunication within official culture. Similarly, I take the recent celebration of the superstars Halle Berry and Denzel Washington in both the Black press and the White critical establishment as symptomatic of a refusal or inability to countenance the long shadow of slavery insofar as it writes a history of the present. That is, the heralding of Black stardom, now disavowing its relation to long-standing cinematic stereotypes, is founded on a belief in not only the possibility of redress under White supremacy, but also its relative ease. Central to this belief is a historical reduction of slavery to the relation of chattel and a formulation of Black emancipation and enfranchisement limited to the most nominal dimensions of civil rights and liberties.

Embracing Black people's agency as subjects of the law (i.e., subjects of rights and liberties), and even their potential to act as or partner with enforcers of the law (i.e., Denzel Washington in *Training Day*), presents itself as an acting out of the historic paradox of Black nonexistence (i.e., the mutable continuity of social death). Here, Black "achievement" in popular culture and the commercial arts requires the bracketing out of that nonexistence in hopes of telling a tale of loss that is intelligible within the national imagination.[18] The insistence on Black personhood (rather than a radical questioning of the terror embedded in that very notion) operates most poignantly in the examples discussed through the problematic coding of gender and domesticity.

In perceiving Black folk as being alive, or at least having the potential to live in the world, the same potential that any subaltern might have, the politics of Black film theorists' aesthetic methodology and desire disavowed the fact that "[Black folk] are always already dead wherever you find them. The nurturing haven of black culture which assured memory and provided a home beyond the ravishing growth of capitalism is no longer. There cannot be any cultural authenticity in resistance to capitalism. The illusion of immaterial purity is no longer possible. It is no longer possible to be black against the system. Black folk are dead, killed by their own faith in willfully being beyond, and in spite of, power."[19]

In short, a besetting hobble of the theorization itself is one which the theory shares with many of the Black films it scrutinizes: both the films and the theory tend to posit a possibility of, and a desire for, Black existence instead of acknowledging the ontological claim of the Afropessimists that Blackness is that outside which makes it possible for White and non-White (i.e., Asians and Latinos) positions to exist and, simultaneously, contest existence. As such, not only is Blackness (Slaveness) outside the terrain of the White (the Master), it is outside the terrain of the subaltern. Unfortunately, almost to a person, the film theorists in question see themselves as (i.e., their assumptive logic takes as given that they are) subjects—dominated, oppressed, downtrodden, reduced to subaltern status, but subjects nonetheless—in a world of other subjects.[20]

The assumptions that Black academics are subalterns in the academy (rather than the Slaves of their "colleagues"), that slavery was a historical event long ended rather than the ongoing paradigm of Black (non)existence, and that Black film theory can harness the rhetorical strategy of simile are most prominent in the work of second wave Black film theorists, who apparently can't bear to live in the impasse of being an object and so turn to hypercoherent articulations of Third Cinema in order to propose a politics for cinematic interpretation. Lott, for example, short-circuits what could otherwise be a profoundly iconoclastic intervention, that is, the proposal that the Third World can fight *against* domination and *for* the return of colonized peoples' land, for they are people with a narrative of repair, whereas Slaves can only fight *against* slavery—the *for*-something-else can only be theorized, if at all, in the process and at the end of the requisite violence against the Settler/Master, not before.[21] Despite having ventured into the first unfortunate move—a need to communicate with other groups of people through the positing of, and anxiety over, Black coherence—Lott's work does make brilliant interventions. Unfortunately, not only does the drive toward a presentation of a Black film canon show a desire to participate in the institutionality of cinema, but the work itself shows a desire to participate in the institutionality of academia. And "participation" is a register unavailable to Slaves. Black film theory, as an intervention, would have a more destructive impact if it foregrounded the impossibility of a Black film, the impossibility of a Black film theory, the impossibility of a Black film theorist, and the impossibility of a Black person except, and this is key, under "cleansing" conditions of violence.[22] Only when real violence is coupled with representational "monstrosity,"[23] can Blacks move from the status of things to the status of . . . of what, we'll just have to wait and see.

In thinking the Black spectator as exploited rather than accumulated, the Second Wave of Black film theorists failed to realize that Slaves are not subalterns, because subalterns are dominated, in the ontological first instance, by the machinations of hegemony (of which cinema is a vital machine) and then, after some symbolic transgression, in other words in the second instance, by violence. Blackness is constituted by violence in the ontological first instance. This, Hortense Spillers reminds us, is the essence of Black being: *"being* for the captor"—the very antithesis of cultural expression or performative agency.[24]

Lacan's Corrective

What is the essential arrangement of the subject's condition of unfreedom? Every film theorist seems to have an answer (stated or implied) to this question. Though theorists perceive the field of these "answers" to be of a wide variety (which they are at the level of content), we could say that the structure of the subject's condition of unfreedom is imagined along one or two shared vectors: the dispossession and stagnation within political economy (Marx) and the dispossession and stagnation within libidinal economy (Lacan). The two are sometimes combined, but rarely are they weighted equally. This is the rebar of the conceptual framework of film studies; and I would not be surprised if it was the same for other theorizations that seek to theorize (a) dispossession and (b) specific cultural practices (e.g., countercinema or performance art) as modes of accompaniment for the redress of said dispossession.

The remainder of this chapter interrogates the efficacy of aesthetic gestures in their role as accompaniments to notions of emancipation within the libidinal economy (as opposed to Gramscian emphasis on political economy). This is a high-stakes interrogation because so much film theory (White, or, non-Black—i.e., Human—film theory) is in fee to Lacan and his underlying thesis on subjectivity and psychic liberation. It does not seek to disprove Lacan's underlying theory of how the subject comes into subjectivity via alienation within the imaginary and the symbolic; nor does it seek to disprove his understanding of psychic stagnation (described as egoic monumentalization) as that condition from which the subject (and by extension, the socius) must be liberated. Rather than attempt to disprove Lacan's (and, by extension non-Black film theory's) evidence and assumptive logic I seek to show how, in aspiring to a paradigmatic explanation of relations, his assumptive logic mystifies rather than clarifies a paradigmatic explanation of relations. Although it vividly accounts for the conflicts between genders, or, more broadly, narcissistic contemporaries and contemporaries who have learned to live in a deconstructive relation to the ego—that is to say, although it offers a reliable toolbox for rigorously examining intra-Human conflicts (and for proposing the aesthetic gestures, i.e., types of filmic practices, which either exacerbate or redress these conflicts, as do Hollywood movies and countercinema, respectively)—it cannot give a paradigmatic explanation of the structure of antagonisms between Blacks and Humans. I argue that the claims and conclusions which Lacanian psychoanalysis (and by extension non-Black film theory) makes regarding dispossession and suffering are (1) insufficient to the task of delineating Black dispossession and suffering, and (2) parasitic on that very Black dispossession and suffering for which it has no words.

In "The Function and Field of Speech and Language in Psychoanalysis," Lacan illustrates what remains to this day one of the most brilliant and comprehensive scenarios for attaining what some believe to be the only bit of freedom we will ever know.[25] Lacan's value to psychoanalysis in particular and critical theory in general was that he removed fear and loathing from the word *alienation*. Alienation, for Lacan, is what literally makes subjectivity possible. Unlike Brecht, who saw alienation (some prefer *distancing*) as the ideological effect of false consciousness, Lacan saw it as the necessary context, the grid which makes human relations possible and divides the world between those with sociability (subjects) and those without it (*infans*—children, say, prior to eighteen months of age). On the grid of sociability, however, it is possible to imagine that one exists in relation to signification as though words were windows on the world—or, worse yet, the very things they signify. These, of course are the speech acts through which subjects monumentalize their presence in disavowal of the very loss of presence (lack) which alienation has imposed on them in exchange for a world with others. This is the meaning of "empty speech,"

> which Lacan consistently defines in opposition to full speech. [Empty speech] is predicated upon the belief that we can be spatially and temporally present to ourselves, and that language is a tool for effecting this self-possession. But instead of leading to self-possession, empty speech is the agency of an "ever-growing dispossession." When we speak empty speech, we lift ourselves out of time, and freeze ourselves

into an object or "statue." . . . We thereby undo ourselves as subjects. . . . [Empty speech's] refusal of symbolization in a second sense [is] what the analysand literally or metaphorically utters when he responds to the figural forms through which the past returns as if their value and meaning were immanent within them.[26]

In short, the analysand collapses the signifier with that which is signified and in so doing seeks to " 'entify' or 'fill up' the signifier—to make it identical with itself." This entification (or monumentalization) is the subject's refusal to surrender to temporality, "the fact that every psychically important event depends for its value and meaning on reference to an earlier or a later one. The analysand also fails to see that with his object-choices and other libidinal acts he is speaking a language of desire. Empty speech is what the analysand classically utters during the early stages of analysis."[27]

But just as language, on the grid of alienation, can be assumed as the method through which signifiers are entified and egos are monumentalized to "shield" the subject from the fact of alienation, so language can also be that agency through which the subject learns to live in a deconstructive relation to this alienation—learns to live with lack. Rather than monumentalizing the image of a present and unified self, subjects can learn instead to comprehend the symbolic relation that has positioned them.

The later stages of the analysis ideally bring the subject to full speech. The analysand engages in full speech when he understands that his literal and metaphoric words are in fact signifiers—neither equivalent to things, nor capable of saying "what" they are, but rather a retroaction to an anticipation of other signifiers. Full speech is also speech in which the analysand recognizes within what he has previously taken to be the 'here and now' the operations of a very personal system of signification—the operations, that is, of what Lacan calls his *primary language*."[28]

As a description of and a prescription for emancipation from suffering, the Lacanian notion of full speech was a brake on what, in the 1950s, was becoming psychoanalysis's slippery slope toward idealism and essentialism. Lacan cited three basic problems with the psychoanalysis of the

1950s: object relations,[29] the role of countertransference, and the place of fantasy.[30] In all of them, he noted "the temptation for the analyst to abandon the foundation of speech, and this precisely in areas where, because they border on the ineffable, its use would seem to require a more than usually close examination."[31]

The "wall of language" is one that, for Lacan, cannot be penetrated by the analysand except in his or her a-subjective state, that is, either as an infans (that state of being prior to alienation in the symbolic) or as a corpse (that state of being after alienation—Death). Within the analytic context, there is nothing meaningful on the other side of language. "Beyond this wall, there is nothing for us but outer darkness. Does this mean that we are entirely masters of the situation? Certainly not, and on this point Freud has bequeathed us his testament on the negative therapeutic reaction."[32] Analysands jettison their projected and imaginary relation to the analyst and come to understand where they are finally in relation to the analyst (which is outside of themselves) and from the place of the analyst (a stand-in for the symbolic order); they come to hear their own language and become auditors in relation to their own speech. "The analysis consists of getting him to become conscious of his relations, not with the ego of the analyst, but with all these Others who are his true interlocutors, whom he hasn't recognized." All these Others are none other than the Lacanian contemporaries or, in the vernacular most salient to the Slave, Whites and their junior partners in civil society—Humans positioned by the symbolic order. "It is a matter of the subject progressively discovering which Other he is truly addressing, without knowing it, and of him progressively assuming the relations of transference at the place where he is, and where at first he didn't know he was."[33] Again, there is no locating of subjectivity within oneself. Lacan is clear: one cannot have a relationship with oneself. Instead, one comes to understand one's existence, one's place outside of oneself. In coming to understand one's place outside of oneself one can hear oneself and assume one's speech—in other words, assume one's desire.

Lacan was alarmed at the increasing concern of psychoanalysis with exploring the analysand's fantasies—a practice which, again, subordinated exploration of the symbolic to exploration of the imaginary.[34] The imaginary relation puts the analysand in an identificatory relation to the Other, whether that Other be his or her own image, an external representation, or an outside Other. This relation is one in which the analysand allows the Other to have only a fraction of "otherness": the analysand can barely apprehend the otherness of the Other, because the psyche says, "That's me." But this is the worst kind of ruse and induces feelings of disarray and insufficiency, putting the analysand in an aggressive relation of rivalry to the Other, for this (imaginary) Other occupies the place the analysand wants to occupy. Through such processes, analysis intensifies rather than diminishes the analysand's narcissism.

Many psychoanalysts in Great Britain and the United States extolled the virtues of an encounter between the analysand and analyst which culminated in an emboldened ego that fortified the monument of a strengthened psyche able, as these claims would have it, to brace itself against the very onslaughts which had produced its crippling frustration. These psychoanalysts' views were underpinned by the rhetorical scaffolding of common sense and, so it seemed, empirical "evidence" of cured analysands. What, then, made Lacan so steadfast in his conviction to the contrary?

> This ego, whose strength our theorists now define by its strength to bear frustration, is frustration in its essence. Not frustration of a desire of the subject, but frustration by an object in which his desire is alienated and which the more it is elaborated, the more profound the alienation from his *jouissance* becomes for the subject. . . . to identify the ego with the discipline of the subject is to confuse imaginary isolation with the mastery of the instincts. This lays open to error of judgment in the conduct of the treatment: such as trying to reinforce the *ego* in many neuroses caused by its over forceful structure—and that is a dead end."[35]

The process of full speech, then, is one that catalyzes disorder and deconstruction rather than order and unity, "the monumental construct of [the analysand's] narcissism."[36] Countering psychology's practice of fortifying the ego in an effort to end the frustration of neurosis, Lacan proposed a revolutionary analytic encounter in which the analysand becomes

> engaged in an ever growing dispossession of that being of his, concerning which—by dint of sincere portraits which leave its idea no less incoherent, of rectifications that do not succeed in freeing its essence,

of stays and defenses that do not prevent his statue from tottering, of narcissistic embraces that become like a puff of air in animating it—he ends up by recognizing that this being has never been anything more than his construct in the imaginary and that this construct disappoints all certainties. . . . For in this labor which he undertakes to reconstruct *for another*, he rediscovers *the fundamental alienation* [my emphases] which made him construct it *like* another, and which has always destined it [the ego] to be taken from him by another.[37]

This notion of "labor" which the analysand "undertakes to reconstruct *for another*" and thereby rediscovers "the fundamental alienation which made him construct it *like* another, and which has always destined it [the ego] to be taken from him by another" returns us to the thorny issue of "contemporaries." Now we must take it up, not in a context of universal, unraced subjects (Whites), or in a culturally modified context of specific identities ("dark" Whites and non-Blacks), but rather in a context of positional polarity which structures civil society and its nether region—namely, the polarity of Human and Black, the context of Masters and Slaves.

The analytic schema of Lacan's breakthrough known as "full speech" posits a subject whose suffering is produced by alienation in the image of the other, or captation within the imaginary, and whose freedom must be produced by alienation in the language of the other, or interpellation within the symbolic. The subject is constituted as subject proper only through a relation to the other. For Lacan, alienation, either in the imaginary or in the symbolic, is the modality productive of subjectivity for *all* sentient beings. In other words, subjectivity is a discursive, or signifying, process of becoming.

Psychic disorder, by way of the death drive, is that mechanism in Lacanian analysis that brings the analysand to his or her understanding of him- or herself as a void. For Lacan, the problems of speech and the death drive are related; the relationship presents the irony "of two contrary terms: instinct in its most comprehensive acceptation being the law that governs in its succession a cycle of behavior whose goal is the accomplishment of a vital function; and death appearing first of all as the destruction of life."[38] But Lacan is clear that though death is implied, it is life through language which is the aim of analysis. (This too bears heavily on what, I argue below, is the poverty of full speech's political or emancipatory promise.) Only by being alienated within the Big A, language, or the symbolic order, does the *moi*, small a or ego, come to be the *je*, the subject of lack, the subject of a void. Prior to the analysand's realizing full speech, she or he projects onto the analyst all of the fantasms which constitute his or her ego. The emancipatory process of Lacan's psychoanalytic encounter is one in which the analysand passes from positing the analyst as the small a, to one in which the analyst occupies, for the analysand, the position of the Big A, a position synonymous with language itself. For Lacan, these two moves complement each other. It bears repeating that this intersubjectivity, alienation in the other, exists whether the subject grasps it or not, whether or not she or he is the subject of full speech or empty speech. But we are still left with alienation as the structuring modality for subjectivity. Whether, by way of description, we posit the analysand as being either alienated in the imaginary (ego, small a) or as being alienated in the symbolic (language as structure, as the unconscious of the Other)—or even if, in addition, we recognize the fact that full speech as prescription demands alienation within the symbolic—we remain left with the fact that, where *becoming* is concerned, alienation is subjectivity's essential modality of existence. Alienation is, for Lacan, an essential grammar of political ontology.

As I stated above, I am not arguing that the unconscious does not exist. Nor am I claiming that sentient beings, whether Human or Black, are not indeed alienated in the imaginary and the symbolic. I am arguing that whereas alienation is an essential grammar underpinning Human relationality, it is an important but ultimately inessential grammar when one attempts to think the structural interdiction against Black recognition and incorporation.[39] In other words, alienation is a grammar underwriting all manner of relationality, whether narcissistic (egoic, empty speech) or liberated (full speech). But it is not a grammar that underwrites, much less explains, the absence of relationality.

Fanon and Full Speech

Jacques Lacan and Frantz Fanon grappled with the question *What does it mean to be free?* and its corollary *What does it mean to suffer?* at the same moment in history. To say that they both appeared at the same time is to say that they both have, as their intellectual condition of possibility, France's brutal occupation of Algeria. It is not my intention to dwell on Lacan's lack of political activism or to roll out Fanon's revolutionary war record. My intention is to interrogate the breadth of full speech's descriptive universality and the depth of its prescriptive cure—to interrogate its foundation by staging an encounter between, on the one hand, Lacan and his interlocutors and, on the other hand, Fanon and his interlocutors. To this end alone do I note the two men's relation to French colonialism, as the force of that relation is felt in their texts.

Fanon's psychoanalytic description of Black neurosis, "hallucinatory whitening," and his prescriptions for a cure, "decolonization" and "the end of the world," resonate with Lacan's categories of empty speech and full speech. There is a monumental disavowal of emptiness involved in hallucinatory whitening, and disorder and death certainly characterize decolonization. For Fanon the trauma of Blackness lies in its absolute Otherness in relation to Whites. That is, White people make Black people by recognizing only their skin color. Fanon's Black patient is "overwhelmed . . . by the wish to be white." But unlike Lacan in his diagnosis of the analysand, Fanon makes a direct and self-conscious connection between his patient's hallucinatory whitening and the stability of White society. If Fanon's texts ratchet violently and unpredictably between the body of the subject and the body of the socius, it is because Fanon understands that "outside [his] psychoanalytic office, [he must] incorporate [his] conclusions into the context of the world." The room is too small to contain the encounter. "As a psychoanalyst, I should help my patient to become conscious of his unconscious and abandon his attempts at a hallucinatory whitening." Here we have a dismantling of all the fantasms that constitute the patient's ego and which she or he projects onto the analyst; this process resonates with that of attaining what Lacan calls full speech. But Fanon takes this a step further, for he wants the analysand not only to surrender to the void of language, but also to "act in the direction of a change . . . with respect to the real source of the conflict—that is, toward the social structures."[40]

As a psychoanalyst, Fanon does not dispute Lacan's claim that suffering and freedom are produced and attained, respectively, in the realm of symbolic; but this, for Fanon, is only half of the modality of existence. The other half of suffering and freedom is violence. By the time Fanon has woven the description of his patient's condition (i.e., his own life as a Black doctor in France) into the prescription for a cure (his commitment to armed struggle in Algeria), he has extended the logic of disorder and death from the symbolic into the real. "Decolonization, which sets out to change the order of the world, is, obviously, a program of complete disorder. . . . It is the meeting of two forces, opposed to each other by their very nature. . . . Their first encounter was marked by violence and their existence together . . . was carried on by dint of a great array of bayonets and cannons. . . . This narrow world, strewn with prohibitions, can only be called in question by absolute violence."[41]

This is because the structural, or absolute, violence, what Loïc Wacquant calls the "carceral continuum," is not a Black experience but a condition of Black "life." It remains constant, paradigmatically, despite changes in its "performance" over time—slave ship, Middle Passage, Slave estate, Jim Crow, the ghetto, and the prison-industrial complex.[42] There is an uncanny connection between Fanon's absolute violence and Lacan's real. Thus, by extension, the grammar of suffering of the Black itself is on the level of the real. In this emblematic passage, Fanon does for violence what Lacan does for alienation: namely, he removes the negative stigma such a term would otherwise incur in the hands of theorists and practitioners who seek coherence and stability. He also raises in Lacan's schema of suffering and freedom a contradiction between the idea of universal unraced contemporaries and two forces opposed to each other, whose first encounter and existence together is marked by violence. In short, he divides the world not between cured contemporaries and uncured contemporaries, but between contemporaries of all sorts and Slaves. He lays the groundwork for a theory of antagonism over and above a theory of conflict.

If Lacan's full speech is not, in essence, a "cure" but a process promoting psychic disorder, through which the subject comes to know her- or himself, not as a stable relation to a true "self"—the imaginary—but as a void constituted only by language, a becoming toward death in relation to the Other—the symbolic—then we will see how this symbolic self-cancellation is possible only when the subject and "his contemporaries" are White or Human.[43] The process of full speech rests on a tremendous disavowal which *re*monumentalizes the (White) ego because it sutures, rather than cancels, formal stagnation by fortifying and extending the interlocutory life of intra-Human discussions.

I am arguing (1) that civil society, the terrain on which the analysand performs full speech, is always already a formally stagnated monument; and (2) that the process by which full speech is performed brokers simultaneously two relations for the analysand, one new and one old. The process by which full speech is performed brokers a (new) deconstructive relationship between the analysand and his or her formal stagnation within civil society and a (pre-existing or) reconstructive relationship between the analysand and the formal stagnation that constitutes civil society.

Whereas Lacan was aware of how language "precedes and exceeds us,"[44] he did not have Fanon's awareness of how violence also precedes and exceeds Blacks. An awareness of this would have disturbed the coherence of the taxonomy implied by the personal pronoun *us*. The trajectory of Lacan's full speech, therefore, is only able to make sense of violence as contingent phenomena, as effects of "transgressions" (acts of rebellion or refusal) within a symbolic order. Here, violence, at least in the first instance, is neither senseless (gratuitous) nor a matrix of human (im)possibility; it is what happens after some form of breach occurs in the realm of signification. That is to say, it is contingent.

Implied in this gesture toward Lacan's trajectory on violence are several questions regarding full speech. First, can Lacanian full speech, wedded as it is to the notion that there is no world to apprehend beyond the realm of signification, adequately theorize those bodies that emerge from direct relations of force? Which is to ask, is the logic of full speech too imbricated in the institutionality of anti-Blackness to be descriptively or prescriptively adequate for thinking Black positionality? In trying to read Human suffering and its effects (what Lacan calls empty speech), as well as Human freedom and its effects (what he calls full speech), through the figure of a Blackened position, can one simply assume that, despite relations of pure force which distinguish one "epidermal schema"[45] from another, relations of signification have the power to cast webs of analogy between such disparate positions? Do webs of analogy exist strong enough to circumscribe relations of pure force, so that all sentient beings can be seen as each others' "contemporaries"? Put another way, is full speech for the Master full speech for the Slave? What would it mean for a Master to live in a deconstructive relation to his *moi*? Is "liberated Master" an oxymoron or, worse yet, simply redundant? Through what agency (volition? will?) does a Slave entify the signifier? Which is to ask, can there be such a thing as a narcissistic Slave? Or, what is full speech for a Slave? Lacan seems to take for granted the universal relevance of (1) the analytic encounter, (2) the centrality of signification, and (3) the possibility of "contemporaries." But can a Blackened position take up these coordinates with merely a few culturally specific modifications, or does blackening these coordinates precipitate crises writ large?

I contend that the web of analogy cast between the subject of analysis and her or his "contemporaries," in the process of full speech, is rent asunder by insertion of the Black position, who is less a site of subjectification and more a site of desubjectification—a "species" of absolute dereliction, a hybrid of "person and property," and a body that magnetizes bullets.[46] I intend to scale upward (to the socius) the implications of Lacanian full speech to illustrate its place as a strategy which fortifies and extends the interlocutory life of civil society, and scale downward (to the body) the implications of Fanonian decolonization to illustrate the incommensurability between Black flesh and the body of the analysand. Full speech is a strategy of psychic disorder, within Human limits, and decolonization is a strategy of complete disorder, without any limits.[47] The implications of this dilemma are profound, for it suggests that Lacanian full speech—like film theory, so much of which stands on its shoulders—is an accomplice to social stability, despite its claims to the contrary.

At the crux of this critique is (a) the unbridgeable gap between the ethical stance of Lacanian full speech and the ethical stance of Fanonian decolonization—in other words, the method by which Lacanian full speech intensifies a disavowal of a violence-structuring matrix—and (b) the question of the analysand's "contemporaries," the language of which, according to Lacan, the analysand speaks when she or he shatters the monuments of the ego's "formal stagnation." To what extent can the analysand become the Slave's contemporary as the latter seeks to shatter civil society? To which call to arms would the analysand be compelled to respond?

What constitutes the ground on which the analysand is able to do the deconstructive work of full speech? My contention is that prior to, and contemporaneous with, the analytic encounter, the Black body "labors" as an enslaved hybridity of person and property so that the analysand may "labor" as a liberated subject.[48] Furthermore, it is the matrix of violence which divides the enslaved from the unenslaved, just as the matrix of alienation divides the infans from the subject: violence zones the Black whereas alienation zones the Human. But whereas "becoming toward death," which results from the Lacanian analytic encounter, allows analysands to deconstruct their monumentalized presence in the face of alienation and a life papered over by language, analysis additionally allows analysands to take for granted (be oblivious to) the matrix of violence which zoned their terrain of "generalized trust,"[49] that terrain euphemistically referred to as "civil" society. "Generalized trust" (racialized Whiteness), along with relative stability, are the preconditions for the analytic encounter, or any other "civil" encounter. Fanon makes clear how some are zoned, a priori, beyond the borders of generalized trust: "This world divided into compartments, this world cut in two is inhabited by two different species. . . . When you examine at close quarters the colonial context, it is evident that what parcels out the world is to begin with the fact of belonging to a given race, a given species. In the colonies the economic substructure is also a superstructure. The cause is the consequence; you are rich because you are white, you are white because you are rich."[50]

When I say that the analysand can take for granted the matrix of violence which zoned his terrain of "generalized trust," I mean that unless the world is parceled out—unless there are two species—she or he cannot commence the work of becoming toward death, nor could Lacan have theorized the work. In short, violence—the "species" division, the zoning, of the enslaved and the unenslaved—is the condition of possibility on which subjectivity (the empty- vs. full speech paradigm: the imaginary vs. symbolic dialectic) can be theorized (i.e., the writing of *Ecrits*) and performed (the analytic encounter). But this theorization and performance, by ignoring its relation to the species zoning which "labors" for its condition of possibility, deconstructs the monuments of the analysand's ego, while simultaneously fortifying and extending the ramparts of civil society which circumscribed those monuments. In short, the trajectory of disorder toward full speech deconstructs what prohibits relations between the analysand and his "contemporaries" while simultaneously entifying and unifying what prohibits relations between species (between Masters and Slaves). Despite Lacan's radical interventions against the practical limitations of object relations and the ideological pitfalls of ego psychology, the process of full speech is nonetheless foundational to the vertical integration of anti-Blackness.

I said above that I wanted to scale upward the implications of Lacanian full speech to illustrate its place as a strategy which fortifies and extends the interlocutory life of civil society, and scale downward the implications of Fanonian decolonization to the level of the body to illustrate the incommensurability between Black flesh and the body of the analysand—how those two positions subtend each other but, like a plane to an angle, mutually construct their triangulated context. Before unpacking, at the level of the body, what this relationship makes (im)possible, I am compelled to extend the cartography of this very intimate encounter, that is, to ratchet the scale up from the body to the socius—where civil society subtends its nether region.

Civil Society and Its Discontents

As I noted above, before the "healthy" rancor and repartee at the cornerstone of civil society can get underway (whether in the boardroom, the polling booth, the bedroom, or the analyst's office), civil society must be relatively stable. But how is this stability to be achieved, and for whom? For Black people, civic stability is a state of emergency. Fanon and Steve Martinot and Jared Sexton explain why the stability of civil society is a state of emergency for Blacks.[51] Fanon writes of zones. For our purposes, we want to bear in mind the following: the zone of the Human (or non-Black—notwithstanding the fact that Fanon is a little too loose and liberal with his language when he calls it the zone of the postcolonial native) has "rules" within the zone that allow for existence of Humanist interaction—that is, Lacan's psychoanalytic encounter or Gramsci's proletarian struggle. This stems from the different paradigms of zoning mentioned earlier in terms of Black zones (void of Humanist interaction) and White zones (the quintessence of Humanist interaction).[52] "The zone where the native lives is not complementary to the zone inhabited by the settler. The two zones are opposed, but not in the service of higher unity. Obedient to the rules of pure Aristotelian logic, they both follow the principle of reciprocal exclusivity. No conciliation is possible, for of the two terms, one is superfluous. . . . The settler's town is a town of white people, of foreigners."[53] This is the basis of his assertion that two zones produce two different "species." The phrase "not in service of higher unity" dismisses any kind of dialectical optimism for a future synthesis. Fanon's specific context does not share the same historical or national context of Martinot's and Sexton's, but the Settler/Native dynamic, the differential zoning and the gratuity (as opposed to contingency) of violence which accrue to the Blackened position, are shared by the two texts.

Martinot and Sexton assert the primacy of Fanon's Manichaean zones (without the promise of higher unity) even when faced with the facticity of integration in the United States: "The dichotomy between white ethics [the discourse of civil society] and its irrelevance to the violence of police profiling is not dialectical; the two are incommensurable whenever one attempts to *speak* about the paradigm of policing, one is forced back into a discussion of particular events—high profile homicides and their related courtroom battles, for instance."[54]

It makes no difference that in the United States the "casbah" and the "European" zone are laid on top of each other, because what is being asserted here is the schematic interchangeability between Fanon's Settler society and Sexton's and Martinot's policing paradigm. (Whites in America are now so settled they no longer call themselves Settlers.) For Fanon, it is the policeman and soldier (not the discursive or hegemonic agents) of colonialism that make one town White and the other Black. For Martinot and Sexton, this Manichaean delirium manifests itself in the U.S. paradigm of policing which (re)produces, repetitively, the inside/outside, the civil society/Black void, by virtue of the difference between those bodies that do not magnetize bullets and those bodies that do. "Police impunity serves to distinguish between the racial itself and the elsewhere that mandates it. . . . the distinction between those whose human being is put permanently in question and those for whom it goes without saying."[55] In such a paradigm White people are, ipso facto, deputized in the face of Black people, whether they know it (consciously) or not.

Until the tapering off of weekly lynching in the 1960s, Whites were called on as individuals to perform this deputation.[56] The 1914 PhD dissertation of H. M. Henry (a scholar in no way hostile to slavery), "The Police Control of the Slave in South Carolina," reveals how vital this performance was in the construction of Whiteness for the Settlers of the 1600s, 1700s, and 1800s, as well as for the Settler-scholar (Henry himself) of the 1900s:

> The evolution of the patrol system is interesting. The need of keeping the slaves from roving was felt from the very first. Among the earliest of the colonial acts in 1686 is one that gave any person the right to apprehend, properly chastise, and send home any slave who might be found off his master's plantation without a ticket. This plan was not altogether effective, and in 1690 it was made the *duty* of all persons under penalty of forty shillings to arrest and chastise any slave [found] out of his home plantation without a proper ticket. This plan of making it everybody's business to punish wandering slaves seems to have been sufficient at least for a time.[57]

Today this process of species division does not turn Blacks into species and produce Whites with the existential potential of fully realized subjectivity in the same spectacular fashion as the spectacle of violence that Henry wrote of in South Carolina and that Fanon was accustomed to in Algeria. In fact, Martinot and Sexton maintain that attention to the spectacle causes us to think of violence as contingent on symbolic transgressions rather than thinking of it as a matrix for the simultaneous production of Black death and White civil society: "The spectacular event camouflages the operation of police law as contempt, police law is the fact that there is *no recourse to the disruption of* [Black] *people's lives by these activities.*"[58] By "no recourse" the authors are suggesting that Black people themselves serve a vital function as the living markers of gratuitous violence. And the spectacular event is a scene that draws attention away from the paradigm of violence. It functions as a crowding out scenario. Crowding out our understanding that, where violence is concerned, to be Black is to be beyond the limit of contingency. This thereby gives the bodies of the rest of society (Humans) some form of coherence (a contingent rather than gratuitous relationship to violence): "In fact, to focus on the spectacular event of police violence is to deploy (and thereby affirm) the logic of police profiling itself. Yet, we can't avoid this logic once we submit to the demand to provide examples or images of the paradigm [once we submit to signifying practices]. As a result, the attempt to articulate the paradigm of policing renders itself non-paradigmatic, reaffirms the logic of police profiling and thereby reduces itself to the fraudulent ethic by which white civil society rationalizes its existence."[59]

"The fraudulent ethic by which white civil society rationalizes its existence" endures in articulations between that species with actual *"recourse to the disruption"* of life (by the policing paradigm) and another member of the same species, such as the dialogue between news reporter and a reader, between a voter and a candidate, or between an analysand and his or her contemporaries. "Recourse to the disruption" of life is the first condition on which a conflict between entified signification and a true language of desire, a nonegoic language of contemporaries, full speech, can be staged: one must first be on the policing side, rather than the policed side, of that division made possible by the violence matrix. In other words, where violence is concerned, one must stay on this side of the wall of contingency (just as one must stay on this side of the wall of language by operating within the symbolic) to enable full speech. Both matrixes, violence and alienation, precede and anticipate the species.

Whiteness, then, and by extension civil society's junior partners, cannot be solely "represented" as some monumentalized coherence of phallic signifiers but must, in the first ontological instance, be understood as a formation of "contemporaries" who do not magnetize bullets. This is the essence of their construction through an *a*signifying absence; their signifying presence is manifest in the fact that they are, if only by default, deputized against those who do magnetize bullets: in short, White people are not simply "protected" by the police, they *are* the police.

Martinot and Sexton claim that the White subject-effects of today's policing paradigm are more banal than the White subject-effects of Fanon's Settler paradigm. For Martinot and Sexton, they cannot be explained by recourse to the *spectacle* of violence. "Police spectacle is not the effect of the racial uniform; rather, it is the police uniform that is producing re-racialization."[60] This "re-racialization" echoes Fanon's assertion that "the cause is the consequence; you are rich because you are white, you are white because you are rich."[61] Whereas in Fanon's settler paradigm this rich, White/White, rich circularity manifests itself in the automatic accrual of life producing potential, in Martinot and Sexton's paradigm of policing it manifests itself in the automatic accrual of life *itself*. It marks the difference between those who are alive, the subjects of civil society, and those who are fatally alive, or "socially dead," the "species" of "absolute dereliction."[62]

Again, the subject of civil society is the species that does not magnetize bullets, though the members of this species do not necessarily perform any advocacy of police practices or of the policing paradigm the way they had to in Henry's nineteenth-century South Carolina. As Martinot and Sexton argue, the civic stability of the twenty-first-century U.S. Slave estate is no longer every White person's duty to perform. In fact, many Whites on the left actually progressively oppose the police, but each performance of progressive opposition encounters what Martinot and Sexton call

> a certain internal limitation. . . . The supposed secrets of white supremacy get sleuthed in its spectacular displays, in pathology and instrumentality, or pawned off on the figure of the "rogue cop." Each approach to race subordinates it to something that is not race, as if to continue the noble epistemological endeavor of getting to know it better. But what each ends up talking about is that other thing. In the face of this, the Left's antiracism becomes its passion. But its passion gives it away. It signifies the passive acceptance of the idea that race, considered to be either a real property of a person or an imaginary projection, is not essential to the social structure, a system of social meanings and categorizations. It is the same passive apparatus of whiteness that in its mainstream guise actively forgets [in a way settlers of the first three centuries simply could not] that it owes its existence to the killing and terrorizing of those it racializes for the purpose, expelling them from the human fold in the same gesture of forgetting. It is the passivity of bad faith that tacitly accepts as "what goes without saying" the postulates of white supremacy. And it must do so passionately since "what goes without saying" is empty and can be held as "truth" only through an obsessiveness. The truth is that the truth is on the surface, flat and repetitive, just as the law is made by the uniform.[63]

A truth without depth, flat, repetitive, on the surface? This unrepresentable subject-effect is more complex than Henry's early Settler performances of communal solidarity in part because the gratuitousness of its repetition bestows upon white supremacy an inherent discontinuity. It stops and starts self-referentially, at whim. To theorize some political, economic, or psychological necessity for its repetition, its unending return to violence, its need to kill is to lose a grasp on that gratuitousness by thinking its performance is representable. Its acts of repetition are its access to unrepresentability; they dissolve its excessiveness into invisibility as simply daily occurrence. Whatever mythic content it pretends to claim is a priori empty. Its secret is that it has no depth. There is no dark corner that, once brought to the light of reason, will unravel its system. . . . its truth lies in the rituals that sustain its circuitous contentless logic; it is, in fact, nothing but its very practices.[64]

To claim that the paradigm of policing has no "mythic content," that its performance is "unrepresentable," and that there is no "political, economic, or psychological necessity for its repletion" is to say something more profound than merely, "Civil society exists in an inverse relation to its own claims." It is to say something more than what the authors say outright: that this inversion translates today in the police's making claims and demands on the institutionality of civil society and not the other way around. The extended implication of Martinot's and Sexton's claim is much more devastating. For this claim, with its emphasis on the gratuitousness of violence—a violence that cannot be represented but which positions species nonetheless—rearticulates Fanon's notion that, for Blacks, violence is a matrix of (im)possibility, a paradigm of ontology as opposed to a performance that is contingent on symbolic transgressions.

Alienation, however, that Lacanian matrix of symbolic and imaginary castration, on which codes are made and broken and full (or empty) speech is possible, comes to appear, by way of the psychoanalytic encounter, as the essential matrix of existence. We are in our place, Lacan insists, on this side of the wall of language.[65] It is the grid on which the analysand can short-circuit somatic compliance with hysterical symptoms and bring to a halt, however temporarily, the egoic monumentalization of empty speech. Thus, the psychoanalytic encounter in general, and Lacanian full speech in particular, works to crowd out the White subject's realization of his or her position by way of violence. It is this crowding-out scenario that allows the analysand of full speech to remain White but "cured" (a liberated master?). And, in addition, the scenario itself weighs in as one more of civil society's enabling accompaniments (like voting, coalition building, and interracial "love") for the production of the Slave—that entity: "insensible to ethics; he represents not only the absence of values, but also the negation of values. He is, let us dare to admit, the enemy of values, and in this sense he is the absolute evil. He is the corrosive element, destroying all that comes near him; he is the de-forming element, disfiguring all that has to do with beauty or morality; he is the depository of maleficent powers, *the unconscious and irretrievable instrument of blind forces.*"[66]

Unlike Fanon's baseline Black, situated a priori in absolute derelic-tion, Lacan's baseline analysand is situated a priori in personhood and circumscribed by "contemporaries" who are also persons. Lacan's body of subjectification is not of the same species as Fanon's body of desubjec-tification. I am not suggesting that Black people's psyches are free from machinations of the *moi* and therefore have no impediments in a process of "becoming toward death." What I am asking is: How are we to trust a Lacanian assessment of Black narcissism? Half of this contradiction could be solved if we simply renamed full speech "White speech" (or Human speech) and attached to the analyst's shingle *Blacks need not apply.* "They may not need apply but they are still essential in positing difference."[67] But coupled with this gesture of full disclosure regarding full speech, we would have to acknowledge that even in the White analysand's becom-ing toward death, that is to say, even after the stays and defenses that heretofore had kept his or her ego from tottering are all stripped away, yes, even after the narcissistic embraces of formal stagnation are hewn into kindling, and even after the labor through which the analysand has rediscovered his or her fundamental alienation, there will still be a nigger in the woodpile.

What Masters Rediscover in Slaves

The difference between Jesus and Buddha is that, though some people may become Christ-*like*, the church does not take kindly to the idea of Jesus being mass-produced. There is only one Jesus. He came once. One day, so goes the legend, he will come again. Amen. In the meantime we will just have to wait. A psychoanalysis modeled on Christianity would have a hard row to hoe. But by becoming toward death in a most unflinching manner anyone can become a Buddha. Small wonder Lacan's prescription for the analytic encounter looks toward this (non)religion with neither a church nor a god. Toward the end of "The Function and Field of Speech and Language in Psychoanalysis," Lacan acknowledges the debt full speech owes to Buddhism, but he adds, curiously, that psychoanalysis must not "go to the extremes to which [Buddhism] is carried, since *they would be contrary to certain limitations imposed by [our technique], a discreet application of its basic principle in analysis* seems much more acceptable to me . . . in so far as [our] technique does not in itself entail any danger of the subject's alienation. For [our] technique only breaks the discourse in order to deliver speech."[68] Unlike ego psychology, and more like Buddhism, Lacan embraced the death drive as the agency that could deconstruct discourse in order to deliver speech and thereby disrupt the corporeal integrity, presence, coherence—the egoic monumentalization—of stagnated subjectivity (or empty speech, a belief in oneself as occupying a position of mastery in the imaginary rather than a position of nothingness in the symbolic).

Many White film theorists and White feminists, such as Mary Ann Doane, Constance Penley, Kaja Silverman, Jacqueline Rose, Janet Begstrom, and Luce Irigaray, embrace the utility of the death drive as well, for it is only through an embrace of the death drive that "normative" male subjectivity, the bane of women's liberation, can free itself from the idiopathic as opposed to heteropathic identifications of formal stagnation. As Silverman points out, psychic death or self-cancellation is no small matter. Her description of the process as a kind of ecstasy of pain is noteworthy: "Masochistic ecstasy . . . implies a sublation of sorts, a lifting of the psyche up and out of the body into other sites of suffering and hence a self-estrangement. It turns . . . upon a narcissistic deferral and so works against the consolidation of the isolated ego." For Silverman, the emancipatory agency of this kind of psychic death enables "a kind of heteropathic chain-reaction . . . [as] the [subject] inhabits multiple sites of suffering." Thus the "exteriorization of one psyche never functions to exalt another and identity is stripped of all 'presence.'"[69]

This exteriorization of the White male psyche in a quest to inhabit multiple sites of suffering, that is, White women, has its costs. The political costs to White men stripped of all presence in relation to White women are death-like but not deadly. Nor do most White feminists wish it to be deadly. Silverman's caution, "I in no way mean to propose catastrophe as the antidote to a mass *méconnaissance*," diverges dramatically from Fanon's demand that "morality is very concrete; it is to silence the settler's defiance, to break his flaunting violence—in a word, to put him out of the picture."[70] The same settler will not weather both storms in quite the same way. Fanon's brand of "full speech" makes this clear: "The violence which has *ruled over the ordering* of the colonial world . . . will be *claimed and taken over* by the native at the moment when, deciding to embody history in his own person, he surges into the forbidden quarters."[71] For feminists like Silverman, full speech is that process through which the analysand has "claimed and taken over" the alienation which rules over the ordering of her world. The analysand comes to hear and assume her speech, in other words, as she assumes her desire. This is not simply a quest for personal liberation but instead the assumptive logic that underwrites two (imbricated) revolutionary projects: the political project of (for Silverman et al.) institutional, or paradigmatic, change, coupled with an aesthetic project (i.e., countercinema) that accompanies the political project. The two, then, work in relay with each other, a mutually enabling dialectic. In *The Acoustic Mirror: The Female Voice in Psychoanalysis and Cinema*, Silverman underscores the crack in the armor of the Oedipal paradigm (that point most vulnerable to attack in what for her is a world-ordering paradigm). Her close reading of Freud's *Ego and the Id* reminds us that there are "two versions of the Oedipus complex, one . . . which . . . works to align the subject smoothly with heterosexuality and the dominant values of the symbolic order, and the other . . . which is culturally disavowed and organizes subjectivity in fundamentally 'perverse: and homosexual ways.'"[72] Oedipus, therefore, can be claimed and taken over for a revolutionary feminist agenda.

Fanon, however, demonstrates that the tools of species division are "claimed and taken over" by the species of absolute dereliction; how violence is turned to the Native's advantage. This notion of embodying "history in his own person" can be likened to a subject becoming lost in language (recognition of the void). But it is important not to lose sight of the difference between the Fanonian implications of "species" and the Lacanian implications of "subjects" because history, for Fanon, is in excess of signification. In addition, for the Lacanian subject, the grid of alienation holds out the possibility of some sort of communication between subjects—a higher unity of contemporaries. Whereas for Fanon, "To break up the colonial world does not mean that after the frontiers have been abolished lines of communication will be set up between the two zones. The destruction of the colonial world is no more and no less than the abolition of one zone, its burial in the depths of the earth."[73]

To say, as Silverman does, "I in no way mean to propose catastrophe as the antidote to a mass *méconnaissance*" is, I contend, to say that the two antagonists are of the same species—they have been zoned not apart but together. So, they are not really antagonists. To be precise, violence as it pertains to and structures gender relations between White men and White women (and it does!) is of a contingent nature: White women who "transgress" their position in the symbolic order run the risk of attack. But as Saidiya Hartman (and Fanon) makes clear, contingency is not what structures violence between White men and Black women, White women and Black women, White women and Black men, or White men and Black men. These White on Black relations share, as their constituent element, an absence of contingency where violence is concerned. The absence of contingency eliminates the necessity of transgression which is a precondition of intra-Settler (White men to White women) violence.

More is at work here than the monumentalization of White supremacy through the imposition of cultural signifiers. Important questions emerge regarding the possibility of full speech, the possibility of an analysand speaking in the language of his "contemporaries" when the field is made up of Whites and Blacks. Put another way, how does one defer the narcissism of a *real* relation? How can speech alone strip Whites of all presence in the face of Blacks? What is the real danger entailed in lifting the White psyche up and out of the body into Black sites of suffering? In short, what kind of performance would that be? We have come up against Lacan's caution not to take Buddhist techniques beyond "*certain limitations imposed by* [*psychoanalysis*]," the limitations of speech.

In examining the spectacles of the slave coffle, the plantation slave parties, the musical performances of slaves for masters, and the scenes of "intimacy" and "seduction" between Black women and White men, Saidiya Hartman illustrates how no discursive act by Blacks toward Whites or by Whites toward Blacks, from the mundane and quotidian, to the horrifying and outlandish can be disentangled from the gratuitousness of violence that structures Black suffering. This structural suffering, which undergirds the spectrum of Black life, from tender words of "love" spoken between slave women and White men to screaming at the whipping post, is imbricated in the "fungibility of the captive body."[74] Black "fungibility" is a violence-effect that marks the difference between Black positionality and White positionality, and, as Hartman makes clear, this difference in positionality marks a difference between capacities of speech.

The violence-induced fungibility of Blackness allows for its appropriation by White psyches as "property of enjoyment." What's more remarkable is that Black fungibility is also that property which inaugurates White empathy toward Black suffering.[75] We might say Black fungibility catalyzes a "heteropathic chain-reaction" that allows a White subject to inhabit multiple sites of suffering. But, again, does the exteriorization of one psyche,[76] enabled by Blackness, successfully strip White identity of all presence? Hartman poses this question in her critique of a Northern White man's fantasy that replaces the body of slaves with the bodies of himself and his family, as the slaves are being beaten:

> By exporting the vulnerability of the captive body as a vessel for the uses, thoughts, and feelings of others, the humanity extended to the slave inadvertently confirms the expectations and desires definitive of the relations of chattel slavery. In other words, the case of Rankin's empathetic identification is as much due to his good intentions and heartfelt opposition to slavery as to the fungibility of the captive body. . . . In the fantasy of being beaten . . . Rankin becomes a proxy and the other's pain is acknowledged to the degree that it can be imagined, yet by virtue of this substitution the object of identification threatens to disappear.[77]

Hartman calls into question the emancipatory claims (for both the individual psyche and the socius) of heteropathic identification and masochistic self-cancellation (loss of self in the other, a process germane to full speech) when these claims are not circumscribed by a White social formation—when they claim to be more than intra-Human discussions. For no web of analogy can be spun between, on the one hand, the free body that mounts fungible flesh on an emancipatory journey toward self-cancellation and, on the other, the fungible being that has just been

mounted. The two positions are structurally irreconcilable, which is to
say they are not "contemporaries." Hartman puts a finer point on it: "The
effort to counteract the commonplace callousness to black suffering requires that the white body be positioned in the place of the black body
in order to make this suffering visible and intelligible. Yet, if this violence
can become palpable and indignation can be fully aroused only through
the masochistic fantasy, then it becomes clear that empathy is double-
edged, for in making the other's suffering one's own, this suffering is occluded by the other's obliteration."[78]

It's worth repeating the lessons of cultural historians: that the Black
experience is a "phenomenon without analog," that "natal alienation" is a
constituent element of slavery, that Black people are socially dead, and
natal alienation endows the species with a past but not a heritage.[79] Therefore, even if, through the iconoclasm of becoming toward death, the analysand dismantles his monuments, even if he deconstructs his heritage,
he will still exist in a relation to heritage, however deconstructed, and
it is the possibility of heritage itself, a life of not magnetizing bullets,[80]
a life of contingent (rather than gratuitous) violence, which divides his
species from those with a life of gratuitous violence. By sifting through
the object choices of his meaning-full heritage, rather than a Black and
sense-less past, he comes to assume his desire where he is (the goal
of full speech). But though where he is may not be where he began in
his relationship (before heteropathic identification with Blackness) to his
"contemporaries," it is indeed even more intensely where he began in his
relationship to Blacks.

Conclusion

Anti-Blackness manifests as the monumentalization and fortification of
civil society against social death. "Narcissism can be deconstructed in
pursuit of subjectivity but civil society remains strengthened."[81] Whereas
Lacan's analytic encounter, the process of full speech, deconstructs narcissism internal to civil society, it is one in a wide range of encounters
(from voting to coalition building to "innocent" filial encounters) that re-
constitute civil society's fortification against social death. If, in contrast,
White supremacy's foundations were built solely on a grid of alienation,
where entified signification wards off the encroachment of deconstruc-

tive signification, then full speech would hold out the revolutionary promise of White supremacy's demise much the way many White film theorists and feminists have demonstrated that full speech can hasten the demise of intra-Human patriarchy. But, as Fanon so vividly warns, White supremacy's and Humanism's foundations are *also* built on a grid of violence, where positions of contingent violence are divided from positions of gratuitous violence (from the Slave position). Here two kinds of "species" are produced and zoned beyond the pale of speech. The social distinction between Whites (or Humans) and Blacks can be neither assessed nor redressed by way of signifying practices alone because the social distinction between life and death cannot be spoken. "It is impossible to fully redress this pained condition without the occurrence of an event of epic and revolutionary proportions . . . the destruction of a racist social order."[82] In life, identification is limited only by the play of endless analogies, but death is like nothing at all. Perhaps psychoanalysis and the promise of full speech are not ready for the end of the world.

2

Antwone Fisher and
Bush Mama

THREE

Fishing for Antwone

"Peaches" and "Brown Sugar," "Sapphire" and "Earth Mother." . . . I describe a locus of confounded identities, a meeting ground of investments and privations in the national treasury of rhetorical wealth. My country needs me, and if I were not here, I would have to be invented.
—HORTENSE SPILLERS, *Black, White and in Color: Essays on American Literature and Culture*

WE NOW TURN our attention to the distance between Slave cinema that claims to be socially and politically engaged and the Slave's most unflinching metacommentary on the ontology of suffering. In other words, through the lens of Afro-pessimism we will scrutinize Black cinema's insistence that Blackness can be disaggregated from social death. By Slave film, I mean feature films whose director is Black and whose narrative strategies must intend for the films' ethical dilemmas to be shouldered by central figures who are also Black and, for our purposes, elaborated by the conditions of the Western Hemisphere. But again, it must be stated that though the social and political specificity of our filmography and concerns are located in the United States, the argument itself is transnational. Achille Mbembe argues that, once the slave trade dubs Africa a site of *"territorium nullius,"* "the land of motionless substance and of the blinding, joyful, and tragic disorder of creation," even Africans who were not captured are nonetheless repositioned as Slaves in relation to the rest of the world, the absence of chains and the distance from the Middle Passage notwithstanding. Though these "free"

Africans may indeed still know themselves through coherent cultural accoutrements unavailable to the Black American, they are known by other positions within the global structure as beings unable to "attain to immanent differentiation or to the clarity of self-knowledge."[1] They are recast as objects in a world of subjects. To put a finer point on it, Saidiya Hartman writes: "Indeed, there was no relation to blackness outside the terms of this use of, entitlement to, and occupation of the captive body, for even the status of free blacks was shaped and compromised by the existence of slavery."[2] In the main, Black cinema deploys a host of narrative strategies to slip the noose of a life shaped and compromised by the existence of slavery.

The aim of this chapter is to explore how films labeled "Slave" by the position of their director and of their diegetic figures labor imaginatively in ways which accompany or abandon the ethical dilemmas of a captive and fungible thing. Specifically, we will examine moments in the diegesis and within the Slave film's social and historical context which indicate, on the one hand, a capacity to dramatize a wish to destroy civil society and its founding episteme (what Antonio Gramsci calls revolutionary "good sense") and, on the other hand, moments where the film is overwhelmed with dissembling gestures and as such "consents" to a structural adjustment as it takes up the Settler/Master's (a.k.a., the Human's) ensemble of questions (what Gramsci calls the "common sense" of ruling-class hegemony).[3] At the heart of our deliberations on Slave cinema is this question: *Can film tell the story of a sentient being whose story can be neither recognized nor incorporated into Human civil society?*

A View from the Void

Variety is a Hollywood tabloid with the good sense not to promote itself as being on the cutting edge of philosophical inquiry. But in its December 1968 review of Jules Dassin's *Up Tight!*, it hit on another question central to our pursuits: *How can cinema narrate a void without filling it in?* The *Variety* reviewer did not share the more politically empathetic assessment of *Up Tight!* offered by the *New Republic*'s Stanley Kauffmann, who seemed not to flinch as he explained how "the film moves unequivocally toward a finale of revolutionary resolve, with the inevitability of race war as its conclusion."[4] *Variety* panned it as "a film hammered to capitalize upon, rather than explore the complex facets of racial problems" and labeled *Up Tight!* "merely [a] social polemic." Since *Up Tight!* had such a short theatrical run, never found its way to video, and has long been out of circulation as a 35-millimeter print, it is all but impossible to adjudicate such divergent claims regarding its aesthetic quality or its social complexity. But midway through *Variety's* four-column disapproval, one finds the following: "The too-facile parallel drawn [between the IRA and *Up Tight!'s* Black underground fighters] . . . involves violence-oriented Negro militants in this country, as though America once was a Negro country, conquered by whites. In contrast, were Mexican-American, or, better, American Indian minorities more in vogue, the literary parallel [between *Up Tight!* and its narrative model Liam O'Flaherty's novel *The Informers*] might have the smattering of historical analogy, totally missing here" (*Variety Reviews*, Dec. 18, 1968). The writer is neither astonished nor enraged in revealing that 35 million people in the United States are barred, structurally, from the rhetorical strategies of analogy that might otherwise suture them into an ensemble of national names. Nonetheless, she or he has unwittingly reiterated Hartman's caution that "every attempt to emplot the slave in a narrative ultimately resulted in his or her obliteration."[5] For indeed, the United States is not "a Negro country conquered by whites." Again, if the rebar of cinematic and revolutionary narrative requires that the figure within the diegesis possesses an analogic historiography, then the *Variety* writer is correct, the slave revolt cannot be mapped onto the postcolonial struggle. Where, then, does that leave the celluloid Slave? What pitfalls await a film that attempts to fill in the void? In another review of *Up Tight!*, a *Village Voice* writer observes, "It's still a shock to see blackness as a frame of reference on the screen" (March 6, 1968). Much like the *Variety* reviewer, the *Village Voice* writer says more than she or he means. The *Variety* writer draws our attention to the ruse of analogy—the limit end of its absurd implications. The *Village Voice* reviewer draws our attention to how destructive recognition and incorporation of the Slave would be for all those Others who are endowed with analogic capacity, that is, to the catastrophic "shock" that would result from a coincidence of slaveness (Blackness) and the constituent elements of political ontology ("a frame of reference").

Denzel Washington's *Antwone Fisher* is the story of a Slave in search of a frame of reference. Or is it? Perhaps the hubris of the film makes it more audacious than that. For *Antwone Fisher* compels the spectator to suspend another layer of disbelief. The film is not quite so self-reflexive as to interrogate what I have argued is an unbreachable chasm between Humanness and Blackness and then lay claim to a coincidence of the two. Its audaciousness rests in its assuming Antwone Fisher's Humanity and taking for granted his place in a frame of reference. Curiously, what gets projected onto the screen and what the spectator experiences is not a shock. Unlike with much of the Black cinema of the 1960s and 1970s, the spectator is not left shivering from anxiety; there is no horrifying contemplation of the "what if" of Blacks entering the frame of Human civil society. On the contrary, the film is widely thought of as having therapeutic properties (much like a Barack Obama rally), as can be gleaned from sampling the "User Comments" on the Internet Movie Data Base (IMDB) Website:

> I'm a 55 year old guy that teaches in Cleveland and I never thought I would cry, but there I was with tears streaming down my face, all alone in my living room late at night.... This was a life-changing experience—not a movie. God bless you all for putting this together....

> Much like his performance as a compassionate lawyer in *Philadelphia*, Denzel Washington's screen presence in Antwone Fisher commands our attention and emotions, leaving few dry eyes in the theater.

> Heartbreakingly poignant and all too knowing in its depiction of the triumph of the human spirit.

> Every one should see this movie because each one of us is broken in some way and it may help us realize 1) My life isn't as bad as I thought it was and 2) How important it is to adopt a child in need. There are so many out there. To think that the movie was actually based on a real person made us think deep [sic] about life and how the world has and always will be [sic]. Corrupt, but that corruption doesn't have to reach your home. We all have a choice!

The consensus around the film-as-therapy resonates with the glaringly unraced précis written by anonymous commenters on the IMDB Website. One writes: "A sailor prone to violent outbursts is sent to a naval psychiatrist for help. Refusing at first to open up, the young man eventually breaks down and reveals a horrific childhood. Through the guidance of his doctor, he confronts his painful past and begins a quest to find the family he never knew." Another follows with: "Things work out, as Antwone is able to convince the doctor to keep on working with him. Antwone's past is revealed in detail. The abuse he suffers at the hands of Mrs. Tate, his foster mother, is brutal, to say the least. The attempt at the hand of an older woman in the Tate's household of a sexual molestation, gives Antwone a bitter taste that stays with him throughout his adult life, as he has been scarred by the shame he carries with him."

Among spectators in the United States, there is a strong tendency to "see" anything and everything in a film except race, to intuitively crowd out or simply forget any manifestation of structural antagonism by speaking about the plot at the lowest scale of abstraction—a sailor with an anger problem meets a naval psychiatrist who stands in as his father—and by psychologizing not just the forces that set the plot in motion but the effects of the cinematic experience on themselves as spectators: "This was a life-changing experience—not a movie." "It may help us realize 1) My life isn't as bad as I thought it was and 2) How important it is to adopt a child in need. . . . We all have a choice!" The elaboration of such symptomatic speech as a means of crowding out social contradictions that were raised by the film or as a way of ratcheting down those contradictions to a manageable scale of abstraction are remarkable feats when one considers the fact that the cast was nearly 100 percent Black, and the mise-en-scène and dialogue frequently touched issues of poverty, homelessness, the frayed relations between Blacks and law enforcement, and even slavery.

The film was also lauded by Oprah Winfrey (not surprisingly) and received two Stanley Awards from the Political Film Society in 2002, "Best Film Exposé" and "Best Film on Peace." Peace between whom? The United States was not once a Negro country that was conquered by Whites.

Antwone Fisher, in which Blacks feature prominently in both the diegesis (Navy psychiatrist and commander Dr. Davenport, played by Washington, and Seaman Antwone Fisher, played by Derek Luke) and the cinematic apparatus of enunciation (director Washington and screenwriter and memoirist Fisher), argues, narratively and cinematically, against Frantz Fanon's claim that the Black is a void beyond Human recognition and incorporation. The film's thesis is that no structural prohibition exists that forecloses on a subjective relationship between Blacks and Humans. The screenplay rejects the claim that the only way the Black and the Human can meet, structurally, is when Blacks are forced into a structural adjustment through which they can be known as anything but Black—worker, woman, man, gay, lesbian, and so on. Thus, Black "institutionality," whether filial as in Black family or *affilial* as in Black community, is not simply impossible; it is unthought and unimaginable.

From viewing *Antwone Fisher*, one would think that the terms *Black family* or *Black masculinity* are not oxymorons and can indeed be established and authenticated as something other than "borrowed institutionality."[6] *Antwone Fisher* makes the case for the possibility of Black kinship structures, freed temporally and protected cartographically from the open vulnerability of an object's accumulated and fungible status. The film asserts that Antwone Fisher, Commander Davenport, and all the "barren Black women who populate the film" do in fact possess the capacity to transform limitless space and endless time into place and event, into something other than borrowed institutionality.[7] It presumes the young man's relational capacity.

Before *Antwone Fisher* can deliver the Slave into relational presence it must clear the hurdles Fanon puts in its path: (1) the nigger is ontological excess; (2) the Slave has no resistance in the eyes of the Other, which is not, however, the same as saying the Slave does not suffer, but that, like the tree that falls in woods where no person is present, Black suffering has no auditor; and (3) whatever ethical dilemmas can be constituted in such an auditory void are constituted without analogy. The film, then, cannot overcome these hurdles by simply dressing Antwone Fisher up as a cultural or historical being. It must refute Fanon by bringing the position of the Slave "into view" instead of just camouflaging it and, once in view, render the Slave "a locus of positive value."[8] But lacking *authentic* indigenous, proletarian, or gendered attributes with which "to fill in the void,"[9] *Antwone Fisher* is burdened with the task of obliterating the list of Fanonian claims, not by deploying Antwone to perform what he *is*, that would be futile, but through a series of narrative strategies that "convince" the spectator of what Antwone Fisher is not. Rather than strain the suspension of disbelief by positing the young man as a specific cultural or historical *someone*, the film simply reconstructs him as "not a nigger." Only then can his dilemmas of filial loss and his quest to restore masculinity be dramatized and believed. But, for this to happen, three Black women must take the rap for his void. It is Black femininity that delivers him from niggerhood, so that his ethical dilemmas can be negotiated within a frame of reference.

Like so many films about loss and recovery, *Antwone Fisher* is bracketed by a rather melodramatic declaration of what has been lost and what must be regained. The opening bracket is a dream sequence in which a small (abandoned?) boy runs alone through a field of wheat until he comes upon a barn. He enters the barn and takes the hand of a paternal figure who leads him to a long table of culinary abundance (see figure 1). But this is not all. Thirty to fifty people are seated and standing around the table and the vestmentary codes of this mise-en-scène blossom with abundance as well: garments, accessories, and hairstyles spanning two hundred years of slavery, Jim Crow, and Civil Rights—though, oddly enough, the vestments are not coded by Black Power, which also exists in this costumed time span! In this dream, the slave community has been liberated and is restored to unfettered filiation; the name of the father can now function, not merely as domestic head, but as that paternal signifier indexical of the promise of cultural inheritance. There is no more terror. There is no captivity. The boy is in the bosom of his "true" relations and not abandoned to the apparatus of roundup. Domesticity is possible. Kinship is possible. Which is to say, culture is possible. Put another way, the Black has transcended absolute dereliction and is now instantiated as a subject among subjects.

The same scene is resurrected for the closing bracket of the film, except this time it is not the boy in a dream whose loss is recovered and restored, but the grown man in real life. Denzel Washington, as director (as a figure within the apparatus of enunciation), is onto something as he calls our attention, at the very beginning of the film and at the very end, to the breadth and depth of slavery's toll: what has been stolen is the "flesh"[10] and the very semantic field on which one can be *imagined* to be Human, which is why the price tag on reparations would not merely bankrupt the world economy but would obliterate a global frame of reference—one which makes articulation (from war to diplomacy) between myriad nations and cultures possible.

But as we move from the opening dream sequence of abundance through the violence that catalyzes loss, we find not one White hand at

1　Antwone as a child facing a plate of pancakes in the opening dream sequence of *Antwone Fisher*

the end of all the literal and figurative whips that cut deep into Antwone Fisher's back and psyche. Instead, we have the figure of three Black women. In fact, as we travel with Antwone Fisher from the sleeping dream of loss to the waking realization of recovery, a journey through scenes of captivity and abandonment, as we follow Antwone into and out of the hell of "open vulnerability,"[11] we find that the staging of this open vulnerability is completely internal to the Slave community. The image track and the mise-en-scène locate the technologies of Slavery in the body of Black femininity—always, and never in either the body of Black masculinity or Whiteness, on the one hand, or "mulatta" femininity, on the other. Light complexion and racial ambiguity do not code the femininity of the Black women who abuse him, though they code the femininity of the Black women who are "acceptable" romantic partners and who represent the hope of filial restoration.

In this three-cornered hell of (unambiguous) Black femininity, where does the film locate the terrain of Black male respite? This is to ask not merely how and where Antwone can catch his breath in his flight from loss to recovery, but on what terrain the film imagines that Black masculine liberation can be strategized, reflected on, discussed, dreamed about, imagined. The answer is the U.S. Navy, which is to say, the police: in this "Black film," the apparatus of roundup writ large (what used to be known as *the pigs*) stands in for the Underground Railroad in a relentless nightmare where Black women not only administer the technologies of slavery but embody its estate. If not for the glory land of the apparatus of roundup (Antwone's military "safe haven"), a million cute and cuddly little Black boys might still be shackled in one-room plantations all over Cleveland, plantations owned and operated by big, dark, lecherous Black women like Mrs. Tate and her daughter. The screenplay first inverts the world, and then makes it spin backward on its axis. The mind boggles.

In addition, the film's cinematic strategies contribute to this inverted tailspin. This "old-fashioned, crowd-pleasing holiday tear-jerker" selects vestmentary codes of military attire and combines them with radiant Black male faces set within the grandeur of a mise-en-scène of bustling base life, close-but-inviting below deck quarters, lots of "sho' good eatin',"[12] and panoramic shots of long, blue-gray destroyers and warm red, white, and blue flags waving in the wind in order to crowd out the idiom of power that explains the essential dynamic between Blackness and policing. Though off-screen the police are everywhere the Black body is not (meaning that Blacks are the objects, not the subjects, of policing even when in uniform), popular cinema is able to invert the world so that, on screen, through selected iconographic and acoustic combinations, Blackness can embody the agency of policing. In fact, few characters aestheticize White supremacy more effectively and persuasively than a Black male cop.[13] Denzel Washington has played a police officer seven times—eight, if one includes, as I do here, his role as a naval commander and psychiatrist in *Antwone Fisher*. While Black masculinity is harnessed to make the law look good, a certain iconic configuration of Black femininity is harnessed to make racial reconciliation within civil society seem not only possible but necessary for any kind of transcendental redemption. Washington's Commander Davenport and Luke's Seaman Antwone Fisher help sustain the illusion that Blacks can indeed exist off screen as Human beings, rather than as beings "for the captor."[14] In cinema such as this, the Black body is portrayed as something other than "a toy in the White man's hands."[15] It is this "something other" which allows cinema to portray as universal the ethical dilemmas of which in real life only Whites and non-Blacks are allowed to partake.

If one were to inventory the catalysts for Antwone Fisher's suffering—in other words, if one were to list the ways in which he was dispossessed—one might say: first, a Black woman blew his father away with a shotgun, depriving him of the paternal signifier as well as the possibility of culture writ large (what Antonio Negri calls the "commons," Michael Hardt calls "life time," Vine Deloria Jr. calls "sovereignty," and Kaja Silverman calls "positive and negative Oedipus"). Then, in the guise of a "welfare queen," she gave birth to him behind bars and abandoned him to the state, forcing him to spend his toddler time in an orphanage. After that, a second Black woman—Mrs. Tate, his foster mother—takes him in only to make his body the object of repetitive lynching pageantries in her basement where she ties him to a post and tortures him with flame and beats him unconscious with wet rags (see figures 2, 3, and 4). Finally, a third Black woman, Mrs. Tate's daughter, habitually slaps and rapes or molests him (it is never clear) when he is six years old, in the same basement.

This is the chronology that unfolds in his sessions with Dr. Davenport:

1 *Gratuitous violence and spectacular death*: The murder of his father by his pregnant mother. Flashback of his father being blown away and tumbling down the stairs from by blast of a shotgun.

2 *Captivity and abandonment*: His birth in prison. A life begun in, and administered by, an apparatus of roundup (the prison-industrial complex and the foster care system).

3 *Being made fungible for the purposes of punishment and pleasure— a being for the captor*: His childhood and adolescence with Mrs. Tate and her daughter. Antwone Fisher as the object of spectacular bodily mutilation and spectacular illicit sexual gratification—a body to be used in any way imaginable and a body available for use in ways as yet unimagined.

The condition of the Slave, then, if we are to be hailed by the film's narrative and cinematic strategies, is not an outgrowth of structural and externally induced violence. It is an effect of social pseudopodia. As biological organisms, amoeba are capable of moving by effecting temporary protrusions of the cytoplasm through which they are able to ingest food and, to the point of our analogy, change their own life forms in indefinite varieties. They are self-generating catalysts. For Denzel Washington and the character he plays, the Slave's condition bears striking similarities to those of amoeba, in that the violence constitutive of accumulation and fungibility arise from their own necessities. Slaves birth slavery and morph its terror through the *internal* dynamics of autoinstitutionality: "The God-fearing foster mother who takes in Fisher and two other boys pits the fair-skinned boy with good hair against his nappy-headed, darker

2 Long shot of Mrs. Tate with torch in torture scene from *Antwone Fisher*

3 Medium close-up of Mrs. Tate with torch

4 Medium low-angle shot of Mrs. Tate

foster sibling. . . . She never calls the boys by their names, instead varying vocal inflections when she calls Nigger! in order to differentiate among the three. And in one of the film's sharpest insights . . . Dr. Davenport identifies the violent beatings the boys frequently endured as a legacy of slavery that black folk have incorporated as a cultural norm."[16] "A cultural norm"?! Beatings and bondage, torture and verbal abuse are only accepted by civil society as both cultural and normative in an ethnography of Blackness. Oddly enough, it is Ernest Hardy's use of the word *legacy* which vouchsafes such terror as cultural and normative. Slavery, after all, is "a thing of the past." Slavery's technologies, which hang on so tenaciously to Black culture and norms, are the product of a self-generating social organism, divorced from the press of civil society—the result of social pseudopodia.

If the Slave estate is neither a historical legacy nor an amoeba-like cultural norm which self-mutates wherever Blacks are gathered, then how does it exert the technologies of accumulation and fungibility on the Black while giving the appearance that the technologies emerge from within the Black? And how does *Antwone Fisher* appropriate these strategies and bring Blackness into view? How does it fill the void? A clue is provided by the uncanny resonance between the logic of anti-Black legislation (for which the 'rule of law' is a euphemism) and the logic of the screenplay.

How Massa Got His STEP Back

In 1988, the state of California intensified and recodified its capacity to capture the Black body within a "carceral continuum"[17] when it passed the Street Terrorism Enforcement and Prevention Act 186.22/186.22a (STEP). It made law an existing practice whereby the authorities focused their attention on the parents of suspected "gang members." California was not the first state to transpose such de facto practice into de jure law: "In one Arkansas town an ordinance was passed permitting the jailing and public humiliation of parents whose children violate curfew. The law was passed in response to increased street gang activity." But STEP went a step further. Not only did it "permit . . . the persecution of parents under a parental responsibility theory," but it "creat[ed] a nuisance provision aimed at buildings in which criminal gang activity takes place"[18]:

"Every building or place used by members of a criminal street gang for the purpose of the commission of the offenses listed in subdivision (e) of Section 186.22 or any offense involving dangerous or deadly weapons, burglary, or rape, and every building or place wherein or on which that criminal conduct by gang members takes place, is a nuisance which shall be enjoined, abated [meaning reduced or removed], and prevented, and for which damages may be recovered, whether it is a public or private nuisance."[19]

There are two key problems buried in this portion of the statute and in the rhetorical arc of antigang legislation more broadly. First, an anti-Black tautology is already at work in such terminology as "gang member" or "gang-related" offense, because the "need" for the legislation cannot be disaggregated from prior "knowledge" of the depravity of Black urban spaces or from a private and quotidian construction and interpretation of images of young Black men. A "zeal to obliterate" is elaborated out of these knowledge and image formations. The fact that the textual heat of the legislation, as it is written, seems to register not this zeal to obliterate, but a wish to protect, should not fool the reader. For if gangness was not overdetermined by Blackness, a long-standing definitional hole in the terms "gang member" and "gang-related offenses" would have been filled in an effort to have the terms pass muster with respect to due process and at levels acceptable to the legislators and their kin. Instead, as Susan Burrell notes: "There is still a good deal of subjectivity in who is considered a 'gang member' and what is considered a 'gang related' offense. One need look no further than recent Los Angeles 'sweeps' to be satisfied that officers are less than careful in arresting 'suspected gang members.' Moreover, case statistics are sometimes altered, simply to meet the needs of law enforcement. . . . Furthermore, as criminological theory changes over time, the characterization of what is gang related may shift."[20]

Burrell's training as a lawyer, or perhaps the need for her article to work within the parameters of a law review, render her text incapable of interpreting this shifting characterization as part and parcel of civil society's requisite capacity to stabilize its frame of reference. "Due process," she writes, "requires that a criminal statute provide both fair notice and fair warning of the act which it prohibits." She even cites the relevant court rulings in support of this assertion, as though the judiciary were an institution that acted as a check on, rather than a conduit for, gratuitous violence. "Notice is important," she continues, "for both the person who may violate the law as well as for those who must enforce it." Like the narrative and cinematic logic of *Antwone Fisher*, Burrell's jurisprudential logic assumes a world in which the site of Blackness is not a priori criminalized and sites of enforcement and adjudication are not a priori anti-Black. Nonetheless, the real of structural violence erupts into the symbolic, despite her efforts to disavow this eruption. "Several terms used in California Penal Code 186.22 may well sweep in innocent persons simply by virtue of their association with persons or groups coming within the statute."[21] Again, it is not a problem of guilt or innocence or, as Burrell would have it, a problem out *there* in corrupt performances—it is not a miscarriage of justice but the very essence of justice. Furthermore, the problem is ensconced within her text as having confused the plantation with civil society, as having read the cartographic and temporal inscription in "carceral continuum"[22] not as an ontological guarantee for the Human race, but as a place in the South and a time in the past.

There is another problem buried in the portion of the statute under consideration. The drafters of STEP have insured that the breadth and vagueness of its terms leave no room for Black maneuver, buttressing it with "parental responsibility theory" and the mapping of "public or private nuisance" monikers on "every building or place used by members of a criminal street gang for the purposes of the commission of . . . offenses" (remember: "member" and "offense" are shifting categories to be determined by the police at the point and time of the encounter). The next moves the law makes are (a) to draw parents into slavery through their children (an amazing reverse symbiosis of the process during chattel slavery when enslaved mothers gave birth to slave children; now, enslaved children are capable of giving birth to slave parents) and (b) to transform the home from a civic sanctuary into a cabin in the quarters of a plantation.

STEP should have been all the evidence the Black intelligentsia needed to acknowledge the repetition compulsion of civil society, which can only be assured of its own cartographic integrity to the extent that it continuously marks and remarks a spatial void across Black domesticity, Black bodies, and Black psyches. By the mid-1990s, when laws such as STEP proliferated across California and across the country—wherever concen-

trations of Blacks are found—even Cornel West, one of the more hopeful
Black intellectuals and certainly the most coalition-minded Black po-
litico, made an assessment of hegemony and the impotent promise of
counterhegemonic resistance when the Slave is under consideration:

> A central preoccupation of black culture is that of confronting can-
> didly the ontological wounds, psychic scars, and existential bruises
> of black people while fending off insanity and self-annihilation. . . .
> This is why the "ur-text" of black culture is neither a word nor a book,
> not an architectural monument or a legal brief. [And it is why hege-
> monic domination is the essential problem of workers not slaves.] In-
> stead, [the "ur-text" of black culture] is a guttural cry and a wrenching
> moan—a cry not so much for help as for home, a moan less out of
> complaint than for recognition.[23]

In the 1980s and 1990s, intellectuals, musicians, artists, and novelists
were once again compelled to meditate on the void of Blackness with a
pessimism uncharacteristic of the Civil Rights and Black Power eras.[24]
Laws like STEP and the meteoric increase in the Black prison population
reminded Black scholars, activists, and artists that Blacks could find neither respite nor recognition within the elastic "contrariness of liberal civil
society."[25] By the 1980s, the post–Civil Rights, post–Black Power backlash
laid to rest the illusion that such Gramscian contrariness (e.g., machinations of hegemony) held out any hope of accommodating Blackness, just
as it had been laid to rest between 1800 and 1850, in the first twenty years
of the twentieth century (e.g., the Red Riots), and again between 1944
and 1964.[26]

Between 1992 and 2002, *Antwone Fisher* was written, produced, directed and distributed as a bold disavowal of the era in which it emerged,
the era of STEP. The word *disavowal*, however, is imprecise. For, in point
of fact, the film does avow the assumptive logic of STEP, but it avows it
in bad faith. The film reproduces the assumptive logic that a Black spatial
void is enabling of a civil spatial presence, but it does so by acknowledging only one of the law's two embodied derelictions: STEP, as a genuine
gesture of civil society, ascribes absolute dereliction to both the "welfare
queen" and to the "gangbanger." *Antwone Fisher* can only bring one pro-
totype along for the ride of self-actualization in civil society, so it selects

the potential "gangbanger" over the "welfare queen" as the figure that can mobilize its tropes of modernity and temporal and conceptual anxiety regarding the Black race's identity and moral standing in the world.

In this way, *Antwone Fisher* is one of the more profound and sophisticated integrationist films to hit the theaters since *Guess Who's Coming to Dinner*. Its sophistication rests in its ability to render an integrationist drama that does not depend on the emotionally charged political pathos, the socially controversial sexual desire, or interracial violence which threaten the diegesis whenever Blacks and Whites are projected together onto the screen. Will they kiss? Will they screw? Will the Black kill the White? Will the White kill the Black? The visual field is so saturated with such questions when Blacks and Whites are intimate on screen that philosophical reflection on the ethical dilemmas bound up in questions of access to civil society is often clouded if not completely obscured. In other words, even if the social contradictions are smoothed over by the end of the film, the spectator may be compelled to contemplate, albeit in fragmentary fashion, the antagonism between Blacks and the world, as were the *Variety* and *Village Voice* reviewers. *Antwone Fisher*, by crowding out the antagonism between Black and White, is able to turn "the narrative of defeat [life within the carceral continuum] into an opportunity for celebration" that subjects of civil society might "find a way to feel good about [themselves]."[27]

The "best" integrationist film, therefore, would be one without Whites, a film with only Blacks. *Antwone Fisher*, as the cinema of what Hartman calls an "integrationist rights agenda," is safe politically and unsullied philosophically because it is able to deploy the Black (male) not as a creature desiring access to White beds, nor as a social opportunist desiring access to White institutions (e.g., money, fame), but as an ontological entity in the "true," "universal," sense of the word, someone who seeks only to realize his own *being*. Unlike Sidney Poitier, who stumbled through the 1940s, 1950s, 1960s, and 1970s trying to prove the existence of his being to the law so that he might experience the nature of that being despite the law, *Antwone Fisher* begins by assuming that Black masculinity *is* the law (naval officers and ensigns) rather than a void created by the force of law. The law, then, is not an impediment to Antwone's access to civil society's ensemble of questions, to the ethical dilemmas of his existential being. But if the Black male "gangster" is to be redeemed from the void of Blackness and access his putative presence in civil society, then the film must work to secure the double dereliction of the Black woman—his and hers. It must mimic, and ruthlessly so, STEP's assault on the female parent.

Not only did STEP act out the repetition compulsion that commonly reterritorializes the body of the Black child, from teenager to "terrorist," it reterritorialized the body of the Black caregiver from "parent" to "accessory" to terrorist:

> After [Gloria] Williams's 15-year-old son was picked up and charged in the gang rape of a 12-year-old girl, police showed up at her house in South Los Angeles. They noted graffiti and paraphernalia of the Crips gang. They flipped through a photo album showing [her] posing with gang members. . . . Then they accused Williams of failing her maternal duties by allowing the son to join a gang and arrested her under the state's Street Terrorism Enforcement and Prevention Act (STEP), which treats street-gang activity as a form of organized crime. . . . STEP allows an expansive prosecutor to argue deductively toward the new crime of faulty child supervision.[28]

STEP's cartography did not end with the body of the parent; it also reterritorialized what was once the only semblance of civil society, other than the church, in the Black community: "Every building or place used by members of a criminal street gang . . . is a nuisance which shall be enjoined, abated, and prevented and from which damages may be recovered whether it is public or private."[29] This was how Section 186.22a read in 1990 because, after 1988, when the statute was first passed, it was amended to delete the restriction "other than residential buildings in which there are three or fewer dwelling units." In the original, this phrase had, in fact, appeared twice following the phrase "building or other place." But once the phrase was deleted the housing grid of the plantation was unambiguously reinscribed. There was no after-hours evening sanctuary in the nineteenth century. With the advent of STEP, there was no evening sanctuary away from policing and punishment in the twentieth century.

Antwone Fisher fails to acknowledge that the existence of civil society depends on this sort of repetition compulsion, through which it maps and remaps a grid of captivity across spatial dimensions of the Black "body," the Black "home," and the Black "community." The guarantee of coherence for civil society requires that, for the Black, there be no inside to civil society and no outside to policing. If there is no outside to policing then there can be no outside to guilt or criminality, there can be no contemplation of civil access, of life in a world of "contemporaries." The integrationist narrative is therefore a narrative of disavowal.

In order to produce an artificial subjectivity outside of guilt and criminality so that a legible "Black" story can be told—in short, for the film to contemplate the young naval serviceman's life as the life of a citizen and not as a Slave—*Antwone Fisher* follows the same steps as STEP: it reterritorializes the Black home as slave quarters. But it also liberates Black male characters from a priori and paradigmatic criminality (1) by exalting and celebrating their embodiment as agents of state violence and policing (in this film it is the Navy), (2) by reproducing a vertical continuum of Black femininity (from tragic "mulatta" down to Sapphire and Aunt Jemima), and (3) by ascribing to the "lower" registers of that continuum the administration and embodiment of the Slave estate (dark-skinned Black women who raped him, chained him to a post, and whipped him, who shot and killed his father, who birthed him in prison, and who abandoned him to the world). Such is the "brilliance" of its social pseudopodia.

Like the district attorney armed with STEP, the film is an "expansive prosecutor." It argues "deductively toward the new crime of faulty child supervision." But the film may be more effective, if not more powerful, than the statute. Millions of people saw *Antwone Fisher*, whereas very few are aware of STEP's existence; and only a smattering of them actually read the statute. It is safe to assume that a statistically insignificant number of that smattering can claim to have laid the statute down after perusing it and sighed, "Heartbreakingly poignant and all too knowing in its depiction of the triumph of the human spirit."[30]

The film's "brilliance" is further enhanced by its understanding of the world of cinematic exhibition, a world of movie theaters that exceeds and anticipates the film, a world predisposed to the loopy, Alice in Wonderland logic on which it stakes its claim. Historically, *manumission* and *incarceration* do not function in the English language as synonyms. Alas, there is no time in the unconscious. In his memoir *Finding Fish*, Antwone Fisher "escaped" from the Tates to reform school and eleven years in the military (as alternatives to the homeless shelter he was living in and the prison he was headed for), to the state penitentiary where he became a correctional officer, to the Sony Pictures lot where he was a security

guard. What the film and the memoir fail to let break in on the spectator and the reader is that it was the L.A. Rebellion of 1992 that may have
"saved" the real Antwone Fisher.

After leaving the Navy, Antwone was clearly on another downward
spiral—just one step from the Sony lot back to the homeless shelter where
veterans, more often than not, would end up. But after the L.A. Rebellion, an army of White do-gooders descended on South Central, just as
they had after the riots of the 1960s. They came to "dialogue" with Blacks.
One such dialogue was a screenwriting class held in a Black church and
conducted by a White Hollywood screenwriter. The screenwriter was a
former college roommate of Todd Black (who is also White), a Hollywood producer. The screenwriter was "moved" by Antwone's story and
knew Todd Black would be moved as well. Todd Black set Fisher up in
an office and paid him to write the script over a period of more than two
years. Then Todd Black contacted Denzel Washington and executives at
20th Century Fox. But in the telling of this story,[31] Todd Black and his
roommate became its catalysts and the L.A. Rebellion fell out of the narrative. It is well known in America that Black violence is a precondition
for genuine dialogue between Blacks and civil society, but such knowledge rarely gets in the way of a good story.

Judging by the way this trajectory is imagined, visually, acoustically, and
narratively in the film—and here I am returning to the diegetic story of the
character, not the extradiegetic story of the man himself—incarceration
(captivity at birth followed by reform school), homelessness, and the
military all function as something more than synonyms for manumission. The film proffers captivity as the highest form of freedom, and it
dramatizes life with unambiguously Black women as the lowest form of
bondage. The most remarkable thing about the perversely inverted logic
of the film is that it does not need to argue its case through the realism of
cinéma vérité or docudrama. It simply has to select and combine sounds
and images from civil society's private and quotidian "knowledge" about
Blackness and femininity, to which the average gathering of spectators is
already predisposed. It selects large, dark, full-featured Black women and
then combines them with kerosene-doused newspapers lit at one end
and jabbed close to the face of six-year-old Antwone, rope used to tie him
to basement posts for long damp hours, or rags wrung and twisted into
flesh-cutting whips. No one sees the sleight of hand through which moral

judgments about Black women are substituted for institutional analyses about White power, because it is not a magic trick but a relay of consent between the spectator and the screen.

During the film's first forty-five days in theaters across the country, sniffling and sobs sometimes drowned out the dialogue. No one seemed to mind. This was true in theaters whether the audience was primarily Black, as in Emeryville, California, or racially "balanced," as in downtown Berkeley.[32] Ernest Hardy offers insight as to why the cinematic strategies of the film contributed to the success of its "argument," especially for Black spectators: "Credit first-time director Washington for being among the few to employ a cinematographer, Philippe Rousselot, who actually knows how to light dark skin."[33] This is certainly true of the homosocial world composed of Antwone and Dr. Davenport (the long segments of dialogue between them during psychiatric sessions, Thanksgiving at Davenport's house, and their encounters aboard Seaman Fisher's destroyer). In fact, the lighting, along with the slow fades, the dissolves, and the frequent shot-reaction shots between the two of them—framed as close-ups and medium close-ups—are so poignant and tender, so lushly lit to enhance the beauty of Black skin, that this same archive of shots could be used to direct a love story between Fisher and Davenport (see figure 5).

It would seem as though the film anticipates (which is not the same as "welcomes") the possibility of such a reading when, during one of the sessions, Antwone, about to embark on his first date with a seawoman named Cheryl, reveals that he is both shy and a virgin. Davenport decides to guide him through a first-date role-play. "You play yourself," the good doctor instructs. "I'll play Cheryl." "You'll play Cheryl?" says Fisher with an anxious chuckle. "Hey! I'm man enough to play, Cheryl, all right." Naval Commander and psychiatrist Davenport may be reassuring Fisher; Washington appears to be reassuring the spectator. This reassurance falters, however, because, as the role-playing continues, Davenport insists that the date between Antwone and Cheryl not "escalate." This warning, albeit coded, should be enough. But Davenport has forgotten that Fisher is a virgin. Fisher asks him, also emphatically, escalate into what? To which the good doctor dissembles, "Marriage." The lighting which projects these two men onto the screen together produces a visual discontinuity between romantic visualization and narrative prudence.

5 Antwone and Dr. Davenport, in a therapy session from *Antwone Fisher*

Moreover, what Hardy, a Black film critic who appreciates the lighting of Black skin, has missed in his admiration of the film's cinematographer is the way the film reverts back to Hollywood's standard anti-Black lighting traditions when Antwone's foster sister and his birth mother and foster mother appear. In fact, the lighting of these three women is decidedly ghoulish. The warm glow of Rousselot's cinematography is briefly cast on light-skinned and racially ambiguous women, like Cheryl and Berta, Davenport's wife, when it is shared with women at all.

Much like the prison-industrial complex, cinema is an institution called on to pull its weight as an apparatus for the accumulation and exchange of Slaves. But the libidinal economy of cinema has resources which the political economy of prisons does not: it can make an offering of Black flesh for the psychic accumulation of civil society in a way that not only hides the dimension of gratuitous violence and force necessary to bring about this offering but, like those spectacles of lynching in which a Black penis is cut off and then the victim is not only forced to eat it but must tell his murderers how good it tastes,[34] cinema can give civil society the pleasure of seeing Blacks maimed as well as the pleasure of Blacks taking pleasure in this process.

Fanon quotes Bernard Wolfe on this score: "It pleases us to portray the Negro showing us all his teeth in a smile made for us. And his smile as we see it—as we make it—always means a gift."[35] Blacks are so comprehensively fungible that cinema can make them die and smile at the same time. As I noted above, the gift of *Antwone Fisher*'s broad and complex cinematic smile was so pleasing "to portray" that it won two Stanley

Awards from the Political Film Society. In awarding it the prize for Best Film Exposé, the Political Society wrote:

> Few in the audience knew until seeing *Antwone Fisher* how locating birth parents . . . can be so important to someone who feels that he was once abandoned. The film can be seen as a plea for governments in the fifty states to open up records so that those who suffer psychologically can become whole. More explicitly the film is an exposé of what Dr. Davenport (Denzel Washington's character) calls "slave mentality," that is, the tendency for generations of African Americans to engage in ethnic self-hate by abusing one another, just as they were once abused by their white masters, a masochistic "identification with the aggressor" that was identified by Theodore Reich as an explanation for the transformation of ordinary Germans into militant anti-Semites after Hitler came to power.[36]

As a first impression, one is struck by the resilience, stamina, and durability of the Jewish Holocaust as the "affective destination" of rhetorical strategies that seek to appreciate suffering and recognize a dispossessed body. What is amazing here is how one small gift can bestow on the world the capacity to talk about anything and everything: child abandonment, filial and reproductive anxiety, responsible government, national identity ("ordinary Germans"), anti-Semitism, the rise of dictatorships, psychoanalysis, and the Jewish Holocaust. The gift of slavery fortifies and extends the interlocutory life of a wide range of ethical dilemmas from which Slaves themselves are barred: questions about access to institutionality, discontent over the crisis of filial and affilial relations, meditations on the loss of individual autonomy, nostalgia for a once robust democracy and vibrant public sphere. Once the list begins to proliferate it takes on a life of its own. One knows the celluloid Negroes have done their duty when citizens leave the film with teary eyes, extolling it as "The best psychological drama since *Ordinary People* and *Good Will Hunting*."[37] A gift that goes on giving, *Antwone Fisher* is a fifty-two-tooth salute to the American Dream.

FOUR

Cinematic Unrest

Bush Mama and the Black Liberation Army

Now the problem is to lay hold of this violence.
—FRANTZ FANON, *The Wretched of the Earth*

THROUGHOUT THE EARLY works of filmmakers like
Charles Burnett, Haile Gerima, Jamaa Fanaka, and Julie
Dash (known as "the L.A. Rebellion School of filmmakers") one is struck by their cinematic translations of the
various ways civil society is a non-Black space—somewhere over there, far away from and inaccessible to
the life of their characters. In Burnett's *The Horse*, for
example, this unbridgeable gap is rendered more immediate and profound than merely the zonal division
between Compton and Beverly Hills. The unbridgeable
gap between civil society and the Slave estate is filmed
at and examined along the scales of the body and domesticity. In this short film, one sees not only that the
formal aspects of cinema are called on to recognize the
degrees to which civil society is barred to Blackness, but
also that civil society's ethical dilemmas are murderous
projections that threaten Blackness at every turn.

This "moody enigmatic [film] depicts a bleached rural
landscape where various characters, including a young
[Black] boy, anticipate an inevitable act of violence."[1] The
aerial establishing shots show a barren, arid landscape
made harsher by the light. This gives way to tight shots

of a house and medium close-ups of the three (White) brothers who will spend most of the film in menacing anticipation on the porch. The house is in shambles, open, dilapidated, and uninhabitable. The kinesic or bodily code of the mise-en-scène positions the patriarch away from his sons— off camera for much of the film. This composition of lighting, camera angles, mise-en-scène, and sound, if left to its own devices, would inter- pellate us to the ethical dilemmas of civil society and its discontents—the questions of shattered domesticity and a barren civic sphere, connoted by the barren landscape.

But there is also a little Black boy in the field, tending to a horse. For nearly the entire film, the boy stands in the field with the animal, which is about to be put to death by the patriarch and his sons: here, not only are the "flesh" of the Slave and the bestiality of the horse barred from the ethical dilemmas of civil society, but the machinations of civil society's discontent—the failed filiation of a homosocial world, in other words, intra-White turmoil—make the Black boy vulnerable to the same vio- lence that this familial formation of civil society will project onto the horse. In fact, the horse is just an alibi and the boy and the spectator know it, though little in the dialogue gives this away.

Hollywood cinema and White political cinema would have staged this differently. Hollywood cinema would have brought the Black boy and the White brothers in contact with each other either for reconciliation or to cast Black attention on White ethical dilemmas. White political cinema may have brought the Black boy and the White brothers in contact for more "noble" intentions. But neither cinema would have been able to bear the psychic costs of contemplating a structural noncommunicability between White and Black, which is to say, neither cinema would own up to the presence of the twentieth-century Slave estate in contradistinction to the presence of civil society.

Between 1967 and 1977, Black cinema was pulled closer to the dream of gratuitous freedom than any genre since Nat Turner's night of gratuitous violence. Films such as Haile Gerima's *Bush Mama* (1976), Robert Alan Arthur's *The Lost Man* (1969), Ivan Dixon's *The Spook Who Sat by the Door* (1973), Krishna Shah's *The River Niger* (1976), and Jules Dassin's *Up Tight!* (1969) resolutely translated the violent historiography of the 1960s and 1970s, which had moved from street life to political awareness to armed insurgency. Gerima's *Bush Mama* is the story of Dorothy (played by Barbara O. Jones), "a welfare mother who gradually comes to political consciousness while facing economic, political, and social oppression. . . . [She] is forced to violent action as a means of protecting [her daughter] against a sexual assault committed by a member of the LAPD. The violence serves a particular purpose in indicating [her] political transformation," and it emphasizes that "both Gerima [the director, writer and editor] and [Charles] Burnett [the cinematographer] were concerned 'with the politics of resistance within the family which emerged after the Watts Rebellion.' "² Dassin's *Up Tight!* tells the story of the assassination of a ghetto informer who was part of an underground Black army spawned by urban unrest in Cleveland.³ *The Spook Who Sat by the Door* ends with a street gang, the Cobras, having trained other gangs around the country, finally unleashing its violence against the police and the National Guard, as the Black ex-CIA agent who trained them "raises his wineglass in a solitary toast to the offensive he has begun."⁴ And eighty minutes into *The River Niger*, an entire Black working-class family (played by Cicely Tyson, James Earl Jones, and Glynn Thurman) and their family doctor (Louis Gossett Jr.) has been inducted into a Black underground army and imbricated in a plot to ambush police officers. Even "Sidney Poitier, eager to revive and update his image, starred in *The Lost Man* (1969) as a revolutionary executing an armed robbery to finance the black takeover of Philadelphia."⁵

The relationship of such films to the era's upsurge in Black-on-civil-society violence was not merely reflective but was also symbiotic: "Reluctantly released by United Artists, *The Spook Who Sat by the Door* attracted lines that went around the block at the back-alley theaters in which it was booked. Weeks later, after a National Guard Armory in California was robbed (much in the same way that had been depicted in the movie), the film was snatched off the screen and pulled from distribution."⁶ In fact, the film was almost "pulled" before it was released. The director, Ivan Dixon, and the screenwriter, Sam Greenlee, beat the pavement from Hollywood studios to the homes of Black millionaires to the ministries of foreign governments in search of funds, to no avail. At last, it appeared that a group of Nigerian financiers and dignitaries would put a package together. "There were ten or twelve" Nigerians discussing the deal at the Bank of Nigeria, in London: "And all of a sudden this white man walked into the room. They said they don't know how he even got through security.

But he came in the room and said, 'I'm here from the American government. We hear you are about to do business with a gentleman named
Dixon. . . . you do not want to do business with this gentleman.' And then
he turned and walked out."[7]

Film scholars routinely acknowledge the impact of the ethos of Black
Power and urban rebellion (the 384 uprisings in 298 cities between 1967
and 1968, characterized as much by sniper attacks as by mass looting)[8] on
films that came out of the "L.A. Rebellion School" (*Killer of Sheep, Bush
Mama, The Horse*), as well as on films that are more difficult to classify
(*The Spook Who Sat by the Door* and *Sweet Sweetback's Baadasssss Song*).
My purpose here is not to rehearse these arguments.[9] I submit, however,
that such arguments, though historically accurate, are too mired in the
conceptual framework of postcolonial theory for the actual analysis of
the films themselves to sufficiently attend to and appreciate the radical
way these films grappled—if not narratively, at least cinematically—with
the ethical dilemmas of the slave: (1) the structure of gratuitous violence
(as opposed to the postcolonial subject's subjugation to a structure of
contingent violence), and (2) questions of gratuitous freedom and the
necessity of gratuitous violence that might bring it about (what Frantz
Fanon called "the end of the world").

While I concur completely with one of the two components of the
common arguments noted above, that "the intellectual and cultural coordinates of [the] Black independent film movement [and many Blaxploitation films] are inseparable from the political and social struggles
and convulsions of the 1960s," I want to supplement and ultimately de-
viate from the other component: Blacks—off screen and on—were in
violent revolt for politically achievable and philosophically legible ends.
This component is stated most emphatically by Ntongela Masilela, who
writes, "Fanon's *The Wretched of the Earth* . . . was a central text, for it
clarified the historical moment in which these filmmakers found themselves."[10] No doubt, *The Wretched of the Earth* was a central text; interviews with directors Gerima, Burnett, and Dixon attest to this, as do the
pronounced goals and objectives of heroic figures within the diegesis of
the era's films. In Gerima's *Bush Mama*, a poster placed on Dorothy's wall
by a young militant woman who lives in the complex is meant to catalyze
"Dorothy's growing consciousness of her figurative imprisonment. . . .
[It is] the image of an African woman holding a gun in one hand and a

baby in another. . . . The poster was produced by the Movimento Popular de Libertação de Angola (MPLA), which was formed in 1956 and fought for self-determination and the withdrawal of Portuguese troops from Angola."[11]

Narratively, these films are predicated on Fanon's postcolonial paradigm. But contrary to the view of many film scholars, this conscious paradigm was not what clarified the historical moment. Rather, this paradigm gave an object who possesses no contemporaries, the Slave, the alibi of a subject who in fact possesses contemporaries, the postcolonial subject, so that the Slave might project his or her violent desire, cinematically, in a manner that could be understood and perhaps appreciated by spectators who were not Slaves. But as we saw in the Slave cinema that followed three decades later (*Antwone Fisher*), the ruse of analogy had its price.

Was It Just a Fantasy?

Consider what appear at face value to be two wildly divergent interpretations of *The Spook Who Sat by the Door*. In a *New York Times* article, "This Spook Has No Respect for Human Life," Meyer Kantor complained that Dixon's film lacked respect for the police and the military ("the enemy"), civil society ("the system"), and human life (the Whites killed by the Cobra insurgents), and that it portrayed "anger without reason." He said that the film failed "to present a clear indictment of white society's treatment of third world people [and this] causes the film to drift from meaningful outrage to senseless James Bond–like violence." Kantor concluded by saying the film had some social value despite its violent "excesses."[12] Although Dixon's own comments on the film suggest a different political orientation, the intractability of the word *excess* is implied in both their statements. "It really wasn't a solution," Dixon concedes, reflecting on his interviewer's suggestion that the film offered a political solution to Black oppression in America. "I've got to tell you. . . . It was a fantasy." Here, Dixon's assessment of his own film converges with Kantor's accusation of "anger without reason." Dixon goes on to say, however, that this "was a fantasy that everybody felt."[13]

The problem, then, is twofold: first, the discontinuity between Kantor's White "human" and Dixon's Black "everybody," which presents itself to us as a political and aesthetic divergence, in fact produces ontological questions that embrace the ethical dilemma of the Black. What Kantor describes as the violence of anger without reason, Dixon describes as a fantasy without "objective value."[14] Regardless of the fact that these two men have different aesthetic sensibilities and are so far apart politically that they could not agree on lunch, they have in fact both stumbled on the ontological problematic of the Black, just as *Variety* magazine stumbled on it when it panned Jules Dassin's *Up Tight!* as a film full of "violence-oriented Negro militants in this country, as though America once was a Negro country, conquered by whites."[15] I am arguing that this contradiction disturbs the generally accepted readings of political violence, the ethical dilemmas of Black Power, and the political fantasies of Blacks more broadly.

The second problematic aspect of the contradiction between Kantor's view and Dixon's is how it disturbs our reading of the era's "ur-text," *The Wretched of the Earth*. In this book, Fanon makes two gestures concerning violence. The first is that violence is a precondition for thought, meaning that without violence the reigning episteme and its elaborated social structures cannot be called into question, paradigmatically. Without revolutionary violence, politics is always predicated on the ensemble of existing questions. The other is that this absolute, or in our parlance gratuitous, violence is not so absolute and gratuitous after all—not, that is, in Algeria. It comes with a therapeutic grounding wire, a purpose that can be articulated: the restoration of the native's land. Whether we read the second gesture as an alibi for or a concession to his hosts, the Algerians, is unimportant. What does matter is the inapplicability of the gesture when we try to reflect on the violence of the Slave and the significance of political violence in Slave films. The vulnerability of postcolonials is open but not absolute: materially speaking, they carve out zones of respite by putting the Settler "out of the picture," whether back to the European zone or into the sea. There is no analogy between the postcolonials' guarantee of restoration predicated on their need to put the Settler out of the picture—the Fanon of *The Wretched of the Earth*—and Slaves' guarantee of restoration predicated on their need to put the Human out of the picture—the Fanon of *Black Skin, White Masks*.[16]

This failed analogy has other implications. It also means that the postcolonial's psychic vulnerability is not absolute: one can dream, legitimately, of a land lost and, legitimately, contemplate a land to be restored. In this respect, Dorothy (in Gerima's *Bush Mama*) is not quite the woman in the MPLA poster whom the film suggests she channels before and after killing the policeman.[17] However, although Dorothy does not share the postcolonial's capacity for cartographic restoration, what they have in common is a "cleansing" relationship to violence: "This narrow world, strewn with prohibitions, can only be called in question by absolute violence."[18] But film scholars, film critics, and the scripts of most of the films themselves have been decidedly uncomfortable with embracing, fully, what is called into question by the absolute violence of the Slave: an epistemological violence unaccompanied by the psychic grounding wires of postcolonial restoration, fantasies anchored by cartography.

In *Bush Mama*, Dorothy (Barbara O. Jones) struggles to navigate Los Angeles's policing, welfare, and sterilization agenda for Black women. Shot in black and white cinéma vérité, the film is a work of fiction, but the opening scene, in which Gerima and his crew are hassled, pushed, frisked, and verbally assaulted by the LAPD, is not a dramatization. The police simply saw Black people with cameras and descended. Gerima left this footage in the film. Here the fictional diegesis of state violence (the script Gerima intended) is forced to encounter the extradiegetic violence of the state (the script the state intended).

This kind of documentary-inspired encounter was not uncommon during the 1960s and 1970s. Several White socially and politically engaged directors took their cinematic apparatuses into the streets in search of the "revolution." While shooting *Medium Cool* (1969), Haskell Wexler took his actors to a National Guard military base and had them pretend to be the newsmen they played in the diegesis so that he might record the antics and behavior of soldiers in the presence of "reporters." He also wrote the script to coincide with the Democratic Convention of 1968. Rather than stage the drama in a park either before or after the convention, he once again had the actors perform the script in the midst of Chicago's police riot.[19] But whereas White filmmakers like Wexler deliberately transported their apparatuses of enunciation (their cameras and crew) in search of the state, Gerima and his crew had barely taken their cameras out of the car when their apparatus of enunciation magnetized State violence. *Bush Mama* opens with a police brutality scene which, unlike similar formal encroachments on the mise-en-scène of White films like *Medium Cool*, was neither anticipated nor sought. It emerged from the ontological condition of the filmmakers themselves, not from their aesthetic or political intentions. One could say it erupted from the "fact of Blackness."[20] *Medium Cool's* apparatus of enunciation invites the state into its diegesis to bolster the film's hegemonic impact, but the state simply invades both the diegesis and the apparatus of *Bush Mama* because, like its main character, like the flesh of Black bodies, and like the narration of Black stories, the institutionality of Black cinema is vulnerable in absolute terms. Black film is the one cinema in which the subject of speech (characters in the diegesis, Dorothy) and the speaking subject (the apparatus of enunciation, Gerima and his crew) are both beings for the captor.

Given this state of open vulnerability—given Blackness as the always already available prey of civil society and the state—the two most difficult psychic gestures for Black politics and Black cinema to make are those gestures that (a) acknowledge civil society's gratuitous violence against the Black body and (b) legitimate the Black's violent response against civil society. *Bush Mama* is one of several films, almost all of them shot and released between 1967 and 1977, that liberate the Black political imaginary in its quest to make those two essential gestures. *Bush Mama*, of course, could not have catalyzed these gestures on its own, but rather it was indebted to the specter of the Black Liberation Army. That is to say, to the spirit of the Slave revolt.

I am interested in Black filmmakers of the 1970s, like Charles Burnett, Haile Gerima, Julie Dash, Ivan Dixon, and Jamaa Fanaka, not as auteurs, or brilliant individuals, but as cinematic prisms. I believe that, regardless of the political views these filmmakers may or may not hold, their bodies and their aesthetic sensibilities became ciphers for a rather special, intense, and rare phenomenon of Black people on the move politically. Of course, this movement was a long time coming and a long time building. But I think that this moment in history was special because it culminated in an embrace of Black violence which had not been seen before. I propose that the specter of the Black Liberation Army—and by specter, I mean the zeitgeist rather than the actual historical record of the BLA—provides us with both a point of condensation for thinking Black people on the move and a structure of articulation between the unflinching movement of Blacks, politically, and the unflinching fantasies of Blacks, cinematically. In the remainder of this chapter I would like, first, to take the credit for a shift in the politics of cinematic thought, and the cinematic unrest that it catalyzed, away from the Black filmmakers as auteurs and place it at the feet of Black people on the move. Second, I would like to suggest that the political antagonism that was explained and the insurgent iconoclasm that was harnessed by these filmmakers, in their films' acoustic strategies, lighting, mise-en-scène and image construction, and camera work, marked an ethical embrace of the Slave's ensemble of questions regarding the Slave estate's structure of violence and the Slave revolt's structure of feeling. This was the case even though the narrative logic of their films often were inspired by the personal pronoun *we* and, as such, genuflected to the ethical dilemmas of the postcolonial (or proletariat, White feminist, or colored immigrant).

   Bush Mama is one of the more exemplary points of condensation between cinema and that special moment of Blackness on the move, the late 1960s to mid-1970s. It is an impressionistic view of L.A. ghetto life in the 1970s, well written and performed, but shot on a shoestring budget. However, the resulting low production values work for it. The tragic, banal, and horrifying encounters among the Blacks in the film (the long political conversations or the humorous and sad interpersonal commentaries and soliloquies) are so "real" that they do not "prepare" us for the rape of Luann (Susan Williams) by a policeman the way, for example, a high-budget Hollywood film would have.

   This is how the sequence unfolds: after listening to Simmi (Simmi Ella Nelson), an older Black woman, counsel a young man on Black militancy and the need for Black "togetherness," Dorothy, the protagonist, and her friend Molly (Cora Lee Day) have a heated and abrupt disagreement about what Simmi has been saying. Then, while waiting for her mother to come home from work, Luann, Dorothy's ten- or eleven-year-old daughter, is raped by the policeman (Chris Clay). Dorothy walks in as the rape is in progress and kills the policeman. Dorothy is incarcerated and then beaten in her cell by a White detective when she refuses to sign a police-prepared confession that says she killed the cop in cold blood, chained her own daughter to the bed, and then pulled the dead policeman's pants down in order to incriminate him. Two or three sequences prior to the film's climatic ending, Dorothy's partner, T. C. (Johnny Weathers), a Vietnam veteran, is sent to prison for a crime he did not commit. We have also learned that Dorothy is pregnant with T. C.'s baby. The significance of this is that the blood on the floor of her cell is hers and probably that of the baby aborted during the beating.

There is a correspondence between the intimacy of the policeman's violence and of Dorothy's killing of him. Like the rape, the killing is body to body—or, more precisely, the rape is body to "flesh" (subject to object, Human to Slave) and the killing is "flesh" to body. The cinematic strategies do not rob the spectator, who is positioned as a Slave, of this delicious moment but savors it well beyond the duration of both real time and the borders of Bazinian naturalism. Dorothy does not blow the officer away with an automatic weapon but crawls on top of him—as he has been on top of her daughter—and stabs him to death with the blunt point of her umbrella. As he has exhausted, relieved, and renewed himself sexually at the expense of her daughter, she now exhausts, relieves, and renews herself through the repeated thrust of her umbrella. To paraphrase Fanon, the violence cleanses her. Here the intimacy between Blacks and Whites, which has been the hallmark of the American imaginary since slavery, cannot be denied, but the idiom of that intimacy—the ontological nature of that uniquely modern relation—has always been the victim of anxious euphemisms. Toward the end of *Bush Mama*, Dorothy's "flesh"-to-body encounter with the policeman calls that intimacy by its proper name: murder.

Political ontology is thought through two ensembles of questions: a descriptive ensemble asks "What does it mean to suffer?" and a prescriptive ensemble asks "How does one become free of suffering?" *Bush Mama* articulates these two ensembles in a manner emblematic of this moment in Black cinema and Black struggle. The descriptive ensemble can be thought of as questions related to how gratuitous violence structures and positions the Black. Burnett's *The Horse* invests nearly all of its points of attention with the descriptive ensemble. The prescriptive ensemble can be thought of as questions concerning the turning of the gratuitous violence that structures and positions the Black against not just the police but civil society writ large.

Let us think about the film and cinematic form in relation to an ensemble of descriptive questions. Dorothy's vulnerability to gratuitous violence is absolute. This is conveyed subtly, at the level of the image, whereby tight shots of Dorothy at home, Luann at home, T. C. in prison, and Dorothy in prison emphasize the disintegration of every infrastructure they inhabit. In all these scenes the spectator faces chipped paint, dirty and battered walls, and graffiti carved and written with sharp objects. In one scene in particular, Angie (Renna Kraft), a young neighbor and Black militant, reads one of T. C.'s letters from prison to Dorothy, who, we realize, cannot read. At the start of the scene, the low camera angle foregrounds the chipped paint of the walls and the doorway. This spectacle remains foregrounded, with Dorothy lying exhausted on the couch in the back: the door opens abruptly and we see the feet and legs of a person entering the room. The next shot shows the person to be Angie.

As Angie reads the letter her voice slowly gives way to T. C.'s voice and we cut to him speaking the letter in a soliloquy through the bars—the bars with their chipped paint and the cell walls carved with graffiti. The camera pans right, along the row of cells, and T. C.'s voice becomes a voice-over for a series of images of captured Black men, close-up and medium close-up shots of them looking directly at the camera through the bars. As the scene concludes, T. C.'s soliloquy draws to a close, and the camera pans back, left, along the cells in T. C.'s row—except, instead of ending where it began, on T. C., the pan ends with a tight close-up of Dorothy resting her chin on the back of her hands the way some of the men in prison have been doing. The camera holds on this image for at least two or three beats before we realize that Dorothy is not also incarcerated. The image is cut so tightly that the window frame looks to us like prison bars. Then the wind blows the curtain across Dorothy's face, and we realize that she is at home, but also that "home" is no different than prison.

Luann's encounter with the policeman confirms, through the spectacle of child rape, what the film's cinematic form has worked so diligently to build: the fact that "Black home" is an oxymoron because this notion has no structural analogy with a notion of White or non-Black domestic space. The absolute vulnerability of Black domesticity finds its structural analogy—if it can be metaphorized as an analogy—with that domain known as the slave quarters: a "private" home on a Master's estate: a building with walls and a door, the vulnerability of which is so absolute that it can be considered neither "private" nor "home." Home then, offers no sanctuary in the film's libidinal economy because captivity is a constituent element of the characters' lives.

The film's acoustic strategies also evoke this structural position of the Black as one of unmitigated vulnerability to violence. Throughout the film, Dorothy hears voices in her head. They are the voices of welfare agency workers who have impaled her on the horns of a dilemma: *Since you are not married to T. C. and since you already have a child, we demand that you have an abortion if you want to go on receiving your check.* The questions, *Do you agree?* and *Do you understand?* which Dorothy hears in the sequence are similar to those she has been hearing throughout the film. The gratuitous violence of sound, to which Dorothy is vulnerable throughout the film, the voices demanding she abort her second child, are important to contemplate, especially considering the historical moment of this film, the early to mid-1970s: the moment of *Roe v. Wade* and the White feminist movement's cries, "Our bodies, ourselves!" and "A woman's right to choose!" I have no interest in debating the social or moral pros and cons of abortion. Dorothy will abort her baby either at the clinic or on the floor of her prison cell, not because she fights for—and either wins or loses—the right to do so, but because she is one of 35 million accumulated and fungible (owned and exchangeable) objects living among 230 million subjects—which is to say, her will is always already subsumed by the will of civil society. Her will is inessential to the machinations of hegemony.

Bush Mama raises disturbing questions about the degree to which hegemonic struggles within civil society are, ultimately, meaningful to the Slave's liberation. My thesis is that questions regarding the structural incompatibility between the worker and the Slave or between the woman and the Slave could be raised cinematically because such questions had already emerged as in full-blown contradiction within the ranks of armed insurgents. These questions echo in commentary on the relationship between Black revolutionaries and White revolutionaries. In September 1979, Jalil Muntaquim, a Black Panther turned Black Liberation Army soldier, wrote:

> It must be stated, a major contradiction was developing between the Black underground and those Euro-American forces who were employing armed tactics in support of Vietnamese liberation struggle. . . . By 1973–75, this contradiction became full blown, whereby, specific Euro-American revolutionary armed forces refused to give meaningful

material and political support to the Black Liberation Movement, more specifically, to the Black Liberation Army. Thereby, in 1974, the Black Liberation Army was without an above-ground political support apparatus; logistically and structurally scattered across the country without the means to unite its combat units; abandoned by Euro-American revolutionary armed forces; and being relentlessly pursued by the State reactionary forces—COINTELPRO (FBI, CIA and local police department). . . . It was only a matter of time before the Black Liberation Army would be virtually decimated as a fighting clandestine organization.[21]

One need only try comparing the structure of feeling of David Gilbert, a White member of Students for a Democratic Society and the Weather Underground (and who went on to become a dedicated member of the Black Liberation Army), with the structure of feeling of Black Panther Party cadres to discover how incompatible the structures of feeling were between Black revolutionaries and even the tiny handful of Whites who allowed themselves to be elaborated by Blackness when the Vietnam War ended. Gilbert, speaking to White interviewers and camera crew for a film that was edited and produced through the ethical dilemmas of White activism and consumed by a White progressive audience, has this to say:

I found out [that in] street fighting situations my defensive reflexes were very good [but] my offensive reflexes were pretty hesitant. . . . There were times when for the purposes of demonstration I should have been more offensive or aggressive and it just wasn't me. It just didn't happen. . . . So many of us had such little experience with violence and so little relationship to violence and [had] led really relatively sheltered lives. And as I said, for my first seven years of activism I was philosophically a pacifist."[22]

The words of the underground Panthers "Dynamite" and "Obatunde," along with those of Ericka Huggins, Fred Hampton, and Judy Douglas—words written in a Black newspaper, consumed by a primarily Black readership—echo from a completely different zone from those of Gilbert. In "Open Warfare in Berkeley," "Dynamite" writes: "The Black Panther Party is making the revolution. . . . We see that the white mother country radical is willing to lay down a life. We ask is he willing to pick up the gun?" (May 25, 1969). In "No Jive Revolution," "Obatunde" asserts, "Revolution destroys everything that gets in its way. . . . if you are going to move on some money [he has been writing about bank expropriations for the purposes of financing political activities], move on some money. Think big, act bad, and be deadly. Strike as much terror in the white boy's heart as possible" (Nov. 16, 1968). Huggins writes: "This is . . . the year of the Panther. This is the beginning . . . of revolutionary struggle . . . the world of guns and political direction. . . . This is the dawning of the age of revolution! guns! bloodshed!" (May 25, 1969). Douglas writes: "Four pigs were offed this week . . . a victory for the people" (April 11, 1970). In the same article, she notes that the shootout was precipitated by straight-up criminal activity, and she states that it would "have been a great event if we could attribute this act to some brothers who righteously got down and went out to deal with the oppressor's troops in the community." But her unwillingness to condone criminal activity did not make Douglas look a gift horse in the mouth: she took a dead cop any way she could get it. The remarks of Hampton, perhaps the most respected Panther beyond the terrain of Blackness, go unapologetically to both the heart of Black political pleasure and to the center of the terrifying promise through which the specter of Blackness haunts civil society. On pedagogy, pleasure, and desire, Hampton writes: "If you kill a few, you get a little satisfaction. That's why we haven't moved. We have to organize the people. We have to teach them about revolutionary political power. And when they understand all that we won't be killing no few and getting no little satisfaction. We'll be killing 'em all and getting complete satisfaction" (July 9, 1969). These articles and editorials may seem chilling and even inhumane to some, but in every metropolis in this country there are to this day apartments, prison cells, and street corners full of Black men and women for whom the emotional and political protocol of the Panther editorials is exhilarating, inspiring and true, rich with symbolic value.[23] Why, in this political milieu, when Black people were at the center of political praxis which moved on this apparatus of roundup—the period of the Panthers and the subsequent period of the BLA—were White radicals so taciturn and scarce?

The distance between the structure of feeling articulated by White radicalism, in the example of David Gilbert, and the structure of feeling articulated by Black radicalism, in the Panther editorials, reproduced itself in the form of an irreconcilable gap between the ethical dilemmas of that period's White political cinema and films like *Bush Mama*, *Killer of Sheep*, and *Soul Vengeance*. So what explains the taciturn absence of White radicalism in the face of Black ethical dilemmas? Is it the difference between laying down one's life and picking up the gun, or between supporting the Vietnamese thousands of miles away and the Black Liberation Army right here at home, or the difference between defensive reflexes and offensive reflexes? How do we explain a White political cinema genuinely anxious about government corruption, the integrity of the press, a woman's right to choose, the plight of turtles and whales, or the status of the public square, and a Black political cinema calling for the end of the world?

I believe that when we contemplate a grammar of suffering through the machinations of libidinal economy—those largely unconscious identifications with correspondences overdetermined by structural positionality—we find that the imaginative labor of White radicalism and White political cinema is animated by the same ensemble of questions and the same structure of feeling that animates White supremacy. Which is to say that while the men and women in blue, with guns and jailers' keys, appear to be White supremacy's front line of violence against Blacks, they are merely its reserves, called on only when needed to augment White radicalism's always already ongoing patrol of a zone more sacred than the streets: the zone of White ethical dilemmas, of civil society at every scale, from the White body, to the White household, through the public sphere on up to the nation. Anti-Blackness, then, as opposed to White apathy, is necessary to White political radicalism and to White political cinema because it sutures affective, emotional, and even ethical solidarity between the ideological polar extremes of Whiteness. This necessary anti-Blackness erects a structural prohibition that one sees in White political discourse and in White political cinema. It prevents Whites from being authorized by the ethical dilemmas of the Slave.

I drew on the White revolutionary figure of David Gilbert and not the figure of a countercultural flower child of the time so as not to succumb to the relative ease of strawperson strategies, and because comrades like David Gilbert and Marilyn Buck were so sincere and forthright in their active commitment to the Black Liberation Army that the state recast them as Black and threw them in prison and threw away the key.[24] But as sincere and true as his words ring when he tells the viewer that "for my first seven years of activism I was philosophically a pacifist," I simply don't buy it. This is not to say that he is consciously lying, but rather that the structure of his testimony partakes of a collective disavowal. I do not accept that the structure of feeling foundational to White radicals has so much pacifist baggage to declare that they find it hard to assume the Slave's structure of feeling. Rather, I believe they unconsciously prefer the violence of the state to the violence of Blacks. This preference is essential to White gendering, White domesticity, and all aspects of White civic life. It is a phenomenon which White political cinema fortifies and extends, and one which Black political discourse and cinema struggle to contend with, deconstruct, and, in rare films like *Bush Mama*, ultimately break through.

White Policing from the Left

Bush Mama's editing strategies, its use of sound, and its imagistic composition invite us to view the absolute vulnerability of Dorothy's captivity socially, politically, and libidinally—what Fanon would call her "absolute dereliction." The acoustic strategies, the voices ringing in her ears (and ours) are emphatic in their assertion that even her unconscious is held captive by the Slave estate. And the prison cell where she washes about in her own blood and that of the fetus uncannily resembles the Middle Passage horror of a slave ship's hold. The film invites us to ponder the image of Dorothy beaten and alone in her cell and the battering of her womb as the a priori captivity and sexual destruction that distinguishes Black women from the women of civil society.

I want to return to the Black Liberation Army by way of its recently deceased soldier, Safiya Bukhari-Alston. Bukhari-Alston spent from April 1975 to June 1978 trying to get medical treatment from authorities at the Virginia Correctional Center for Women. Her ordeal, anthologized in Joy James's *Imprisoned Intellectuals*, is chilling. In 1979, while still incarcerated, she wrote:

> The "medical treatment" for women prisoners here in Virginia has got to be at an all time low, when you put your life in the hands of a "doc-

tor" who examines a woman who has her right ovary removed and tells her there's tenderness in her right ovary; or when the same "doctor" examines a woman who has been in prison for six months and tells her she's six weeks pregnant and there's nothing wrong with her and she later finds her baby has died and mortified inside of her; or when he tells you you're not pregnant and three months later you give birth to a seven pound baby boy; not to mention prescribing Maalox for a sore throat that turns out to be cancer.[25]

From this macabre description of the state's policing of female sexuality, Bukhari-Alston moves to the specificity of her own sexuality and its relation to the state:

In December 1976 I started hemorrhaging and went to the clinic for help. No help of any consequence was given, so I escaped. Two months later I was recaptured. While on escape a doctor told me that I could either endure the situation, take painkillers, or have surgery. . . . I finally got to the hospital in June of 1978. By that time it was too late, *I was so messed up inside that everything but one ovary had to go.* Because of the negligence of the "doctor" and the *lack of feeling* of the prison officials, they didn't give a damn, I was forced to have a hysterectomy.[26]

I want to locate Bukhari-Alston's state-induced hemorrhaging and the subsequent destruction of her womb outside of and prior to the prison walls, spatially at the symbolic plentitude of the White woman's womb, and temporally at White femininity's moment of possibility. This rich semantic field of White female sexuality, which spreads its tendrils through the conceits of civil society, depends, even for its discontents, on a repetition of the always already mutilation and destruction of Black female sexuality. For White women to embrace patriarchy as its celebrated dupe or to rail against it, for them to celebrate the confinement of domesticity or agitate for access to the workplace, for them to acquiesce to church doctrines of sexuality or proclaim "Our bodies, ourselves"—for all such conflicts to have coherence, find semiotic correspondence, cash in on symbolic value, and cultivate a semantic field, there must occur, in the first instance of ontological time, the reification and destruction of Bukhari-Alston's womb. White thought, even at its most radical outposts, is not possible without the unmooring of Black femininity. And this accumulated and destroyed sexuality (to recall the 1914 dissertation of H. M. Henry) is every White person's business to patrol, not only through the spectacular violence of a prison hospital, but also through White struggles over ethical dilemmas in civil society: the selection of topics, the distribution of concerns, emphasis, the bounding of debate within acceptable limits, and the propensity for the affective intensity of no more than everyday life[27]—so that Whites may be saddened by the spectacle of ghetto life in their own backyards yet find no joy at the thought of four dead cops. Everyday life, which is the backdrop, the hum, the private, and the quotidian of civil society, can only cohere by way of the imaginative labor which genocided and banished the object it constructed as "Savage" to the reservations of White ethics and by way of a simultaneous imaginative labor that keeps the gratuity of Black genital accumulation and destruction from occurring between White legs.

The courts and the prison authorities said that they locked Bukhari-Alston in isolation for three years and seven months because she was "a threat to the security of the free world."[28] In the political economy of U.S. institutionality that statement is dialogic with the state's more empirical and nameable anxieties with respect to security. After all, Bukhari-Alston had been a cadre in the Black Panther Party, which had ten-thousand above-ground activists at its peak, and which J. Edgar Hoover called "the greatest threat to national security." Later, in the 1970s, she had been a soldier in the Black Liberation Army, which according to the police had four hundred members throughout urban America and which launched more than sixty attacks on law enforcement.[29] In this way she can be imagined as a specific threat to the tactile infrastructure and political economy of the state. But in the libidinal economy of institutionality in the United States, she threatened something much more fundamental than the men and women in blue, for as I stated earlier they are only the police in reserve. She stood before her jailers as a threat to the security of the free world because her existence, or more precisely her living death, threatened the conceptual framework of White sexuality writ large, which is to say, only through her death can White women know themselves as women and White men know themselves as men. Her structural position threatens the security of the White domestic scene, the White home—the purest distillation of the state.

I want to ponder the image of Bukhari-Alston in her isolation unit, lying on her back at the Virginia Correctional Center for Women waiting for "help" that, when it comes, will wreak even more havoc, as a means through which to ponder *Bush Mama*'s Dorothy, also alone in a prison cell. The familiar images of blood and destruction between their and every other Black man and woman's legs are seldom thought of as essential to the imaginings of both White progressives and White racists. I want to juxtapose those carceral images of Dorothy and Bukhari-Alston with another set of 1970s images: White women burning bras in Harvard Square, passionately debating in a Madison consciousness-raising circle, marching in Washington with signs defending *Roe v. Wade*, or in Manhattan agitating for the Equal Rights Amendment. I juxtapose these images not to present them as zones which hold out the promise of some dialectical unity or synthesis, but so we can visualize the Manichaeism that divides Black ethical dilemmas and White ethical dilemmas into irreconcilable zones. But it would be as intellectually shoddy to read the lame libidinal economy of Betty Friedan's and Gloria Steinem's feminism against the unflinching libidinal economy of Safiya Bukhari-Alston and Assata Shakur as it would have been to read a flower child's structure of feeling regarding violence against the structure of feeling which animated the Panthers.[30]

Leopoldina Fortunati and the Marxist feminists of Italy's Autonomia movement are perhaps the most provocative, iconoclastic, and dedicated White female intellectuals and street fighters alive today—which is to say they are as sincere as David Gilbert and Marilyn Buck. A glimpse of their admittedly bold and subversive analyses highlights how the correspondence between White feminism's ethical dilemmas and White supremacy work to structure solidarity between White radicalism and White supremacy, even at some of White activism's most radical outposts.

What is remarkable about the Italian feminists is that their work is impelled by the same call for the destruction of the state articulated by the Panthers and the Black Liberation Army. But their understanding of the ontology of the one who suffers and how that suffering is manifested is as White as the assumptions found in the more disappointing common sense of feminists in the United States (such as Friedan and Steinem) who do not call for the destruction of the state but simply want access to and transformation of its existing institutions.

What I am saying is that the imaginative labor—the work—of this most radical outpost of White feminism polices the terrain of suffering and patrols Black feminism by suggesting that the ultimate form of suffering is that imposed on women by way of the wage relation. This is a crowding-out scenario because, as the most incisive and probing Black feminists, like Hortense Spillers, insist, the Black woman's relation to capital is not, in the first ontological instance, the wage relation of a subject but rather the fungible, violent, relation of an object. White Italian feminism imagines, much like White U.S. feminism, an exploited and alienated body. But Spillers reminds us that Blacks cannot form bodies; they are ontologically deprived of the body.

"Motherhood as female birthright," Spillers recalls, "is outraged, is denied [Black women] *at the very same time* that it becomes the founding term for [White women's] human and social enactment." Spillers reinforces this point when she says that for the Black woman "'mother' and 'enslavement' are indistinct categories," synonymous elements which define "a cultural situation that is father-lacking." Fortunati understands the sexual rubric differently, writing, "Within reproduction, the exchange [of labor power] takes place on three different levels. It, too, is an exchange of nonequivalents between unequals, but it does not appear even formally as an exchange that is organized in a capitalist way. Rather, it is an exchange that *appears* to take place between male workers and women, but in reality takes place between *capital* and women with male workers acting as the intermediaries."[31] For Fortunati, capital has the female subject ensconced within a symbolic illusion in which it appears that the reproductive subject (mother/wife) confronts the productive subject (father/husband) when in fact they are both productive subjects confronted by capital. And the sooner they both realize it, the sooner they can get on with the workers' revolution. The same counterhegemonic, antiillusionary tactics that animate social movement theory and alternative cinema are implied in Fortunati's analysis.

However, gratuitous violence relegates the Slave to the taxonomy, the list of things. That is, it reduces the Slave to an object. Motherhood, fatherhood, and gender differentiations can only be sustained in the taxonomy of subjects. A reading of Italian feminist thought through Spillers reminds us that the foundation of all White feminist thought maintains its coherence not primarily through a conscious understanding of how the White female body is exploited, but through the unconscious libidinal understanding that, no matter how bad exploitation becomes, the White body can never fall prey to accumulation and fungibility: "Simple enough one has only not to be a nigger."[32] In this way, the most radical White politics function as the patrols did during slavery. Like the grand emancipatory rhetoric of the American Revolution, White feminism is inessential to and parasitic on the grammar of *Bush Mama*'s suffering. It polices and crowds out Dorothy's and Bukhari-Alston's ethical dilemmas because its emancipatory imperative is predicated on a refusal to relinquish its body to the ripped-apartness of *Bush Mama*'s Black flesh.

For Black people, the structure of essential antagonisms cannot be attributed, as Fortunati attributes it, to the illusory nature of the reproductive sphere (laws like STEP incarcerate "Black home" with scare quotes) where the woman's subordination to patriarchal capital is brought on by the illusory mystification of her mother-to-child, wife-to-husband relations (mystified and illusory because, as Fortunati would have it, the objective conditions of the woman's oppression stem from the fact that her waged relation to capital is hidden by capital). On the contrary, the ontological core of Black suffering is not lost in a labyrinth of production posing as a reproduction posing as natural motherhood. Nor, at the core of Black suffering, is the Black woman's (or man's) ontology erroneously gendered by patriarchal castration fears and masculine desire as in an Oedipal drama. For the production of Black suffering, as Spillers notes, no such hall of mirrors is necessary: "Gender, or sex-role assignation or the clear differentiation of sexual stuff, *sustained elsewhere in the culture* [i.e., available to White and non-Black women], does not emerge for the African-American female in this historic instance [an "instance" which Spiller reminds us spans from the Middle Passage to the Moynihan Report to the present] except indirectly, except as a way to reinforce through the process of birthing 'the reproduction of the relations of production.'" Spillers goes on to acknowledge the symmetry between the Black woman and Fortunati's working-class mother/wife, in that the birthing process is indeed one of the first steps in the reproduction of the relations of production. In other words, like White mothers, Black mothers, if they can be called mothers, can also help Black babies reproduce both themselves and the values and behavior patterns necessary to maintain civil society's system of hierarchy. But Spillers steadfastly insists that although Black "mothers" indeed experience the same "naturalized" attachments to their children (and to their partners) as mothers of the working class, the Black woman cannot "claim her child."[33] Black children do not belong to Black mothers (or fathers), just as Black men and women don't belong to, and thus cannot claim, each other: flesh is always already claimed by direct relations of force.

As a result, the conflicts that arise between the disparate ideological elements within civil society (i.e., the White Left and the White Right) ultimately strengthen White solidarity within the libidinal economy. The greater the intensity of the conflict, the more intense the unconscious reminder of what they can all agree on: that bodily reification and mutilation is not one of their dilemmas. It's a Black thing. And when this unconscious agreement is made available to speech and therefore becomes conscious, it is displaced onto a myriad of investments—one may call it environmentalism, multiculturalism, pacifism, or feminism, but I call it anti-Black policing.

Invitations to the Dance

If the structure of political desire in socially engaged film hopes to stake out an antagonistic relationship between its dream and the idiom of power that underwrites civil society, then it should grasp the invitation to assume the position of objects of social death. If we are to be honest with ourselves, we must admit that "the Negro" has been inviting Whites and civil society's junior partners to the dance of death for hundreds of years. Cinema is just one of many institutions that have refused to learn the steps. In the 1960s and 1970s, as White radicalism's (especially the Weather Underground's) discourse and political common sense was beginning to be authorized by the ethical dilemmas of embodied incapacity (i.e., Blackness), White cinema's historical proclivity to embrace dispossession through the vectors of capacity (alienation and exploitation) was radically disturbed. In some films, this proclivity was so profoundly ruptured that while they did not surrender to the authority of incapacity (i.e., did not openly signal their having been authorized by the Slave), they nonetheless failed to assert the legitimacy of the White ethical dilemmas.[34] The years when COINTELPRO crushed the Black Panthers and then the Black Liberation Army also witnessed the flowering of the political power of Blackness—not as institutional capacity but as a zeitgeist, a demand capable of authorizing White (Settler/Master) radicalism. By 1980, White radicalism had comfortably re-embraced capacity—that is to say, it returned to the discontents of civil society with the same formal tenacity as it had from 1532 to 1967, only now that formal tenacity was emboldened by a wider range of alibis than just free speech or Vietnam; it included, for example, the women's, gay, antinuclear, and environmental movements.

Cinema has been, and remains today—even when most politically engaged—invested elsewhere, away from the ethical dilemmas of beings positioned by social death. This is not to say that the desire of all socially engaged cinema today is pro-White. But it is to say that it is almost always anti-Black—which is to say it will not dance with death.

Black liberation, as a prospect, makes radicalism more dangerous to the United States not because it raises the specter of some alternative polity (like socialism, or community control of existing resources) but because its condition of possibility as well as its gesture of resistance function as both a politics of refusal and a refusal to affirm, that is, it functions as "a program of complete disorder."[35] *Bush Mama* was able to embrace this disorder, this incoherence, and allow for its cinematic elaboration. For a brief moment in history, Black film assumed the Black desire to take this country down.

The cinematic strategies of films like *Bush Mama* were able to contend with, deconstruct, and ultimately break through the zeitgeist and political common sense which normally reify White civil society under the banner of the universal "we" and open a portal through which the descriptive and prescriptive registers of Black ethical dilemmas could be raised without apology—that is, without the need to comfort the Human spectator by justifying the violence as a response to an inessential grammar of suffering. The descriptive register can be imagined as an ensemble of questions through which cinema and political discourse face without blinking an unflinching analysis of the Black's "absolute dereliction," a complete abandonment by the cartography of civil society. The descriptive imaginary of these filmmakers which accrued to them and their films in the 1970s held them in good stead even beyond the 1970s. Witness Julie Dash's *Daughters of the Dust*. What prevents this film from having the life sucked out of it by some grandiose pabulum proclaiming its "universal" message (e.g., the "universal" message of immigration and all its trials and tribulations) is that *Daughters of the Dust* makes the spectator painfully aware that what is essential about the journey being contemplated and argued over by various members of the family is the impossibility of reducing it to an analogy. Certainly, immigrants all over the world leave one country (or one place) for another. But only Black folks migrate from one place to the next while remaining on the same plantation.

Like Dash's *Daughters of the Dust*, Gerima's editing and Burnett's cinematography of *Bush Mama* are skeptical about the universality of migration. While eating dinner one evening, T. C., Dorothy, and Luanne joyously muse about the possibility of emigrating to somewhere, anywhere, outside of the United States. They believe that mobility will be greatly expanded as a result of T. C.'s first job since he came back to the world from Vietnam. The editing and the cinematography work in a black-inspired shorthand which squashes the necessity of a narrative or storyline explanation for what is about to happen. The next morning, after this joyful dinner scene, T. C. leaves the apartment for his new job. There's an abrupt edit in which we cut from Dorothy, waving a smiling goodbye, to T. C. being escorted down seemingly endless prison corridors to a cell. Rather than script the how or why of his incarceration, the cinematography and editing know what all Black people know, that the circuit of mobility is between what Jared Sexton calls the social incarceration of Black life and the institutional incarceration of the prison-industrial complex—so much for the cinematic elaboration of the descriptive register of Black ethical dilemmas.

The prescriptive register, in contrast, might be called the Nat Turner syndrome. Blacks articulate and ruminate on these ensembles of questions, in hushed tones, in back rooms, quietly, alone, or sometimes only in our dreams. Save for in a select few films like *Up Tight!*, *The Lost Man*, *The Spook Who Sat by the Door*, and *Soul Vengeance*, this ensemble of questions has rarely found its way into the narrative coherence of a screenplay. Even in *Bush Mama*, one gets the sense that whereas Burnett's cinematography and Gerima's editing and acoustic innovation acknowledge the gratuitousness of violence that simultaneously structures the chaos of Black life and the relative calm of White life, the screenplay insists on contingent and commonsense notions of police brutality and therefore is only willing or able to identify policing in the spectacle of police violence (e.g., Luann's being raped) and not in the everyday banality of ordinary White existence. Still this is a shift, a breakthrough, and we have every reason to believe that this cinematic breakthrough finds its ethical correspondence not in the archive of film history but in actions such as those taken by the BLA and by the random, angry, and motivated Black people who were emerging all across America at this time, often with no more than a brick and a bottle and never with more than a rifle and a scope.

As sites of political struggle and loci of philosophical meditation, cultural capacity, civil society, and political agency give rise to maps and chronologies of loss and to dreams of restoration and redemption. The Marxist, postcolonial, ecological, and feminist narratives of loss followed by restoration and redemption are predicated on exploitation and alienation as the twin constitutive elements of an essential grammar of suffering. They are political narratives predicated on stories which they have the capacity to tell—and this is key—regarding the coherent ethics of their time and space dilemmas.

The Slave needs freedom not from the wage relation, nor sexism, homophobia, and patriarchy, nor freedom in the form of land restoration. These are part and parcel of the diverse list of contingent freedoms of the "multitudes."[36] The Slave needs freedom from the Human race, freedom from the world. The Slave requires gratuitous freedom. Only gratuitous freedom can repair the object status of his or her flesh, which itself is the product of accumulation's and fungibility's gratuitous violence. But what does the Slave's desire for gratuitous freedom mean for the Human's desire for contingent freedom? This difference between contingent freedom and gratuitous freedom brings us to *Bush Mama* and the specter of the BLA, to the irreconcilable imbroglio of the Black as a social and political being and the Human as a social and political being—what Jalil Muntaquim termed, a bit too generously, as "a major contradiction . . . between the Black underground and . . . Euro-American [revolutionary] forces."[37] The inability of the Human's political discourses to think gratuitous freedom is less indicative of a "contradiction" than of how anti-Blackness subsidizes Human survival in all its diversity.

Given this state of affairs, the only way the Black can be imagined as an agent of politics is when she or he is crowded out of politics. Politics, for the Black, has as its prerequisite some discursive move which replaces the Black void with a positive, Human, value. Thus, if the Black is to *be* politically within the world, rather than against the world, she or he only reflects on politics as an ontologist, pontificates about politics as a pundit, or gestures politically as an activist or revolutionary, to the extent that she or he is willing to *be* structurally adjusted. Since exploitation and alienation's grammar of suffering has crowded out the grammar of suffering of accumulation and fungibility—whipped a police action on it—the Black can only meditate, speak about, or act politically as a worker, as a postcolonial, or as a gay or female subject—but not as a Black object.

One might perform an "anthropology of sentiment" on the Black and write "ontological" meditations, political discourse, or agitate politically, based on how often the Black feels like a man, feels like a women, feels like a gendered subject, feels like a worker, or feels like a postcolonial, and those feelings are important, but they are not essential at the level of ontology. They cannot address the gratuitous violence which structures what is essential to Blackness and suffering, and they are imaginatively constrained in their will: they cannot imagine the kind of violence the Black must harness to break that structure. There is nothing in those Black sentiments powerful enough to alter the structure of the Black's seven-hundred-year-long relation to the world, the relation between one accumulated and fungible thing and a diverse plethora of exploited and alienated Human beings. In other words, there are no feelings powerful enough to alter the structural relation between the living and the dead, not if feelings are pressed into the service of a project which seeks to bring the dead to life. But one can imagine feelings powerful enough to bring the living to death. Whenever Black people walk into a room, spines tingle with such imagination. Will they insist on a politics predicated on their grammar of suffering or will they give us a break and talk about exploitation and alienation? Will they pretend to join the living or will they make us join the dead? The work of exploitation and alienation labors to make politics both possible and impossible. It is a two-pronged labor: it must both animate the political capacity of the Human being and police the political capacity of the Black.

In the 1960s and 1970s, cinema benefited from the specter of the BLA's power to wrench the question of political agency from the grasp of the Human being. Transposed by the ethical dilemmas of the Slave, the question of political agency began to go something like this: *What kind of imaginative labor is required to squash the political capacity of the Human being so that we might catalyze the political capacity of the Black?* If one were a Gramscian, the word *hegemony* would spring to mind, and from that word, the political ontologist would begin to meditate on and brainstorm around various ethical dilemmas implied in the phrase *hegemonic struggle.* This, of course, would be ontologically and ethically misguided, because struggles for hegemony put us back on the terrain of Human beings—the ground of exploited and alienated subjects—whereas we need to think this question on the terrain of the accumulated and fungible object. Again, a more appropriate word than *hegemony* is *murder.*

If, when caught between the pincers of the imperative to meditate on Black dispossession and Black political agency, we do not dissemble, but instead allow our minds to reflect on the murderous ontology of chattel slavery's gratuitous violence—seven hundred years ago, five hundred years ago, two hundred years ago, last year, and today, then maybe, just maybe, we will be able to think Blackness and agency together in an ethical manner. This is not an Afrocentric question. It is a question through which the dead ask themselves how to put the living out of the picture.

Through its use of imagery, camera work, editing, mise-en-scène, and its acoustic innovations, *Bush Mama* unflinchingly articulates the Slave's descriptive ensemble of questions. In other words, it manages to articulate the ethical dilemmas of the Slave's position without—and this is key—appeal to some shared proletarian or White feminist ensemble of questions. One could say that its cinematic form shits on the inspiration of the personal pronoun *we.* But how unflinchingly does the film embrace the Slave's prescriptive ensemble of questions?

Clearly, Burnett's cinematography, as it lingers and zooms in on Dorothy's repeated stabbing of the cop, claims for the Black the gratuitous violence which positions and repositions the Black. Here and elsewhere, the nonnarrative work of the film engages, in good faith, Fanon's invitation to "lay hold of the violence."[38] But Gerima's script seems to want to work contrapuntally to the film's formal (that is, cinematic) embrace of the structural antagonism. In other words, the script needs the "event" of police brutality as a justification for Black on White violence. Whereas the cinematic form is content with a structural and ontological argument for Black on White violence (for instance, the repetition of the stabs and the camera's fascination with that repetition), the narrative can only meet the form halfway. The script requires the moral and juridical persuasion of the "event" of police brutality—something Steve Martinot and Jared Sexton have argued is a way of mystifying rather than clarifying the issue. The script thus responds to and imagines White on Black violence as though such violence was individuated and contingent, as though it had everything to do with the police in Compton and nothing to do with White women burning bras in Harvard Square, as though it were not structural and gratuitous.

Nonetheless, this tension between the complete antagonism of the film's cinematic form and the "principled" militancy of the film's narrative is important and not to be taken lightly or dismissed. It is a tension we cannot even hope for anymore in today's cinema, as our analysis of *Antwone Fisher* suggests. The cinematic tension itself owes much to the fact that in this period Black folks had taken up arms, that is, taken up the tension in a concrete way, taking their tensions to the streets.

Black cinema's ability to distinguish between the story of the Slave estate and the story of civil society, the power of its cinematography to embrace and harness the violence of accumulation and fungibility—however embryonic and emergent in films such as *Bush Mama*—did not come easily, nor was it epiphenomenal or autodidactic. It was the outgrowth of aesthetic meditations written in blood—the blood of Black folks on the move and the blood Black folks spilled while on the move. Without the contradictions between White progressivism and Black radicalism being played out with deadly force, with life-and-death consequences, it is doubtful that films such as *Bush Mama*, *The Horse*, *The Lost Man*, *The Spook Who Sat by the Door*, *Up Tight!*, or even their supposed ideological nemeses, the films of Blaxploitation, could have elaborated in their sound, image, camera work, and editing strategies the "anger without reason" that gave Whites like Meyer Kantor pause and fueled the fantasies of Ivan Dixon's "everybody." Without such eruption of desire on the ground, Black cinema might not have engaged the gratuitous violence bound up in the postemancipation ethics of gratuitous freedom. Instead, these films might have become both narratively as well as cinematically mired in the "responsible" postcolonial ethics of contingent freedom (e.g., land restoration).

According to the Justice Department, the first BLA action occurred on October 22, 1970, when an antipersonnel time bomb exploded outside a White church in San Francisco, showering shrapnel on mourners of a patrolman slain in a bank holdup. No one was injured. The political and subjective significance of this action is not to be found at the level of facticity—at the level of the event. What is important for the elaboration of Black antagonistic identity formation is not such operations' success or failure but rather their mere occurrence and frequency from 1967 to 1981. Like Nat Turner's interventions, the specter of BLA-like activity in the 1960s and 1970s allowed for a certain concrete correspondence between Black fantasies and Black life—from which films like *Bush Mama* benefited immensely. The milieu of this brief Nat Turner moment in the twentieth century provided Black fantasies with what David Marriott has called "objective value" in a country where Black fantasies ordinarily have no objective value and where White fantasies have endless and exponential objective value—today a White fantasy, tomorrow a new law.[39] This objective value can be tested by White ability to take up spectatorship at a wide array of spectacles of Black death, from a back-row position at a South Carolina lynching to a front-row seat at a Berkeley theater for a matinee tearjerker like *Antwone Fisher*.

Films of the 1970s like *Bush Mama*, *The Spook Who Sat by the Door*, *Soul Vengeance*, and *The Horse* were in large part elaborated by this historical conjuncture in which Black militants were slowly but steadily developing the consciousness, the conviction, and perhaps even the comfort level needed to read the most "innocent" and banal terrains and activities of White civil society—like the church and the sanctity of a funeral—merely as different scales of police activity. Again, this represents no small shift in thinking but a major reconfiguration of consciousness by way of the unconscious, for in the end it removes the psychic encumbrance of contingency from the contemplation of Black on White violence, an encumbrance that has never existed in the contemplation of White on Black violence—whether on the slave ship or on the screen.

3

Skins

FIVE

Absurd Mobility

> For indigenous people, civil society is . . .
> a creation of settler colonizers.
> —HAUNANI-KAY TRASK,
> *Notes from a Native Daughter*

WE NOW TURN to the articulation between "Savage"
cinema that self-consciously engages political ethics
and the "Savage's" most unflinching metacommentary on the ontology of suffering. By "Savage" film I
mean a film where the director is American Indian.
In addition, to qualify as a "Savage" film the narrative strategies of the film must intend for the film's
ethical dilemma(s) to be shouldered by a central figure
who is Native American. Though the number of fiction feature films directed by Native Americans in the
United States is small compared with films directed by
Blacks or Whites, they could all be considered part of
our filmography because their scripts and directorial
intentions proclaim to be engaged socially and politically, unlike most White-directed films (especially those
made in Hollywood) and a growing number of Black-
directed films which proclaim themselves to be apolit-
ical—"just" comedy, drama, or suspense.

Most non-White and nonheterosexual people in the
United States exist in social and political conflict within
its structure. Throughout this book I have been at pains
to point out that this is not the same as existing in social

and political antagonism to its structure. The "Savage" and the Slave are positioned as antagonisms because ethical restoration of their essential losses would obliterate the cartographic and subjective integrity, respectively, of the Americas, if not the world. There is, however, a caveat to which I alluded to in chapter 1. Whereas the "Savage" demand for the return of Turtle Island—the restoration of sovereignty—would surely obliterate the cartographic integrity of the United States, it is not a foregone conclusion that this demand would obliterate the subjective integrity of the Settler/Master. By dismantling the cartographic institutionality of the nation-state, a return to Native American paradigms of sovereignty need not destroy the spatial and temporal capacity (the anthropological and historiographic power) of Human existence. In fact, as the most prolific ontologists of indigenous sovereignty are quick to point out, such a restoration, while bad for the United States as a settlement, would ultimately be good for its Settlers. This is why so many left-leaning and progressive Settlers take such solace in Native American customs and forms of governance—but only after they have "settled" in. The political common sense of Settler radicalism has drawn freely on the ontological grammar of indigenous sovereignty, from Ben Franklin to antiglobalization activists and intellectuals in Seattle.

My argument in part 3 is, first, that sovereignty, as one modality of the "Savage" grammar of suffering, articulates quite well with the two modalities of the Settler/Master's grammar of suffering, exploitation, and alienation. The second thrust of my argument is that whereas the genocidal modality of the "Savage" grammar of suffering articulates quite well within the two modalities of the Slave's grammar of suffering, accumulation, and fungibility, Native American film, political texts, and ontological meditations are not predisposed to recognize, much less pursue, this articulation. To put a finer point on it, one could safely say, first, that "Savage" ontological meditations are animated by the network of connections, transfers, and displacements between the constituent registers of indigenous sovereignty (governance, land stewardship, kinship structure, custom, language, and cosmology) and the constituent registers of Settler/Master meditations (Marxism, environmentalism, and psychoanalysis); but these ontological meditations do not explore the being of the Indian as a product of genocide (except in the work of a handful of metacommentators on ontology such as Ward Churchill and, to a lesser extent, Leslie Silko). And these meditations are certainly not explorations of a network of connections, transfers, and displacements between Red ontological death and Black ontological death.

Second, one could argue that the small corpus of socially engaged films directed by Native Americans privileges an ensemble of questions animated by sovereign loss. However, the libidinal economy of cinema is so powerful that the questions catalyzed by genocide as a grammar of suffering often force their way into the discourse of these films with a vengeance that exceeds their meek appearance in (or omission from) the scripts, which, nonetheless, tend to exert their authority by policing the cinematic exploration of genocide with the sovereign power of the narrative.

Heretofore, little has been written which comments on the disinclination of "Savage" ontological meditations to explore the network of connections, transfers, and displacements between Red death and Black death. This section will end with an analysis of this disinclination and its alarming consequences for "Savage" cinema. Most alarming is the fact that half of the seven or eight feature films directed by Native Americans in the past thirty years, Peter Bratt's *Follow Me Home* (1996), Lou Diamond Phillips's *Sioux City* (1994), Sherman Alexie's *The Business of Fancydancing* (2002), and Chris Eyre's *Skins* (2002), are not content to balance the pathos of their ethical dilemmas solely on the back of White supremacy. In these films the aesthetic argument as regards the history (and continuation) of Native extinction rests as much on the iconography and symbolism of Blackness as it does on the iconography and symbolism of White supremacy. When I say "as much" I do not mean a quantitative, one for one, pilgrim's progress in which Indian films envision Native encounters with Black people as being historically, or even empirically, the source of their extinction—cinema is seldom called to such a rational and conscious account. By "as much" I mean that these films sometimes seek to persuade the spectator that the suffering of Indianness is untenable, cannot be justified, and should not be endured. None would argue with the political and economic reasoning of such claims. But their libidinal "reasoning," manifest in some of the most emotionally charged scenes, relies on Settler civil society's long-standing commonplace and quotidian phobias inspired by the image- and acoustic-based iconography of Blackness as an unspecified and undisputed threat: for example, the quotidian depravity of Black rap music (*Skins*), the figure of the cold and aggressive Black woman (*The Business of Fancydancing*), the loud and impossible Black male taskmaster (*Sioux City*),[1] and the vestmentary and kinesic codes of mise en scène commonly accrued to Black youth qua criminal (*Skins*). The Black in both "Savage" and Settler cinema is commonly imagined as a threat to sovereignty and civil society, respectively. Furthermore, the imaginative labor around this threat in common secures coherence for the grammar of "Savage" sovereignty. My argument here is one never before made in film studies, Native American studies, Black studies, or, for that matter, comparative ethnic studies. It will proceed not only by examining what a benchmark film like Chris Eyre's *Skins* yields symptomatically but also by extensively exploring Native American ontological commentaries. In short, whereas the coherence of Native American cinema may not reproduce the White supremacy of Settler/Master cinema, its grammar of suffering, and the way that grammar labors cinematically, depends on what I will call "Savage" Negrophobia—a Native American brand of anxiety as regards the Slave, which is foundational not only to the emerging filmography of "Savage" cinema but also to the more substantial and established archive of Native American political common sense and metacommentaries on "Savage" ontology.

Why does the Black in "Savage" cinema cause anxiety when, in point of fact, the "Savage," like the Slave, is a structural antagonist of the Settler/Master—and when this anxiety is the lifeblood of Settler/Master cinema? As we saw in chapter 2, Blackness does indeed pose a real threat to civil society, yet it would seem not to pose a threat to the reservation, that *terra nullius* on the border of civil society. Why, then, does Blackness appear in cinema to be as threatening to the death zone of the "Savage" as it is to the life zone of the Settler? The answer to this question is imbricated in the way Native American ontological meditations, political common sense, and films privilege the sovereign modality of the "Savage" grammar of suffering to the near exclusion of the genocide modality.

My aim is to illustrate how a film marked as "Savage" by the position of its director and diegetic figures labors imaginatively in ways which accompany the discursive labor of "Savage" ethics—ethics manifest in the ontology of genocide and sovereignty. I also will explore those cinematic moments when the "Savage" film becomes so invested in the register of "Savage" ontology animated by questions of sovereignty that it crowds out its own existential register of genocide and thus reproduces aesthetic gestures that articulate all too well with Settler civil society's touchstones of cohesion.

The crowding out, or disavowal, of the genocide modality allows the Settler/"Savage" struggle to appear as a conflict rather than as an antagonism. This has therapeutic value for both the "Savage" and the Settler: the mind can grasp the fight, conceptually put it into words. To say, "You stole my land and pilfered and appropriated my culture" and then produce books, articles, and films that travel back and forth along the vectors of those conceptually coherent accusations is less threatening to the integrity of the ego, than to say, "You culled me down from 19 million to 250,000."[2] Books, articles, and films, bound up as they are in the semiotics of representation, are simply scandalized by such an accusation. The modes of address and rhetorical conventions of symbolic intervention (i.e., the machinations of hegemony) seem too small for the task. But the always already disabled condition of symbolic intervention when confronted with genocide—the fact that hegemony has no symbols for genocide (and I do not mean the event of genocide which a people might experience at one time or another, but rather genocide as an idiom power which literally produces two positions out of two peoples: one as subjects, the other as objects)—in no way lessens its status as a constituent element of "Savage" ontology. We will explore the work of director Chris Eyre in order to see, inter alia, where a more antagonistic formulation of sovereignty attempts to break through, where it is disavowed in the cinematic articulation of "the Treaty," and to what degree Eyre is able to embrace genocide as a structural lack.

Eyre's films (*Smoke Signals* and *Skins*) are among the most socially engaged and politically emphatic films on the cinematic landscape of the forty-eight contiguous states (whether Red, White, or Black). He is also acknowledged as the most widely distributed Native American director working today. Despite his films' varying plots, they are noted for their attention—whether humorous, sullen, sardonic, or enraged—to the intractable dichotomy between civil society and the "rez" (reservation).

In *Smoke Signals*, two Native women who live on the reservation drive their car only in reverse, never forward. They sip Coca-Cola, their recent substitute for beer, as they drive, in reverse, through the reservation's mise-en-scène of poverty. This is interesting for what it signifies about how genocide reterritorializes space and about the reservation as a space beyond civil society. If the automobile is one of the Settlers' most emblematic icons of mobility and progress, and one of their most profound and egoic monuments, then two Native women driving backward in this icon of mobility, across the cartography of terra nullius (the reservation), is a cinematic moment that compels the spectator to meditate, albeit humorously, on the antagonism between the "somewhere" of civil society—that place where cars drive forward—and the "nowhere" of the reservation.

The American automobile is so malleable and transpositional within the multitude of narrative combinations of Settler cinema that it can animate the pleasures of both White masculinity, which Kaja Silverman refers to as the "coherence of the male ego,"[3] as well as White feminist gestures of resistance to that consolidation, as the most cursory comparison of "male" and "female" road films like Terry Gilliam's *Fear and Loathing in Las Vegas* and Ridley Scott's *Thelma and Louise*, respectively, will bear out. In *Smoke Signals*, however, the American automobile is reconfigured as a medium, not of civic aggrandizement, but as a lens through which "Savage" ontology can be illuminated and through which (tangentially) the Settler is reconfigured from a subject of agency into an object, a specimen of the "Savage" gaze. This occurs despite the Settler's actual absence from the film during the reservation driving-backward scenes.

The (absent) Settler becomes an object of the "Savage" gaze due to the fact that, in *Smoke Signals*, the American automobile, with a reservation woman behind the wheel, is disabled. It can signify neither access to, nor mobility across, civil society's plenitude of promises and discontents. The American automobile is now the "rez" automobile, and as such cannot be pressed into the service of an ensemble of questions elaborated by questions of "citizenship," "freedom," "autonomy," "sexual prowess," or "sexual attraction"—it cannot secure, for the "Savage," agency within civil society's touchstones of cohesion. Since this is the case, *Smoke Signals* stands the icon on its head, makes light of it, and in so doing turns a "Savage" gaze on the ethics of civil society and its "settled" subjects.

In *Smoke Signals* the automobile exhibits the raw absurdity of "mobility" as an element constituent of ontology on the reservation: how, indeed, is it possible for the dead to move? Where, one could ask, are the dead able to go? If civic "mobility" reveals its absurdity (a car moving backward across a barren plain) within the constraints of the rez, then "mobility" is ethically bankrupt—and so are Settlers in their elaboration via its attendant dilemmas. What begins to unfold is an understanding of how the relationship between, on the one hand, two Native women and, on the other, two women in civil society (my example of Thelma and Louise) is an antagonistic relationship rather than a conflictual one. This is because the American automobile in *Thelma and Louise* simultaneously symbolizes the myriad of conflicts that White women face in civil society and also carries them forward, thus symbolizing their mobility in civil society—it complicates the push/pull of civic contrariness that Settlers are so fond of calling "change." In other words, the automobile can be imagined as what allows Thelma and Louise to struggle with and negotiate their symbolic value in the libidinal economy of civil society, despite their characters' physical death at the end of the film. But a genocided "Savage" cannot negotiate her symbolic value in White civil society precisely because her death was and is one of the preconditions from which value can be contested, negotiated, or hierarchized in the first ontological instance. In *Smoke Signals*, the automobile cannot assist the Native women in negotiating life as it does White women in Settler cinema because the automobile would have to first bring the two Native women back *to* life, before it could assist them in their negotiation *of* life. This, as I have just indicated, is impossible because the automobile's symbolic capacity in civil society is, a priori, dependent on these two Native women's death. Eyre's *Smoke Signals* looks on this condition with humor, but the implications are deadly serious.

Eyre's second full-length feature film, *Skins*, presents us with ontological challenges and dilemmas at which the prescient but lighthearted *Smoke Signals* only hinted. In *Skins*, the implications of that dead body from which civil society draws its capacity for symbolic (and economic) life are rendered humorously as well. But here the humor is anything but "light": it is sardonic and unflinching. Unlike the two Native women who appear in *Smoke Signals* only briefly, as minor characters providing comic relief, *Skins* provides us with a main character, Mogie Yellow Lodge (Graham Greene), who fills the screen and takes no prisoners. In the face of this enormous presence of death, neither civil society's bad faith ethical dilemmas (questions of access and mobility) nor Native American sovereignty's aspirations of cultural restoration are safe—nor, for that matter, can Mogie Yellow Lodge be spared from Mogie Yellow Lodge.[4]

What is curious about *Skins* is how the screenplay surrenders to the story of Mogie's brother Rudy (Eric Schweig), a Bureau of Indian Affairs (BIA) policeman who embodies the ensemble of sovereignty's ethical dilemmas, rather than the ensemble of genocide's ethical dilemmas. Mogie's embodied genocide makes its way into the film largely by way of discourse rather than story: that is, through the formalism of cinematic strategies (lighting, sound, camera angle, editing, mise en scène). But this formalism is so insistent that it exceeds and anticipates Mogie: it intrudes on the story long before either brother appears on screen.

The opening credits roll with voice-overs, moving and still images, a pastiche of documentary-esque material that precedes the film's scripted narrative. The opening shot of a ramshackle trailer house perched on parched, lacerated earth was culled from the documentary *Incident at Oglala: The Leonard Peltier Story*, produced by Robert Redford and directed by Michael Apted. From this image of individuated deracination we cut to aerial footage of row on row of desolate housing grids, a shot overlaid with the voice of a television newscaster . . .

MALE NEWSCASTER [*voice-over*]: In the shadow of one of America's most popular tourist attractions, South Dakota's Mount Rushmore, some sixty miles southeast lies the poorest of all counties in the U.S.: the Pine Ridge Indian Reservation. Pine Ridge is just two miles from the Nebraska border.

The viewer is then shown destitute and intoxicated Native men beached on the perimeter of White-owned liquor stores in Whiteclay, Nebraska (population: twenty), civil society beyond the reservation, where 4 million cans of beer a year are sold to Pine Ridge residents. "I don't call that capitalism," Eyre comments. "I call that merchants of death. . . . It has the feel of the kind of treatment animals would be given."[5] This is followed by a montage of still photography: the 1890 massacre at Wounded Knee; a modern-day Native woman bleeding from the nose, looking into the camera while cradling her baby; a young Leonard Peltier being extradited from Canada to the United States in handcuffs; and an Indian man face down on the floor in a pool of blood.

MALE NEWSCASTER [*voice-over*]: Wounded Knee, located in the
middle of Pine Ridge; the place where hundreds of men, women,
and children were killed by the U.S. Army in 1890. Today it's
known as the massacre at Wounded Knee. Forty percent of
residents here live in substandard quarters. The $2,600 average
yearly earnings are the lowest. Seventy-five percent unemploy-
ment. Death from alcoholism is nine times the national average.
Life expectancy here, fifteen years less than most Americans.

We then see President Bill Clinton glad-handing on the reservation. He
wades gregariously through the crowd—as ever, in his element.

CLINTON: We're coming from Washington to ask you what you want
to do. And to tell you that we'll give you the tools and the support to get done what *you want to do* for your children and their
future! [*Applause*]
[*Reverse shot to Milo Yellow Hair (Pine Ridge resident/activist)*]
YELLOW HAIR: I believe that America is big enough, it's powerful
enough, it's rich enough to really deal with the American Indian
in the way it should be done.

The reverse shot of Milo Yellow Hair's commentary oscillates between
Yellow Hair (speaking outside with a group of people around him) and
Bill Clinton (also outside in a crowd). Clinton is nodding, as though in
agreement. The editing strategy makes it appear as though Yellow Hair
and Clinton are together in the center of a group of Indians where Clinton
is being subjected to Yellow Hair's critique. Whether the two were actually engaged in this dialogue or whether *Skins's* editing strategy spliced
these two shots together to stage their interlocution is unclear. The sequence passes too quickly to ascertain the degree of continuity or discontinuity between shots and reverse shots. Nor does Eyre satisfy our
curiosity with a long- or even a medium-shot which would place the two
men in the same frame. It is the selected and combined truth of the film's
construction and not the "natural," or historical, truth of where Yellow
Hair and Clinton are "really" positioned in relation to each other that
matters here.

We are less than two minutes and fifty seconds into the film and
the grammars of suffering that position the "Savage," sovereignty and

genocide, have already been established. This attests both to the brilliance of Eyre's aesthetic sensibilities and to the ontological necessity of those grammars within the structure of U.S. antagonisms. Not only do the establishing montage and the editing of Yellow Hair and Clinton suggest that the relationship between civil society and the Pine Ridge Reservation is more genocidal than sovereign—a litany of treaties notwithstanding—but, through the film's initial sound and image strategies, the grammar of genocide breaks in on the spectator before the film's more deliberate and privileged grammar of sovereign loss. Some of these voices and images return in emotionally associative ways which punctuate and interrupt the screenplay's sovereign bias.

Now *Skins*, the story, a "blend of character study, sociology[,] . . . whodunit" suspense and drama, begins.[6] We are treated to a long shot of Rudy coming home from one of his lone vigilante actions. He is weary as he drives his BIA police patrol car. "It's taken years off of his life to be a tribal cop."[7] Cut to interior of car. Medium close-up of Rudy, his face blackened with shoe polish. His head and face are completely covered with a pantyhose stocking.

As the film progresses, we learn that during the night, when Rudy Yellow Lodge's shift ends, he often covers his face with black shoe polish, pulls a pantyhose over his face, grabs a baseball bat, or a gasoline can, some rags, and a book of matches. He goes out into the Pine Ridge night and performs his sovereign acts. Rudy's nocturnal vigilantism is intended as a kind of alchemy: he imbues his imaginary maps of a sovereign territory with the material force of violence in what he believes to be a trajectory that will someday remap the political and material terrain of Settler civil society into a material terrain predicated on the imaginary of Indigenism. Rudy's vigilantism is a pure distillation of the sovereign power he wields by day as a Bureau of Indian Affairs police officer.

His job as a policeman, however, cannot represent the imaginary restoration of indigenous governance, and the cinematic strategies as well as the narrative remind the viewer of this. There are at least three sustained close-ups and seven medium shots of Rudy, framed in such a way that the U.S. flag patch on the left shoulder of his BIA police uniform is always prominent and assertive. Narratively, the script proclaims a high degree of sovereign autonomy for Rudy and his fellow Indian police officers. This autonomy breaks down not only when Rudy crosses the border into Whiteclay, Nebraska (where he has no authority), but when capital crimes are committed on "his" terrain. In the latter example, there is always an in-house FBI agent lurking about, with whom Rudy must check in and to whom he must defer. In short, what the film realizes, however unintentionally, is that Rudy's official sovereign power has little "objective value."[8] In addition, his nocturnal violence, his vigilantism, gives his sovereign fantasy the illusion of objective value. To maintain the fantasy of that objective value, his rationalizations morph into obscene distortions of logic: Native American youth who are, in Rudy's eyes, criminal blights on his sovereignty must have their kneecaps broken by his baseball bat in order that the reservation might one day re-embrace Native culture and restore Native sovereignty.

Skins's tension between the ethical dilemmas of sovereignty and those of genocide culminates in an expression of "Savage" liminality within the structure of antagonisms. The liminality of Redness in the triumvirate of antagonisms (Red, White, and Black) stems from a tension in its ontological structure, a tension expressed in the way "Savage" ontology is imagined in film and by Native American ontologists. By examining Native American film and metacommentaries on ontology, we will see how, although the "Savage" modality of genocide disarticulates the machinations of Settler hegemony (civil society's sinews), those same machinations can be recomposed and rearticulated through a network of connections, transfers, and displacements provided by the "Savage" modality of sovereignty.

An articulation between civil society's ensemble of Human questions and Indigenous sovereignty's ensemble of "Savage" questions occurs because Settler suffering and "Savage" suffering share a common grammar. Thus, the Settler and the "Savage" sustain a degree of ontological relationality even as the Settler massacres the "Savage." Granted, the Red is always already "Savage" in relation to the White, and the White is always already Settler in relation to the Red. But this does not mean that the idiom of power which characterizes the relation between Settler and "Savage" is always an antagonistic relation of irreconcilable positions.

One embodiment of the "Savage" is able to transform space and time into place and cartography. Rudy Yellow Lodge—virile, masculine, conserving, and conservative—is, at the very least, the locus of a nameable loss. Here, the "Savage" is no more an antagonist to the Settler than the

Palestinian is to the Jew or than the Iraqi is to the American. In short, Rudy Yellow Lodge embodies the position of the postcolonial subaltern. The ethics of this postcolonial stance are predicated on a coherent semiotics of loss, for example, territorial integrity, political self-determination, economic independence, and religious freedom. This loss, whether spatial (as in land) or temporal (as in language or kinship structure), stages a drama between two Human communities. In addition, this drama is not an antagonism because the shared grammar of suffering of "Savage" and Settler cannot also be shared with the Slave. And if the "Savage" and Settler imaginaries find agreement at moments when their grammars of loss threaten to diverge, this is because the agreement is sutured by their common anxiety toward a body in bits and pieces, the threat of incoherence that sentient objects (Slaves) pose to subjects—that is, by their common Negrophobia.

Skins also struggles with the genocide modality of "Savage" ontology in the same way as many Native American metacommentaries on "Savage" ontology. It is difficult, if not impossible, to find a language—cinematic or otherwise—able to dramatize five hundred years of genocide. The majority of "Savage" cinema, political discourse, and ontological metacommentary contains, rather than explains, genocide. It does so by attempting to account for genocide through the modality of sovereignty.

I am not suggesting that there is no relation between the Native Americans' sovereign loss of land and the loss of 85 to 99 percent of the Native population—that (loss of) sovereignty and genocide are unrelated grammars of suffering. Rather I am attempting to make two points. First, the film's subordination of genocide to sovereignty enables the dream of a cultural alliance between the "Savage" and the Settler (however tenuous and fraught with contradictions the ontologists claim that dream is), while it simultaneously crowds out the dream of a political alliance between the "Savage" and the Slave. Second, the subordination of genocide to sovereignty lends coherence and rationality to the modality of genocide which, if it were to be contemplated on its own terms, would be otherwise incomprehensible. Though such gestures may have intermediate therapeutic value—in the way that speech provides the grounding wires for trauma in psychoanalysis—they stunt the explanatory power and political force of the "Savage" position as an antagonism. Put more crudely, wallowing in the incomprehension of genocide could, ultimately, not only be productive for Native American studies and the political demand embedded in films like *Skins*, but could also raise the stakes of Native American revolutionary theory and practice.

Work remains to be done on the plenitude of White (and Latino and Asian) subjectivity from behind the lens of Red genocide, work to be done through a Red gaze on immigration. One question that such work might attend to is how the banality of Settler ontology (family, sexuality, spirituality, civic practice) is structured by, and indebted to, the gratuitousness of "Savage" genocide. This question is large and important enough to fill a wing of any decent library. The Red ontologists would be asking, *How does our absence from civil society elaborate your (White, Latino, and Asian) presence?* If this could be asked without the therapeutic recourse to the scaffolding of sovereignty, a singular kind of rage could be catalyzed—Red rage: a rage which could not be contained through analogy to postcolonial anger.

Before exploring these tensions in *Skins*, we must embark on a substantial schematization of sovereignty itself: what it means in "Savage" ontological metacommentaries and how its grammar of suffering underwrites key aspects of Native American political and celluloid texts. This requires us to suspend, for one chapter, our consideration of *Skins*'s ideological tensions in order to stage a conversation between the most prolific and revered Native American ontologists.

SIX

The Ethics of Sovereignty

[Our] cultural heroes . . . never become the object of individual attention as to the efficacy in either the facts of their existence or their present supranatural ability to affect events.

—VINE DELORIA JR., *God Is Red*

Consider that every inch of stolen ground recovered by . . . Native Americans comes directly from the imperial integrity of the U.S. itself.

—WARD CHURCHILL, *Marxism and Native Americans*

KINSHIP STRUCTURE and naming practices, religion and spirituality, governance, and land are key elements that scaffold the "Savage" narrative of sovereign loss. My purpose is not to reenact a thorough and precise ethnographic study of these elements of Indigenous sovereignty in their various tribal specificities. Rather, I want to point out that these are the scaffolding elements agreed on by a range of the most prolific and respected Native American thinkers north of the Mexican border. What is important for this study is how these elements are imagined and authorized.

Indigenous scholars do not compartmentalize or separate the various elements of sovereignty: land, religion, kinship, and governance. However, metacommentaries often treat these elements separately. Vine Deloria Jr., Taiaiake Alfred, Haunani-Kay Trask, and Ward Churchill provisionally break down these elements for two reasons, one methodological, the other political. First, the deracination of Native American culture on U.S. soil has been almost as complete as the deracination of African culture on U.S. soil. All of these writers not only meditate on a grammar of "Savage" suffering, in the way that Marxist and psychoanalytic scholars meditate on a grammar of Settler suffering, but they also participate in the restoration, reinvigoration, and, in some cases, reconstitution of Native culture for Native youth. (This latter mission is expressed most explicitly in the work of Deloria and Trask.) This pedagogic process is part of an ongoing psychic as well as physical reconstruction of a people.

Between 1500 and the 1890s, Settler genocide against Indigenous people in the forty-eight contiguous states and Hawaii had reduced the population from between 15 to 19 million to 250,000. Today the Native American population stands at 4,119,000—a sixteenfold population increase over the period of one century. This figure is even more amazing when one considers that genocidal practices have continued, transmogrified and, in some cases, intensified over the twentieth century and that, consequently, the life expectancy of Native American men living on reservations is forty-four years. Small wonder that the most prolific meta-commentators of "Savage" ontology view their work as integral to the ongoing fight, as Trask puts it, "against our planned disappearance."[1]

Deloria's methodological separation of land, religion (including language and kinship), and governance allows Indian readers, especially youth, to contemplate the various components of deracinated Native American sovereignty. It is a provisional separation in service to a cultural and political movement that seeks to reconstruct and restore sovereignty in a more comprehensive way.[2] As Deloria concludes:

> At least part of the motivation for [*The Metaphysics of Modern Existence*] comes from the reception that some young Indians gave to *God Is Red*, [which] attempted to outline the areas of difference between Western religious conceptions and a generalized theory of Indian beliefs. In the years since *God Is Red* was published, a number of young Indians have thanked me for writing it, saying they always believed the migration, creation, or revelation stories of their tribe but were unable to defend the reality they experienced in the face of disbelieving non-Indians."[3]

Here Deloria explains how his (and others') methodological isolation and elaboration of various elements of Native American sovereignty embolden and politically enfranchise Native American youth—thus contributing to collective restoration. He continues:

That a catastrophic theory of interpretations could be used to verify their tribe's traditions and, in some instances, could show them how to relate their traditions to modern developments in physics, medicine, psychology, and religion encouraged me to attempt a more thorough outline of the differences that exist between traditional Newtonian and Darwinian interpretations of the world and new ideas now surfacing. I thus firmly believe that the newly emerging view of the world will support and illuminate Indian traditions and that Indian traditions will prove extremely useful and accurate when cast in a new and more respectful light.[4]

This passage indicates the overall political necessity for treating the elements of "Savage" sovereignty separately: this particular gesture enables the metacommentators to disarticulate the ethics of the Settler's ensemble of ontological questions, the fundamental factor that "keeps Indians and non-Indians from communicating [being] that they are speaking about two entirely different perceptions of the world."[5] But this disarticulation is also provisional: it gives Native ontologists hope for an eventual ethical articulation between the elements of "Savage" sovereignty and the elements of Settler ontology elaborated in the work of exceptional Settler intellectuals, organizers of what Deloria calls a newly emerging view of the world.[6] (It should be noted here that the degree of investment in this hope varies from ontologist to ontologist: Deloria is high on this hope, Silko dreams of it in fiction, Churchill acknowledges it with cold intellectualism, and Trask will not countenance it at all.)[7] Let us now examine the imaginative labor common to "Savage" ontology's meditations on governance, religion, and land.

Governance

All of the metacommentators on "Savage" ontology attribute the destabilization of energy (power) in the universe to the coming of the *haole*, the destroyer or predator: the White, the Settler.[8] The harmonic balance of *waken, orenda, manitou,* or *mana* has yet to be restored in the universe, but Silko, Churchill, and Trask point to a moment in recent Native American history when Indigenous people in Canada and the United States began to reconnect with the power of the universe on a grand, communal scale. They all agree that this period of rearticulated spiritual power commences in the late 1960s and early 1970s, and extends for some (especially the Hawaiians) into the 1980s. Trask suggests that, as a result of a groundswell of political activism, coupled with the reinvigoration of tribal customs—in other words, with the revitalization of Indigenous demands for decolonization—mana was reasserted as a defining element of cultural and political leadership in the sovereignty movement.[9] Trask and Deloria emphatically seek to distinguish power as it occurs in the schema of "Savage" sovereignty from power as it occurs in the schema of Settler sovereignty. They suggest that, where Settler sovereignty is concerned, power can be vested as spiritual, as in the hegemony of Christian deities and ecclesiastics, or secular, as in the power of money, civil rights, or force of arms. But the manifestation of Settler/Sovereign power differs from that of mana in that Settler power is either completely secular or, in the case of Christianity, asserts supreme dominance over the elements of the universe rather than balance within the elements of the universe. The implications of this difference for the ontological modality of sovereignty, though nuanced, are profound.

Trask points out that a high chiefly line (whose opposite number would manifest itself as some sort of sanctioned leadership in civil society—that is, as a member of the clergy or a public official) "may bequeath the potential for *mana*, but the actualization or achievement of *mana* . . . requires more than genealogy, *it requires specific identification by the leader with the people* . . . [and] presupposes that the people acknowledge *mana* as an attribute of political leadership."[10] It would be all too easy to suggest that Trask's description of Native power (mana) and its legitimation is but a reconfiguration of the hegemony in Settler civil society (i.e., the communicability of Christian faith, the power of the press, the interpellation of advertising and media, the plebiscite's production of consensus). But this is not the case.

Taiaiake Alfred lays such misreading to rest by reminding us that the constituent subjects of Native sovereignty consist not only of the Human (the sole subject position of Western metaphysics) but of all the animate and inanimate creatures in the universe: "In indigenous philosophies, power flows from respect for Nature. In dominant Western philosophy, power derives from coercion and artifice—in effect, alienation from nature."[11] This is a significant difference between the manifest content of tribal society and civil society, but more important, it is an effect of the latent difference between "Savage" and Settler ontologies.

Trask hints at this difference when she writes, "Both the people and their leaders understand the link between mana and *pono*, the traditional Hawaiian value of balance between people, land, and the cosmos." Although *pono*, balance *in* the universe, and *mana*, the power *of* the universe, are two distinct concepts, they are in fact inextricably bound. The combined restoration of the articulation of mana and pono in the people of the tribal community, and the articulation's subsequent restoration in the leadership—by way of the people—are both necessary if Native governance is to be not only legitimate but coherent. Without both of these the idea of the tribe is not possible. These interwoven necessities index a glaring irreconcilability between the structure of Settler sovereignty (whether spiritual or secular hegemony) and that of "Savage" sovereignty: "Only a leader who understands [the] familial genealogical link between Hawaiians and their lands can hope to re-establish *pono*, the balance that has been lacking in the Hawaiian universe since the coming of the *haole*. The assertion of the value of *pono* then, awaits the leader with *mana*."[12]

Trask goes on to state in no uncertain terms that reclamation of mana, Native power, is achieved through a process of decolonization which directly "opposes the American system of electoral power": "*Mana* . . . [is] a tremendous challenge to the colonial system which defines political leadership in terms of democratic liberalism. . . . [Indigenous] leaders embody sovereignty only if they are *pono*, that is, only if they believe in and work for the well being of the land and the people. In this way Hawaiian leaders exhibit *mana* and increase it if they speak and represent the needs of Hawaiians not the needs of all citizens of Hawai'i, or of legislative districts, or of bureaucratic institutions."[13] In other words, mana and pono not only make tribal society irreconcilable with civil society, but they make tribal society and civil society disarticulate one another; furthermore, mana and pono, as foundational to both the conceptualization and functioning of tribal society, bar the subject of civil society— ontologically—from the Indigenous world: the Settler would have to lose hegemony as the element constituent to his or her ontology in order to gain access to a world whose foundation is the interweaving of mana and pono. In short, the Settler would have to die.

Deloria, much like Trask, makes an important intervention when he splits the hair of the Settler/"Savage" conflict between the level of existence ("We have been taught to look at American history as a series of land transactions involving some three hundred Indian tribes and a growing United States government. This conception is certainly the picture that emerges when tribal officials [on the reservation] are forced to deal with [state] officials, clams commissioners, state highway departments, game wardens, county sheriffs and private corporations") and the level of ontology ("Yet [this is] hardly the whole picture. Perhaps nearly accurate would be the picture of settlement phrased as a continuous conflict of two mutually exclusive worldviews"). Deloria goes on to explain how the most banal and benevolent impositions of civil society made the "natural" reinscription of "Savage" ontology impossible. He begins by reminding the reader that tribal organization itself did not elaborate a collective imaginary of industrial-scale social relations characteristic of Settler civil society. Europeans looked on various tribal groups who had similar language patterns and customs in common and imagined they were encountering "nations." Deloria argues that instead of "nation" the more appropriate simile would have been "band." Although these bands sometimes came together for ceremonies, to share war parties, or to sign treaties, they would break apart whenever they became too large to support themselves and needed a large game source to feed everyone. "For political decisions, religious ceremonies, hunting and fishing activities, and general community life both the political and religious outlook of the tribe was designed for a small group of people. It was a very rare tribal group that was larger than a thousand people for any extended period of time."[14]

Clearly, Deloria draws here largely from the specificity of his own Lakota people in order to make comprehensive structural generalizations regarding the touchstones of cohesion which position Indigenous subjectivity. But the specifics he gives should not distract us. He is speaking of a scale of sociability that internally disarticulates the scale of industry whenever the latter encroaches on it. Manageability and decentralized autonomy, rather than a nation-state ideology sutured by hegemony, is the primary organizing characteristic of Native life. The "banal" and "benevolent" introduction, as well as the violent and militarized introduction of hegemony as a social foundation, all but destroyed the conceptual

framework of "Savage" sovereignty. Pono was replaced by constitution-
ality. Mana surrendered to Gramscian hegemony. "Today tribal con-
stitutions define who shall represent the tribe in its relations with the
outside world. No quality is needed to assume leadership, except the ability to win elections. Consequently, tribal elections have become one of
the dirtiest forms of human activity in existence."[15]

The imposition of civil society on the Native body politic is both devastating and parasitic, devastating in that it cripples the ability of Native people to think their bodies and their subjective relations through
rubrics of their own cultural imaginary, and parasitic in that it requires
Native people to perform a pageantry of social mimicry. Settler civil society feeds off of this mimicry, but not in obvious and straightforward
ways. In other words, Settlers do not develop a sense that the content of
the Settler/"Savage" conflict has been miraculously laid to rest. The affective intensity of White progressive and conservative ire catalyzed by
the recent development of gambling casinos or land use disputes evinces
civil society's awareness that "the Indian Wars" are ongoing. What Settler
civil society is able to feed off of, however, is a condition in which Indians
must now compose their imaginary of the centuries' old conflict between
Settler and "Savage"—in other words, they must enunciate their Sovereign demands—through hegemony's ensemble of questions and ethical
dilemmas that ontologically enable the Settler and devastate the "Savage."
The content of the conflict is of little importance when the modality of
simply having the conflict fortifies and extends the interlocutory life of
only one combatant. Indian governance, then, not only functions as the
corpse of tribal society in the ways described by Deloria and Trask, but
lays its body down as a host on which White ethical aggrandizement can
feed and through which the collective ego of Settler civil society can be
monumentalized. As we saw in chapter 2, something similar transpires
between the analysand (the Master) and the Black (the Slave), though
there are essential differences between the two rubrics.

Religion

If Ward Churchill is the most prolific and profound metacommentator
on the ontological modality of genocide, then Vine Deloria Jr. is the most
prolific and profound metacommentator on Indigenous religion. My em-

phasis on profundity and production requires qualification. Deloria and Churchill would be the first to admit that Native elders, medicine people, and everyday Indians (what Verdell Weasel Tail [Gary Farmer], Mogie's best friend and drinking buddy in *Skins*, calls "grassroots Indians") are as prolific and profound as they are, just as Frantz Fanon, Hortense Spillers, Saidiya Hartman, and the Afro-pessimists would not cathedralize their own wisdom but instead confess to channeling the wisdom of the likes of Harriet Tubman, Nat Turner, Malcolm X, and Assata Shakur, and the hundreds of thousands of unknown Slaves. The ontologists are prolific because they write books and articles. But they are profound because they channel the wisdom of their people's knowledge. Rather than "lead" with "original" discoveries, they secure mandates of desire.

Deloria's influential works, *God Is Red* and *The Metaphysics of Modern Existence*, are attentive to two large tasks. First, Deloria maps the coordinates of religion common to all those positioned (in the Western Hemisphere at least) as Indigenous. In so doing, he says that no clear or desirable distinction exists between spiritual and material, or physical and psychical, notions in metaphysical meditations on Indigenism. Second, he maintains that at a plethora of nodal points the constituent elements of Indian religion articulate with nodal points of Western theology and psychoanalysis. This is neither the mark of a contradiction nor an error in Deloria's work. Though he is often pessimistic about, and hostile to, the general framework of Western metaphysics, he finds points of ontological coalition in what are for him "progressive" White social formations, as well as in the writing of "enlightened" White ontologists.

Among his favorite examples of such Settler exception are the Jew, the Amish, the Mormon, and the work of Carl Jung. This notwithstanding, Deloria maintains that Native touchstones of cohesion are by far more ethical than Settler metaphysics, be those metaphysics spiritual, as in the case of Christianity, or secular, as in the case of psychoanalysis and Marxism: "The minds and eyes of Western man have . . . been rather permanently closed to understanding or observing religious experiences. Religion has become a comfortable ethic for Western man, not a force of undetermined intensity and unsuspected origin that may break in on him."[16]

Skins's repeated references to the sacredness of the Black Hills and the cosmological power of animate and inanimate forms of tricksters, its extradiegetic reliance on sacred music at key moments when emotional arguments need to be made and won, and its emphasis on the centrality that sweat lodges and offerings should play in Rudy's life (even if they have not done so in the recent past) are all representational supports of a screenplay driven by Deloria's argument that religion is a force of "undetermined intensity and unsuspected origin" that may, at any moment, break in on the subject. Again, Rudy Yellow Lodge is designated by the script to shoulder the ethical dilemmas this force elaborates. Through him, the narrative introduces Iktomi (a spirit force and trickster) and deciphers its form and meaning. Iktomi, in the form of a spider, first bites him when he is a young boy. Later in the film, he sees a spider in his bathroom sink as he is blackening his face for a vigilante outing. At another point, a medicine man says that Iktomi may have come to Rudy in the form of the rock on which he hit his head while chasing one of the reservation's youth offenders.

The film is not as conscious as Deloria is of the differences between Christianity and Marxism, on the one hand, and Indigenous religion, on the other. But Iktomi accrues, adjectivally, to Rudy's plotline, and not to Mogie's, because the film passionately agrees with Deloria that liberation is inextricably bound to cultural (especially religious) restoration. "Skins," the medicine man tells Rudy, "have forgotten the forces around them." That Rudy, and not Mogie, receives this bit of cautionary and imploring information is significant.

When I say that the idea of liberation qua religious restoration does not accrue, adjectivally, to Mogie's character, I am not arguing that the real Mogies of this world, the "grassroots" Indians, are less concerned about this ethical dilemma than are Deloria and the real Rudys of this world. What I am saying is that, as far as "Savage" cinema in general and *Skins* in particular are concerned, Mogie's position of red dust and ruin, his embodied genocide, is not a persona to whom the ensemble of questions which animate this ethical dilemma accrue. Subsequently, questions of filial and communal survival versus those of pleasure and release (such as the gratification of adultery)—questions animated by sweat-lodge cleansing, sage burning, spirit offerings, and prayer versus the prolonged angst of brooding or the rush and "certainty" of vigilantism—not only cluster around Rudy, to their near exclusion of Mogie, but their presence is so overwhelming as to crowd out the narrative's ability to sustain forays into the ethical dilemmas of genocide.

When, at the end of the film, Rudy confesses his vigilante activities to Mogie, he says they were for "our people." "Our people," says Mogie, with pronounced sarcasm and incredulity. "Who's our people?" "You know, our *Tiospaye*, our *Oyate*," answers Rudy. "Our Oyate," Mogie laughs. "You gotta be kidding me."

There is intimation here that, although Rudy has launched vigilante attacks against troublemakers, Mogie is the one who has blasphemed, for *Oyate* implies more than "people" in the sense of a body politic. It has spiritual significance, whereby the sensory self is intimately bound with the group. One is said to carry (or not carry) the welfare of Oyate in one's heart. Oyate is that vessel through which the sensory self can sacrifice itself for the good of the nation and "be connected with all creation, both the present universe and the spirits of those who have gone before."[17] The narrative does not necessarily imply that Mogie is a cultural scandal (he has too many facts and figures regarding Indian massacres, even in his most inebriated moments, for him to be a scandal), but it does maintain that he is in desperate need of help (because he does not embrace the values of Oyate)—help which only someone like Rudy can provide. Therefore it is imperative that the Rudys of the world restore their own spirituality, so that the Mogies will not be lost completely. What is astounding is the film's inability to grasp the organicity of Mogie's intellectual and political project. It sees Mogie only as an effect of sovereign deracination. The narrative's reluctance to allow the modality of genocide either to ponder its ethical dilemmas or to stage a conversation between the genocide modality and the sovereignty modality, let alone a critique of the sovereignty modality by way of the genocide modality, is mirrored in Deloria's metacommentaries on "Savage" ontology.

Deloria's primary reader is Native American; his secondary reader is the Settler. His texts address Settlers as though they are simultaneously his enemies and his possible allies. In other words, he treats the Settlers' secular Manichaeism, their spiritual monotheism, and their gratuitous violence as threats to the very possibility of Indigenism. But he also sees profound structural articulations between Indigenism and more promising and "progressive" adventures among Settlers. As I noted above, these adventures include Jungian, as opposed to Freudian, psychoanalysis and the religious practice and spiritual inheritance of the Amish and Jews.[18]

Carl Jung, Deloria asserts, did not fall into the Freudian trap of attributing human instincts and intuitions to nonhuman species: sex, individual survival, and a "social inheritance [no] larger or more complex than the family group." Deloria appreciates the basic tenets of Jungian psychoanalysis for the same reasons he celebrates the touchstones of Indigenous religious cohesion: Jung "recognizes the existence of instincts but . . . also transcends instinctual problems to draw conclusions from the study of the human mind which have universal implications." This expansive gesture that Deloria experiences in the work of Jung allows for a Western metaphysics of the human mind which not only has implications "universal" enough to embrace the Indigenous subject but can also work hand in hand with an Indigenous religious embrace of what Native people call "all my relations"—in short, inanimate and animate beings that are not human.[19] Put another way, for Deloria, Jungian psychoanalysis is one of modernity's few metaphysical meditations which have ethical capacity.

The potential for ethical capacity is also found in the structure and practice of Amish and Jewish spirituality. Deloria claims that the Amish, like spiritually centered Indians, lack the social alienation found elsewhere in Settler civil society. This, he believes, "stems from their tight communal ways, the fact that they settled on definite lands and are related to those lands."[20] This is one of the many instances when Deloria presents land, conceptually, as the capacity to transpose space into place. In other words, he gives value to land, subordinating—or outright rejecting—its commercial value for its ontological value. In this way, the stewardship relationality of "Savage" sovereignty sets the ethical standard against which only one or two Settler meditations and formations can measure.

In addition, language, much like land, is imbued by Deloria with both a temporal and a spatial capacity. He maintains that the ethicality of language is ensconced in its binding power. Prior to contact and conquest, Indian languages vouchsafed each Indian tribe's "discernable history, both religious and political" and bound "each tribe . . . closer" together. Such power has been lost to the Settler due to the alienating interventions of Western metaphysics; colonization threatens Indians with a similar loss. The Jews, however, are a notable exception among Settlers. "Only with the use of Hebrew by the Jewish community, which in so many ways perpetuates the Indian tribal religious conceptions of community, do we find contemporary similarities. Again conception of group identity is very strong among the Jews, and the phenomenon of having been born into a complete cultural and religious tradition is present, though many Jews, like many Indians, refuse to acknowledge their membership in an exclusive community."[21] Language, then, is a temporal capacity, the power to transpose meaningless and unspecified time into the meaningful and specific "event" known as the tribe. The "event" is not a single instance but rather a temporal coherence which perpetuates "the Indian [and Jewish] tribal religious conception of community." The temporal power of language must not only have been transposed in the past but must *re*inscribe itself in the time of the present if the event of the tribe is to cohere as "an exclusive community" in the future.

Deloria's outlines of Indigenous religion (as a constituent element of "Savage" sovereignty) move back and forth between three registers: (1) spatial capacity to transpose *terra nullius* into nameable place, coupled with a stewardship, rather than a proprietary, relation to those place names, (2) temporal capacity to transpose meaningless time into coherent chronology—the elaboration of the tribe as "event" through the reification of language, and (3) a series of celebrations of the holistic dimensions of Indigenous religion in contradistinction to the isolating, alienating, and atomizing dimensions of Western metaphysics.

For Deloria, the holistic impetus of Indigenous religion stems from several attributes, one of which is the lack of doctrine. Since tribal religions are not doctrinaire there can be no religious heresies in Indigenous spiritualism: "It is virtually impossible to 'join' a tribal religion by arguing for its doctrines. People could care less whether an outsider believes anything. No separate standard of religious behavior is imposed on followers of the religious tradition outside of the requirements for its ceremonies—who shall do what, who may participate, and who is excluded from which part of the ceremony, who is needed for other parts of the ceremony." The importance of Deloria's claims above should not be reduced to a mere comparison of Indigenous and Christian religious practices. Rather, his analysis alerts us to an incompatibility between important elements of "Savage" existence and Settler existence: "One could say that the tribal religions created the tribal community, which, in turn, made a place for every tribal individual. Christianity, on the other hand . . . created the solitary individual who, gathered together every seven days, constitutes the 'church,' which then defines the extent to which the religion is to be understood and followed." Deloria throws a spanner in the works of not just Christianity but Western metaphysics itself by suggesting that Christianity conceives of the individual as an element within the group (society), when in point of fact (the "fact" being the elements of "Savage" ontological thought) it is the group that must be apprehended as an element within the individual. The inability of Western metaphysics to grasp this is central to its internally, as well as outwardly, destructive legacy: "With the individual as the primary focal point and his relationship with the deity as his primary concern, the group is never on certain ground as to its existence but must continually change its doctrines and beliefs to attract a maximum number of followers: it is always subject to horrendous fragmentation over doctrinal interpretations, whenever two strong-minded individuals clash." This clash between strong-minded individuals is a common occurrence systemic to the historiography of Western metaphysics, a hair trigger that threatens, if not the rest of the world, then at least the coherence of "Savage" sovereignty in the Western Hemisphere. In tribal religions, contrary to the built-in dualism of Christianity, "theology is part of communal experiences needing no elaboration, abstraction, or articulation of principles. Every factor of human experience is seen in a religious light as part of the meaning of life." This safeguards against the social manifestation in Christianity and Western metaphysics writ large which distinguishes between the outcast (the heretic) and the flock. "Because the Christian religion is conceived as a person," writes Deloria, "the individual is both victim and victor of the religion."[22]

Indigenous religion cannot accommodate such divine individualism. Deloria maintains that such divine individualism is a key, an internal catalyst to a wide range of social ills in civil society, despite the fact that this divine individualism is known by its euphemism, "salvation." There is "no salvation in tribal religions apart from the continuation of the tribe itself. . . . The possibility of conceiving of an individual alone in a tribal religious sense is ridiculous. The very complexity of tribal life and the inerdependence of people on one another makes this conception improbable at best, a terrifying loss of identity at worst."[23]

The absence of a doctrinaire context for Indigenous religion not only militates against existential isolation common in the West but also allows for a more comprehensive and less atomized experience of, and relationship to, the universe and its powers. This is possible because, as Deloria notes, "tribal religious realities" do not divide the world into dualistic realms of "spiritual and material . . . , this-worldly and other-worldly, and absolute space and time dimensions" but instead "maintain a consistent understanding of the unity of all experience." Deloria is quick to acknowledge, however, the possibility of religious articulation between the "Savage" and the Settler when he points out that in the Western scheme of knowledge there are "some things that have utmost importance" for Native peoples, but they can only be ascertained by what appears to be a symptomatic, rather than a direct, reading of "their system of beliefs, their myths, or their social and political organizations."[24]

Still, Western metaphysics, whether secular or religious, is not imbued with what, for Deloria, is the most common feature of Indigenous awareness of the world, "the feeling or belief that the universe is energized by a pervading power." This common awareness of a pervasive power is a constituent element of "Savage" sovereignty although its manifest content elaborates different ceremonial forms and is known by different names across Native America: *mana* in Hawaii, *waken, orenda,* or *manitou* in North America. These names give tribal members the conceptual framework for meditation and prayer with respect to widely distributed powers in the universe, the "inherent energy," the "field of force" capable of producing extraordinary effects.[25]

The barrenness of Western metaphysics, as opposed to the plenitude of the Indigenous spirituality, lies not only in the former's need to atomize the natural world into realms, but also in its desire to master, rather than experience, what it encounters in that world. Contrary to the claims of Western metaphysics, this need to atomize and desire to master deadens, rather than sharpens, awareness of the universe:

> The observations and experiences of primitive peoples was so acute that they were able to recognize a basic phenomenon of the natural religiously rather than scientifically. *They felt power but did not measure it.* Today we measure power, are unable to feel it except on extremely rare occasions. We conclude that energy forms the basic constituent

of the universe through experimentation. For primitive peoples, on the other hand, *the presence of energy and power is the starting point of their analyses and understanding of the natural world, it is their cornerstone for further exploration.*[26]

Power—such as waken, orenda, manitou, or mana—also has specific resonance in the way Indigenous people imagine and structure governance (tribal society).

Land

In delineating "Savage" ontology through the element of land, Indigenous scholars emphasize that a relationship (a) to the land in general and (b) to the land which any given tribe inhabited at the time of contact, is a relationship constituent of ontology. Most writers are also quick to distinguish between their relationship to the land and that of the Settler. Land thus becomes a pivotal element in a semiotics of "Savage" loss and Settler gain: "We are all land-based people . . . who are attuned to the rhythms of our homelands in a way that assumes both protection of, and an intimate belonging to, our ancestral places. . . . [But we are] surrounded by other, more powerful nations that . . . want our land and resources. . . . [This is an] ongoing colonial relationship."[27]

"Savage" sovereignty qua land is distinguished from Settlerism in how it imagines *dominion* and *use*. Indigenous dominion is characterized by the idea of "stewardship" rather than the idea of ownership:

Indigenous philosophies are premised on the belief that the earth was created by a power external to human beings, who have a responsibility to act as stewards; since humans had no hand in making the earth, they have no right to "possess" it or dispose of it as they see fit—possession of land by man is unnatural and unjust. The stewardship principle, reflecting a spiritual connection with land established by the Creator, gives human beings special responsibilities in the areas they occupy as Indigenous peoples, linking them in a "natural" way to their territories.[28]

Stewardship impacts on *use* in that the land—what Western metaphysics refers to as "nature"—is viewed as source rather than resource. This not only gestures to the unethical spiritual and political character of the capitalist profit motive but also posits "resource development" and industrialization as paradigms of dominion and use which are irreconcilable with Indigenism's paradigms of dominion and use. It not only marks a conflict between Indigenism and the heinous and exploitive desires of capitalism but also between Indigenism and the emancipatory and revolutionary desires for a Marxist proletarian dictatorship.

Ward Churchill illustrates the split between Indians and Marxists regarding "conclusions to be drawn from analyses of what is wrong with the capitalist process; with a vision of an alternative society. . . . the redistribution of proceeds accruing from a systematic rape of the earth is, at best, an irrelevancy for . . . Indians."[29] Metacommentaries of "Savage" ontology continually make the point that Native people share and watch over the land in concert with other creatures that inhabit it. Settlerism's structural imposition on the Indigenous system of relationality (one in which all inhabitants of the land are the Indian's "relations") is tantamount to the dismantling of Indigenous subjectivity. This dismantling of subjectivity, Churchill and others point out, cannot be repaired by a Marxist revolution (found, for example, in Negri's and Hardt's idea of "time redeemed" or the commons restored), for such a revolution neither reinstates "stewardship" nor returns kinship relations among animate and inanimate to the paradigm of dominion and use.[30]

The Settler's ontological degradation in the form of capitalism, and his or her emancipation in the form of communism, entails the beginning and the continuation of Indian land dispossession—a dispossession far more profound than material larceny: "Abandonment of their land base is not an option for Native Americans, either in fact or in theory. The result would simply be 'auto-genocide.'"[31]

"Savage" sovereignty's notions of stewardship and source are presented as ethical alternatives to Settler sovereignty's notions of dominance and resource. The counterpoint offered by Deloria, Trask, Alfred, and Churchill to Marxists and Settler progressives is twofold. First, civil society cannot become ethical simply by adjusting its paradigm of resource accumulation and distribution; instead, the entire ensemble of questions which orient the Human in relation to the natural world have to be "Indigenized." This also means—as Churchill, Trask, and Silko, but not Deloria and Alfred, are quick to point out—that the Indigenous subject, and not the Settler, is the quintessential revolutionary subject-position. The Indigenous subject, and not the proletariat, is the sine qua non of revolutionary subjectivity because the semiotics of loss which positions the Indigenous (dispossession of a culturally and spiritually specific land base wherein all creatures were their relations and of which they were stewards) is an essential modality of dispossession. Dispossession of labor power, at the site of the wage relation, is an important but ultimately inessential form of dispossession. Not only is it inessential but it takes place in an a priori unethical ontological formation: Settlers and civil society. This is a schematization of the difference between a vital aspect of "Savage" sovereignty and Settler sovereignty. Churchill puts a finer point on it by suggesting that not only is the proletariat not the essential placeholder for the revolutionary subject, but the proletariat's struggle to obliterate the wage relation and democratize ownership of the means of production (of which land is a primary component) is at best inadequate, and at worst unethical, in comparison to a struggle to re-Indigenize the land.

> The potential for oppositional action centering upon tangibles such as landbase rather than abstracts on the order of "class interest" . . . should be starkly evident. Concomitantly, the threat to the stability of the status quo should be readily apparent. A whole body of anti-colonial theory should spring to the mind of any well-read leftist and serve to underscore this [point]. . . . Consider that every inch of stolen ground recovered . . . by Native Americans comes directly from the *imperial integrity* of the U.S. itself. By any definition, the mere potential for even a partial dissolution of the U.S. landbase should be a high priority consideration for *anyone* concerned with destabilizing the status quo.[32]

In this passage Churchill is not simply asserting a tactical distinction between Marxist politicos and organizations like the American Indian Movement. Rather, his examination of the Marxist answer to the question *What is to be done?* critiques the question itself at a paradigmatic level, while offering an alternative, a paradigmatic shift predicated on Indigenism. In short, Churchill claims that if Settler revolutionaries shift the spatial paradigm of Marxism from the wage/labor nexus (where surplus value is extracted on the Gramscian factory floor or from within the

Negrian libidinal "commons") to the land/spirit nexus (the domain where all objects are related to each other as subjects and where source cannot be denigrated as resource) then the revolution would possess an essential, rather than merely an important, ensemble of questions—questions of Native power (mana, waken, manitou, or orenda) rather than Settler hegemony (influence, leadership, and consent).[33] This shift from the wage/labor nexus to the land/spirit nexus, Churchill implies, would make the movement a better and more ethical fighting machine, and, most important, give the Settler the ontological integrity she or he could never achieve through the machinations of hegemony.

Sovereignty and the Structure of Antagonisms

The meditations on "Savage" ontology which are weighted heavily toward the modality of sovereignty reproduce a network of connections, transfers, and displacements—articulations—between themselves and meditations on Settler ontology. I am not suggesting that the content of Marxism, or even of Christianity and psychoanalysis, for that matter (meditations foundational to the range of ethical questions one can conceptualize in civil society), can be reconciled with the content of Indigenous religion, land cathexis, and governance. Trask, Deloria, Churchill, and Silko persuade me when they argue that Marx, Freud, and Jesus have lost (usurped?) the road map to Turtle Island.

I borrow the notion of triumvirate articulation (connections, transfers, and displacements) from Peter Miller's and Nikolas Rose's article "On Therapeutic Authority: Psychoanalytical Expertise under Advanced Liberalism." Miller and Rose reject the trend in scholarly writing about psychoanalysis that attempts to explain the discourse "by locating its origins in general social and cultural transformations." Their strategy of analysis differs from dominant trends in scholarship in that they are "*concern[ed] with therapeutics as a form of authority.*" This means that their analysis focuses on the rhetorical strategies through which the discourse of psychoanalysis (in an historical milieu of advanced liberalism) becomes authoritative. Their analysis is animated not by the *why* but by the *how* of therapeutics.[34] Similarly, we have asked ourselves how, rhetorically, the Settler/Master's grammar of exploitation and alienation functions. In what way is this grammar authoritative in discourses as disparate as feminism, Marxism, and Western aesthetics?[35] We asked ourselves why there is no articulation between the Slave's grammar of suffering and the Settler/Master's grammar of suffering. What prevents them from being simultaneously authoritative? Now, we find ourselves faced with sovereignty as a modality of the "Savage's" grammar of suffering, with the network through which sovereignty's authority functions, and with the possibility or impossibility of its articulation with the Settler and the Slave.

Deloria, Churchill, and others insist on the incompatibility of both Marxist and psychoanalytic utopianism as projects of emancipation for Native people. Churchill goes so far as to say that "Marxism [constitutes] as great a threat to native sovereignty and self-determination as capitalism."[36] In addition, there seems to be a radical disarticulation between the Settler's and the "Savage's" topographies of the soul: the secular mediations and processes through which a psychoanalyst "punctuates" (as Lacan would put it) the analysand's empty speech, thereby guiding the analysand to a nonegoic relationship with his or her contemporaries (the attainment of full speech), are apparently dumbstruck when confronted by the mediations and processes through which the medicine man or medicine woman heals the tribal member and thereby reharmonizes him or her with the universe and all its relations. Deloria links this besetting hobble of psychoanalysis's healing power to the bankrupt ethics of Christianity: "The original [Christian] perception of reality becomes transformed over a period of time into philosophies and theologies which purport to give a logical and analytical explanation of ultimate reality [i.e., Freudian psychoanalysis]. These explanations, of course, have eliminated the human emotions and intuitive insights of the original experience and in their place have substituted a systematic rendering of human knowledge concerning the natural world."[37] Here, Deloria glosses Leslie Silko's assertion that Europeans are spiritual orphans. "The ancestors had called Europeans the orphan people and had noted that as with orphans taken in by selfish and coldhearted people, few Europeans had remained whole. They failed to recognize the earth as their mother."[38] The disturbing result of this abandonment, Deloria argues, is the European

> divisions of the natural world into spiritual and material, eternal and ephemeral, this-worldly and other-worldly, and absolute space and time dimensions. . . . Primitive people do not differentiate their world

of experience into two realms that oppose or complement each other. They ... maintain a consistent understanding of the unity of all experience. Rather than seeking underlying causes or substances, primitives report the nature and intensity of their experience. Carl Jung clarified this approach to experience when he wrote that "thanks to our one-sided emphasis on so-called natural causes, we have to differentiate what is subjective and psychic from what is objective and 'natural.' For primitive man, on the contrary, the psychic and the objective coalesce in the external world."[39]

Deloria and others thus make it clear that the network of connections, transfers, and displacements which authorize and articulate Settler ontology and the sovereignty modality of "Savage" ontology is not a network of relays between the content of their respective rhetoric, for they do not map the soul with the same vision of spatial and temporal cartographies. How, then, is the articulation sutured if not by the content of their visions? Why is it that the struggle between one half of "Savage" ontology (sovereignty) and the complete ontological frame of reference of the Settler/Master (exploitation and alienation) cannot be characterized as an antagonism? Why, instead, must it be thought of as a conflict? How can we name this rubric of articulation between these two mortal enemies?

What the Settler and the "Savage" share is a capacity for time and space coherence. At every scale—the soul, the body, the group, the land, and the universe—they can both practice cartography, and although at every scale their maps are radically incompatible, their respective "mapness" is never in question. This capacity for cartographic coherence is the thing itself, that which secures subjectivity for both the Settler and the "Savage" and articulates them to one another in a network of connections, transfers, and displacements. The shared capacity for cartographic coherence ratchets the Settler/"Savage" struggle down from an antagonism to a conflict. In other words, this struggle succumbs to the constraints of analogy, is captured and made into a simile by the word *like*: like the war in Iraq, like the Palestinian struggle, like women's liberation, and so on. At best, the "like" makes the Settler/"Savage" struggle legible in the discourse of postcolonial theory. At worst, the simile grants the Settler/"Savage" struggle the tepid legibility of various junior partner struggles in civil society.

Of course, the "Savage" ontological modality of genocide ratchets the Settler/"Savage" struggle up from a conflict to an antagonism and thus overwhelms the constraints of analogy. Suddenly, the struggle between the Settler and the "Savage" is "like" nothing at all, which is to say it becomes "like" the struggle between the Master and the Slave. Suddenly, the network of connections, transfers, and displacements between the "Savage's" semiotics of loss and the Settler's semiotics of gain is overwhelmed—crowded out—by a network of connections, transfers, and displacements between a genocided *thing* and a fungible and accumulated *thing*. Unfortunately, ontological meditations in which Native American theorists muse on genocide as an ontological modality are found, for the most part, only in the work of Churchill and, to a lesser extent, Silko. Without more work on this articulation, there can be no hope of theorizing the partial object status of the "Savage" in conjunction with the absolute object status of the Slave.

If Native American theorization embraced its structural nonpresence, one could begin to look for an articulation between the object status of the "Savage" and that of the Slave. The diagnostic payoff of this would manifest in a further and more decisive crowding out of any ethical pretense that the ontologists of White civil society could claim (having lost their Indigenous interlocutors, they would only have the power of their empty rhetoric and their guns), and there is no telling what kinds of unflinching revolutionary prognostications could result over the years. For this to happen, a handful of Native American theorists must join that handful of Black theorists and dialogue in the empty space and temporal stillness of absolute dereliction. What, we might ask, inhibits this analytic and political dream of a "Savage"/Slave encounter? Is it a matter of the Native theorist's need to preserve the constituent elements of sovereignty, or is there such a thing as "Savage" Negrophobia? Are the two related?

Skins is a film whose ontological *authorization* struggles in uneasy tension between the monumentalizing imaginary of sovereignty and the absolute dereliction of genocide—between the authority of Rudy Yellow Lodge and Mogie Yellow Lodge. This tension is anxious and brittle, ill at ease with its competing authorizations. This anxiety manifests in the modality of genocide's entrance through the backdoor, so to speak—by way of Graham Greene's performance, and his rewriting of the dialogue, and by way of the formal, rather than narrative, cinematic strategies. In other words, the film knows, unconsciously, Mogie's genocided body as the quintessence of "Savage" ontology, but the narrative only recognizes, consciously, Rudy's sovereign body as the quintessence of "Savage" ontology.

As I have noted, only a small number of Native American ontological meditations are given over to genocide; most meditations on the grammar of "Savage" suffering focus on sovereignty and its semiotics of loss. Furthermore, most of the Native American writing that reflects on genocide as an ontological modality (instead of simply recording it as experience) has been done by two authors: Leslie Marmon Silko and Ward Churchill. Although the works of Silko and Churchill often meditate on sovereignty through the same semiotics of loss found in Trask, Alfred, and Deloria, their prose and analysis often grapple with an ensemble of questions central to extermination. Silko's method of conveyance and argumentative strategy is poetic, narrative, associative, and impressionistic; Churchill's is marked by a strong, highly rhetorical prose style and evidentiary argument strategies; his books sometimes have almost as many pages of footnotes as they do pages of prose.

In "Concerning Violence," Fanon splits an important hair between structural position and political discourse when he writes that natives "do not lay a claim to the truth; they do not *say* that they represent the truth, for they *are* the truth." For Fanon, this ontological truth makes "morality [i.e., political action/discourse/aesthetics] very concrete; it is to silence the settler's defiance, to break his flaunting violence—in a word, to put him out of the picture."[40] I intend to proceed in such a way as to trouble Fanon's assertion of Native ontology when the U.S. "Savage" is the native in question. For the bifurcation of "Savage" ontology often works, cinematically and in the ontological meditations and political common sense under consideration here, to put Settlers back into the picture (makes them present on screen), and, however unwittingly, defers indefinitely an ethical encounter between the "Savage" and the Slave.

In this regard, Taiaiake Alfred's *Peace, Power, Righteousness: An Indigenous Manifesto* is an interesting exception which presents us with a semiotics of sovereignty that should not be labeled "sovereignty" since it attempts to disturb, rather than suture, touchstones of cohesion between the "Savage" and the Settler. Alfred goes so far as to assert that sovereignty is an inappropriate concept for Indigenism because the notion of an Indian "state" is an oxymoron. Traditionally, Indigenous governance elaborates no absolute authority, coercive enforcement of decisions, hierarchy, or separate ruling elite. Sovereignty, for Alfred, is an exclusionary concept rooted in adversarial and coercive Western notions of power.[41] His book stages an intramural conversation between a cross-section of Native thinkers. In it, he presents his own work and also invites Native scholars (from Audra Simpson, a twenty-nine-year-old Kanien'kehaka graduate student in anthropology, to Atsenhaienton, an international spokesperson for the Kanien'kehaka people, part of the Iroquois Confederacy, to well-known authorities on ontology such as Deloria) to muse with him on the ways the Indigenous position is imagined.

To Audra Simpson he puts the question of sovereignty directly, asking her if there is a difference between sovereignty and the Native concept of "nationhood." Her response is worth quoting at length.

> The concepts are quite different. I find it hard to isolate, define, and then generalize what a "Native" concept of nationhood would be without it sounding contrived. This is a tired point: we are different people, different nations, and would have different ideas about what nationhood is and what it means to us. The Sechelt conception or Northern Cree conception will certainly depart from Mohawk ideas about who we are. Each people will have a term in their own language that will mean "us." I think that is what our concept of nationhood is.
>
> My opinion is that "Mohawk" and "nationhood" are inseparable. Both are simply about *being*. Being is who you are, and a sense of who you are is arrived at through your relationships with other people—your people. So who you are is tied with what we are: nation.
>
> Now, sovereignty—the authority to exercise power over life, affairs, territory—this is not inherited. It is not part of being, the way our form of nationhood is. It has to be conferred, or granted—it's a thing that can be given and thus can be taken away. It's clearly a foreign concept, because it occurs through an exercise of power—power over another. . . . [42]

Skins presents us with a paradox, manifest in its simultaneous embrace of indigenous *being* in intra-tribal (cosmological, inanimate, and non-human) relations and institutionality (the logic of policing) deployed through rugged individualism (Rudy's persona: tall; broad shouldered; burdened with isolated rather than communal, angst). Granted, it is not altogether clear that the film's intentions are to condone openly Rudy's vigilantism (one could argue that the narrative condemns it just as easily as one could argue that it merely condemns its excesses). But it is clear that the film imagines the loss of what Alfred and Simpson call communal, or tribal, "being," as an ethical dilemma to be struggled over, not by the tribe or communal entity, but by one man; a man whose authority has been "conferred, or granted," by the logic of policing, "the authority to exercise power over life, affairs, territory."

> This is not to say that the valuing of sovereignty, of having control over territory has not been indigenized. We've used it in a rhetorical and political way time and again. But I think there is a difference between the *being* of who we are—Mohawk—and the defense mechanisms that we have to adopt in the neocolonial context—sovereignty.[43]

Here Simpson suggests that the Rudy-phenomenon, which appears in "Savage" cinema, political tracts, and ontological meditations, may be a compensatory gesture, a form of strategic essentialism geared to help the Native American antagonist over the immediate hump of whatever conflict she or he is pressed into at the moment. I believe that exploration of the libidinal economy—that is, the unconscious reflexes, selections, and combinations detected in cinema—render her explanation too generous and thus in need of further elaboration.

It is important to note that Alfred and Simpson are Native Canadians. True, they are both Mohawk and part of the Iroquois Confederacy, which spans across Southeastern Canada and the Northeastern United States. But Alfred writes as though he is in conflict primarily with Canadian Settlerism. His book concretizes his structural claims, politically and anecdotally, by way of Canadian versus Indigenous conflicts. This does not put Alfred's assumptive logic, or the basis of his claims, at variance with those of Indigenous thinkers in the United States, such as Trask, a Native Hawaiian, or Deloria, a Lakota.[44] I submit, however, that the difference between deconstructive proclivity in Alfred and Simpson as regards the idea of "Savage" sovereignty, and the intensity with which sovereignty is invested by U.S. scholars and activists, stems from a combination of political, material, and libidinal factors.

To begin with, Canada is a vast country covering 3,852,000 square miles, compared to the United States of America's 3,615,211 square miles. Yet Canada has only 33 million people, 3.3 million of whom are Indigenous. Of the 288 million inhabitants of the United States, 4.1 million are Indigenous. In other words, 10 percent of Canadians are Indigenous whereas only 1.6 percent of people in the United States are Indigenous. This has impacted the social reality profoundly: Native people in Canada have various forms of governmental autonomy and their own television channel. In addition, although Whites in Canada can know Whiteness in contradistinction to Native Canadian genocide, the number and frequency of genocidal campaigns never approached the scale that they did south of the border.

None of this accounts, however, for the fact that Trask's ontological meditations are charged with the same unflinching political rhetoric as that in the work of Churchill, a Cherokee whose people were massacred on the Trail of Tears, or Deloria, a Lakota whose people were massacred at Wounded Knee in 1890 and attacked there again, as part of a reign of terror on Pine Ridge, in the 1970s, or Silko, a Laguna whose reservation is known as the single most radioactively contaminated area in North America outside of nuclear bomb test sites.[45] Trask is a Hawaiian. As such, her people's victimization by U.S. genocidal practices mirrors that of Alfred and Native Canadians more than it does Indigenous people trapped within the forty-eight contiguous States—decimated, as they were, from 19 million to 4.1 million. In other words, one can look to the empiricism of material (tactile) conditions and say Native Canadians are 10 percent of a national population in a vast and mostly uninhabited land. Thus, the hydraulics of Settler repression need not be as deracinating as those in a Settler society with roughly the same amount of territory but with roughly eight times as many Settlers.

Again, in the United States, the "Savage" equals 1.6 percent of the population and the Settler equals 80.6 percent. Since contact, genocide has reversed the "Savage" to Settler ratio with nearly perfect symmetry. Herein lies the Manichaeism of the Settler/"Savage" antagonism, a Manichaeism manifest far more emphatically in the United States than in Canada. In the United States, the symbiosis between the material production of living zones (scaled up from White bodies to civil society) and dead zones (scaled up from Red flesh to the reservation) is so pervasive that one need not belong to a specific tribe which has directly experienced the events of genocide in order for one's own Indigenism to be underwritten by the historical trauma of genocide. (Like "Savage" ontologists from Hawaii or Canada, Saidiya Hartman makes a similar case with respect to the Slave, explicitly arguing that the spatial condition of chattel slavery is not bound by the borders of the plantation, but also territorializes the world of Blacks in the North. And she implicitly argues that the temporal condition of chattel slavery did not end in 1865 but followed generations of Blacks 140 years into the future.)[46]

The historical relationship of Trask's Hawaiian people to genocide (in terms of scale, intensity, and duration) is closer to that experienced in Canada than that suffered in the United States. Still, Hawaiians came to know themselves as belonging to a group of people whose ontology was predicated on genocide. In addition, the Manichaeism between the Master and the Slave (between exploited bodies and accumulated flesh) added to the intensity of the Manichaeism between the Settler and the "Savage."[47] The Master/Slave antagonism put further libidinal pressure on the social structure of relations with which Indigenous Hawaiians had to contend psychically and politically. The unflinching analysis, politics of refusal, and acerbic method of conveyance, taking no prisoners, in the work of Hawaiian thinkers like Trask, and which is not found in the work of Native Canadians like Taiaiake Alfred, is a reflection not of differing ontological structures but rather of variant social intensities. To put a finer point on it, if, as I have argued, the Master/Slave dynamic is an ontological, and not simply a historical condition, then Canada cannot be said to be "free" of that dynamic simply because there are no plantations in Canada.

The structure of Canadian antagonisms (Red, White, and Black) is isomorphic with the structure of antagonisms elsewhere in the hemisphere. But the Canadian socialization of that structure has "allowed" Blacks and some Native Americans to consider Canada as a safe haven from the "excesses" of the United States.[48] This may account for Taiaiake Alfred and Audra Simpson's casual deconstruction of sovereignty versus its reification beyond the sort of strategic essentialism (what Simpson calls "indigenized sovereignty") in the works of Trask, Deloria, Churchill, and others south (and west) of Canada's borders. However, Trask's ontological meditations share, with Silko's and Churchill's, an unflinching hatred for the United States of America, a hatred uncharacteristic of Alfred's discussion of Canada.

Most important, Trask, Churchill, Deloria—and, to a lesser extent, Silko—have an ossified and possessive relationship to the idea of colonialism which Alfred's and Simpson's more relaxed and contemplative writing is able to deconstruct. Oddly enough, it is the success of their struggles with the Canadian government, admittedly limited and driven by the logic of postcolonialism (extensive self-governed territories inside of Canada, a national television station, royal commissions dedicated to negotiating expanded sovereignty), which has, over time, given Canadian First Peoples the space to be critical of and live in a deconstructive relationship to that very logic.

Simpson says, "The valuing of sovereignty, of having control over territory, has . . . been indigenized."[49] This is her way of answering the question of whether "control over territory" is or is not an element constituent of "Savage" ontology. But rather than answer the question, I believe that Alfred's and Simpson's dialogue has just begun to pose it. *Skins* takes up this question more substantially, and so do the metacommentators on "Savage" ontology south of the Canadian border.

There are of course political and spiritual differences between the cosmology of the "Savage" and the cosmology of the Settler. The question before us, however, is if those differences are essential, as Simpson and others seem to argue, or important, as I would suggest, when one considers them not only through the way Settler/"Savage" relationality is imagined, but through the way "Savage"/Slave relationality is (un)imagined. I make this suggestion not by offering evidence which contradicts what Simpson, Alfred, Deloria, and others press into service of their arguments regarding the essential division between Settler and "Savage," but by demonstrating how the antagonistic disarticulation which *seems* to occur between the Settler and the "Savage" is recomposed as a conflictual articulation in the presence of the Slave. This claim will be taken up in the remaining chapters of part 3, in a close reading of *Skins*.

SEVEN

Excess Lack

> We are maintained alive at all primarily as a matter of utility . . .
> and then only in a form considered acceptable to them.
> —WARD CHURCHILL, *A Little Matter of Genocide*

TOWARD THE END of *Skins*, we find Mogie Yellow
Lodge (Graham Greene) home from the hospital. His
face has been burned almost beyond recognition. The
camera tracks him as he walks from the sofa to the
kitchen table and back again to the sofa, where Rudy
Yellow Lodge (Eric Schweig), his younger brother, will
tell him that it was he, Rudy, who burned his face and
body to the third degree (see figure 6). In this scene it
is Mogie, rather than Rudy, who interpellates the spectator. In fact, it would be safe to say that Mogie interpellates spectator identification in every scene in which
the two brothers appear together as grown men. This
is remarkable for two reasons. To begin with, both the
script and the contextualizing discourse that circu-
lates around the film (the director's commentary, actor's commentary, online and print media film reviews,
as well as the poster art of the lobby card and the DVD
cover) are unanimous that *Skins* is Rudy's story. Rudy,
and not Mogie, is the film's protagonist.

Rudy cares for his people, the largely indigent Lakota of the Pine Ridge Indian Reservation in South Dakota, and for his brother, "a one-time football hero and

6　Medium close-up of Mogie with burned face (sitting on sofa)

decorated Vietnam vet, now ravaged by alcoholism and broken dreams," the best way he knows how: through a "vigilante crusade to clean up their squalid surroundings."[1] Rudy's bodily coordinates are represented as intact and unscarred (the antithesis of Mogie's body ravaged by Vietnam, alcoholism, and arson), coded with the kind of masculine virility and rugged individualism found most often in Settler/Master cinema, from White socially engaged films like Marc Forster's *Monster's Ball* and John Sayles's *Lone Star* to aggrandizing and unapologetic Westerns like John Ford's *Stagecoach*. This is celebrated by the intentionality of the script. Even the director, Chris Eyre, comments on how pleased he is with Eric Schweig's masculine charisma: "Eric has such presence. He's a handsome man. He feels like he has a wealth of experience in his demeanor. He's a great actor. I love working with him and I know that there are several other roles that I would love to do with him just because he has such great presence. He's six foot two or three [and] a good weight here [in *Skins*]."[2] Mogie, on the other hand, is a mixture of red dust and ruin. Mogie is the film's embodiment of a lost soul who does not signify sovereign plenitude. He has opted, that is, "for the non-ego over the ego, the threatening outside over the coherent inside, and death over life." Rudy, in contrast, epitomizes egoic monumentalization of cultural, political, and sexual sovereignty. In the case of Kaja Silverman's (White) male, such monumentalized positions manifest themselves in the unconscious through a "binding" of the "paternal imago" through which the subject can recognize himself. White masculinity, then, is secured by way of repetitive and "gradual reaffirmation and reconstitution of the dominant fiction" which occurs "at the level of a wide range of textural practices, from Hollywood cinema, to advertisements for kitchen appliances, to Dior's 'New Look.'" Silverman advocates the "ruination" of this dominant fiction through textual encounters with the death drive, that "the typical male subject, like his female counterpart, might learn to live with lack." This often happens, she reminds us, after civil society has waged war (e.g., World War II and Vietnam).[3] But Mogie has encountered a violence too vast and timeless for the nomenclature of war to signify; he embodies something extratextual and hence more emphatic than the kind of ruination of masculinity and corporeal lack which Silverman and other White feminists have offered as what disarticulates the consolidation of the White male ego.

Mogie Yellow Lodge's body is not simply a body of phallic lack. In other words, he has not simply been "feminized" by the film's adjectival strategies and by his character's counterpoint to Rudy—which is the modus operandi of film noir, that is, White women to White men. Rather his body is an ontological placeholder for genocide. In this way the stakes of "Savage" ethics are ratcheted up beyond the dilemmas of civil society's internal conflict between men and women, up to the dilemmas of the antagonism between Settler and "Savage." But in the body of the "Savage" this upward ratchet is never complete or absolute. This is because Rudy and his corporeal coherence, his sovereign integrity, are always waiting in the wings.

It is important to remind ourselves that Mogie is probably as much a creation of actor Graham Greene's on-location interventions as he is of the official script. Greene (characterized by more than one reviewer as the Indian version of the stereotypical "angry Black man") told Eyre, "I hope you know, I made your movie for you."[4] I take this in the spirit that Eyre took it, not as ridicule or as an aesthetic put-down, but as a joke between "Skins" which indicates mutual appreciation: on the one hand, Greene's appreciation of Eyre for providing him with a vehicle to communicate dimensions of Native American pathos and antagonism which few other Indian actors have been allowed to communicate. Greene reflected, "I haven't been able to stretch as an actor for a long time and [Skins] is a really tough nut to chew; I'm pulling a lot of muscles with Mogie":[5] on the other hand, Eyre's appreciation of Greene, manifest in Eyre's becoming

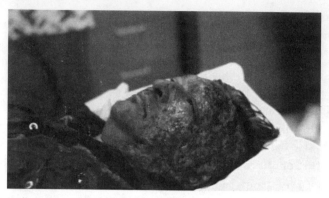

7   Medium close-up of Mogie burned on gurney, in a scene from *Skins*

a "pliable" director, to the point of allowing Greene to rewrite, edit, and improvise Mogie's lines.[6] But my claim above—that when Rudy and Mogie appear on screen together the spectator is "hailed" by the ethical dilemmas, the ensemble of questions, elaborated by Mogie rather than those elaborated by Rudy—is not based on the synergy between Eyre and Greene, or on the humor and intensity which Greene brought to the project.[7] Rather, I believe two other, essential, variables are at work here, one ontological and the other aesthetic or experiential.[8]

When Rudy and Mogie are on screen together the social, experiential narrative of colonialism is overwhelmed by the ontological (anti)narrative of genocide. But Mogie, which is to say Greene in his performance of him, does not do all this work by himself; in fact, his labor may be relatively less significant than the aesthetic formalism of *Skins*, which often breaks ranks with its putative allegiance to narrative (i.e., breaks with classical cinema's rules requiring the subordination of sound and image to story). Such ontological disturbance of the narrative's sovereign imperatives occurs spatially in cinematic strategies that include, but are neither limited by nor wedded to, Greene's laconic performance.

This ontological disturbance of sovereign coherence also occurs temporally. After he torches the Old Chief liquor store, Rudy meets with Dr. Fitzgerald (played by the Native Canadian actor Tina Keeper) to inquire about Mogie's burns (see figure 7). The hubris of this inquiry lies in Rudy's belief that he has caused his brother's injuries through one of his hypersovereign acts—his vigilantism—gone awry.

8 Close-up of Rudy in his BIA uniform, in a scene from *Skins*

In other words, Rudy, like the narrative itself, is so absorbed by and cathected to the violence of coherent intentions, the ensemble of questions scaffolded by the grammar of cultural loss, that he is blindsided by the gratuitous violence of incoherent genocide (see figure 8).

DR. FITZGERALD: Mogie will get over the burns but something else has come up. When we did the blood work we found that he had elevated levels of macrocytes and spur cells. So we decided to do a biopsy. Rudy, I'm afraid that Mogie's got cirrhosis of the liver.

RUDY: How bad?

DR. FITZGERALD: It's terminal.

RUDY: What if he quit drinking? [*Dr. Fitzgerald shakes her head.*] What about a liver transplant?

DR. FITZGERALD: Rudy, I'm afraid that potential transplant patients don't include practicing alcoholics. And besides his liver problems, his stomach is thoroughly ulcerated. He's borderline diabetic. And his kidneys are only functioning at 50 percent.

RUDY: What am I gonna to do now?

DR. FITZGERALD: Help him say his peace, Rudy. I'm really sorry, but that's all you can do.

At this point in the film it becomes clear to us that the topography of Mogie Yellow Lodge's body is the place where "vectors of death" meet.[9] His body is the hub of these vectors of death. As such, "terminal" takes on a double meaning. It is the space of death, a *place* where multiple deaths meet, unnaming the named place, decomposing it as dead, unrepresentable *space*. And it is a time of death, that is, the destruction of temporality. Mogie Yellow Lodge is not only terminal but he was terminal prior to his burns, a time and space of genocide long before Rudy set fire to the liquor store—five hundred years before, to be exact. The exchange between Rudy and Dr. Fitzgerald catches the hubris of Rudy's sovereign agency off guard. Even if the script does not intend this painful comeuppance, the film's spectator experiences the prognosis that Dr. Fitzgerald imparts to Rudy like a punctuation mark at the end of a sentence: what has gone before begins to make sense, albeit in a less than conscious fashion. It suddenly becomes clear why Mogie's power of spectator interpellation is greater than Rudy's when the two are on screen together. Mogie is the "living" embodiment of death, whereas Rudy is the living embodiment of culture. The authenticity of culture (i.e., sovereignty) is always contested, whereas death is beyond contestation for it is beyond the symbolic.

When Mogie appears on screen, we must turn and look away. No one wants to die, or, more precisely, be "hailed" by this body of bits and pieces of death. Nonetheless, we are compelled and riveted to his every word and gesture, fixed by Mogie's authority, derived from the universality of his authenticity. Mogie's universal authenticity is not founded on the statement *We all have our cultures* but rather on the statement *We will all be dead*. Mogie Yellow Lodge is one of two creatures in the Western Hemisphere (the "Savage" and the Slave) for whom death is the meaning of life. Many generations before Mogie was a burn victim he was a victim of gratuitous violence, violence beyond the scope of symbolism and its powers of comprehension. "At Wounded Knee . . . three hundred and fifty-odd unarmed terrified immobilized Lakota were rained with Hotch-kiss guns by a reconstituted Seventh Calvary and blown to pieces. They were chasing children three miles up snow-filled ravines in order to hack them apart with sabers and hatchets at the end; and then dragged them back to the concentration point [where they were] carefully counted and dumped . . . into a mass grave."[10] Such violence is too immense for sovereignty's imaginary of cultural restoration, the cinematic labor which Rudy's character is called on to perform.

Not only is Mogie's condition always already terminal, but the violence that precipitates his condition exceeds and anticipates any individuated, representable, or nameable violence such as, in this case, Rudy's act of arson. *Genocide* is not a name for violence in the way that "arson" is; *genocide* is a linguistic placeholder connoting that violence which outstrips the power of connotation. To represent it we have to dismantle it, pretend that we can identify its component parts, force a name into its hole—macrocytes, spur cells, kidneys at half-throttle, a thoroughly ulcerated stomach, Wounded Knee, Sand Creek—and make it what it is not, the way one fills the tucked sleeve of a one-armed boy. But these fillers, these phantom limbs of connotation, can only be imagined separately, and as such they take on the ruse of items that science, love, aesthetics, or justice—some form of symbolic intervention—can attend to and set right. They become treatable, much like the massacre at Wounded Knee were it not for the fact that to comprehend Wounded Knee, three hundred-plus men, women, and children in a snow-filled ravine, one must comprehend those three hundred synchronically over three thousand miles (the forty-eight contiguous states) and diachronically over five hundred years. Here, madness sets in and the promises of symbolic intervention turn to dust. We are returned to the time and space of no time and space, the "terminal." Mogie Yellow Lodge is a refusal of such symbolic assistance; he laughs, sardonically, in the face of its bad faith.

Rudy Yellow Lodge, on the other hand, is a placeholder for a kind of disavowal that believes the "Savage" body, home, or "nation" should be imagined, more appropriately, through a cluster of representable and nameable losses: a burned body, a stolen and occupied territory, and assault on cultural supports (such as language and spiritual customs). This is the project of "Savage" sovereignty. A grammar of suffering elaborated by the constituent elements of anthropological coherence (i.e., language, body, home, territory) grants the "Savage's" suffering and his or her attendant ethical dilemmas the power of analogy. The power of analogy subsequently constructs the "Savage" as Human, but only up to the point of genocide.

Analogy positions the "Savage" in discursive proximity to the Settler. This, as I argued in chapter 1, is the essential conflictual harmony between the "Savage" and the Settler. Rudy goes through the motions; the lines, movements, and motivations of his character are meant to "argue" a litany of causal, rational, and symbolic explanations for Mogie's burns:

1   White merchants in Whiteclay, Nebraska, engage in hyperexploita-
    tion of Native Americans by selling 4 million cans of beer a year to
    Pine Ridge residents.

2   The U.S. government has a long history of collusion with such mer-
    chants: directly, by corralling Indians into reservations, followed by
    "indirect" collusion which legislates the reservation as "dry," mak-
    ing the nearest White towns "oases" of alcohol.

3   Rudy witnesses the way such exploitation manifests in subjective
    alienation and in the outright colonization of his people. Thus, he
    intervenes with force, arson, against a tangible time and space co-
    ordinate of that exploitation, a Whiteclay, Nebraska, liquor store.
    He makes a coherent response (arson) to coherent oppression
    (colonization).

Clearly, if Rudy Yellow Lodge were a Palestinian, or an Iraqi, the film's
fidelity to exploitation, and to the priority of sovereign loss over and
above genocidal death, would be both correct and ontologically exhaustive. Here, however, in the case of the "Savage," while the force of Rudy's
fixation on exploitation motivates him to destroy the liquor store, it
simultaneously cathedralizes that ensemble of questions elaborated by
sovereignty's semiotics of loss and as such widens, rather than narrows,
the chasm between sovereignty and genocide. Rudy's ethical dilemmas
and their attendant force (arson and, more broadly, vigilantism) act in
concert as a crowding-out scenario of the film's ability to embrace and be
authorized by genocide and all its mad antagonism.

This imbues Rudy (and the narrative more broadly) with the hubris of
faith in his own (sovereign) agency, his sense that he had it in his power
to kill another Indian. Rudy approaches another Indian, Dr. Fitzgerald, as
though he is genuinely the cause of Mogie's injuries. More pointedly, he
assumes that his brother was already alive and therefore could indeed be
killed, that within Mogie resides a life force that can be threatened with
loss. For this to be the case, however, one's ontological apparatus would
have to be overdetermined by sovereignty and not genocide. I am not
calling Rudy (or the film itself, for that matter) mendacious. What I am
noting is the manner and frequency (a frequency approaching something
like 99 percent) with which "Savage" discourse notes genocide as an on-

tological constituent and then proceeds to treat it as a past or passing "event."

What is more, the hubris of sovereignty and its rhetorical work, which crowd out a more emphatic ethical dimension, give Rudy a special kind of alibi. Sovereignty allows Rudy an alibi for his own genocided body, because only a living subject, and not a genocided object, could be charged with the task of first registering, and then redeeming, a nation's coherence. The film's narrative, in its allegiance to and in its elaboration of Rudy Yellow Lodge, labors to redeem (restore, rescue, manage, and constrain) the rigor mortis of genocide through the benevolence of sovereignty. This is the film's intended project.

At one point in the director's commentary, Eyre talks about how Mogie is a burden on Rudy. He is not suggesting that Rudy jettison Mogie. Rather, he tells the viewer, "We [Indians] all have a Mogie in our families." This bit of information the director gives us in the spirit of a lament. He implies that the duty of films like his, and the duty of people like Rudy, is to save the Mogies physically and redeem them psychically. Nowhere in this lament do we hear the corollary: that the Rudys of this world should give themselves over to the organicity of Mogie and be redeemed. Eyre does not lament Rudy as a social metaphor, or see his kind as a material blight on Indigenism. He doesn't say, "We all have a cop, a policy wonk, or a sell-out to White civil society, someone like Rudy, in our families."

Rudy's plenitude is not thought of as a liability, but Mogie's lack is. In his statement, Eyre both acknowledges and disavows genocide as what positions him (and the characters of *Skins*) ontologically. Only the living can struggle through a semiotics of loss. Rudy's fixation, or rather the fixation embodied in Rudy and in the force of his actions, gives him a perfect alibi, it places him somewhere, anywhere, other than at the scene of the genocide. The film maintains its sanity, its willful and dubious coherence, by scripting Rudy as somehow alive. This is one effect, however unintentional, of sovereignty's representational labor as an element of "Savage" ontology. And it speaks to the liminality of the "Savage" position in the structure of U.S. antagonisms.

We can think this liminality of the "Savage" position—its suspension between a conflict and an antagonism—through *Skins*'s formal and narrative articulations at three sites of territorialization and deterritorialization:

1   The political and material territorialization of Settler/Master civil
    society, scaled downward from the monument at Mount Rush-
    more, to the town of White Clay, Nebraska (pop. 20), to the Settler/
    Master's civic embodiment: the Asian American TV news anchor-
    woman, the White father and son liquor store owners in White-
    clay, the local FBI agent, and the White Bill Clinton, who appears
    in the film, by way of documentary outtakes, as the president of the
    United States.

2   The libidinal territorialization of "Savage" sovereignty, scaled
    downward from the sacred Black Hills, to the Pine Ridge Reserva-
    tion's police station, gas stations, and shopping mall, to Rudy Yellow
    Lodge's modest but immaculate home, to the sweat lodge, to the
    sovereign "Savage" body itself: the medicine man, the Indian cops,
    the Native American doctor. Here I am attentive to the libidinal,
    rather than the material, coherence of these examples of sovereign
    territorialization brought to life by the film, because the coherence
    of their political materiality hangs in the balance of Settler/Master
    civil society and its murderous whimsy.

3   The political, material, and libidinal deterritorialization of "Savage"
    genocide, scaled downward from the film's aerial establishing shots
    of Pine Ridge's desolate grid of housing tracks, to the no-place space
    of curbsides, back walls of buildings and the like where inebriated
    Indians drink, stagger, fall, and die, to the interior of Mogie's shack
    and its mise-en-scène of ruin, to the genocided "Savage" body it-
    self: the teenage murder victim, Corky Red Tail (Yellow Pony Pet-
    tibone), kicked to death in an abandoned shack, the alcoholics
    waiting outside gas stations and liquor stores—waiting for spare
    change, Mogie himself with third-degree burns as the least of his
    worries.

Like most Native American political common sense and metacommentaries on "Savage" ontology, the narrative preoccupations of Eyre's
Skins are attentive to the conflict between the political and material territorialization of White civil society and the libidinal territorialization of
Red sovereignty. Most of the film's narrative strategies are pressed into
service of this conflict. But the film's narrative (its script and the various
director and cast commentaries found in the DVD's special features) is

not nearly as committed to engaging the antagonism between the political and material territorialization of White civil society, on the one hand, and the combined political and material deterritorialization of "Savage" genocide, on the other.

Fortunately, however, the film's formal cinematic strategies break in on the conservative and conserving intentions of sovereign coherence intended by the narrative and the vision of the director. In other words, genocide as an ontological grammar of suffering is formally immanent throughout the film, so much so that sovereignty's grammar of suffering (reified and politicized cultural touchstones) cannot always contain or surmount it.

EIGHT

The Pleasures of Parity

> Indeed, applying . . . standards of "pay back" vis-à-vis American
> Indians . . . would require a lethal reduction in the U.S. population . . .
> of between 96 and 99 percent. —WARD CHURCHILL,
> *On the Justice of Roosting Chickens*

THERE IS THEORETICAL work to be done on the plenitude of White (as well as Asian and Latino) subjectivity from behind the lens of Red genocide. *Skins* attempts this theorization by asking how the banality of Settler ontology is structured by the gratuitousness of "Savage" genocide.[1] I have suggested that "grassroots Indians" like Mogie Yellow Lodge embody this lens, an ensemble of questions through which that work could be done. This is illustrated in a sequence that begins, not with Mogie, but with a medium close-up of Rudy Yellow Lodge sitting on his sofa, burning sage. Extradiegetic sacred Native American music fades and a chorus of Indian voices swells as the camera slowly zooms in on Rudy seated on his sofa burning sage and making his offering. We are interpellated by a sense that Rudy's offerings, while they may not cure the turmoil around and within him, are at least a beginning. Furthermore, they alert the spectator to the intentionality of the script: Rudy is the main character and, as such, he is the one authorized by the ensemble of questions regarding sovereignty's project of cultural restoration.

From here we cut to an exterior, medium close-up

9   Medium close-up of an Asian American anchorwoman, in a scene from *Skins*

of a young Asian American anchorwoman (Jenny Cheng) beginning a
broadcast with microphone in hand (figure 9). The poor resolution of
the image—its waviness and grainy quality—tells us we are seeing the
image twice mediated. In other words, the constructedness of the image
is brought to our attention, the suddenly impoverished quality of both
sound and image making clear that we are seeing the image of a television
screen as our primary perception and the image of an Asian American
anchorwoman as our secondary perception. This is important because,
as a formal, nonnarrative, cinematic strategy, it allows *Skins* one of its
rare antagonistic moments: the film briefly turns the news media, one of
Settler civil society's primary apparatuses of enunciation, into an object
of the "Savage" gaze. (This is similar to the kind of disturbance the director, Chris Eyre, was able to wreak on Settler civil society through his
inversion of automobility [the car] in *Smoke Signals.*) The media, along
with hegemony—the Gramscian glue of civil society—is thus dethroned
as the ruler of knowledge.

The question then becomes through whose eyes this deconstructive
critique is taking place, Rudy's or Mogie's. In other words, which ethical dilemma, genocide or sovereignty, do the formal strategies want us
to embrace; which position are we maneuvered into assuming? I believe
that the formal strategies of this shot and the subsequent movements
of the sequence serve Mogie's ethical dilemmas of genocide, but as the
sequence progresses, the narrative usurps Mogie's authority through
Rudy's ethics of cultural restoration, sovereignty.

As we cut from the flat, grainy television screen close-up to a soft, richly textured film image (a wide shot of the Asian American anchorwoman), and then back to the television graininess, the anchorwoman tells us that "this is the first in a three-part series on the Oglala Sioux. Tonight's subject: the multimillion-dollar liquor business generated in this small town of Whiteclay, Nebraska."

The cut from the medium close-up of the anchorwoman on the television screen, to a wide shot of the same scene (this time on film) indicates the gaze through which this deconstructive act is taking place. Mogie sits on the porch of the liquor store with his chin resting on the railing. He stares at the anchorwoman and the cameraman, unimpressed. The cutting back and forth between the grainy, mediated image of the television and the "true" image of film disrupts the spectator's contract of suspended disbelief. There is no guarantee, however, that this cinematic strategy will disrupt the spectator's "faith" in the power of hegemony; in other words, it does not automatically dethrone the media as enunciator of, or its methods of conveyance as essential to, the machinations of ontology. When I suggest that, for the spectator, hegemony as a form of relational glue is essential to the machinations of Human ontology, I am not contradicting contemporary Marxists' observations about the withering away of civil society and the diminishment of hegemony's heretofore essential role in forming Human ontological relations.[2] There is some disagreement among White ontologists as to whether the Settler has passed the Gramscian moment or not. Silverman, for example, in *Male Subjectivity at the Margins*, transposes Antonio Gramsci's notion of hegemony from what operates on the level of preconscious interest to what operates on the level of unconscious desire. It is still nonetheless an essential glue of Human (Settler) ontology. Whether hegemony *is* the glue or *was* the glue is not a score I am trying to settle.[3] My point is that in this "Savage" film we reach a point in which the "Savage" gaze murders not hegemony's past or its present, but its claim to an essential status.

This murderous deconstruction is secured through Mogie Yellow Lodge as he stares at the apparatus of enunciation. It is important to note that, in this sequence, civil society is dealt a blow by the "Savage" in his genocided embodiment. The same iconoclastic rupture might not have been achieved by the "Savage" in this sovereign embodiment (e.g., if the setting were a church, or a Native community center, or a Bureau of

Indian Affairs police station—Rudy's favored haunts—instead of a liquor store), and if we cut between the grainy TV image and Rudy gazing at the anchorwoman and the cameraman. Were Rudy the index of the gaze, the cinematic strategies would connote a critique of media practice (a constellation of concerns bandied about, primarily, by White progressives such as Michael Moore and Amy Goodman). But here, through Mogie's eyes, the strategies coalesce in a more comprehensive, existential condemnation of civil society itself. Our eyes are drawn to Mogie's eyes. Unlike the other Indians who mill about the liquor store, he holds a cigarette, not a drink. Though his gaze cannot be named definitively, the words *hard, sarcastic, unimpressed, sardonic,* or even *bored* would certainly trump words like *compassionate, curious,* or *empathetic.*

The anchorwoman tells us that the town of Whiteclay—which sells 4 million bottles of liquor a year to reservation Indians—has a "population of only twenty people. Some accuse these white liquor store owners of being bloodsuckers who make a living off of Indian misery." As she speaks, we witness a montage of documentary footage: Indians carrying crates of beer out of liquor stores, intoxicated Indians drinking in the back seat of a scrap metal car, Indians drinking while seated on the dusty ground in front of a liquor store, Indians lying face down at night on the pavement with beams from a patrol car lighting on their bodies. Then comes a sound bite of a young Native American woman saying, "They all drink; they all do drugs because it's hard to live down here in Pine Ridge. There's just not anything here." Anchorwoman: "Indians drinking beer and cheap wine. This sad cliché is brought to stark reality every Friday night, payday on the Pine Ridge Indian reservation. [They] then flood border towns like this one to buy alcohol, which is outlawed on the reservation."

More documentary footage follows in another montage of broken lives and destitution. The collision and associational montage overpower and consume the thin and rehearsed commentary through which the anchorwoman tries to frame the unframeable. Then we return to Mogie on the porch, as though the entire montage of living deaths have been shot through his eyes and projected onto the Asian American anchorwoman, her microphone and wires, the White cameraman, the (implicit) crew that supports them, and their documenting narrative and its attempt to give the anchorwoman's commentary meaning, authority, legitimacy, and, above all, ethics.

Up to this point, the nonnarrative construction of the sequence has progressed by way of a murderous juxtaposition between the images and editing techniques deployed in adjectival support of Mogie's sardonic contempt for Human (Settler) ontology, on the one hand, and the anemic language of the anchorwoman's reporting, on the other. The tension bound up in the juxtaposition of Mogie's contempt and her deluded sense of capacity and ethics gathers intensity. But the film, and this sequence, does not allow that intensity to spill over—formally or narratively—into a (re)enactment, or at least acknowledgement, of the murder that brought civil society and the "Savage" together. Were it to do so, at this particular moment, given this particular sequential construction, it would do so on Mogie's terms: those of the genocided "Savage." But this "Savage" film is not entirely comfortable with what the "Savage" has to say about genocide. Instead, we cut abruptly from Mogie (the sound of death stirring water!) in front of the liquor store to the scrubbed and well-kept exterior of Rudy's home later that evening.

The abrupt and anxious shift in location repositions the spectator from the madness of genocide's ensemble of questions to the comparative stability of sovereignty's ensemble of questions. It is a night shot and over the image of his house we hear the sound effects of gunfire, galloping horse hoofs, and someone calling for "a couple of deputies." We cut to the home's interior and witness Rudy seated on the sofa. Only one lamp is lit; the room is dark, meditative, and inviting. The lighting codes of this interior mise-en-scène augment the way the room's colors and lines have been selected and combined: we experience Rudy's domesticity as a kind of sanctuary. The drapes behind him are soft white and their creases fall in lush, pleasing lines to the floor. Spread end-to-end on the sofa where he sits is a handmade Native American blanket with exquisite shapes and designs, a tapestried hermeneutics that hails the viewer to culture's ensemble of coordinating and often therapeutic touchstones of cohesion (kinship, homeland, custom, language).

Rudy is visibly tired after another hard day of policing and forty-five minutes of film in which Iktomi (a trickster in the form of a spider and a rock) has destabilized his spiritual balance. Absent-mindedly, he points his remote and channel-surfs until he hits on the voice of the Asian American anchorwoman: "And you, sir, what would you suggest the government do to improve the living conditions here on the rez?"

10 Medium close-up of Mogie (inside Rudy's tv console)

Rather than match her voice with the continuity of her image, the camera zooms in, slowly, on Rudy. He is shocked and angered by what he sees on the screen. The shot cuts back to his television set and the surrounding stereo console. Mogie is the interviewee (figure 10). Mogie: "I'd like the Great White Father in Washington to send me a *big* woman. Big *fat* woman! So that when I sleep with her she'll cover up all the cracks in my shack and keep the wind from blowing through. Hey! You wanna see me piss in my pants?"

In the midst of Mogie's response we hear the fade-in of sad, mournful music; and the camera cuts from Mogie expressing his demand from within his confinement, the small box of Rudy's television, to Rudy expressing his anger, disappointment, and embarrassment at Mogie as spectacle. What is key here is that the film's cinematic strategies—for example, its mournful music, the slow zoom in on Rudy's face, the screen-within-the-screen capture of Mogie at the moment he utters his most intransigent demand, and the mise-en-scène's proxemics and lighting codes, which send up representational supports of cultural and domestic legitimacy all around Rudy and thus mark him with sovereign authority—all labor to contain and ameliorate the otherwise murderous gesture of the genocided "Savage." In this way, the murder that marks the meeting of civil society and the "Savage" can indeed be reenacted and acknowledged but only as a sad joke. Now, the zoom in on Rudy is slightly faster, more deliberate. We see him with his head in his hand, as the screen grows darker.

Hegemony, reeling from the existential blow that Mogie's scrutiny dealt it, is now on its way to recovery. In the beginning of the sequence, the libidinally powerful cinematic strategies of sound, image, and editing had been deployed in such a way as to derail the narrative of civil society, to rupture the thin and rehearsed commentaries through which the anchorwoman tries to frame the unframeable, commentaries founded on the belief that access to information, citizen education, public disclosure, and investigative journalism can change the lives even of those who are only "fatally alive," Indians.[4] In the beginning of the sequence, this aspect of civil society's axiomatic faith is singed by the gaze of the "Savage": it is shown to be wholly inadequate to genocide's grammar of suffering. But then the sequence is jerked—by way of the abrupt cut from DAY-EXTERIOR-The Old Chief's Liquor store to EVENING-EXTERIOR-Rudy's Home—from genocide to sovereignty. Articulation with the Settler is rescued by the other modality of "Savage" ontology.

The genocided object's desire for the obliteration of civil society writ large is captured and incarcerated, not by Settler civil society—the Asian American anchorwoman and the White cameraman are not selected, by the film, to perform this labor—but by the superego of the sovereign subject. This is a form of intra-Indian containment, self-governance. As a result, the film's political allegiance to the project of antagonistic identity formation, that is, to Mogie's unflinching demand (for a big fat [White] woman to cover the holes in his shack) is diminished and dismantled by Rudy's project of cultural, territorial, and genealogical restoration and integrity. Sovereign integrity, we are instructed, must be called on, if for no other reason than to stop-gap what appears as madness and incoherence, which is to say, a coherence too pure to ponder.

The problem with this formulation is that the sovereign gesture's aspirations of "integrity" are realized by severing itself (and thus distracting the spectator) from Mogie's embrace of Native peoples' genocidal ontology. The sovereign "Savage's" coerced repositioning of the genocided "Savage" means that the dead Indian cannot assume his desire from within the *terra nullius* where he is positioned, but must instead accommodate the structural adjustment that the living Indian insists on.

The scene ends with Rudy facing the bathroom mirror, covering his face with shoe polish, then at the garage fetching a canister of petrol, now in his van en route to torch the Whiteclay liquor store. But this ending of

one sequence and segue into another, while attempting to signify determination and direct action, is in effect a cinematic disavowal, a manifestation of the film's unwillingness to follow through on its exploration of
murder as an idiom of power that structures the relation between White
skins and Red skins. If Rudy's postcolonial angst has limited explanatory
value when confronted with the idiom of power that truly separates the
reservation from civil society, the dead from the living, how might this
idiom be best explained?

Well over twenty thousand Westerns and frontier films have been shot
and released since the dawn of cinema.[5] Even though they may only appear in a small percentage of the films and for relatively few minutes, Native Americans are central to the libidinal economy of the entire genre.
The Western's cinematic imaginary casts the "Savage" as a "clear and
probable" danger lurking just beyond the Settler's clearing. The clearing, then, is imagined by the Western as a space whose safety is under
constant, if sometimes unspoken threat from "Savages" who inhabit the
"frontier" or who, typically at the beginning of a film, have inexplicably
"jumped the reservation." *Clearing*, in the Settler/"Savage" relation, has
two grammatical structures, one as a noun and the other as a verb. But
the Western only recognizes *clearing* as a noun. Westerns call on us to
bow our heads reverently, to give this noun a proper name and refer to
it fondly, the way Christians gave the child a proper name and called it
"the Little Baby Jesus." Similarly, the Western interpellates us with such
reverence to the clearing, whose proper name might be the Little Baby
Civil Society, a genuflection bestowed on the clearing by, for example,
Stagecoach and other films by John Ford.

But prior to the clearing's fragile infancy, that is, before its cinematic
legacy as a newborn place name, it labored not *across* the land as a noun
but as a verb *on* the body of the "Savage," speaking civil society's essential
status as an effect for genocide. What would happen to the libidinal economy of civil society if, over the course of one hundred years, it had been
subjected to twenty thousand cinematic mirrors, films about itself in
which it was cast not as an infant cartography of budding democratic dilemmas, but as a murderous projection, a juggernaut for extermination?

Given the centrality of the White child, the infant, to the Western's
cinematic solicitation of faith in the ethics of the Little Baby Civil Society, how shattered might that faith become were the films to reveal that

the newborn babe suckled Indian blood instead of White breast milk?[6] The sinews of civil institutionality could not sustain themselves libidinally under such conditions. And civil society would lose its mid- to late twentieth-century elasticity. There would be, for example, no social space for the White cultural progressive who revels in Native American lore, studies Indian place names, or otherwise derives pleasure and an enhanced sense of purpose from his or her respect for Indian culture—just as there would be no social space for the White person who romanticizes the history of the pioneering West while neglecting the genocide that clears the space for this history. (These two personas are not so far apart.) Anyone who was White and did not speak, socially and libidinally, in what would be a hyperarticulate and thoroughly self-conscious anti-Indian fascism would find him- or herself unable to broker relations with other members of civil society, for the ruse of social, sexual, and political hybridity which Whiteness manages to convince itself of, would become untenable at best, treasonous at worse. One could not, for example, be in favor of Native American sweat lodge ceremonies, fishing or gaming rights and be, simultaneously, enfranchised within civil society. Such postcolonial or democratic questions would become structurally impossible: one would either be among the living or among the dead—but not, as is assumed today, both.

Cinema comes into existence during the 1890s, precisely when the Little Baby Civil Society was being weaned from its self-image as a murderous projection and establishing itself as a site where the leadership of ideas (hegemony) replaces direct relations of force, a place where a robust political, sexual, and social hybridity counteracts crude Manichean negotiations of violence. Early cinema is on the cusp of that attempt. A moment when the "we" of White subjectivity is moving from "We are murderers" toward "We are citizens." What is important for our investigation is the centrality of "Savage" ontology and the institutionality of cinema to the rhetoric, rather than the actual history, of this transition (where, as I have indicated, "transition" is merely a euphemism for disavowal).

In 1894, less than four years after the Seventh Calvary had massacred more than three hundred Lakota, ostensibly for persisting in performing the Ghost Dance, a "ceremony which included calling upon ancestors to help clear the land of white invaders," Thomas Edison screened his production of *Sioux Ghost Dance* in the Edison Company's first kinetoscope parlor. The film was twenty seconds long and featured men and boys, beaded and bare chested, dancing around in front of a "stark black backdrop common to all early films shot in Edison's one-room studio in West Orange, New Jersey." On this macabre, ironic, and fateful day in September 1894, several Oglala and Brule Sioux were brought to the Edison Company kinetoscope parlor, where *Sioux Ghost Dance* was screened for them. They were part of a group of "nearly a hundred Sioux survivors of Wounded Knee [who] had been recruited by William F. 'Buffalo Bill' Cody for his Wild West show for a season after 1890. . . . Twenty-three of [them were] designated 'prisoners of war' [by the U.S. government]."[7] This symbiosis linked Wounded Knee to public spectacle (Buffalo Bill's traveling show) and public spectacle to cinema; between genocide and the collective pleasures that constitute membership in, and the coherence of, civil society, this symbiosis was unabashedly avowed in 1894. The headline in the *New York Herald* read "Red Man Again Conquered."

> A party of Indians in full war paint invaded the Edison laboratory at West Orange yesterday and faced unflinchingly the unerring rapid fire of the kinetograph. It was indeed a memorable engagement, no less so than the battle of Wounded Knee, still fresh in the minds of the warriors. It was probably more effective in demonstrating to the red men the power and supremacy of the white man, for savagery and the most advanced science stood face to face, and there was an absolute triumph for one without the spilling of a single drop of blood.[8]

The *Herald* acknowledges that Wounded Knee is "still fresh in the minds of the warriors," which means that it is also still fresh in the minds of Whites whose sense of belonging is constituted by their status as spectators of Cody's rodeos and Edison's cinema exhibitions, and as readers of the daily newspapers. This "still fresh in the minds" fragment is symptomatic of civil society's late nineteenth, early twentieth-century capacity to appreciate the acute proximity between the tranquility *in* their clearing—Edison's first kinetoscope parlor—and the blood-soaked horror *of* their clearing—the massacre at Wounded Knee three and one half years before Edison's screening. But the *Herald*'s avowal of *clearing* as a verb is corrupted by symptoms of what, over the next one hundred years, would become comprehensive disavowals of *clearing* as a verb.

The *Herald* refers to Wounded Knee as a "battle," insinuating something akin to the mutual exchange of gunfire or extraction of casualties instead of genocide. It does, however, raise the specter of genocide in its opening sentence: "Indians in full war paint invaded the Edison laboratory." Here, the unconscious language of the prose has spoken in good faith: essential to the Settler/"Savage" relation is the repetition of a scene where a civil site is indeed set on by a militarized force. But the conscious language of the prose has spoken in bad faith, by suggesting that in this essential relation the "Savage" is militarized ("Indians in full war paint invaded") while the Settler is civilized ("the Edison laboratory at West Orange"). The rhetorical labor of the article thus proceeds to move from the sublime to the absurd as it attempts to insinuate the genocided object into civil society as civil subject (that is, as a subject of discourse and interlocution) by suggesting that any given aspect of civil society's hegemonic apparatus (be it the persuasive power of science and technology or the interpellative power of cinematic sound and image) is up to the task of subordinating the "Savage." In other words, the *Herald* would have us believe that the "Savage," like the White woman or the immigrant, occupies a subordinate position *within* civil society, and it would have us believe this while simultaneously making no distinction between the ontological moment when the "Savage" is genocided and the ontological moment when the "Savage" is sovereign. It draws on the dead genocided object by gesturing to Wounded Knee but adorns this corpse in the accoutrement of a living subject with "full war paint." This cross-dressing, I maintain, benefits the Settler, not the "Savage."

We know that the symbolic power of the wage relation structures the relationship between the proletariat and the boss and that, furthermore, violence is contingent on the proletariat's spatial or temporal resistance to that relation. This is how the Human suffers. But the violence of Wounded Knee has no structural contingency. It is not contingent on resistance to the deracination of spatiality—what Antonio Negri and Michael Hardt refer to as the commons' slide into the dead zone of capital—nor is it contingent on resistance to capital's deracination of temporality—what Hardt calls the loss of living time and the imposition of "prison time." For the "Savage," genocide is not contingent on resistance.

When, in 1894, the *New York Herald* linked a demonstration of White superiority (the article's reference to film and science as apparatuses of hegemony coupled with its inference that hegemony itself is the web of social relations and the force of social change) and the subordination of the "Savage" (Cody's twenty-three official "prisoners of war" and his seventy-seven captive genocide survivors who came to screen the film), it began to lay the groundwork for the coming one hundred years, for the rhetorical strategies of the twentieth century which would disavow the structuring power of gratuitous violence by attempting to bring the "Savage" into the purview of hegemony.

The "absolute triumph" which allowed "savagery and the most advanced science" to stand face to face in Edison's first kinetoscope parlor "without the spilling of a single drop of blood" was not, contrary to the *Herald*'s delusional claim, contingent on conflict that can be rendered symbolically. The quote has all the trappings of cognitive dissonance. One moment it speaks of Wounded Knee, genocide, and notes it as being essential. The next moment it diminishes its essential status by describing it as a "battle." Finally, the article notes its desire to be rid of Wounded Knee, that is, to be rid of genocide as a modality that structures the ontology of the "Savage." Why this sudden urge at the end of the quotation and at the end of the nineteenth century?

If the various apparatuses of hegemony (the news media, the cinema, etc.) were to name genocide as that which positions the "Savage" ontologically, then it would have to name the way genocide positions the Settler ontologically as well. Thirty-nine years prior to Edison's screening of *Sioux Ghost Dance*, civil society did not consider itself to be balancing on the cusp of such a dilemma. It acknowledged, indeed reveled in, the structural necessity of itself as a murderous projection on the body of the "Savage." In 1853 San Francisco's *Daily Alta California* explained "how incoming Angloamericans were handling their 'Indian question': 'people are . . . ready to knife them, shoot them, or inoculate them with smallpox—*and all have been done.*'"[9] By 1860, extermination of Indians was routine coast to coast. It was "so commonplace that it was no longer a military specialty. Rather it had been adopted as a method of 'pest control' by average civilians."[10] The *San Francisco Bulletin* of 1860 described it as a conscious strategy to "effect the ultimate extermination of the race by disease."[11] And in 1891, within a year of the Wounded Knee massacre and less than three years prior to the *New York Herald*'s report on the Edison screening,

L. Frank Baum[,] famed "gentle" author of *The Wizard of Oz* and writer [for] the *Aberdeen Saturday Pioneer*[,] called for the army to "finish" the job and exterminate *all remaining Indians*. "The nobility of the Redskin is extinguished. . . . The whites, by law of conquest, by justice of civilization, are masters of the American continent and the best safety of the frontier settlements will be secured by the total annihilation of the few remaining Indians. Why not annihilation? Their glory has fled, their spirit broken, their manhood effaced; better that they should die than live as the miserable wretches that they are."[12]

In three short years, from 1891 to 1894, the press, exemplar of the enunciatory apparatus of civil society, began its transition from an open assumption of civic desire (Baum's call for "the total annihilation of the few remaining Indians") to a monumentalization of hegemony (the *New York Herald*'s celebration of "an absolute triumph for [civil society] without the spilling of a single drop of blood"). What is noteworthy is the pivotal role played by cinema, Edison's *Sioux Ghost Dance*, in this conjunctural recomposition of civil society's self-presentation. Cinema is vital to an imaginary which seeks to widen, exponentially, the distance between civil society's grammatical structure and the actual words it is willing to use to describe itself—the vast distance between *clearing* as noun and *clearing* as verb. This is a necessary recomposition, or more precisely a disavowal, for it allows the Human subject of civil society— the Asian American anchorwoman and the White cameraman on whom Mogie's sardonic gaze is fixed—to console themselves with the illusion that the structure of the relation between themselves and the "Savage" is forged by the force of hegemony and not the force of genocide. Again, one hundred years after the *New York Herald*'s tilt from genocide toward hegemony, at the other end of the twentieth century, White radicals' and progressives' faith that such generic principles and practices as access to institutionality, full disclosure, and fairness and accuracy in reporting are pivotal to meditation on, and mediation for, social change has never been stronger. The surgical gaze of Mogie Yellow Lodge shreds this faith in the essential nature of hegemony into thin strips of ridicule. Hegemony remains essential to the idiom of power between, for example, the Asian American anchorwoman and the White cameraman;[13] and the film, through Mogie and the formalism that accrues to him, understands this, but this understanding is akin to an insult: "Send me a *big* woman. Big *fat* woman!" And through the gaze, Mogie will not allow the spectator the cultural solace of mapping hegemony as an idiom of power onto the relation between Settler (Human) and "Savage"—until, that is, Rudy's presence reasserts itself and makes amends.

Today the United States is no longer self-consciously fascistic but instead self-consciously democratic. *Clearing* is completely disavowed as a verb. Instead, *clearing* as a noun makes itself known through the narrative of sovereign gain, civil society, and its external threat (the "Savage"). The imaginary of "Savage" positionality more often than not articulates (dialogues) with this Settler imaginary. In other words, the "Savage" narrative of sovereignty (Rudy's plot points in the film) is dialogic with the Settler narrative of sovereignty (the Western's genuflection to the Little Baby Civil Society). The narratives are disparate at the level of manifest content but dependent rhetorically on the same semiotics of gain and loss. Thus, even the "Savage's" semiotics of sovereign loss fortifies and extends the interlocutory life of the Settler's disavowal of *clearing* as a verb. Ironically, they work hand in hand to crowd out the ensemble of questions, and thus the ethical dilemmas, of genocide's ontological imperatives.

A semiotics of loss cannot be reconciled with a semiotics of genocide (provided genocide could even be apprehended through a semiotics, and there is no evidence that it can) because semiotics implies the possibility of narrative; and narrative implies the possibility of both a subject of speech and a speaking subject. Genocide, however, has no speaking subject; as such it has no narrative. It can only be apprehended by way of a narrative about something that it is not—such as sovereignty. (This is why a number of Jewish Holocaust films end up—or begin—in Israel: the impossible semiotics of genocide must be compensated for by way of a gesture of coherence, even if that coherence distracts the spectator from the topic at hand.) No single film could represent the clearing of a hemisphere. And no hemisphere, let alone a country, could maintain egoic consolidation of its psychic coordinates under the weight of the number and kind of films that it would take to even attempt to represent *clearing* as a verb. Though it is precisely the impossible "narrative" of genocide that positions the "Savage," ensembles of questions that could elaborate more or less coherent ethical dilemmas regarding genocide—even if a coherent story of genocide could not be told—are often managed, constrained, marginalized, and disavowed in political discourse, meta-commentaries on ontology, and the cinema of Native Americans. *Skins*'s simultaneous elaboration of and uneasiness with Mogie Yellow Lodge is emblematic of how this management, constraint, marginalization, and disavowal are rendered cinematically.

Mogie's surrealist demand, "Send me a big . . . fat woman . . . [to] cover up all the cracks in my shack," goes to the heart of the matter. Red flesh can only be restored, ethically, through the destruction of White bodies, because the corporeality of the Indigenous has been consumed by and gone into the making of the Settler's corporeality. Mogie wants what he has lost, not just his labor power, not just his language or land, but the raw material of his flesh. And, like most "grassroots Indians," he knows precisely where it went—into the Settler's "body"—and thus he knows precisely from where to repossess it.

Though Mogie's shack is small, we know from earlier scenes that it has at least two rooms. Therefore, to stretch a woman across its interior, window to window, wall to wall, corner to corner, and then stretch her across the door, would be to reconfigure her body into grotesque and unrecognizable dimensions. There are serious doubts as to whether a woman, even as large an (implicitly White) woman as Mogie Yellow Lodge is demanding from the president, "the Great White Father in Washington," would survive such an ordeal. Imagine such a demand being made, such wallpapering taking place, en masse, on a scale which even Mogie's inebriated imagination has not yet grasped.

[General Andrew Jackson] instructed his troops to cut the noses of the corpses so that no one would be able to challenge the body count. They had bushel baskets full of noses that they brought back. This [practice] got him elected President. [He] campaigned on the basis that he had never met a recalcitrant Indian that he had not killed and never killed an Indian that he had not scalped and that anybody who wanted to question the validity of what he was saying was invited to tea in his parlor that evening so he could display the scalps and prove his point. [He] rode with a saddle bridle made out of the skin of an opposing Indian leader. This is the President of the United States.[14]

One begins to see how wallpapering or insulating one's room not with "bushel baskets" of White female skin but with even one White woman is simply out of the question. Mogie's demand, then, is laughed off—managed, constrained, marginalized—by the script. "Hey! You wanna see me piss in my pants?" are the words he is made to utter next. His words are thus portrayed as the surreal ruminations of an Indian who has reached the end of his inebriated tether, and not as the wisdom of a man who could lead his people. The film is nervous in the face of Mogie's demand not because of its absurdity but because of its authority. But Mogie is demanding no more of the Great White Father, no more of civil society, than he has already given. In fact, he is demanding less.

His surrealism indicates a qualitatively similar ontological relationship between the Red and the White as exists between the Black and the White. The Middle Passage turns, for example, Ashanti spatial and temporal capacity into spatial and temporal incapacity—a body into flesh. This process begins as early as the 1200s for the Slave.[15] By the 1530s, modernity is more self-conscious of its coordinates, and Whiteness begins its ontological consolidation and negative knowledge of itself by turning (part of) the Aztec body, for example, into Indian flesh.[16] In this moment the White body completes itself and proceeds to lay the groundwork for the intra-Settler ensemble of questions foundational to its ethical dilemmas (i.e., Marxism, feminism, psychoanalysis). In the final analysis, Settler ontology is guaranteed by way of a negative knowledge of what it is not rather than by way of its positive claims of what it is. Ontological Whiteness is secured not through its cultural, economic, or gendered identities but by the fact that it cannot be known (positioned) by genocide (or by accumulation and fungibility).

As Churchill observed in a book tour speech in Berkeley, California on July 31, 2004, this negative knowledge has its pleasures.

> [Unlike Jackson's army of the early nineteenth century, the sixteenth-century Dutch] didn't take the noses and they didn't take the scalps. They took whole heads because they wanted to identify the fact that they had eradicated the entire leadership of the opposition. They brought the heads back to the central square in New Amsterdam [now Manhattan] where the citizenry began to celebrate. They turned it into a sport. People who had participated in the expedition had themselves

a jolly game of kickball using the heads and the citizenry sat around and cheered.

It has a sense of affilial inclusion and filial longevity.

[In 1864, the Third Regiment of the U.S. Calvary] returned to Denver [Colorado] with their trophies [the vaginas of Native American women stapled to the front of their hats] and held a triumphal parade. [They] proceeded down Larimore Street . . . and the good citizenry stood up and cheered wildly. . . . The *Rocky Mountain News* [described it as] "an unparalleled feat of martial prowess that would live forever in the annals of the history and nobility of the race."

And it has a capacity for territorial integrity.

Scalp bounties . . . were officially claimed bounties that were placed on Indians in every antecedent colony in the Eastern Seaboard—French, English, and Spanish. I don't know about the Dutch. They killed all the Indians around before they had the chance to need a bounty. But from the antecedent colonies this law transferred to every state and territory in forty-eight contiguous states."

In other words, it has the capacity to transform *clearing* from a verb into *clearing* as a noun.

Every [state in the union] placed a bounty on Indians, any Indians, all Indians. [For example in the] Pennsylvania colony in the 1740s, the bounty [was] forty pounds sterling for proof of death of an adult male Indian. That proof of death being in the form of a scalp or a bloody red skin. . . . Proof of death in that form got the bearer of the proof forty pounds sterling. Forty pounds sterling in the 1740s was equivalent to the annual wage of your average farmer. This is big business. Twenty pounds sterling would be paid for proof of death in the same form of an adult female. Ten pounds sterling for proof of death of a child, a child being defined as human being of either sex under ten years of age down to and, yes, including the fetus. . . . In Texas this law was not rescinded until 1887, [when] the debate in the Texas legislature concluded that there was no reason to continue because there were no longer sufficient numbers of living Indians in the entire state of Texas to warrant the continuation of it. It had accomplished its purpose.[17]

And just like that, the Little Baby Civil Society was walking on its own two feet.

To Grown-Up Civil Society (Mogie's "Great White Father in Washington") Mogie Yellow Lodge submits his own "personal" genocide reparations bill. A bill that accounts for the perfect symmetry through which Whiteness has formed a *body* (from the genitals to the body politic) out of "Savage" flesh. The symmetry's perfection becomes clear when one realizes that today's 1.6 percent-to-80.6 percent "Savage"-to-Settler ratio is a pure inversion of the sixteenth century's "Savage" to Settler ratio.[18] "Send me a *big* woman. Big *fat* woman! So that when I sleep with her she'll cover up all the cracks in my shack and stop the wind from blowing through." This is a demand so ethically pure that the film finds it unbearable and, as such, is unable (unwilling?) to let Mogie state it without irony. And yet, Mogie's outbursts like this—"outbursts" because they are generally infrequent and contained by pity or humor—are the few moments when the film engages the ethical dilemmas of the Settler/"Savage" antagonism (genocide and its impossible semiotics) instead of the ethical dilemmas of the Settler/"Savage" conflict (sovereignty and its semiotics of loss).

Again, it is not that Mogie's demand is absurd and unethical but rather that it is a demand so pure in its ethicality that it threatens the quotidian prohibitions which, in modernity, constrain ethics. The demand is far too ethical for the film to embrace and elaborate at the level of narrative. It is a demand that must be policed by sovereign powers. Exploring *Skins*'s cinematic strategies reveals this containment as an effort to manage the spectator's interpellation by the dilemmas of Mogie's ruination and by the demand that ushers forth from his "flesh."

Mogie's surrealism seeks to cull power directly from the subjectivity of the Settler, what Churchill calls "the imperial integrity of the U.S. itself."[19] This idea of culling power, resources, and Human life directly from the imperial integrity of the United States, especially when we think that imperial integrity through the banality of White bodies (in other words, through the "innocence" of today's citizen), is indicative of the kind of unflinching paradigmatic analyses which allowed Churchill to embrace the 9/11 attack on the World Trade Center within forty-eight hours of its occurrence, a moment in time when Settler Marxists and Settler progressives either suddenly became mute or stumbled over their own tongues in half-hearted attempts to simultaneously condemn the attack and explain its political and historical rationale. Churchill's embrace of the event is not synonymous with either celebration or condemnation. It goes without saying that Churchill also refused to be interpellated by the pageantry of mourning that followed in the wake of 9/11. But Settler radicals and progressives assailed him for meditating on the attack from within the questions of the genocided "Savage" rather than from within an ensemble of questions allied with Settler's grammar of suffering, exploitation, and alienation.

People on the left tried to shame Churchill for embracing incoherent terror (suicide bombers) instead of morally and politically sanctioned revolutionary action (like the Zapatistas or the Sandinistas). Others chided him for advocating violence in any form. Many said that now is not the time for a scathing critique; "our" nation is in mourning. And others wagged their fingers and reminded him that members of the working class (not just police agents and investment bankers) died in the Twin Towers. These naysayers all made their arguments at the level of experience, and Churchill, rather handily, answered them at this level as well. But I am neither interested in his interlocutors' chiding nor in his response. The Left's attack on Churchill's embrace of the 9/11 attacks is important not for the social issues it raises, the myriad of things it claims it is concerned about, but rather for the grammar of suffering shared across the board, those building blocks through which loss is conceptualized in such a way that makes it impossible for the "Savage" to function, grammatically, as their paradigm of suffering, and even less as its paradigmatic agent for change. Had Churchill's interlocutors been more honest, they would have used fewer words—not draped their rejoinders with the veil of issues from the realm of experience (i.e., tactics)—and said, quite simply, "We will not be led by the 'Savage'; death is not an element constituent of our ontology."

Unlike the narrative and cinematic strategies of *Skins*, Churchill's meditation on 9/11 embraces, rather than contains, Mogie Yellow Lodge's demand. Churchill's work is authorized by Mogie's grammar of suffering which, inter alia, forecloses on Churchill's passing judgment on the tactical ethics of either the attack on the World Trade Center or, for that matter, Mogie's attack on the body of White femininity. Churchill accepts this foreclosure and works off of it. He does not feel constrained by it but finds that it enables a quality of reflection otherwise inconceivable:

There can be no defensible suggestion that those who attacked the Pentagon and the World Trade Center on 9/11 were seeking to get even with the United States. Still less is there a basis for claims that they "started" something, or that the United States has anything to get *even* with them for. Quite the contrary. For the attackers to have arguably "evened the score" for Iraq's dead children alone, it would have been necessary for them to have killed *a hundred times* the number of Americans who actually died. This in itself, however, would have allowed them to attain parity in terms of real numbers. The U.S. population is about fifteen times the size of Iraq's. Hence, for the attackers to have achieved a proportionally equivalent impact, it would have been necessary that they kill some 7.5 *million* Americans.[20]

Churchill reflects on the event of 9/11 in such a way as to make it impossible to talk about it as an event. This is a marker of the philosophical brilliance and rhetorical dexterity foundational to Churchill's thirty-odd books, articles, and recorded speeches. This dexterity allows the work to be conversant with the actual details and "facts" of the event (as presented and cathedralized by White civil society). Yet instead of becoming mired in the bog of concerns which makes the event as "event" (details and common sense ethics), Churchill jettisons common sense and presses the details into service of an ensemble of questions animated by the ethical dilemmas of "Savage," and not Settler, ontology. He can do this on behalf of those who are not even Native Americans (in this passage, Iraqis) because he provides them with the "Savage" as a lens through which they can do ethnographic and political work on the Settler as specimen. In other words, in his chapter on 9/11, his argument is made in such a way that, to be interpellated, the reader must adjust the logic of his or her political experience to fit the logic of "Savage" genocidal ontology—and not vice versa. The reader must be subordinated to, and incorporated by, Redness, or else the reader will experience the piece in the same way that the viewer is meant to experience Mogie Yellow Lodge: as a scandal, as a problem in need of fixing.

Churchill continues to subordinate the "facts" of 9/11 to an ethical examination of Settlerism by reminding the reader that "the U.S. population is fifteen times the size of Iraq's," therefore 9/11 would have had to have killed "7.5 *million* Americans" in order to have "achieved a proportionately equivalent impact." In the very next paragraph, Churchill corrects himself and insists that 7.5 million is the number of American *children* the attackers would have had to have killed in order to achieve parity. This is followed by a list of even more corrections, in which Churchill recalculates the meaning of parity based solely on the U.S. deracination of Iraq since 1990 (further down the correctives will lead him to the "Savage" and to the Slave). True parity would result in 7.5 million dead American children, 15 million dead American adults, the obliteration of "sewage, water sanitation and electrical plants, food production/storage capacity, hospitals, pharmaceutical production facilities, communication centers and much more." The effects of which would be not just mass death but "a surviving population wracked by malnutrition and endemic disease." "Indeed, applying such standards of 'pay back' vis-à-vis American Indians alone would require a lethal reduction in the U.S. population . . . of between 96 and 99 percent." Suddenly, Mogie Yellow Lodge's demand for parity (one big fat White woman "to cover up the cracks in [his] shack") sounds downright generous. Mogie is demanding one Settler, a far cry from demanding parity for ontological death. Were he to demand parity the United States "would run out of people long before it ran out of compensatory obligation."[21]

NINE

"Savage" Negrophobia

AS I STATED in chapter 5, although Native American feature films (still a small corpus) assert that White supremacy, the press of civil society, constitutes the greatest threat to the project of a restored sovereign ontology, they make an emotional argument that Blackness also threatens this restorative project. This is disturbing because if, ultimately, "Savage" social and cultural coherence rests on ethical dilemmas which are animated by anti-Black anxiety—Negrophobia—then this would imply that political solidarity between the "Savage" and the Settler would make more sense than between the "Savage" and the Slave. Hence, the isolation of the Slave would not be sealed by an interest-based political coalition between the Settler and the "Savage" (for the interests of Turtle Island's restoration and the longevity of the fifty states are inimical) or by the shared positivities of sovereign rubrics (for *mana*, *waken*, and *orenda* are incompatible with hegemony). Instead, it would be sealed by a common imaginary as to what constitutes a threat to *being* itself. Leaving aside for the moment the fragility of a "Savage"/Slave political alliance (not because it is irrelevant but because it is beyond the largely structural and descriptive analytic framework of this book), I will address the following question: *Is anti-Black anxiety constitutive of the way "Savage" cinema imagines sovereignty, and if so, why?*

Skins, in keeping with the esprit de corps of the "Savage" filmography to which it belongs, imagines Blackness as a force that threatens the social and cultural coherence of "Savage" sovereignty. *Skins* operates through a myriad of strategies which demonstrate its fidelity to the same project of sovereign restoration that is brought to life in the work of ontologists like Vine Deloria, Leslie Silko, Taiaiake Alfred, Ward Churchill, and Haunani-Kay Trask: Rudy's quest to avenge himself, his family, and his culture. But the film, in its "argument" as regards what exactly puts this project in peril, makes an emotional, if not intellectual, claim that what needs to be avenged is not so much the violence of White Settler supremacy, but rather the (perceived) intrusion of Black "style."[1] In *Skins*'s oeuvre, the cinematic imaginary of the most life-threatening constellation of encroachments to Native American sovereignty (e.g., language, kinship structure, modes of address, and cultural memory) are deployed by what is commonly thought of as Black urban culture (rap music, handshakes, vestmentary codes, dialect, and disrespect for elders). The FBI, the banal freedoms of everyday White life (e.g., White family life in the town of Whiteclay, Nebraska), and the logic of policing (patrols, surveillance, detention) carry neither the intellectual nor the emotional weight—nor are they meditated on with the same intensity—as Black urban "style." Black "style," or Black youth "culture," seems to form the most emotionally charged constellation of threats to Native American sovereignty. Anxiety regarding the violent effects of Blackness on the ontological structure of Red sovereignty blooms to such grandiose proportions that it crowds out the film's capacity to be properly anxious about the violent effects of latter- and present-day agents of genocide—despite the fact that portions of the script, the narrative of conscious reflection, seem to know the true source of the violence. What are the methods of this disavowal and why is it so emphatic?

In the director's commentary on the DVD of *Skins*, Chris Eyre describes a postscreening Q and A session where a member of the audience objected to the film's use of the word *nigger*. Earlier in the commentary he

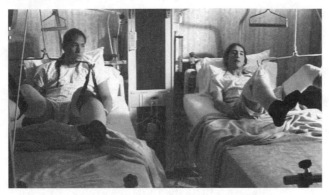

11 The two boys who murdered Corky Red Tail, in their hospital beds, in a scene from *Skins*

expressed his irritation with people whom he describes as complaining that the film is not "PC." "I've always been baffled by the whole political correctness thing. . . . It's never about race. It's about poverty and oppression. . . . This is not a politically correct film." Now, as the word is being spoken on screen, he reiterates his irritation by recounting the story of yet another displeased viewer.

In the scene in question, Rudy has gone to the reservation hospital in his capacity as a Bureau of Indian Affairs police officer to take the statements of the two teenagers whose knees he broke with a baseball bat in his capacity as vigilante (see figure 11). The boys confess to the murder of Corky Red Tail (Yellow Pony Pettibone), a wholesome checkout clerk who works at the reservation shopping mall and whom Rudy and the film seem to like, in contradistinction to the attitude we are "hailed" to assume toward his murderers.

> BLACK LODGE BOY: Look, we already done confessed. What the hell else you want?
> RUDY: I want to know who did your knees.
> MR. GREEN SHOELACES: Look, all I know is he was tall, man. Crazy, crazier 'an hell man. Ugliest, like, ugliest dude I ever saw, man. He had, like, mud on his face [*Rudy had covered his face with shoe polish and a black nylon stocking*]; like, part nigger and ho-sapa guy. I dunno, I ain't never seen him around the rez.
> RUDY: What's your name?

MR. GREEN SHOELACES: Teddy Yellow Lodge, but we're not related;
    my family's from over in Cheyenne River.
RUDY: Hmm, that's where my family's from.
MR. GREEN SHOELACES: You want a medal or what?

There is a curious juxtaposition here of Black urban "style," the word
nigger, and Mr. Green Shoelaces's rebuff of Rudy's suggestion that they
might be related. It is as though the film codes the young man demoni-
cally with Blackness, then it suggests a crack in this code by having one
of them use the word *nigger* in a way that marks his exilic marginality to
Blackness, then it reverberates back to its demonizing strategy by having
the young man show nothing in the way of cultural appreciation at the
prospect of meeting a new relation ("You want a medal or what?"). This
seals the taint of Blackness over our attitude toward the character. As
Rudy stands in front of their hospital beds, Eyre tells us:

> And here we have Tokala and Michael again. This was a really funny
> scene, *really funny scene*. Michael says "hosapa" there. *Hosapa* means
> black. Somebody said to me, "Take the word *nigger* out." And [I said]
> it's a reflection of the characters. I mean this is not a politically cor-
> rect film. It's not intended to be. And, I was again baffled by [some-
> one else's] comment to take that word out. It offended them. And, I
> thought to myself, well, you know what offends me is the poverty and
> the oppression. And that's why we're making the movie—is to dem-
> onstrate, is to illustrate some of that. Um, so, I kind of feel like those
> issues miss the point to a certain degree. Everybody's entitled to their
> opinions but I kind of am a little taken back by [people] not seeing the
> whole.[2]

Eyre's two interlocutors may have been Black and may have truly been of-
fended by the use of the word *nigger*. This is reasonable. But Eyre's "right"
to have characters in his film use the word is also reasonable. In keeping
with the intellectual and political protocol of this book, I have no interest
in adjudicating Eyre's being chafed by the constraints of political correctness or the interlocutor's discomfort with the use of the word *nigger*: the
film could be politically correct (whatever Eyre thinks that means) and
have characters using the word *nigger* without jeopardizing that "correct-

ness." What interests me here is Eyre's and Rudy Yellow Lodge's anxiety in the face of the two young men's relationship to Blackness. Eyre and Rudy Yellow Lodge are anthropomorphic placeholders for the cinematic apparatus and the diegesis, respectively. When Eyre begins his commentary on the hospital scene in which the word *nigger* is used, by saying "This was a really funny scene, *really funny scene*," knowing that in the next breath he will have to acknowledge that Black people do not find it funny at all, he betrays an anxiety about the relationship between Blacks and Indians for which "healthy disagreement" over the proper placement of *nigger* only scratches the surface. If the proper, or improper, placement of this word were all that was at stake, in other words, if the interlocutors' "Take it out," or Eyre's "This is not a politically correct film" could actually explain the dispute, that is if they were not statements symptomatic of a structural divide, then Eyre's unconscious would have allowed him to simply restate the incidents, along with his rejoinder. Or he might have been able to skip it altogether and let the word *nigger* pass, concentrating instead on something banal, like the thespian training of the actors, Michael Spears and Tokala Clifford. Instead, he prefaces his remarks by informing viewers that what they are about to witness is "funny . . . *really funny*." A good joke gets a laugh without any introduction. "I kind of am a little taken back by [people] not seeing the whole," as if to say, *I told you it was a joke, now here's the joke, and here's why nobody laughs.* Rather than contest the truth of either Eyre's or his interlocutors' declarations, we should ask ourselves why a "nigger" joke needs brackets.

The film's displeasure with and anxiety surrounding these two young men cannot be overemphasized. It is a displeasure and anxiety that has been building over the course of the film long before we see them in their hospital beds with their knees busted. Early in the film, we meet one of them by way only of his green phosphorescent shoelaces, which are filmed near the body of Corky Red Tail.

Rudy answers a call regarding a disturbance at an abandoned home where teenagers have been known to hang out and get high. When he arrives, he finds the bloodied body of the wholesome Corky, to whom we were introduced when the film was more light-hearted. Corky's character can be seen as one of the bits of adjectival connotation that accrue to Rudy, thus providing a piece of the ongoing representational support for sovereignty. Like Rudy, Corky holds down a job. Like Rudy, Corky is good-natured and soft-spoken. Corky's affection for Rudy is qualitatively similar to the affection of Herbie (Mogie's son) for Rudy—signifying a filial structure of feeling (kinship and, more broadly, relationality), if not respect for law and order. And, most important for the process of spectator interpellation, Rudy likes Corky. If Rudy's ethical dilemmas are indeed the film's intended dilemmas, then who he has affection for and who he disdains matters immensely.

Then there are the bits of adjectival connotation that do not accrue to Corky Red Tail, fragments that cluster around Mr. Green Shoelaces and Black Lodge Boy: Black urban dialect, the vestmentary codes of urban Black youth, aggressive body language and posturing, and rap lyrics with hip-hop beats. Because Corky was given the film's seal of approval in life, the spectator is called to mourn him in death. What emotion does the film give us for the kneecaps of Corky's peers?

As Rudy shines his flashlight around the perimeter of Corky's body, two figures run down the stairs and through the room. They scurry out the window. He grabs one of them. They scuffle. In the darkness, we see what Rudy sees: the green shoelaces. The sneaker with green shoelaces kicks Rudy in the chest. The assailant tumbles out of the window and runs across the field for the forest. While in hot pursuit Rudy trips and lands, headfirst, on a rock (a rock that, a medicine man will later tell him, may be Iktomi, this time not in the form of a spider). While he is unconscious, Rudy's head begins to fill with visions. These visions are selected and combined from the montage of images we witnessed as the film opened and the credits rolled: photographs of nineteenth-century chiefs, the Wounded Knee occupation of the 1970s, and Leonard Peltier being extradited from Canada to the United States.

Later in the film, Rudy is eating inside the food court of a Texaco gas station on the reservation. His dinner and peace of mind are repeatedly disturbed by the antics of Mr. Green Shoelaces and Black Lodge Boy, who are seated several tables behind him. They are talking loudly, like Black youth as portrayed in popular culture, and in complete contrast to the quiet, respectful, and pleasant tones of Corky or Rudy's nephew Herbie. Rudy grows increasingly annoyed. We are not sure whether it is the way their voices fill the room, the rap lyrics and hip-hop beats pulsing from their boombox, the uncanny mimicry of their speech cadences, their tone, or their pronunciation of words like *shit* ("sheet") or *motherfucker* ("muthafucka") which excites his ire the most.

Eyre's voice-over commentary during this scene shares Rudy's anxiety, if not irritation, toward these two young men. Eyre begins by introducing them as actors—that is, using their real names and not the names of their characters: "This is Michael Spears, [with] the number eighty-two shirt [and green shoelaces] and his sidekick Tokala Clifford." Their music is so loud that none of the patrons can enjoy their meal, but all of them appear too intimidated to say anything. It seems likely that during this scene Eyre's soundperson switched from a unidirectional microphone to a multidirectional microphone. The effect is that the hip-hop beats and rap lyrics from the young men's boombox overpower whatever dialogue is occurring between them. One sees them acting "Black" and one knows from their grunting voices and aggressive body language that they are talking "Black," but one must watch the scene several times in order to ascertain whether or not their "Black" voices and "Black" mannerisms have culminated in anything resembling a "Black" subject matter—or any subject at all for that matter. On replaying the scene one can hear that yes, in point of fact, they are talking about what the popular imagination "knows" Black people talk about—which is nothing at all. One tells the other to get up and get some cigarettes. The other tells him, "I ain't gettin' up to get shit." The first responds, "Stop acting like a bitch," at which point the other says, "Who you callin' a bitch? I ain't no bitch." Then the first laughs and says, "Ooo, did I hurt your feelings?" Before you know it these two friends are on their feet engaged in a full-blown fistfight. Someone watching this scene in a theater would have comprehended none of this. But, after viewing the scene several times, under the more pristine and infinitely less pleasurable conditions of research and close reading, one can only come to the same conclusion that the audio technician arrived at as she or he drowned this dialogue in rap lyrics and hip-hop beats: It does not matter what Black people say because Black people *have* nothing *to* say. What does matter, however, so the logic continues, is the corrosive effect that this seductive and highly stylized "nothing" has on the sovereign "something" of Indigenism. Rap lyrics, dialect, and Black male body language have pulled these two young men into a pit of absolute dereliction and cultural abandonment. There is a trajectory, so the film-cum-cautionary tale would have it, from the corrosive effects of this abandonment to the death of Corky Red Tail—a "good" Indian. Blackness causes Skins to murder Skins. Blackness is at the heart of Native American autogenocide.

The only time Rudy shows any genuine anger at a personification of White civil society is when the resident FBI agent cavalierly comments that Corky probably hung out with the "wrong" crowd. Rudy is so incensed that his superior, the Native American chief of police, gives him a restraining look as if to say: Remember, Rudy, this guy is the real police. Rudy hisses at the FBI agent that Corky Red Tail did not hang out with the wrong crowd, to which the agent responds, again cavalierly, "Well, he did once." The narrative has not positioned Rudy and the FBI agent to be at loggerheads around an issue more structurally critical than the specter of Black stylistic imposition and its corrosive properties with respect to Native American youth. For example, they could have had a nice little scuffle over some comment the script might have had the agent make about Leonard Peltier and the FBI's role in the Jumping Bull incident, or they might have come to blows over territorial constraints which the FBI agent's constant presence imposes on Indian cops who are just trying to do their jobs, or they could fight, not over the stylistic imposition of Blackness, but over the truly deadly cultural imposition of White civil society, to name but a few episodic effects of the "Savage"/Settler antagonism that are not taken up. Instead, the angst of genocide and colonialism undergoes the most bizarre form of condensation and displacement: the FBI agent makes the mistake of calling a "good" Indian a "Black" Indian and suddenly another "good" Indian is ready to fight. True, the film is not happy about the presence of the FBI, but there is a dearth of cinematic animus about this occupation compared to the haunting specter of Blackness.

Now, in the Texaco food arcade, two "bad" Indians are fighting over the things Black youth presumably fight over: who is a bitch and who is not, who will buy cigarettes and who will not. Rudy turns from his meal in anger, rises, walks down the aisle, grabs both young men and throws them apart, effectively breaking up the fight (see figure 12). Mr. Green Shoelaces mouths off to Rudy and then slowly and, we are led to understand, wisely backs off as Rudy approaches. We are treated to a medium shot of Rudy as he walks toward the camera, getting larger and closer,

12 Rudy moving to break up a fight of two boys, in a scene from *Skins*

the image of his anger at having recognized the shoelaces rising to over-power the beats of the boombox.

Then, something miraculous happens: the two young men, having just flown at each other with mutual barbarism, start laughing and joking. They speak to each other, but, again, it is difficult to figure out what is being said. They rise, shake hands like soul brothers, strut out into the sunlight with their boombox blaring, and drive away. Again, after watching the scene several times, one is able to discern that one suggests to the other that they both go get some drugs or alcohol and then go somewhere and get high. To which the other replies, "Ahm down wid dat shit!" That evening, they sit in front of a campfire on the outskirts of the rez. They are high, drunk, and exhilarated. Black Lodge Boy takes a swig of alcohol and says, "Ahma let all deese faggot-ass fools know what's up! Not to be fuckin' around wid me an' ma money." This explains why they murdered Corky Red Tail. Rudy is hiding behind a grassy knoll in back of them. He crawls back to his truck, blackens his face with shoe polish, pulls a nylon stocking over his head and face, and returns (taking advantage of their inebriated stupor) to destroy their legs with a baseball bat (figures 13 and 14).

"Here's Rudy as he goes over the top and becomes Iktomi," Eyre tells us in the commentary. "He's the trickster. But really he's just a man who's tired of—he's a vigilante. He's taken the law into his own hands now." The director's commentary emphasizes what the film makes abundantly clear: our empathy is to be directed toward Rudy and not Mr. Green

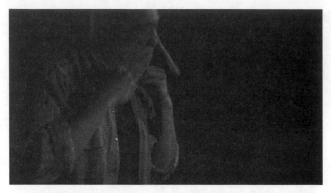

13   Rudy putting a stocking cap on his head and face

14   Rudy beating boys with a baseball bat

Shoelaces or Black Lodge Boy. As the film would have it, what is painful about this scene is not the physical terror of having one's kneecaps
destroyed or the psychological terror of being set on when one is intoxicated, but Rudy's burden of *Weltschmerz*, his melancholy over the fragile
state of Indigenous sovereignty. Two things are at play here, two symptomatic gestures which suture spectator identification with Rudy and not
with the two young men. The first gesture is the legitimation of Rudy
by collapsing the iconography of sovereignty onto him, both diegetically,
and, as we have discussed, extradiegetically, through Eyre's commentary,
which gives him "trickster," that is, spiritual status (however troubled and
conflicted that status might be, for we must remember that hegemony is
strongest when it has the power to ask the questions, not when it imposes
the answers). The second gesture is that the two young men, prior to their

"execution," are sufficiently "tarred" with the always already of criminality: Blackness.

Earlier in the sequence, as they strutted out of the Texaco station, Eyre's voice-over grows increasingly emphatic. "They both speak Lakota," he tells us. "Both very knowledgeable." We must be made aware that Blackness has subsumed the characters not the actors. "Real good young men," he continues. "They know their histories and know their culture and their past." We know from Taiaiake Alfred, Haunani-Kay Trask, Leslie Silko, and others that the touchstones of cohesion which underwrite the idea of private property and the system of capitalism are deadly poisons to the principles that underwrite Indigenous values of land stewardship, of giving one's most precious belongings away to others, of use-value in contradistinction to surplus value. And yet, when Corky Red Tail appears on screen as a checkout clerk behind a cash register in a huge department store, Eyre is surprisingly free of anxiety. He is not compelled to reassure us that Yellow Pony Pettibone (the actor who plays Corky) is not, in real life, in danger of becoming a capitalist scumbag, despite the fact that the character Pettibone plays handles money, assumes the posture and body language of a good employee, and even speaks like a retail aficionado, joking with the customers that they might find shopping a pleasant experience and thereby return to the scene of what Marx, as well as Silko, Deloria, Trask, and Churchill call a "crime"—the scene of profit extraction. Eyre chooses not to assuage our fears by saying something like: "Off screen, Yellow Pony Pettibone is a real good young man who speaks Lakota, is very knowledgeable, and knows his history, his culture, and his past." Nor does Rudy's tête-à-tête with the FBI agent suggest that, on screen, Corky Red Tail is a scandalous example of Native youth straying from the values of Indigenous sovereignty. Corky, Rudy informs the FBI agent, "was a good kid!"

In the structure of antagonisms, ontology comes with its ledger: on one side, life, on the other side, death. But the "Savage" exists liminally on this ledger. Unlike Silko and Deloria, who meditate on the ledger analytically, Chris Eyre and Rudy Yellow Lodge understand it is aesthetic and intuitive, respectively. On one side of the ledger, there are the taxonomies of history and culture—time and space capacity. On the other side of the ledger, there is Blackness—time and space incapacity. So deracinated are the time and space capacities of Blackness that Black "style" (the performances or masks projected onto death) need not be represented as coherent. In *Skins*, the audio and visual strategies of the film give a wink and a nod to the spectator, as if to say: *We all know how Blacks are, talking loud and saying nothing (so there is no need for a unidirectional microphone)—one minute sober, the next minute high, now happy, now sad, one minute friends, the next minute enemies, like animals with no relations (so there is no need for narration).*

Again, it is important to understand that two Indians who are, off-screen, well versed in their culture and history have agreed to wear the world's most corrosive vestments so that they might collaborate with the cinematic apparatus of "Savage" cinema in telling this cautionary tale. We know from the work of "Savage" ontologists that, since Predator came, the foundation of "Savage" sovereignty has been fragile. But how does sovereignty's rhetorical structure authorize an aesthetic through which "Savage" cinema can dream the specter of Black "style" as being more deadly than capital and the police? This question has two components, one historical and the other philosophical.

In her analysis of nineteenth-century tourist guidebooks for visitors to the U.S. Capitol, Susan Scheckel shows how the imaginative labor performed by the recurring "insistence of the Indian" fortified and extended the interlocutory life of the United States and cast "'the citizen' as audience and actor in an ongoing national drama":

> The history of contact between Euro-Americans and Indians is a dominant theme of the Capitol's commemorative artwork. The appeal of this subject . . . [is that] it allows a young nation to locate its origins in a (relatively) distant past. Benedict Anderson's argument that the idea of the nation is imagined to be rooted in time immemorial and to extend into the immeasurable future is particularly apt in connection with the Capitol, where the past and future meet to create its meaning as symbol and nation.[3]

This articulation of imaginative labor (a drama of value in which two nations meet and make war: one winning, the other losing; one emerging on the world stage, the other vanishing except as ghosts) is rendered through a network of connections, transfers, and displacements between "Savage" and Settler anthropological touchstones of cohesion. The guidebooks make the struggle between "Savage" and Settler legible to the nineteenth-century tourist by presenting that struggle as a conflict between competing cultural and political systems, but not as a matter of genocide.

Scheckel illustrates this semiotic coherence by demonstrating how anthropological touchstones of cohesion find their correspondences in the articulation of words and concepts like *council house* versus *the Capitol*, *council of elders* versus *National Legislature*, and *Indian nation* versus *American nation*:

> Jonathan Elliot's 1830 guidebook begins by linking the rise of the United States with the history of Indian decline. As Elliot informs the reader, the Capitol is built upon the same land "where councils were held among various tribes." He goes on to direct the reader's response to this fact: "The coincidence of the location of the National Legislature, so near the scite [sic] of the council house of an Indian Nation, cannot fail to excite interesting reflections in the mind of an intelligent reader." Thus, Elliot presents a vision of one nation superseding another, with Indians consequently removed from the land where the Capitol now visibly stands and from history except insofar as they form the foundation of the rising American nation.[4]

Randall Robinson's *The Debt: What America Owes to Blacks* begins by attempting to find similar articulations between Master and Slave in the same cultural objects that hold Scheckel's attention, the Capitol, its guidebooks, and its artwork. But unlike the "Savage," whose figure proliferates in these objects, Slaves are strikingly absent "in the frescoes, the friezes, the oil paintings, the composite art," although they are as materially foundational to the Capitol's existence as the "Savage." In the first stage of the Capitol's construction (1793–1802), the government paid the owners of one hundred slaves five dollars per month per slave. Robinson tells us that slaves also did much of the work "in implementing Pierre-Charles L'Enfant's grand design for the whole of the District of Columbia." For example, they cleared "a broad swath of forest between the sites" of what would become the Capitol and the White House. The visitor guidebooks on which Robinson reflects are of the late twentieth century (*The Greatest Solemn Dignity* [1995] and *Uncle Sam's Architects: Builders of the Capitol* [1994]). In other words, unlike Elliot's guidebook, these books are post–Civil War, post-Jubilee, post-Reconstruction, post–Civil Rights, post–1960s riots (more than three hundred per year during that period), and even post–Black Power. These books were written with the benefit of one hundred years of Black historical uprising and intellectual reflection on that uprising—whereas Elliot's 1830 guidebook only had the Haitian Revolution, Harriet Tubman, and Nat Turner's rebellion to reflect on. Yet "neither book mentioned anything about the use of slave labor."[5]

Discouraged by the absence of the figure of the Slave in the Capitol's frescoes, friezes, oil paintings, composite art, and written literature, Robinson searches for the articulation of the Slave in the oral "literature" of a present-day Settler/Master: a telephone interview he conducts with William Allen of the Architect of the Capitol office. Allen tells him (as Robinson paraphrases) that during the Civil War "slaves dislocated in the turmoil gravitated to Union soldiers, who often brought them to Washington to be put to work on [the third phase of the Capitol's construction— the second phase having occurred after British troops burned it to the ground in 1812]. William Allen called them 'spoils of war' and 'contraband slaves.' When I asked him about the term 'contraband slaves,' he grew quiet as if questioning for the first time the purpose of my general inquiry about the use of black slave labor."[6] At the site where Scheckel unearths a plethora of articulations predicated on violence—the conquest and genocide of Indians—Robinson finds a void of articulations also predicated on violence, this time that of accumulation and fungibility.

There is a similarity between the place Blackness occupies in the private and quotidian imaginary of the Capitol architect William Allen and the place it occupies in the imaginary of Chris Eyre's *Skins*. For both the architect and the film, Blackness is "a vicarious, disfiguring, joyful pleasure, passionately enabling as well as substitutively dead."[7] Although the unconscious of both Allen and *Skins* experience the object status—the fungibility—of Blackness, they do so differently. For Allen, the vicariousness is emphasized; for *Skins*, it is the joyfulness of the pleasure— hip-hop esprit de corps—which ultimately disfigures (the death of Corky Red Tail). But for both the film and the architect, it is Blackness that facilitates the capacity to contemplate egoic monumentalization. Robinson, hyperaware of and hypersensitive to his own object status, his own fungibility, is disturbed not by the truth of his own dead ontics (his book is testament to more than sixty years of living with, and suffering through, nonbeing) but by the fact that it does not disturb Allen the Capitol architect. Allen, for his part, is disturbed by Robinson's disturbance. But the reaction of *Skins* to the "Savage" knowledge of Black fungibility is of a different order than Allen's.

Skins is disturbed not by the prospect of Black rage (or, in this case, Randall Robinson's subdued annoyance) but by the horrifying possibility that Black fungibility might somehow rub off of the Slave and stick to the "Savage." The philosophical anxiety of *Skins* is all too aware that, through the Middle Passage, African culture became Black "style," both a form of "contraband" and one of civil society's many "spoils of war." The object status of Blackness means that it can be placed and displaced with limitless frequency and across untold territories, by whoever so chooses. Most important, there is nothing real Black people can do to either check or direct this process. Both jazz and hip-hop have become known in the same way that Black bodies are known: as forces "liberated" from time and space, belonging nowhere and to no one, simply there for the taking. Anyone can say "nigger" because anyone can *be* a "nigger."[8] What a nightmare indeed, reads the caution of *Skins*, should the fragile coherence of Indigenous sovereignty fall prey to such hopeless and totalizing deracination. "Simple enough one has only not to be a nigger."[9]

Whereas the knowledge of Black fungibility folds easily into Allen's (Settler/Master) reflections, the same knowledge of the object status of Blacks threatens to pull "Savages" perilously close to their own object status, that is, to the genocide modality of their ontology. But rather than surrender to this encounter with the object status of Blackness and form an ontological legion of the dead, a rather curious condensation and displacement occurs.

One pattern of this condensation and displacement can be found in the frequent construction of "Savage" ontological meditations around "Savage" and Settler anthropological similarities and differences, examples of which include the following:

1   Vine Deloria's search for common ground between Amish land occupation principles and Native American land stewardship principles.
2   Leslie Silko's aesthetic meditation on the philosophical convergences and divergences between Native American and Marxist principles of justice and redistribution.[10]

3   Deloria's celebration of the centrality of language and kinship struc-
    ture for both Indigenous people and Jews.
4   Deloria's belief in an essential bond between Indigenous spiritual
    healing and Jungian psychoanalysis.

The historical antecedents for "Savage" ontology's privileging of this particular pattern of condensation and displacement (I am suggesting, in
part at least, a metonymic journey in flight from the harsh ontics of genocide) are mirrored in the Settler's meditations on his or her own social
and philosophical reality. Scheckel demonstrates this in her illustration
of citizenship's iconographic dependency on the figure of the Indian, and
Deloria finds analytic dependency on Indigenous cosmological principles in Jungian psychoanalysis. My point, once again, is that when faced
with the subjective void of Black fungibility, Settlers/Masters, in both of
their ontological modalities (exploitation and alienation), and "Savages,"
in their sovereign modality, are confronted with some*thing* that appears
to be a cultural (i.e., historical and anthropological) being but is in fact a
pure distillation of the political. And their analytic apparatuses, their respective ontics, are shocked by such an unmediated encounter, requiring
their rhetorical gestures to either disavow the encounter or displace its
particulars onto an ensemble of cultural considerations. Examples of this
include Deloria's and Silko's moves, as noted above, and Eyre's emphatic
affirmation of the cultural health of Michael Spears and Tokala Clifford.

The second pattern of this condensation and displacement also takes
the form of a hysterical symptom—speech that speaks away from the
trauma at hand. But here, unlike the radical displacement onto sovereignty, the hysterical speech is in fact imbricated in Blackness. It is imbricated in Blackness, however, in such a way as to speak extensively about
Slaves and about "Savages," but as this speech grows in size, scope, and
duration, the text loses more and more of its explanatory power regarding both the ontics of the Slave and the structural relation between the
"Savage" and the Slave. Silko's *Almanac of the Dead* and Deloria's *God Is
Red* are both examples of this progressive thinning of explanatory power.
Eyre, for example, tells us that he is baffled by the politically correct re-
quest to "take the word *nigger* out." In lieu of working off both the demand and his own bafflement, he suggests that the real issue is "poverty

and oppression"—as though the genealogy of the word *nigger* is somehow tangential to poverty and oppression.

Silko takes Eyre's hysterical symptom and develops it narratively. For
Silko, the fungible status of Blacks—the Black body as a pure distillation
of the political—presents her with a "cultural" scandal too blinding to
be looked at directly, much less embraced on its own terms. Her more
meditative response (it unfolds over 661 pages of prose rather than 90
minutes of celluloid) is similar to Eyre's *Skins.* Like the director and his
film, Silko displaces the potential good faith encounter between the object status of the "Savage" and the object status of the Slave onto a series
of philosophical declarations which subordinate race to class. It must be
emphasized that her novel, much like Eyre's film and his director's commentary, feels the need to make this move strongly and with passion;
furthermore, this compulsion only rears its head when the text stages an
encounter in which the Black is an interlocutor. The same compulsion is
not manifest when the novel stages "Savage"-to-"Savage" encounters, or
"Savage"-to-Settler encounters.

When Angelita, an Indigenous colonel in the Army of Justice and
Redistribution, struggles to explain to Comrade Bartolomeo, a White
Marxist, why "Indians couldn't care less about international Marxism;
all they wanted was to retake their land from the white man," or when
Sterling reminisces on his lifelong banishment from Laguna Pueblo by
the elders (an intra-"Savage" conflict), Silko is not compelled to discipline the dream world of the fiction by reminding us that it is not about
race but rather about poverty and oppression. Curiously enough, these
encounters evince what can only be described as a philosophical about-
face: Angelita is deployed by Silko against Marxism's ethical dilemmas
so that writer and character might demonstrate how puny and inadequate the question of class is to Indigenous dilemmas of land restoration.
And while Sterling is sent into the fictional world by Silko for a variety
of complex reasons central to the sovereign dilemma of cultural restoration, one thing is certain: he is not deployed across 661 pages to convince
the reader that oppression is all about class. Why then, must the Black be
brought to heel? *Almanac of the Dead* is not content to simply ignore that
modality of the "Savage" most analogous to the Slave; nor is it content
to merely displace the dilemma of the object status of the Slave onto the

ethical dilemma of class. Silko is also determined to make the Black over in the image of Indigenism. This is a gratuitous gesture that even *Skins* does not attempt.

The main characters in *Almanac of the Dead* function as placeholders for the various ethical dilemmas imposed on the socius by the structure of modernity's conflicts and antagonisms elaborated by contact. This could be said of *Skins* as well: I have made a case for Mogie as the embodied ethics of genocide and Rudy as the embodied ethics of sovereignty. The difference between *Skins* and *Almanac of the Dead* is that Eyre's cinematic conversation between competing and converging ethical dilemmas is staged incidentally and infrequently, whereas Silko's is staged deliberately and extensively.

As a philosophical tome, *Almanac of the Dead*'s place in the archive of "Savage" ontological meditations has been secured both genealogically and paradigmatically. Native scholars and activists concur that Silko's work is authorized genealogically "in that it draws heavily on Laguna Pueblo myth and lore and thus has significance separate from Western tradition."[11] Her aesthetic and philosophical rearticulation of Laguna Pueblo tradition is what authorizes her work at the micro- or tribal level. The genealogical authorization of her work at the macro-level of the Indian writ large stems from its fidelity to Deloria's ensemble of questions: as Tamara Teale has noted, "Deloria's works of the late 1960s and on into the 1970s are part of the support system, the established preconditions of Silko's aesthetic rendering of indigenous values in *Almanac of the Dead*."[12]

The place of *Almanac of the Dead* in the archive of "Savage" ontological meditations has been secured paradigmatically by her work's relentless striving for an antagonistic stance toward both the material reality of North America, as well as toward the *ideas*, the ethical dilemmas of Western civil society, for example, Marxism and capitalism. Through extended political dialogues between characters, long historical and philosophical third-person digressions, and free-floating internal monologues, *Almanac of the Dead* presents its uncompromising thesis that sexual, environmental, and political relations in North America are either poisonous or dead. The novel gathers steam as its Indians, its lone Black, Clinton, and its smattering of provisionally redeemable Whites arm themselves and prepare to join ranks with the Army of Justice and

Redistribution, an Indigenous force that will march from Chiapas to Tucson and, eventually, across all of North America.

Sterling and Angelita advance across the novel bearing their grammar of suffering and its incompatibility with the Settler's grammar of suffering. Sterling is banished from his reservation because he helped a Hollywood camera crew film a sacred site, although the same elders who banished him also "allowed" U.S. corporate mining interests onto the reservation to mine uranium and, consequently, contaminate the minds and bodies of the inhabitants. The people and places Sterling meets during his wandering exile, as well as his internal monologues, catalyzed by his reminiscences, give Silko the opportunity to reflect extensively on the spiritual impact of Laguna Pueblo myth and lore on a colonized people and on the intra-Indigenous tensions that arise when the credibility of those charged with safekeeping and continuing these traditions comes into question. Angelita's struggle for her own credibility in the Army of Justice and Redistribution and among the Indigenous peoples of southern Mexico allows Silko to critique Marxism through an Indigenous lens and thereby show that its secular excesses (e.g., industrialization) are isomorphic with the religious excesses of Christianity. Silko's argument—by way of Angelita's struggles with Bartolomeo and her dialogues with her people and the elders—is that, at a certain level of abstraction, both the emancipatory logic of Marxism and the conservative logic of Christianity are unethical when confronted with emancipatory Indigenism because both are built on the supremacy of a monolithic entity: either the Human being (Marxism) or the one God (Christianity).

The kind of heavy lifting which Silko requires of characters like Angelita and Sterling (who carry the ethical dilemmas of "Savage" ontology) and characters like Bartolomeo, Rambo Roy, and Seese (who carry the ethical dilemmas of Settler ontology) is rare in U.S. fiction. But Silko is determined to narrativize the structure of antagonisms, rather than simply tell the story of conflicts. The force and self-conscious intentionality of her projects, therefore, makes her dubious rendering of her main Black character even more curious and problematic than Eyre's superficial rendering of vicarious Blackness.

When she deploys Clinton, the struggle with his Blackness is no longer philosophical, concrete, or political. Instead, his struggle is impressionistic, metaphoric, and vague. Ultimately, Silko recreates him as someone on the road to spiritual and cultural redemption, through the rubric of sovereignty. Clinton, the Black, is the only main character who does not come to this ambitious novel with his own philosophical endowments, his own treasure chest of intellectual capital. He is an intellectual magpie: he feeds off of the traditions of others; more precisely, through repeated gestures of noblesse oblige, Silko allows the Native Americans and one of the Whites—those who *are* philosophically endowed—to spoon-feed Clinton. Like the fragments of "Blackness" which make their way into *Skins*, Clinton provides *Almanac of the Dead* with a vicarious pleasure, passionately enabling, although Clinton himself is substitutively dead: "Clinton was the Black veteran with one foot, but he wore the best, the top of the line, the best kind of prosthetic foot you could buy. Clinton had to wear his full Green Beret uniform every day. . . . Clinton's shrine held the knife, or the blade of a knife and what remained of a handle, a skeletal piece of metal. Clinton had kept the blade razor-sharp; he had carried the knife in combat because it had never failed him in the dangerous alleys and streets at home. Clinton's people—women and men alike—all carried knives."[13]

Clinton comes to us as a body in bits and pieces. Psychoanalysis teaches us that, in the unconscious, fear of experiencing one's body in bits and pieces (the traumas that impinge on the psyche as a soldier enters battle and for long periods of time after she or he has left the war) has an even more deconstructive impact on the ego and its capacity to monumentalize the personal pronoun *I* than the fear of death itself. For Silko and Eyre a Black body in bits and pieces (Clinton) and disembodied bits and pieces of "Blackness" (rap, dialect, etc.) produce a common sense of impending doom for their ontological vision and aesthetics: the fragmentation of their sovereign presence. And they have no other way to reflect on Blackness, due to their proclivity for culture over death.

A Black amputee advances across the novel bearing what Silko imagines to be his people's grammar of suffering. But there are several problems here. To begin with, Clinton seems to have no relation to his people. We hardly ever meet them. Unlike with Angelita and her people and elders in Chiapas or Sterling and the elders of Laguna Pueblo, we are not privy to any substantive (scene-generated) interaction between Clinton's Black body in bits and pieces and a collective body of Blacks. Silko, as third-person narrator, tells us all we need to know about them: "Clinton's people—women and men alike—all carried knives." This is one of many instances in which we find Silko's ontological imaginary to be in conflict with her ontological preconscious. Her preconscious logic "understands" that Clinton's politically, culturally, and physically amputated condition is predicated on the Middle Passage and slavery. But her unconscious imaginary repeatedly reveals itself to be more fearful of Blacks ("Clinton's people . . . all carried knives") than of the Destroyers (Europeans). The condensation and displacement that occurs here imposes on the imaginary a sense that the amputated condition of Black life is in fact produced by Black people, regardless of what we know, intellectually, about slavery. Furthermore, not only does Blackness deterritorialize its own, but it also looms large as that bundle of barbaric energies that can deterritorialize the entire socius. "Clinton had to get back to the big cities. He had to try to reach the black war vets before they got misled by fanatics or extremists screaming 'Black only! Africa only!' because Clinton had realized the truth: millions of black Indians were scattered throughout the Americas."[14]

The last clause of the preceding quotation is important, because it is symptomatic of both Silko's and Eyre's inability to (a) meditate on Blackness's grammar of suffering and (b) meditate on how the ethical dilemmas of that grammar of suffering are incompatible with the world's grammar—despite the fact that Silko, at least, demonstrates how the violence of Black slavery and the violence of Red genocide are both foundational to the production of the Western Hemisphere. The claim that "millions of black Indians [are] scattered throughout the Americas" is symptomatic of these two failings and reminds us of the novel's constant third-person tutoring of Clinton, its admonishing of him to learn, respect, and protect Indigenism from the scourge of Blackness.[15] *Almanac* cannot, however, imagine that *Blackness* should be studied, respected, and protected by or from the ravages of anything, much less Indigenism. A refusal to be authorized by the Slave is an effect of the Negrophobia that the "Savage" shares with the Settler/Master.

Silko's *Almanac of the Dead*, unlike Eyre's *Skins*, approves of mass political violence (e.g., Angelita's Army of Justice and Redistribution and the armies of homeless people in Tucson) rather than the violence of the police. For this, I commend her. However, much like Eyre's *Skins* and the political, social, and aesthetic imaginary of nearly every other discursive gesture in the United States, Silko is shocked by the specter of mass Black violence. This is because Black violence is the violence of a people for whom loss cannot be named. Just as Mogie Yellow Lodge cannot name his embodied genocide, the Black cannot name the loss but knows where the loss is located: in the hide of whoever is alive, in the body of the subject. But, as we witnessed above, Mogie Yellow Lodge's violent gesture was handily constrained by the ethics of his own sovereign ontological status. The editing, lighting, and camera work incarcerate Mogie within Rudy's field of vision at the moment he makes his unflinching demand, and they thus rearticulate his demand as a joke or an embarrassment. Black violence, as either gesture, demand, mobilization, or simply desire, cannot be constrained by any ethics internal to Blackness: there is no (internal) subjective status through which any Humanist ethic can make an appeal. Black violence, then, threatens not simply to take land away from the capitalists or to take the vision of land redistribution away from the Marxists; it threatens to take life away from everyone.

As philosophically unflinching as Silko claims to be, she is ultimately far too interested in coalitions and self-preservation to reflect unflinchingly on the ethics of Blackness, much less the violent manifestation of those ethics. Eyre is only a filmmaker, a storyteller who sometimes lucks into philosophy; but Silko is a philosopher who is able to tell stories. Therefore, unlike Eyre, she cannot afford to dismiss the "nigger" joke (which we can now see is no joke at all, but the world's most vexing dilemma) with such flimsy brackets as "people like that miss the point . . . [and are not seeing] the whole," because she has charged herself with explaining structural relations. Nor can she dismiss a "nigger" joke with "this is funny, *really* funny," because humor is not an enduring protocol of her tome. Eyre and *Skins* attempt to bracket the "nigger" joke so the viewer might feel safe enough to laugh. For Silko, the brackets need to become stone walls: she must directly "engage" Blackness in order to first transform it, then to redeem it, and, finally, to render it structurally adjusted: "One whole branch [of Clinton's family] in Tennessee had been married to Indians, 'American Indian.' 'Native Americans.' And not just any kind of Indian either. Clinton had not got over the shock and wonder of it. He and the rest of his family had been direct descendants of wealthy, slave-owning Cherokee Indians. . . . The branch of the family that was Indian always bragged they were the *first* black Indians."[16]

Unable, or unwilling, to embrace Blackness as an embodied distillation of pure political force, Silko dresses Clinton up like an Indian. She adjusts him, structurally, so that she might incorporate Blackness in a way that Eyre's high-handedness had no interest in doing. Needless to say, we are meant to feel grateful for this gesture. The largesse of her prose would indicate that we are to consider this gesture an act of redemption bestowed on Clinton's Black void. Silko can now pass Clinton's political actions off as some sort of Black political agency elaborated by Black ethical dilemmas. We are faced, however, with not simply the mendacity through which Silko has first erased and then rewritten the figure of Blackness, but with the fact that her rather common and typical anxiety regarding the figure of Blackness has short-circuited her ability to meditate on the mass of Blackness. Here she does, in fact, become as cavalier as Eyre. Silko only has the time and the energy to redeem one Black. That Black must then go out and redeem the rest—alas, even an ontologist cannot do it all. But "Clinton wasn't going to waste time with the whiners and complainers who had made wine or dope their religion, or the Jesus junkies, who had made religion their drug." In other words, like the novel, Clinton was not going to "waste" time with ordinary Black people, even though Angelita "wastes" pages upon pages with ordinary Indians, and Rambo Roy and the third-person narrative of the novel "waste" a tremendous amount of time and ink on ordinary White people. "The Hopi had given Clinton a book that the Hopi said might shine some more light on the black Indians. . . . Clinton knew racism had made people afraid to talk about their Native American ancestors but the black Indians would know in their hearts who they were when they heard Clinton talk about the spirits. . . . Clinton had promised the Barefoot Hopi he would spread the word among the brothers and sisters in the cities."[17]

Clinton is the spanner in the works of Silko's analytic apparatus. Her canvas is presented with the enormity of Black loss, coupled with the impossibility of putting that loss into words. Rather than write about the terror (fear without reason or origin) that Blackness both experiences *in* the world and promises to return *to* the world, her prose style and conceptual capacity abandon the poetic erudition with which it deployed the likes of Angelita and slips into solipsistic euphemism. In this way, she makes Clinton ready to join Angelita's Army of Justice and Redistribution and accomplishes, as an ontologist, what Eyre could not accomplish as an artist. She makes the Black safe for sovereignty and rescues sovereignty from the Black.

4

Monster's Ball

TEN

A Crisis in the Commons

The commons is the incarnation, the production, and
the liberation of the multitude.—ANTONIO NEGRI and
MICHAEL HARDT, *Empire*

Can there be a "community" of niggers, as opposed to
a "bunch" or a "collection"?—RONALD JUDY,
"On the Question of Nigga Authenticity"

MY THESIS with respect to the structure of U.S. antagonisms posits violence as an idiom of power which
marks the triangulated relation of modernity (Red,
White, and Black) as the broad institutional effect of
the Western Hemisphere and most pernicious expression of that institutionality, the United States of America.
My claim, building on the explanatory power of the
Afro-pessimists, is that violence is at the heart of
this idiom of power. Violence determines the essential contours of Settler/"Savage" and Master/Slave relations. This notion of violence as a positioning matrix
weakens the heretofore consensual poststructuralist
notions of film studies, feminism, and Antonio Negri's
and Michael Hardt's postindustrial Marxism, all of
which assume symbolic negotiation (discourse) to be
the essence of the matrix that positions subjects. The
thesis seeks to mark film studies, feminism, psychoanalysis, and Marxism as White, and to de-essentialize
the suffering which animates them, humiliating them
in the face of the Slave and that part of the "Savage"
positioned, ontologically, by genocide as opposed to
sovereignty.

In the preceding chapters there has been little discussion of violent "events" (save a brief discussion of genocide endured by Native Americans and how the carceral continuum of Black life morphs and shapeshifts through legislation). This is because the violence constitutive of the idiom of power that positions one U.S. antagonist as Settler/Master, another as Slave, and still another as "Savage" should not be reduced to its spectacle. It is not an event but rather a matrix of elaboration on which temporal and spatial capacity is possible for the Settler/Master, both possible and impossible for the "Savage," and absolutely derelict for the Slave. One can no more "show" the matrix of violence that positions the Slave than one can "show" psychoanalysis's matrix of language, the large object A, the symbolic order that castrates the *infans* and brings (positions) him or her into subjectivity, that is, into a world of "contemporaries."

At the time of this writing, even the most radical and overtly political gestures in film studies have as yet to engage Hardt's and Negri's theories of political economy and its recomposed subject, "the multitude." But this shortcoming plays out Master-to-Master and Settler-to-Settler: it is an intra-Human discussion inessential to the Slave's ethical dilemmas catalyzed by accumulation and fungibility. (The Slave, however, is often brought into the discussion not to advance the analysis but rather to avoid embarrassment.) Still engaging either the assumptive logic of Foucauldian disciplinary regimes (i.e., Kalpana Seshadri-Crooks, Patrice Petro) or Gramscian hegemony (i.e., Stuart Hall, Mary Ann Doane, Stephen Heath, and early Kaja Silverman), film studies has either a minimalist agenda as regards the cinema's socially transformative potential (that is, it is animated by notions of hybridity and change *within* the interstices of civil society), or it is hopeful for a realignment of cinematic practice whose counterhegemonic elements qualify as cultural accompaniment for major social and political change. All this is to say that film studies has yet to become underwritten by an ensemble of Negrian questions as regards the status of the spectator and the cinematic diegesis in a world where now (even) Whites are positioned more and more by what appears to Hardt and Negri as gratuitous violence and less and less by what had appeared to Antonio Gramsci and Michel Foucault as contingent violence. But as poles apart as Negrian Marxism and film studies may be, what binds Negri's and Hardt's unflinching paradigmatic analysis to the most unflinching interpretive film theory is a largely unspoken and unsubstantiated notion that all sentient beings (euphemistically referred to as "humans"—or bona fide subjects) possess the capacity to contest value in some kind of drama—in other words, "faith" in the notion that all people have the capacity for history and anthropology, the power to transform time and space.

The drama of value, then, is underwritten by the inspiration of the personal pronoun *we*. It is this inspiration that throughout this book I have attempted to deconstruct and humiliate. The inspiration of *we*, to use a term from film theory, is a form of *suture*. It papers over any contemplation of violence as a structuring matrix—and weds us to the notion of violence as a contingent event. And the inspiration of *we* also sutures fields of study and political motivations as seemingly far apart as Negrian Marxism and Gramscian/Lacanian film studies, sutures them together by way of two basic assumptions: (1) that all people have bodies and (2) that all people contest dramas of value. Thus, Marxism and film theory operate like police actions: they police our ability to contemplate how the Slave is not a lesser valued entity on a pole of higher valued entities but is instead exiled from the drama of value.

Acknowledgments of this exile are to be found, not in White metacommentary and not in White film theory but, oddly enough, in White films themselves. *Monster's Ball* is a film that attempts to share the inspiration of Marxism and White film theory's *we* but finds itself divided on the matter. It cannot be inspired by the assumptive *we* of its screenplay, that is, its most conscious narrative strategies, because at key moments its images and soundtrack act contrapuntally to the screenplay. The next three chapters are predicated on my claim that whereas the screenplay labors ideologically in support of a notion that exploitation and alienation (the Human's grammar of suffering) explain the essential antagonism of the paradigm, strategies of cinematic form (as well as the irruption of contextual elements into the film's production) labor ideologically in support of a notion that accumulation and fungibility (the Slave's grammar of suffering) explain the essential antagonism of the paradigm (and, through this explanation, render exploitation and alienation the touchstones of a conflict).

Monster's Ball's cinematic form dismantles the political common sense that scaffolds the film's ethical dilemmas and the narrative's argument that Blacks, like Whites, are "among the disparate entities" for which value is an arbiter. For Negri and Hardt these disparate entities face off as proletarian and capitalist, for White film theory the range of entities spans gay/straight, man/woman, postcolonial/empire, and more. In all of these combinations, value, as "an arbitrator among disparate entities . . . labors to naturalize *its very process of arbitration* to the point of sublimation and fetishization."[1]

For Marxists, this sublimation and fetishization is located in "the commodity [which] marks itself as unitary and self-involved. It masks the social relations to which it is inevitably tied and that it equally redacts."[2] For film theory and White cinema (i.e., the political common sense of a screenplay's ethical dilemmas or a White director's auteurial intention) such as *Monster's Ball*, the phallus (Kaja Silverman, Mary Ann Doane), the frame (Stephen Heath), or Whiteness itself (Richard Dyer, or Marc Forster's auteurial intention) are the points of representational coherence through which value "marks itself as unitary and self-involved." Like the commodity-form, the phallus, the frame, and Whiteness (as imagined rigorously by scholars of Whiteness and superficially by the screenplay of *Monster's Ball*) all mask the social relations to which they are tied and which they also redact. But we need to be mindful of two things at once; first, the ways in which this masking and redaction occur: the commodity-form's redaction of exploited labor-power, the phallus's masking of the (White) male's castration by the symbolic order, the frame and the voice-over's alibi for the cinematic apparatus, and the racial labor that Whiteness depends on for its unracialized "normality"; and second, whereas such masking and redaction are essential to the grammar of suffering of the worker, the woman, the spectator, and the postcolonial, they are inessential to the grammar of suffering of the Slave.

Value, Lindon Barrett asserts through his reading of Gayatri Spivak's *In Other Worlds*, is not only a representation that masks and redacts social relations. By opening the lid on value in its fetishized form as money (a "seemingly unitary phenomenon") one sees that money is not only a representation but a differential: Value-Money-Capital. He concludes that: "It is this differential nature that value most successfully secrets when it most fully seems itself. The phenomenon of value—like its particular instantiations in political economy: the commodity, capitalist ideology, money—is most fully *exposed* in terms of acknowledging its occluded differential economy, the *circuit of displacement, substitution, and sig-*

nification that value is always struggling to mask by means of a hypostasized 'form'. In short, the ideal referent and confirmation for value are the forms it is in the process of seeking to substantiate."[3] My argument with the passage above has little to do with the content of Barrett's claims. Certainly, value is both the masking of social relations as well as the masking of its own "circuit of displacement, substitution, and signification." But theories (i.e., Marxism, feminism, and film theory) which unpack the hypostasized "form" that value takes, as it masks both its differential and social relations, experience the humiliation of their explanatory power when confronted with the Black. For the Black has no social relation(s) to be either masked or unmasked—not, that is, in a structural sense. Social relations depend on various pretenses to the contrary; therefore, what gets masked is the matrix of violence that makes Black relationality an oxymoron. To relate, socially, one must enter a social drama's mise-en-scène with spatial and temporal coherence—in other words, with Human capacity. The Slave is not so much the antithesis of Human capacity (that might imply a dialectic potential in the Slave's encounter with the world) as she or he is the absence of Human capacity.

Having recapped the general project, we can begin to closely examine Settler/Master cinema, a cinema elaborated by an ensemble of questions that arise out of an explanatory rubric predicated on exploitation and alienation, a cinema in which the protagonist(s) who shoulders a film's ethical dilemmas is an exploited and alienated Human. The apex of Humanness is Whiteness.[4] Therefore, socially engaged cinema of which the director is White and whose standard-bearer of ethical dilemmas is also White will be the focal point of our investigation. Enter *Monster's Ball*.

Negri and Hardt Dancing at the *Monster's Ball*

Sonny Grotowski (Heath Ledger) is having his portrait drawn. Lawrence Musgrove (Sean Combs, a.k.a., P. Diddy) appears to be drawing it; but Musgrove is really writing to his wife, Leticia. This portrait, the one he is drawing now of Sonny—Sonny who sits and waits on the other side of Musgrove's death-row cell—together with the one he will draw of another guard, Sonny's father, Hank (Billy Bob Thornton), is a letter Leticia (Halle Berry) will not read until the end of the film when it is time to kill Hank. These portraits will take the place of Lawrence Musgrove's last phone call, a call denied him by the warden's proxies, the father and son Grotowski.

Set in Georgia but shot in Louisiana (a continuity glitch for anyone who has spent an impressionable amount of time in the South), *Monster's Ball* is the tale of Hank Grotowski, a racist prison guard who works with his son, Sonny. Both Hank and Sonny live at home with Hank's father, Buck (Peter Boyle), also a template Southern racist. In fact, the only Grotowskis who may not have been bigots are Buck's and Hank's wives, both of whom are dead and both of whom are the recipients of posthumous derision from their surviving husbands. Sonny, who is shown to be partial to Blacks, commits suicide the day after Musgrove is executed. Soon after Sonny's death, Hank, now on the road to Damascus, commits Buck to a retirement home. Damascus, of course, is his love affair with Leticia, who is Black, and his slow but steady acceptance of racial harmony. Hank learns that he is the executioner of Leticia's husband early in the film, but Leticia does not learn this until the film's final sequence when her husband's letter (the portraits he drew just before he was executed) finally arrives.

The execution sequence illustrates the effect of lost historiography and lost cartography as a crisis in the commons, what Negri and Hardt have theorized as capital's subsumption of the entire socius: the world as prison, the prison as world. Such subsumption has changed the dynamics of proletarian relationality almost to the point of obliterating proletarian history, foreclosing on its future and squeezing out the proletariat's last acre of the commons—that patch of autonomous greenery where one can map a zone of respite relatively free from the equation $S/v = C.$[5] In *Monster's Ball* this zone of respite from capitalist coercion has been deracinated by prison modalities at almost every level of civil society, all the way down to the scale of domesticity.

The absence of White women in Hank's household, along with the tombstones of Hank's wife and his mother in the backyard, leave the home wide open to the ravages of political society and all its force.[6] It is a symptom of Hardt's (and Negri's) warning that civil society is withering away.[7] As a result of the home's (domestic cartography's) having been deterritorialized by the absence of White femininity and by the invasion of the prison's coercive modalities of violence (the home as yet another lost zone of proletarian respite), Hank's body is marked as the primary site in the film where the drama of value is staged and contested. White femininity only enters the homosocial world of three generations of prison guards through Sonny's and Hank's brief encounters with the same prostitute and through Buck's defamatory recollections of Hank's wife and his mother (Buck's wife), "weak" figures who "failed" them both. Coercion, rather than consent, overdetermines the arc of the three men's filial encounters: fistfights instead of middle-class family feuds, armed assaults, and a living-room suicide by way of a revolver.

The execution sequence of *The Monster's Ball* is the only one in the entire film that brings together Hank, Sonny, Lawrence, Leticia, and Tyrell (Coronji Calhoun), the Musgroves' son, in the same ten minutes. It takes place less than thirty minutes into the film. If it does not prepare us emotionally for three necessary deaths (Lawrence Musgrove's, Sonny Grotowski's, and Tyrell Musgrove's), it at least foreshadows these deaths and hints at their necessity to the narrative, that is, to the thesis of the director, Marc Forster, on interracial love and redemption.

On Lawrence Musgrove's death walk, Sonny and his father, Hank, walk on either side of him. Lawrence's head has been shaved and the overall vestmentary code of the mise-en-scène—Lawrence in a thin, white T-shirt, with faded jeans with one pants leg cut off, wearing women's house slippers, flanked and followed by the crisp uniforms of the prison-industrial complex—coupled with the continued use of high-angle camera shots, mark Lawrence with diminished and, ultimately, fatal agency. But it bears repeating that Lawrence Musgrove is not *Monster's Ball*'s intended protagonist, Hank Grotowski is. At this point in the sequence a voice-over breaks in on the death walk. "It is ordered and adjudged that the judgment pronounced and set forth in this order, sentencing the defendant to death in a manner and by the authorities as provided by statute, shall be executed at this time."

As a generic strategy of cinematic form, voice-overs are commonly used in television commercials. For example, a White housewife or "woman-on-the-go" has just dramatized her endorsement of a product. Then, as the camera lingers on the final bit of her performance, a disembodied White male voice with the same lilt and enthusiasm she had for the product, but with a firm authority which she, supposedly, would not be capable of, re-endorses the product from his extradiegetic, godlike position of command and control.[8]

Whether the voice-over in *Monster's Ball* is diegetic or extradiegetic is a question I will take up presently. Assuming for the moment that it could be a diegetic voice (assuming that this was Forster's intention), then what becomes striking about this slice of the death walk is the asynchronic nature of the voice-over; that is, its status as sound "which belongs to the world of the image track, but which has a dislocated temporal relationship to the image track."[9]

What is so disorienting about the voice-over is that one assumes that it constitutes "the past in relation to the image," that it is the voice of the judge who has condemned Musgrove to die. But because the film starts *in medias res* we cannot be sure whether this asynchronic diegetic sound "is motivated by the subjective, psychological world of [the] characters, as part of their story space, or whether it exists as a narrator's comment on the characters [Lawrence, Sonny, and Hank] and/or the world they occupy"—which would make it asynchronic *and* extradiegetic. The uncertainty with respect to the space which motivates the voice-over leaves open the possibility that it can indeed be thought of as both asynchronic and extradiegetic. This would "liberate" the voice of the judge from a spatial fix: thus the source of his voice would not be in the world of the film, and the authority would be neither bound to nor threatened by the world of the film. It would mean that not only can the characters not hear the voice-over (hence its asynchronicity), but also that they have *never* heard it, "for it does not belong to their world but is directed at the audience alone." We know that "non-diegetic dialogue . . . in fiction film is unusual . . . because of the tendency to absorb everything into the narrative flow. . . . By definition, non-diegetic sound stands outside the narrativised image."[10] And Forster himself is on record as saying that cinematic sound must be subordinated to narrative. He suggested that the beauty of Asche's and Spencer's musical score lay in the fact that it did not draw attention to itself.[11] But is it possible that in this particular sequence, sound, in the form of this brief but disturbing voice-over, has not been subordinated to the narrative, that it is not only liberated from narrative but returns to police and incarcerate the diegesis and the auteur's intentions? Is some outside force exerting pressure on the story—a force that subdues the diegesis? So subdued by cinematic form is *Monster's Ball*'s storyline in this sequence that it seems as though the film is acting under some directional imperatives other than Forster's. There are profound implications for the commons when the voice of the law is a force external to the frame.

In this death walk, a White male voice-over (with the same authority but minus the lilt of sexist commercials) gives us the final word, as it were. But neither Hank nor Sonny nor the kind White guard with soft fat hands, nor Lawrence Musgrove for that matter, have endorsed these proceedings. The high-angle shots, the sacred, minimalist music score, and the somber, almost grieving, expression on everyone's faces mark them all as victims of this upcoming execution, reluctant participants to a man, coerced and diminished by its necessary rituals, capable (for the guards) of benefiting from this execution not by way of a "victims' rights" or "crime-free society" discourse which permeates so much of the Right's death-penalty arguments, but benefiting, if at all (and if *benefiting* is the right word), through ascendance to a transcendental afterlife cartography. It is a sad and spiritual death walk through which they suffer just as much as Lawrence: here, in this death walk, White and Black are crushed together under the anvil of cinematic form. Hank seems to suffer as much, if not more, than the condemned, and he is neither advertising nor promoting this suffering. His figure seems to be neither emboldened nor repaired by the death that is about to occur; rather, he endures it in anticipation (so the music would suggest) of spiritual redemption. Therefore, the voice-over functions as the pronouncement of a sentence for both Lawrence and Hank (and Sonny and the other guards), with one small caveat: Lawrence will be redeemed (to the extent that redemption can be imagined for Lawrence; his redemption seems strangely immaterial) when he is executed, whereas changing his ways will redeem Hank. And so the words "It is ordered and adjudged that the judgment pronounced and set forth in this order, sentencing the defendant to death in a manner and by the authorities as provided by statute: shall be executed at this time" intensify the hydraulics of suffering which Hank will spend the rest of the film trying to escape and which Sonny will only be relieved of by committing suicide.

The sentence of death is self-referential, for it need not specify who ordered and adjudged it—the state, or "the people" of Georgia?—and it is under no obligation to name either the defendant, the manner of death, the crime and its character, the authorities, or the date and time of death. It is as though these specifications are not only as extradiegetic and asynchronic to the death walk as the voice-over itself, but appear to be also timeless, generic, and ubiquitous, placing them beyond the limits of civil society, that is, beyond the populist and democratic interventions of both its minions and its representatives, locked, as they are, in the witness room of the death chamber.

The voice-over alerts us to the immanence of the state's command and control. The disembodied voice and the circuitous logic of the sentence mark yet another symptom of the postindustrial withering away of civil society. "The democratic and/or disciplinary institutions of civil society, the channels of social mediation, as a particular form of the organization of social labor, have declined and been displaced from the center of the scene. Not the State [the prison, the death chamber, the violence], but civil society [the home, the commons, the machinations of hegemony and its attendant institutionality] has withered away. . . . The social conditions necessary for civil society no longer exist." "The society we are living in today is more properly understood as a postcivil society."[12]

The voice-over's self-referential justification for violence, and the cavalier way in which the formal strategies of the execution sequence, and so much of the film, imagine no need for the state to display itself ethically for the idea of "justice" to emanate from the image track (be it the robed spectacle of a judge, or the common, civil, spectacle of a jury) mark cinema's late twentieth- and early twenty-first-century embrace of postcivil society's ethical dilemmas and its articulation of certain ontological touchstones of cohesion, namely, political economy's crisis of space and temporality, a crisis of the commons. But *Monster's Ball* pushes the envelope of this proletarian crisis more deliberately than do metacommentaries on the proletarian themselves. The film's formal cinematic strategies—here the disembodied voice-over—suggest that state power, which is to say state violence, exists in excess even to the embodied authority of the prison guards and their uniforms. Lawrence Musgrove is about to be executed, but it is Sonny's and Hank's death walk to which the film's formal strategies cathect us most. It is the horrific trauma of civil society, not simply the trauma of its withering away, as Hardt and Negri would have it, but of Hardt's and Negri's nightmare in full bloom, that interpellates our anxiety. We are engrossed in the drama that positions White men at the site of a double lack.[13] We are not engrossed in or interpellated by the anxiety of Lawrence Musgrove, who is not only suffering via the grammar of postcivil society but is also about to stop breathing. His dilemmas seem reasonable, banal, and unremarkable.

The double lack, then, is coded White: the voice-over not only lords its disembodied violence and authority over Sonny and Hank but, by way of intellectual montage, the cross-cut to the witness room, over a diverse ensemble of civil society's institutional representatives. In this the montage cuts between one death walk and another: from Sonny and Hank to the press, the clergy, the elected representative, those place-holders of the "intellectual function" formerly emblematic—in a Gramscian milieu of civil society—of a vibrant commons and a contested institutionality that stood in cartographic distinction (and sometimes revolutionary opposition) to the violent command and control modalities of the state which Gramsci called "political society" (police, prison, army).[14] Here, in the cross-cutting montage from an omnipotent state "voice," the organizers of hegemony are herded into the death chamber's witness room by the same disembodied authority to which they now, in Negri's and Hardt's postcivil dispensation, have as little access to and as little agency in the face of, as Hank and Sonny Grotowski, two lowly proletarians. Capital has incarcerated workers together with their organizers of, and capacity for, hegemonic struggle, those "processes [or that institutionality] . . . variously conceived as education, training, or discipline." It has incarcerated them in the command and control cartography of its self-referential violence and curtailed the possibility of "active engagement with social forces . . . within the context of institutions. What has come to an end . . . in postcivil society . . . [are the] functions of mediation or education and the institutions that gave them form." "The State today has moved beyond Hegel and his dialectic, not limiting but perfecting state rule."[15]

If the private and quotidian of civil society has been deterritorialized by the force of violence (the home subsumed by the prison), so too has the publicly acknowledged of civil society, the commons, been deterritorialized. Incarcerated in the witness room behind the glass of the execution chamber, without the capacity for speech, the symbolic representatives of civil society, assembled to observe Lawrence Musgrove's death, are literally in no position to act as either a check on, or balance against, the extradiegetic voice-over which we hear while watching Musgrove and company on his death walk. The voice-over's circuitous (il)logic signifies a virtual thumbing of the nose at the authority of civil society's symbolic representatives and, therefore, at any socially transformative optimism which had, in eras gone by, accrued to those representatives and their institutions within civil society.[16] That optimism can be traced historically from Gramsci's writings on a hegemonic war of position in *The Prison Notebooks*, to wartime labor solidarity in the United States and across the globe, to the euphoria of postcolonial struggles in the 1950s, 1960s, and 1970s, and up through New Left demands (in Paris, London, and the United States) in the 1960s and 1970s for civil society's expansion and the intensification of its promise of access. When one considers socially engaged White cinema of the 1960s and 1970s, especially the spate of fiction films produced in the wake of the Democratic Convention in Chicago (1968), the Weathermen's Days of Rage (1969), and the post–Kent State national student strike (1970), one sees how cinema of that period would lose all meaning without its faith in the power of a public voice as the linchpin of social transformation.[17]

But there exists today no such optimism, no such socially transformative public voice, and no grand illusions regarding social transformation that a film like *Monster's Ball*, which engages a phenomenon as vast and social as the prison-industrial complex, might embrace. Civil society as a public play and display of struggle and discontent, so alive in the sea of people surrounding Mario Savio at the University of California, Berkeley, in the public discourse surrounding the Pentagon Papers, in the rage after Kent State, and in the public indignation over Watergate, is lost on *Monster's Ball* in general and on Hank Grotowski in particular. My point is this: socially engaged White cinema can no longer articulate civil society's vast and collective ethical dilemmas. Hank Grotowski's ethical dilemmas seem to have fallen from the status of public agent to that of the prisoner. His prototypical dilemmas, once animated by the question *Where are we going?* (in films like *Medium Cool* [1970] and *Coming Home* [1978]), have been crowded out by a more urgent hydraulics of questions like *How do we break out?* For cinema, the power to pose the questions is withering away because, as Negri and Hardt have made so clear, civil society is withering away. Despite this nadir of articulation and articulateness, *Monster's Ball* "knows" something more than do director Marc Forster, White feminism and film theory, and Negri and Hardt. What *Monster's Ball* "knows," in spite of directorial intentionality and in spite of Negri's and Hardt's textual repression and disavowal, is that this debacle (civil society withering down past the scale of domesticity) can be neither imagined, nor thought, nor staged; that is to say, it cannot be made coherent without the Black. The coherence of a White grammar of suffering, even the spatial and temporal deracination of a heretofore robust civil cartography (whether the scene of a domestic commons or the scene of a public commons), cannot narrate its own devastation without calling on the Family Thanatos, that is, without devouring the flesh of Leticia, Lawrence, and Tyrell.

This is true even as the film ratchets the ethical dilemmas of civil society down a notch *below* domesticity, to the scale of the body. Again, throughout *Monster's Ball*, civil society's autonomous cartography, its liberated zone, is much smaller, more private and quotidian than it has ever been in the history of socially engaged White cinema. In fact, the map has been reduced to the oral zone of the mouth, through which Hank is only "free" to suck chocolate ice cream with a white plastic spoon, or, interchangeably, to suck Leticia's vagina under white cotton sheets. The map has been reduced to the ocular zone of the eyes, through which Hank gazes as he meticulously paints the letters "L-e-t-i-c-i-a" on what he tells her is "our" sign above "our" gas station. Civil society, if it can be found at all in what Negri and Hardt call a postindustrial world, no longer flourishes and assembles in the public spaces which hegemony had once territorialized as discursive (i.e., the street, the stump, the union hall, the square, the home) but rather finds itself under permanent lockdown, deterritorialized by command, coercion, and force (as though lost somewhere in Guantánamo, awaiting trial). Such is the fate of civil society's organizers of hegemony, locked as they are inside the prison, in the witness room of the death chamber. The only temporal capacity left to the worker is to be found not in a living heritage of wildcat strikes, public speeches in the square, consciousness-raising meetings, and the like, but in the simple memory of last night's pleasures: the taste of chocolate ice cream, the vision of a coffee-colored woman's body, the gaze on the large black font that spells her name, the touch (and taste) of cunnilingus, and the memory of penetration between her legs.

That which can still be mapped with civil society's cartographic integrity and remembered in its historiographic integrity no longer exists (has no guaranteed coherence) at the scale of domesticity but rather has been reduced to the scale of corporeal integrity. In point of fact, the scenario is even bleaker, for in Negri's and Hardt's postindustrial world, the body, in its reified form as "gender" and "race," can no longer be thought of as a liberated zone, though it is still a contested zone.[18] In a socius that has withered away and become a prison, the last coordinate of spatial and temporal capacity, the last sanctuary of civil society—in that it remains (or can still be imagined as) a coherent vector of "civil" space and time—is the body. And this is something *Monster's Ball* is well aware of. Hank Grotowski's job site and his home are those spaces of work and domesticity where contingent violence is no longer guaranteed; so complete is their postindustrial deracination that they have become vulnerable to gratuitous violence. His *body*, however, is another matter altogether. Here coherence and optimism can be maintained. The body, then, of Hank Grotowski gives both radical feminism and film theory (Butler, Seshadri-Crooks, Silverman, Doane, et al.) and iconoclastic Marxism (Negri and Hardt) a terrain where their assumptive logic can still resonate. The resonance, however, does not bring about an ideological, methodological, or aesthetic (or, for that matter, a conscious) suture between them. It is a rhetorical resonance (symptomatic of a structural kinship) through which all of these discourses know that even in the crisis of a postindustrial world they still have something coherent to hold on to. How, exactly, do they know what they know given the disparate nature of their discourses? How does one know that though the commons may no longer exist, there are still bodies in the world? I maintain that this knowledge of bodies, however peripheral and unconscious, is sustained through the presence of flesh.

Both radical and feminist film theory, on the one hand, and unflinching Marxism, on the other, are rigorous and correct: the body is still a contested terrain—Hank Grotowski is cinematic "proof" of their rigor and insight. But what are Leticia, Lawrence, and Tyrell Musgrove proof of? To put it more crudely, why must Hank Grotowski map, remember, contest, and recompose his body by feeding on Black flesh? In short, the film's ethical dilemmas (interracial love, the burgeoning of the prison-industrial complex, capital punishment, the generative crises in filiation, and the ennui of White masculinity in the twenty-first century) require, for their coherence and animation, the repetition of necrophilic acts: ice cream consumption, cunnilingus, sign-gazing, body gazing, strip-searching, head-shaving, electrocution—death. Through the figure of

Hank, *Monster's Ball* positions the spectator both "as photographer and cannibal." Here "scopophilia and negrophobia come together" so that the flesh of the Black might sustain and rejuvenate the body of the proletarian. But were Blacks to treat the cinematic image "as a mirror (as a point of identification)" they would find that their "face is missing, displaced by a heavily loaded racial icon or figurehead," connected only "to a history of drawn-out abasement." "As the *sign of polluting infection*," Leticia, Lawrence, and Tyrell "can be ripped open and consumed—that is, framed by the eye, taken into the mouth because, in essence, they represent the place where the shame and nausea produced by excreta becomes visible. . . . As reeking tombs in the public life of culture, [they] can be cannibalised, shredded and torn open because, like the living dead, they are imagined as vicious and parasitic, insatiably feeding off the lives of their living, white hosts."[19] We can extend David Marriott's observations by stating that the White parasitism which devours Black flesh, even as it imagines and lives in dread of Black aggression, is the social performance of a structural violence which allows Whites to be entities capable of contesting this or that drama of value. But to say that the flesh of Leticia (or Halle Berry), Lawrence (or Sean Combs), and Tyrell (or Coronji Calhoun) are essential to the White body's drama of value does not mean that this trio, this Family Thanatos, is also among the disparate entities that contest this drama. It means, quite simply, that three pieces of dead meat can start and sustain a story.

This parasitic necessity reveals itself through the contrapuntal gestures of the film's cinematic form, gestures accumulated and sustained profoundly against the imposition of dialogue during the execution sequence. The editing strategies of this sequence allow the structure of U.S. antagonisms, the impossibility of positional relations between Master and Slave, to break in on the film even though the narrative strategies before and after this sequence "argue" tenaciously, if not anxiously, in favor of the possibility of such relations, an argument underwritten by the ubiquitous inspiration of the personal pronoun *we* and by a universalizing mise-en-scène in which disparate entities are staged in dramas of value.

Like a weed, this inspiration chokes the terrain of Western cultural and political common sense. It is an inspiration that underwrites discourses as far afield as film reviews in newspapers and magazines, film theory, screenplays, and White metacommentaries on the grammar of suffering. At every scale of nearly every genre of social meditation on value and its drama, the personal pronoun *we* assumes a fetishized and hypothesized value-form. Simply put, Humankind is taken as a given. Its reification as a rhetorical commodity goes something like this: Through symbolic interventions all people are capable, have the capacity, of transformation and recomposition. This change-power, this subjective transformation and recomposition, happens over time and across space. *We*, then, registers in cultural discourse, albeit superficially, as in *we* all have a language, *we* all have customs, *we* all can dream of home, *we* all have families, *we* all have a heritage, *we* all have a place of origin. The inspiration of *we* is a Humanizing inspiration. It welcomes all to the family of (wo)man except the Family Thanatos.

From *Monster's Ball* itself, to its reviews, to White film theory and the ontological meditations of Negri and Hardt, the textual attitudes, as regards this "universal" capacity and its hypostasized value-form *we* are as disparate as the form and content of the various discourses themselves. For example, the screenplay of *Monster's Ball* is wildly delusional about the project of racial redemption and the prospect of reconciliation. White film theory, in contrast, spans from its political optimism of the 1970s and 1980s to an archive of the 1990s and early twenty-first century that can only be characterized as a kind of political refraction. The 1970s and 1980s was a period in which White film theory sought more than to merely understand cinema but also change "our" receptivity to it and inspire a demand for alternative cinematic practices. In an effort to give some shape to the period's film theory archive, Mary Ann Doane draws our attention to "the intense methodological consciousness of film and literary theory in [the 1970s and 1980s]. This hyperawareness of position and method was an effect of the structuralist, semiotic, and poststructuralist movements which generated the most exciting and intellectually radical cultural work of this period."[20] White film theory's political refraction of the last fifteen years all but sidelined the "awareness of position and method" dominant in the 1970s and 1980s and its desire to radically change the material and ideological construction of culture. Rather than wielding film theory as though it were a neo-Marxist, materialist historiographic, or radical feminist weapon, White film theory's political mandate splintered in so many directions that it no longer resembled a mandate.

The (White) female spectator, once the sine qua non of a subversive subject position, came to be considered "a category now exhausted or superceded . . . and feminist film theory [came to be] seen as tiresome and repetitive." Rather than try to coalesce around, be assimilated by, or attempt to accompany macrosocial dreams of structural disturbance, White film theory since the 1990s broke itself down into bite-sized desires and embarked on reflections of cinema which tried to "account for [what its practitioners thought to be] a more flexible and expansive understanding" of the subject of speech within the diegesis, "as well as issues of race and gender in [the institutionality of] cinema."[21] Despite my weakness for "position and method" over identity and play, my point, as regards the Slave and White film theory, is not one which finds an "ally" in the political ambitions of psychoanalytic and materialist film theory feminists of the 1970s and 1980s, or an "enemy" in the political refracton of postmodern film theory feminists who locate cinema within what they believe to be a more complex matrix of contending identities, impulses, voices, and sensibilities. The milestones along that thirty-year road of transition, from the two-fisted modernism of White film theory's interventionist agenda to its recent reinvigoration—or ennui, depending on one's perspective—are important enough to have been well documented.[22] These differences, however, maintain between them an uncanny solidarity in relation to the "estate of slavery."[23] That solidarity is evidenced by the fact that the Slave remains unthought, foreclosed by the inspiration of we. The Slave is assumed to have been liberated and now is assumed to function like any other disparate entity in the drama of value.

The assumptive logic of this multifaceted, superficial, and commonsense deployment of we is itself supported by a more rigorous and ontological pair of assumptions, regardless of the fact that its commonsense and aesthetic adherents cannot articulate such assumptions. The assumptions can be summed up by this statement: "We" are all imbued with spatial and temporal capacity. Thus, the ground zero of communal inspiration (assumptions shared by the narrative strategies of Monster's Ball, local film reviews, White film theory, and Marxist meditations on the grammar of suffering) is a kind of faith in the subject's ability to, in the first ontological instance, possess spatial and temporal capacity, and, in the second experiential instance, shape or contest cartographic and historiographic coherence (i.e., to be present anthropologically and historically, to be a cultural being). But it is bad faith. For it is this more rigorous and ontological pair of supports that the Black destroys or, more accurately, that the Black "gives" his or her flesh to. White film, in rare moments of narrative exile or neglect, may be the only kind of White discourse that destroys (unintentionally but nonetheless empathically) its own pair of ontological supports.

Of course, if White cinema's destruction of the logic of *we* was not in some way pleasurable, that is to say, if the cinematography's destruction of civic access did not simultaneously feed the unconscious and guilty pleasures derived from beating, mutilating, murdering, caressing, or eating the Black, then White cinema would not be able to function as a cultural accompaniment to the ethical dilemmas of White suffering—its trajectory of subversion would reach a point of no return; it would be useless to civil society and become, *ipso facto*, Black cinema. It might ultimately betray its own dilemmas, namely exploitation and alienation, and articulate the ensemble of questions catalyzed by accumulation and fungibility. In my discussion of *Antwone Fisher* and *Bush Mama*, I explained why such a trajectory is rarely sustained for the length of a single film, even when Blacks control the level of enunciation, the cinematic apparatus; furthermore, in those rare instances when it seems that a complete film can be dubbed Black (that is, shown to accompany the ethical dilemmas of the Slave from beginning to end), such films were generally produced in a period when the Slave had burned down much of urban America (1967–71) or when underground cells of groups like the Black Liberation Army targeted police (1971–81). Given these constraints and conditions for being able to think film as Black, to think film as subversive, my project is not to cathedralize the political wisdom of *Monster's Ball* but rather to remark on its "telling" moments.

Now, Lawrence Musgrove writes his last letter to Leticia. He sits on his death row bed, sketching first Sonny and then Hank. The execution sequence lasts eight to ten minutes and breaks with the more established patterns of the film's formal cinematic conventions. To begin with, through a series of rapid cuts and the foregrounding of its otherwise underscored soundtrack,[24] this particular sequence proves itself to be as void of dialogue as the infamous sex scene between Hank and Leticia. Again, it is also the only moment in *Monster's Ball* when Sonny, Hank, Leticia, Lawrence, and Tyrell are all brought together for a sustained period of time. During the execution sequence, the "disparate entities"[25] of this unlikely collective are not brought into relation with one another by way of narrative (or dialogue), or even a shared mise-en-scène, but by way of cross-cutting at the beginning of the sequence (between the prison where Lawrence prepares to die and the home where Leticia and Tyrell wait in vain for his call) and by intellectual and emotional montage toward the end of the sequence (after his death walk, when the images collide back and forth among Lawrence Musgrove, "his" chair, the representatives of civil society watching him from their chairs, and the apparatus of death being pushed and pulled) (see figures 15 and 16).

Though the cuts between home and prison are paced more swiftly than the cuts in other parts of the film, in the beginning of the sequence they are not swift enough to suppress the dialogue. Seated on the sofa, Leticia and Tyrell are captured by the camera's high-angle shot, connotative of diminished agency, with bodies either disempowered or on the brink of mishap.[26] Leticia discovers chocolate on Tyrell's lip and flies into a rage. She drags him into his bedroom and verbally and physically degrades him. She berates him for being fat and tells him that the chaotic and disastrous spectacle of his bedroom came about "'Cause a fat little piggy lives in this room!" Later in the film, after both Lawrence and Tyrell have been killed, the narrative can proceed toward interracial sex and social redemption from which the optimism of its socially transformative agenda derives so much pride and pleasure. As screenwriter Milos Addica put it: "The story doesn't work if the child doesn't die. . . . [We were] adamant about the boy had [*sic*] to die. We tried to change it to make the boy live, but it wasn't working. . . . The story we wrote becomes pointless if the child doesn't die."[27] In other words, "not only is Leticia's husband executed, but *her son must also die* as the precondition for her new life with her husband's executioner. And the death requirement is rendered as a romance."[28]

To wit, Leticia is beating Tyrell against a mise-en-scène of chaos, the bedroom of "a fat little piggy," and Lawrence is sketching portraits against

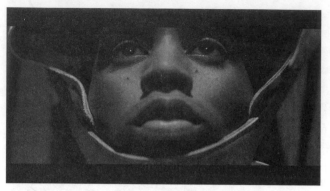

15   Extreme close-up of Lawrence Musgrove in the electric chair,
in a scene from *Monster's Ball*

16   White woman in the witness box (with Lawrence in glass reflection)

the mise-en-scène of death row. The film establishes Tyrell as fat: ex-
panding, dirty, and disorganized, a contagion, the burden of disease on
Leticia. Here the effect of the narrative together with the image track
establishes Tyrell as Black, dirty, a threat without boundaries, a Black
plague in waiting. Contrary to the political and social claims of Forster
and the screenwriters Addica and Rokos, there is no parallel between
the ethical dilemmas of the Grotowski household and those of Leticia's
home. It is true that the narrative insists on the parallelism of Sonny's and
Tyrell's deaths, as if to say both families must experience the death of the
son, a death in the family, in order for the parents to realize a forbidden
but joyous union and the promise of a new world.

But Sonny disturbs Hank intellectually. Sonny's attitude toward the prison is ambiguous, and that ambiguity threatens the coherence of Hank's own institutional commitment. Sonny's relationship to Blacks, to Black children at least, threatens Hank's idea of his place in the world. Sonny dies but his ensemble of questions, the ethical dilemmas posed by his rejection of the prison, his liaison with Black kids, and his suicide, live on and become hegemonic. Sonny is offered, by the film, as a moral challenge to Hank and, by extension, to the rigidity of Southern civil society.

Tyrell, in contrast, is not beaten and berated for the threat he poses to Leticia's ideas. Part of the reason for this is that the film intuits what Hank's father tells Leticia, to her face: she is a "nigger." And as such, she cannot be imagined, cinematically, as having ideas to be challenged. True, Leticia is "our" nigger (the spectator's nigger), whereas Tyrell is just "a" nigger. She is "our" nigger in the sense that to "mulattas" (and "mulattos") accrues a certain pride of place in civil society. But that pride of place does not transform "mullatas" into addressees of civil society, nor into the means for it to organize its hegemony. In addition, and more to Forster's narrative conceit of parallelism, the articulateness and capacity for ideas, convictions, thoughts, or even complex feelings accrue to Tyrell even less than they do to Leticia. His waddling from room to room, his constant wheezing, his voracious and indiscriminate appetite, and his room, suggestive of a site in need of quarantine, connote neither moral superiority nor progressive intellectualism. Tyrell is offered, by the film, as a bodily threat to Leticia and, by extension, to the world. Sonny is the specter of a subject that questions and haunts; Tyrell is the specter of a phobic object. The film's cinematic unconscious is well aware of this schism between the living and the dead, for whereas both sons die, only one of them is treated to a funeral scene, and it is not Tyrell.

Leticia pushes Tyrell onto the scale, he weighs 180 pounds, she elbows him in the stomach, he squeals, doubles over, falls to the bed, sobbing. Now she holds him and consoles him. "Come on," she says, "let's go wait for your Daddy to call." Once Leticia's tirade against Tyrell is over, the film cuts back to death row and the execution sequence starts to move at a more rapid pace, in that "cinematic coherence and plentitude emerge through multiple cuts and negations" and the space of the frame becomes more and more claustrophobic.[29] In other words, the hydraulics of this crisp and swift editing exert a crowding-out pressure on the use of dialogue as a narrative strategy. The credo of the director, Marc Forster, that music (and, implicitly, other formal elements of cinema) should always remain subordinate to the narrative[30] is grossly neglected during the execution sequence. The effect of what I am calling narrative neglect is important here for it hobbles the film's ability to easily jettison a "guilt complex" which White cinema often manages to jettison. As a result, the film can be "written" by an otherwise impermissible knowledge. "There is first of all a sadistic aggression toward the black man, followed by a guilt complex because of the sanction against such behavior by the democratic culture of the country in question." This "sadistic aggression," Fanon informs us, is structural, in that without it Whites could not be positioned as Whites;[31] but the "sanction against such behavior" by a "democratic culture" turns this structural violence into an impermissible knowledge—at least at the level of a film's narrative intentions. This impermissible knowledge is knowledge of the necessity of necrophilia in the maintenance of civil society and for White ontological coherence. But the narrative throughout most films, including *Monster's Ball*, represses it. My claim here is that what the execution sequence "knows" about White ontology (its sustenance of "sadistic aggression") is also repressed by Marxist metacommentaries on the grammar of suffering (Negri and Hardt) and by film theory.

The cut from Tyrell's bedroom is to a brief shot of the witness room. It is empty, separated from the empty electric chair by a huge glass window. Before the viewer becomes unbearably anxious about from what position the shot is being observed, the shot-to-reverse-shot technique kicks in and the camera pans the death chamber and its electric chair. This panning shot comes to rest on a microphone plugged into a modest acoustic console near the electric chair. In this shot the witness room remains unpopulated. We cut back to Lawrence Musgrove having his head shaved by a pair of White hands with fingers fat as bratwursts. These White hands are softly, and "classically" lit in what is known as a "three-point system consisting of a primary light (the key), giving general illumination of the figure, a second, softer light (the *fill*), eliminating some of the shadows created by the key . . . and *backlighting*, which serves to keep the figure separate from the background as well as creating . . . the rim and halo effects of heroic and glamour lighting." The three-point lighting system, by which Forster's cinematography illuminates these large White hands, is most commonly used to "construct the characteristic glow of white women" in cinema. The blending of three points of light imbues the White woman with a soft, unified look which suggests "she inhabits . . . a space of transcendence." Curiously enough, however, both Lawrence Musgrove, the official condemned, and the guards who are shaving his head (not only free agents in relation to Musgrove, but agents of the state's repressive apparatus) are positioned together as diminished, captured agency, fixed as it were by the film's high camera angles and sacred musical score. Given this common location, and given Musgrove's centrality to the ritual, why is his Black face not graced with the three-point blend of transcendent light, whereas the hands of his captor are? Richard Dyer reminds us that in most films the characteristic glow of White women is typically contrasted against the "dark masculine desire" of the White male lead. He goes on to say that, historically, "under the pressure of war propaganda," this dark masculine desire "would also have been felt as racially other."[32]

Monster's Ball's transcendent lighting of White hands in contrast with the banal lighting of the Black face, on the one hand, coupled with the immanence of the sacred music and the way all of the figures are captured by the high-angle shot, on the other hand, are symptomatic of the fact that shared experiences in the realm of the social do not necessarily index shared positions in the realm of the structural. There is a crisis in the commons, a social reality which Black Lawrence Musgrove experiences together with White prison guards: prison and the death penalty diminish the lives of guards, inmates, and civil society's organizers of hegemony (the people who will be seated in the witness room). As Michael Hardt writes: "My life too is structured through disciplinary regimes." The prison's walls have become a phenomenon permeating the private and quotidian of the socius "separating us from our desires, isolating us from contact, prohibiting encounters, seem[ing] to make love impossible." Subsequently, "the sexual deprivation that is one of the center-pieces of the prison regime is only indicative of a more general deprivation of affect." Hardt argues that everyone in this postindustrial milieu, inmate, guard, organizer of hegemony—in short, the entire commons—suffers a common "exile from affect."[33] The common capture of bodies by the high camera angles (Leticia and Tyrell on the couch waiting for Lawrence to call; Lawrence and his captors in the cell and on the death walk) attests to this "general deprivation of affect" and to everyone's suffering the social experience of "prison time." But the three-point blend of light that deifies the White hands shaving a Black head, given its almost exclusive history as an accompaniment to White femininity, is symptomatic of a structural antagonism rarely acknowledged socially.

Hardt is wrong to assume that the "general deprivation of affect," experienced by everyone, has a social *and* an ontological impact, and that it positions everyone as a member of the exploited and alienated multitude simply because it makes everyone *feel* affectively deprived. Within an ontological relation, Lawrence Musgrove (and Leticia and Tyrell) exists "under the pressure of war" in his structural, as opposed to social, relation to Hank Grotowski and the organizers of civil society's hegemony.[34] But the structural violence of this war has no discernable social discourse, no official "propaganda" of "sadistic aggression."[35] Over the past five hundred years, Hank Grotowski (and his colleagues' soft White hands) has *officially* declared war on Native Americans, on the ruling class, on Mexico (1838), Spain, Vietnam, Germany, Afghanistan, and Iraq, to name but a few;[36] but he has never declared war on the Blacks. How could he? Who are they? Where is the Black terrain? And yet . . .

The ritual continues as the soft wooly tufts of Musgrove's hair fall gently to the floor. Now the shot cuts to another pair of compassionate White hands holding a pair of scissors and cutting one leg of his trousers off at the knee. The same hands then shave his leg from the ankle up to the knee. This "compassionate" head- and leg-shaving will allow the electricity to conduct itself from head to toe with greater ease and burn the necessary organs without burning unnecessary hair.

The religiosity of the musical score marks these garment- and body-shaving shots with a kind of transcendent spirituality infinitely more sublime than the transcendence of the large but soft and gentle White hands, were those hands to be abandoned to their own soundless image. And yet, again, as the shot commences, what is most striking is not the musical accompaniment (which becomes apparent in a rather delayed way) but the mark of the condemned which all of the figures—Musgrove as well as his captors—are forced, by the high-angle shot, to bear. Negri and Hardt would find solace here, for it confirms their thesis that civil society is withering away for everyone (regardless of race) and that for the past thirty years of postindustrial death everyone's lives, whether Black or White, have been subsumed by the temporality of prison time. As Hardt puts it:

> Inmates live prison as an exile from life, or rather, from the time of living. . . . The weight of destiny, the fate imposed by the sovereign power of prison time seems to have pushed them out of their bodies, out of existence altogether. . . . Those who are free . . . might imagine their own freedom defined and reinforced in opposition to prison time. When you get close to prison, however, you realize that it is not really a site of exclusion, separate from society, but rather a focal point, the site of the highest concentration of a logic of power that is generally diffused throughout the world. Prison is our society in its most realized form. . . . My life too is structured through disciplinary regimes, my days move on with a mechanical repetitiveness—work, commute, tv, sleep. I do not have the same physical discomfort or the sexual deprivation, but even without the walls and bars my life ends up being strangely similar. . . . I live prison time in our free society, exiled from living.[37]

Hardt might blanch at my suggestion that his meditations on the lost time and space of proletarian ontology are predicated on the same rhetorical scaffolding as Marc Forster's faux racial politics. Nonetheless, there is "a stunning mutuality"[38] between what *Monster's Ball* intends and what Hardt assumes. The screenplay of *Monster's Ball* offers Hank Grotowski's devastated life as cinematic proof that "when you get close to prison . . . you realize that it is not really a sight of exclusion": the close-up shots of Hank's face as he walks with Lawrence to the electric chair, fastens his arms to the arms of the chair, and tightens the screws that fasten the wires to the skull cap on Musgrove's head, are images of pain, of Humane reluctance clashing with the superego of senseless duty: his is the face of exploitation and alienation unto death. And then he pulls the switch.

Prison, Hardt writes, "is not really a site of exclusion, separate from society, but rather . . . the site of the highest concentration of a logic of power that is generally diffused throughout the world." This diffusion throughout the world not only imposes prison time on the homosocial domesticity of the Grotowski home, but it also puts an otherwise vibrant and democratic civil society on permanent lockdown. The only moment in the film when civil society's organizers of hegemony are featured occurs during this execution sequence, as the scene cuts from the sacred religiosity of Lawrence Musgrove's being shaved to a midlevel shot of a White female prison guard standing in a short narrow hallway as though wedged there. She stands next to the door. She holds a clipboard and checks the security tags of various people who represent institutions of civil society (e.g., the press, the clergy). One by one she admits them into the witness room where they remain speechless behind the glass for the remainder of the scene.

As Forster and Hardt would have it, all of civil society lives "prison time in our free society." Everyone is exiled from the time of life. And so, regardless of how much Hardt's revolutionary Marxism may disapprove of Forster's liberal humanism, they share a set of structural assumptions that grants them ontological coherence: Grotowski, like Hardt's proletariat, has been "exiled from living." Not only does he suffer from the grammar of capitalism's basic modalities of exploitation—the intensification of work and the extraction of surplus value—but he endures the hyperalienation of prison time. The structure of their descriptive gestures is the same: exploitation and alienation, by way of capitalist exploitation, intensified by carceral temporality imposed on the proletariat during the last thirty years of globalization. Both the film and the metacommentary assert "that prison time lies at the heart of our social order, and that its destruction is the condition for any revolution"—whether individuated (*Monster's Ball*) or collective (Marxism). In short, both the film and the ontological meditation see the prison as "the paradigm for punishment" consisting of "the loss of [a] most precious asset" which both Forster and Hardt believe *we* all possess equally: time.[39] Subsequently, their prescriptive gestures also correspond, in that for both Forster and Hardt the politics of social and ontological intervention, respectively, turn on the idea of redemption. Hank Grotowski must be socially redeemed and the proletariat must be ontologically redeemed. Put another way, the time of life must be redeemed from the time of prison.

In *Monster's Ball*, living time is redeemed from prison time by the power of love, the liberal humanist "event," rendered aesthetically through the character arc: the Southern racist's refusal of hate and his self-abandonment to the amorous embrace of the Other. Also enabled by the power of the amorous, Hardt's living time is redeemed from prison time through the "event" of revolutionary love, ontologically rendered through "the continuous movement of constituent power" manifest in Hardt's prescription to embrace and transpose Jean Genet's "project" of "saintliness."[40] In *Empire*, Negri and Hardt ground this notion of a common, constituent power in their belief that the postindustrial "abstract and transcendental" evolution of private property coincides with the recomposition of the proletariat into a global, "more radical and profound commonality than has ever been experienced in the history of capitalism."[41] They call this recomposed, radical, and profound commonality, which has been elaborated in the last twenty to thirty years of capitalist exploitation and alienation, "the multitude."

> Just as Empire in the spectacle of its force continually determines systemic recompositions, so too new figures of resistance are composed through the sequences of the events of struggle. This is another fundamental characteristic of the existence of the multitude today, *within* Empire and *against* Empire. New figures of struggle and new subjectivities are produced in the conjuncture of events, in the universal nomadism [here Negri and Hardt are referring to the exponential rise in the number of refugees among Third World people during globalization], in the general mixture and miscegenation of individuals and populations, and in the technological metamorphoses of the imperial biopolitical machine. . . . [Those who comprise the multitude] express, nourish, and develop positively their own constituent projects; they work toward the liberation of living labor, creating constellations of powerful singularities. . . . The multitude is the real productive force of our social world, whereas Empire is a mere apparatus of capture that lives only off the vitality of the multitude—as Marx would say, a vampire regime of accumulated dead labor that survives only by sucking off the blood of the living.[42]

And on the terrain of empire (a terrain on which private property is more and more abstract and transcendental, a terrain of communicative and interactive production) "a new notion of [the] 'commons' will have to emerge" from the "constituent projects" of the multitude, their "liberation of living labor."[43] According to Hardt, "a new species of political activist has been born" of the multitude, "paradoxical" in its "idealism" in that its

> realistic course of action today is to demand what is seemingly impossible, that is, something new. [The constituent projects of the multitude] do not provide a practical blueprint for how to solve problems, and we should not expect that of them. They seek rather to transform the public agenda by creating political desires for a better future. . . . One of the most remarkable characteristics of these movements is their diversity: trade unionists together with ecologists together with priests and Communists. These movements evoke the openness—toward new kinds of exchange and new ideas.[44]

The emergence of a new notion of the commons, a transformed "political agenda" by way of the creation of "political desires for a better future," is Negri's and Hardt's dream for the transformation of capitalist cartography: the redemption of prison space. It goes hand in hand with Hardt's specific dream for new "common names" by way of Genet's saintly project for the redemption of prison time—his "simple affirmation . . . [that] we still do not know what bodies can do."[45] For Hardt, Genet's "divinity" lies in his "revealing our common power to constitute reality, to constitute being. The power of creation, the power to cause our own existence, is divine. . . . If we recognize what is common to [the prisoner's] body and our own, if we discover the way [the prisoner's] body agrees with our own and how our bodies together compose a new body [the multitude recomposed from the worker], we can ourselves cause that joyful encounter to return [hence the emancipatory "event"]."[46]

For Forster's individual and Hardt's multitude—both subsumed by prison time—the "event" or "encounter" in which time is redeemed is inextricably bound in the subject's capacity to be transformed, socially (Forster) and ontologically (Hardt), by abandoning subjectivity to, in the words of Genet, "one long mating, burdened and complicated by a heavy, strange, erotic ceremonial."[47] "And love is the driving force in this constitution [of a new body, the multitude]. The organization of joyful encounters is the increase in our power, our power to act and power to exist. . . . This eternal return to the joyful encounter is a constitution of being, not in the sense that it fixes an immobile identity (far from it), but rather in that it defines a movement, a becoming, a trajectory of encounters,

17 Medium close-up of Lawrence with a White man reflected in the glass
of the death chamber

always open and unforeseeable, continuously susceptible to the intervention of the new events. The return of the joyful encounter is the first
thread from which we will weave an alternative constituent time."[48]

Lest the structural correlation between Hank's susceptibility "to the
intervention of the new events" (his liaison with Leticia) and that same
susceptibility of the multitude, found in Hardt's and Negri's work, be
read as an agreement between *Monster's Ball* and Marxism at the level
of the social, we should bear in mind Hardt's and Negri's contrariness
when confronted with the politics of individuated liberation. "Outside
of a materialist, collective, and dynamic conception of time it is impossible to conceive of revolution";[49] which is to say, the social effect of
Forster's amorous interracial dream cannot have a structural impact on
Hank Grotowski in his capacity as a member of the multitude. Thus, for
Hardt, *Monster's Ball*'s social politics would be weak at best, reactionary at worst. I would agree with Hardt, but it is my task here to add that
the structural impact of Hardt's and Negri's amorous dream shakes not
one pillar on the Slave estate and in fact strengthens, along with Forster's
dream, the Slave estate's foundation. *Monster's Ball* does, however, pose
the question of redemption both in terms of Hank's individuated amorous event, his liaison with Leticia, and in terms of Hardt's constituent
(collective) revolutionary event, the problems posed by both the image
of civil society's organizers of hegemony trapped behind the glass of the
death chamber's witness room and by the gathering of guards suffering
on death row (see figure 17). What is essential, however, is that the power

to pose the question is dependent and parasitic on Black presence, while, simultaneously, the Black is barred from the questions raised.

From the organizers of hegemony locked behind the glass of the witness room, we cut back to Lawrence, the guards, and the preparatory rituals. The opening shot here is cropped in such a way that a headless White guard appears. He is helping the condemned put on his diaper. Like the high-angle shot toward the beginning of this montage, the acephalous subjectivity of the prison guard positions him so that he shares with Lawrence Musgrove, not the fate of physical death, but the fate of social death. It is as if they are positioned, both White guard and Black inmate, by "a fatal way of being alive."[50]

The execution sequence, through a swift succession of compilation shots (spliced together to give a quick impression of the place where the rituals of shaving and diapering take place), cross-cuts Leticia and Tyrell at home; Lawrence, Hank, and Sonny; and the sketches Lawrence has drawn. It then shifts back and forth among the sacred shearing, the witness room, the hallway, the incarceration of civil society's assemblage, and the electric chair itself. It moves us through the death walk during which Sonny vomits, doubles over, and so takes himself out of the proceedings, all the way to the execution itself and the final cut, which brings us back to the Musgrove residence where Leticia is now alone, brushing her teeth (the image of her face split in two between a normal medicine-cabinet mirror and a magnifying mirror that extends out from the wall; see figure 18). On the face of it, the argument of the sequence appears to be in tandem with the ontological assumptive logic that I have suggested, shared by both the aesthetic gestures of White cinema and meta-commentaries on proletarian ontology. In other words, *Monster's Ball*, through the intentionality of its screenplay, seeks agreement with the assumptive logic of Negri, Hardt, film theory, and the plethora of critical attention the film received in local newspapers and magazines; its narrative suggests that, though the experience of suffering varies from person to person (some folks get executed while others grow morose at the thought of execution), the grammar of suffering is universal because a carceral modality now permeates the commons. As Hardt would have it: "My life too is structured through disciplinary regimes. . . . I live prison time in our free society, exiled from living."

18 Leticia in a mirror, in a scene from *Monster's Ball*

Again, accompanying those discourses, which assume a universal grammar of suffering (White film, metacommentaries on ontology, film theory, and film reviews) is a prescriptive political common sense vested in shared convictions regarding the socially transformative power of symbolic action, a notion that the effects of symbolic action can have the impact of a structural intervention powerful enough to liberate the subject positionally. At the end of this socially transformative trajectory, the subject is recomposed and redeemed—in a word, liberated.[51]

Who Took the *Form* Out of Transformative?

Again, throughout the history of film theory, alternative cinema has been held out as the exemplar of the socially transformative trajectory alluded to above. For example, the assumptive logic undergirding the descriptive gestures of much of Kaja Silverman's work has "challenged the phallic identification upon which masculinity depends by insisting upon the lack at the heart of all subjectivity, and by isolating historical trauma as a force capable of unbinding the coherence of the male ego, and exposing the abyss that it conceals."[52] Here, as I argued in chapter 2, alienation is posited not as a negative modality but simply as what happens when the *infans* becomes a subject (your money or your life, as Lacan would say). "The lack," as it were, "at the heart of all subjectivity" is marked by the subject's being given over to the symbolic order and being barred from access to the real, until she or he dies. Exploitation, in this instance, is manifest in what, for Silverman, would amount to Hardt's "prison time," a temporality incarcerated by the "phallic . . . coherence of the male ego," which is manifest most emphatically for Silverman in the hegemony of Hollywood cinema, and for Hardt in the subsumption of civil society by the postindustrial command modalities of capitalism.

Subtending Silverman's descriptive logic one finds a prescriptive gesture—her contribution to a large ensemble of socially transformative trajectories—namely, alternative cinema: celluloid as a time and space vector that can approximate "historical trauma [and here the verb *approximate* is essential, for Silverman makes clear in her opening chapters her nonviolent intentions toward White men] as a force capable of unbinding the coherence of the male ego, and exposing the abyss that it conceals." Silverman locates her political optimism for a socially transformative aesthetics in the countercinema of Rainer Werner Fassbinder. She applauds

> Fassbinder's radical refusal to *affirm*, his repudiation of positivity in any shape or form[,] . . . his aversion to the fictions which make psychic and social existence tolerable. . . . What happens within Fassbinder's cinema is that both the gaze and the images which promote identity remain irreducibly exterior, stubbornly removed from the subject who depends upon them for its experience of "self". . . . Subjectivity is consequently shown to depend upon a visual agency which remains insistently outside.[53]

This prescriptive gesture from film theory echoes Hardt's ontologically based prescription for the multitude to reveal its "common power to constitute reality, to constitute being" by opening itself, collectively, to the "unforeseeable . . . intervention of the new events" through which the body of the nominally free can be recomposed in joyous union with the body of the barred.[54] Silverman's cinematic "visual agency which remains insistently outside" the "phallic . . . coherence of the male ego"—her Fassbinderesque prescription for abandoning the self to the abyss of subjectivity—is an aesthetic prescription predicated on the same ethical dilemmas, the same grammar of suffering, as *Monster's Ball*'s social prescription and Negri's and Hardt's ontological prescription.[55]

In passing, it is worth pointing out that the Silverman quotation also illustrates how film theory is perched liminally between the explanatory power of ontological meditations and the interventionist rhetoric of political manifesto. White film theory's confidence in the explanatory power of Lacanian psychoanalysis and Gramscian questions of hegemony make the scaffolding of its rhetorical structure read at one moment like a metacommentary on the structure of ontology, while its desire to offer film as a weapon for social change make it read at another moment like the rhetoric of political discourse, a political common sense shared even by the assumptive logic of most Black film theory and by the sentiments of Black characters on screen, such as Lawrence Musgrove, when he inscribes himself willfully, if not foolishly, into the symbolic order as a "man"—and a "bad" one at that—and by Leticia Musgrove (and Halle Berry) when she inscribes herself into the symbolic order as "woman" and "mother."

White film, Marxist metacommentaries on ontology, film theory, and film reviews, as well as the delusions of Halle Berry and Lawrence and Leticia Musgrove, are structured by the ontological necessity of Whiteness (more precisely, by Humans) because they either take for granted (in the case of political discourse, film reviews, and film theory) or insist on (in the case of ontological metacommentaries) the a priori nature of the subject's capacity to be alienated and exploited. The form of this capacity is temporal, in the sense that a subject's heritage, his or her history and genealogy, stripped of its particular accoutrement, amounts to that "most precious asset that all [supposedly] possess equally: time."[56] The form of this capacity is also spatial. In other words, it is a contestation over, a composition and recomposition of, cartography that can cohere as determinate place in a way that endless space is not.

Temporal capacity (the heritage of historiography) permits one to think "time can be *redeemed.*" For time to be redeemable, time must have been, at some historical moment, *deemed*. But the most coherent temporality ever deemed as Black time is the "moment" of no time at all on the map of no place at all: the ship hold of the Middle Passage. The capacity for temporal redemption—the bare-bones ability to make coherent the vaguest notion of redeemable temporality—is a basic assumption which the screenplay of *Monster's Ball* shares with Hardt's and Negri's meditations. But the Black has no capacity to analogize the loss of Black time with the multitude's (Hank's) loss of commons time; nor is there a spatial analogy between the commons, whether a public assembly, a domestic scene, or the body, on the one hand, or the hold of a slave ship, on the other. One cannot think loss and redemption through Blackness, as one can think them through the proletarian multitude or the female body, because Blackness recalls nothing prior to the devastation that defines it.[57]

What, then, is the significance of Hank's redemption of time and space in relation to Lawrence, Leticia, and Tyrell? Ontological capacity equals time marked by the power of chronology, and space marked by the power of place. In this chronology and place a drama of value can cohere and inscribe subjectivity at multiple scales circumscribed by the macromovement of class recomposition and the attendant reterritorializing of social cartography. These scales are in turn circumscribed by the body, all the way down to scales circumscribed by the micromovement of celluloid cartography and the borders of the cinematic frame—what Stephen Heath calls "narrative space."[58] That frame has the power to compose and recompose, position and reposition, subjects through the selection and combination of presence and absence:

> In fact, the *composition* will organize the frame in function of the human figures in their actions; what enters cinema is *a logic of movement* and it is this logic that centres the frame. Frame space, in other words, is constructed as narrative space. It is narrative significance that at any moment sets the space of the frame to be followed and "read," and that determines the development of the filmic cues in their contributions to the definition of space frame. . . . *space becomes place—narrative as the taking place of film.* . . . What is crucial is the conversion of seen into scene, the holding signifier on signified: the frame, composed, centred, narrated, is the point of that conversion.[59]

Whereas Kaja Silverman locates the socially transformative power of alternative cinema in its content-oriented ability to recompose and reposition the subject by deconstructing the idiopathic identity predicated on phallic coherence of the (White) male ego and recomposing it at the heteropathic site of masochism, Heath locates the socially transformative power of cinema in the frame's formally oriented ability to compose and recompose the human figure in "a logic of movement," the frame's "conversion of seen into scene." My point is not to suggest a contradiction between Silverman's psychoanalytic interventions as regards the socially transformative power of cinema and Heath's technical attention to the transformative power of the celluloid canvas. These two tendencies may in fact disagree about which aesthetic gestures do or do not constitute a trajectory of emancipatory cinema. What we should note here are the different scales and terrains, from the image of the body and the unconscious of the subject, on the one hand, to a square of celluloid and its movement across a beam of light, on the other, through which film theory is able to suture internal solidarity around its universally, almost piously, held assumption that all sentient beings are positioned in space by way of place and can reference time by way of the "event."

Like the reconstructive (socially transformative) gesture of Lacan's "full speech," the politics of heteropathic cinema is none other than a narrative instance of Whiteness. And the frame, in its internal assemblage—what is known as mise-en-scène—and in its external movement—the shot—is none other than a formal instance of Whiteness. These reconstructive gestures are grounded in what Negri's meta-commentary on proletarian ontology and Heath's meditations on the frame call "composition." Composition is an effect of the temporal and the spatial, a "logic of movement" that "centres the frame" and through which it is "constructed as narrative space." Composition is the effect of a capacity to stamp space and time with coherence, to both assert and be hailed by a "logic of movement" which can compose "eventful" chronology out of endless time, and by a logic of cartography which can compose determinate place out of nameless space. In this way, Heath informs us, the seen is converted into scene, and narrative can literally take (possess) place. But can the Black be framed if the Black, by definition, has no capacity to take place? How can composition "organize the frame in function of the human figures" who have no humanity? In point of fact, the compositional effects of Heath's cinematic frame are not available to the Black unless the Black has been structurally adjusted within the frame, made to *appear* as "man," "woman," "proletarian," "child," "gay," or "straight," and so on. Such a structural adjustment makes the Black "palatable" and allows for his or her cinematic "conversion [from] seen into scene."[60]

Alienation and exploitation depend on temporal and spatial coherence, "logics of movement," as Heath indicated. The cinematic frame is one site where these elements are "composed" ontologically. The frame, then, is not just a square space on a thin strip of celluloid, but a vital junction of time and space, one of the smallest, but by no means least significant, of civil society's scales. We could just as well pull back from our close-up of the frame to a long shot of the frame's double; scale up, that is, to civil society. Just as the frame is bound by the capacity for spatial and temporal coherence—logics of movement coupled with logics of cartography—so too is civil society bound. Again, as Heath observed, the effect of this binding is composition: "Composition will organize the frame [and civil society] in function of the human figures in their actions."

In the frame, the human image is composed and recomposed. In civil society, the human subject is composed and recomposed—from factory worker to global multitude in the space of thirty years, or from idiopathic subject to heteropathic subject in the space of thirty seconds. The metacommentaries on the ontology of the proletariat share an essential "imaginative labor" (as Jared Sexton would put it)[61] with the labor of film theory by Heath and Silverman and others. The recomposition of the proletariat, then, is dependent on a spatial and temporal dynamism in which the terrain of exploitation is first the factory, then the socius at large, and then both the socius and the globe are subsumed by capital in a wasteland of command, what Hardt and Negri call *empire*.[62] Despite the tragic downward spiral of a "story" in which capital and its subsuming tendencies spread their tendrils everywhere, the "story" is still a story, which is to say, Hardt's and Negri's terrain of proletarian recomposition, like Heath's cinematic frame, coheres through the capacity of narrative space. Imbricated in this recomposed cartography are changes in the "story" itself, new acts staged and performed by the "drama of value."[63]

Hence, the recomposition of the proletariat is malleable enough to include the phenomenon of White supremacy; the hydraulics of work intensification, sexual orientation, and gender oppression; ethnic cleansing and population displacement; and so on (just as the analysand was malleable for Lacan and his feminist commentators, especially Silverman). Given this state of affairs, the metacommentators on ontology in the realm of political economy do not deny the franchise of dispossession to Blacks, because for them, although the experience of the Black's "story" may differ from the factory worker's story at the level of accoutrement, it nonetheless shares exploitation as an essential grammar of suffering.

This political democracy of the dispossessed, imagined in the catch-all egalitarianism of Hardt's and Negri's "multitude," achieves a kind of formal democracy in Heath's gloss on the frame: "Composition will organize the frame in function of the human figures in their actions." And it achieves a kind of social and aesthetic democracy in the cinematic frame as film: Lawrence Musgrove, Hank and Sonny Grotowski, and the portly and affectionate guard are assembled together, democratically, as working stiffs (pun intended), framed cinematically, and therefore socially, by the coercion of the high-angle shot, ecclesiastic imperatives of ritual sacrifice, spiritual transcendence manifest in the requiem-like musical score, and claustrophobic mise-en-scène of incarceration. They are in "it" together. But there is a glitch which Hardt's and Negri's democratically dispossessed, the multitude and its constituent power, and Heath's democratic formalism, the frame and its compositional power, cannot account for. It is a problem of structure and position, which is to say a problem of ontology. If, as Ronald Judy has pointed out, the Negro, the Black as modernity's creation, "is an interdiction of the African, a censorship to be inarticulate, to not compel, *to have no capacity to move, to be without effect, without agency, without thought*,"[64] then the frame (cinema) and the multitude's capacity to move, to be with effect, with agency, and with thought, stand in structural opposition to the Negro, the Black. If this is the case, the Black is neither protagonist nor antagonist in Negri's "drama of value" and, in addition, the Black has no subjective presence in Heath's "frame." In other words, the Black can be placed *on* film but cannot be positioned *within* the frame. Like the slaves observing the debate between the Aztecs and the Thomists, the Black bears witness to a space and time she cannot enter: the space and time of the world.

Again, for the Black, "exile from affect," the subsumption of living time by prison time,[65] occurs in the Middle Passage. It is merely re-enacted on the auction block, along the slave coffle, from the lynching tree, in the prison, on the receiving end of a hail of bullets, or, in the cinema, projected onto the screen. The capacity to redeem time and space is foreclosed to the Black because redemption requires a "heritage" of temporality and spatiality, rather than a past of boundless time and indeterminate space.[66] Also, a "general deprivation of affect" cannot be calculated by the Black.[67] Temporally, the Black would have to be able to say when

Blackness and the deprivation of affect were not coterminous. Onto this five-hundred-year obliteration of subjectivity it would be difficult, if not obscene, to try to graft a narrative which imagines, from the Black position, the essence of "ontological malady" as an "exile from affect."[68] Lawrence, Leticia, and Tyrell Musgrove are beyond those exiled from affect; they have been exiled, de jure, from the drama of value. They are not part of Hardt's and Negri's ever-widening democracy of dispossession marked by the ever-expanding recomposition of class. This does not mean that they stand in no relation to the recomposition of class or, for that matter, to the dynamics of the frame's composition (its narrative taking of place). On the contrary, they are essential to both. And *Monster's Ball*—much, I would imagine, to the chagrin of Forster's liberal humanist intentions—illustrates why when Lawrence Musgrove's head is shaved and he begins his death walk.

ELEVEN

Half-White Healing

Gender is the repeated stylization of the body, a set of repeated acts within a highly rigid regulatory frame that congeal over time to produce the appearance of substance, of a natural sort of being.

—JUDITH BUTLER, *Gender Trouble*

The cargo of a ship might not be regarded as elements of the domestic, even though the vessel that carries the cargo is sometimes romantically personified as "she."

—HORTENSE SPILLERS, *Black, White and in Color*

IN THE LAST SCENE of *Monster's Ball*, Hank and Leticia go out to the back steps of Hank's house. As they emerge we see them as two tiny figures in a long shot that places the camera, and the spectator, at the far end of the backyard. Three large, darkly lit tombstones consume the foreground screen-right. We know that these are the graves of Sonny Grotowski and two White women, Hank's wife (Sonny's mother) and Hank's mother (Sonny's grandmother). Still in the background, Hank and Leticia close the door and sit on the small back steps. The camera pans down and pulls back a little further. This is significant because until now the image has been cropped so as to sever the base of the three tombstones. Now, as the ground on which the tombstones stand is revealed, we see that there is a soft dark mound of toiled earth in front of the stone closest to the spectator. It is the grave of Sonny Grotowski, too fresh for grass to have grown over it.

We cut to a medium shot of Hank and Leticia sitting on the steps. She is still dazed from the experience of finding Lawrence Musgrove's sketches of Hank and Sonny in Sonny's room: Lawrence's letter has finally arrived. Its impact is still breaking in on her—although something has mitigated the rage she felt while waiting for Hank to return with the chocolate ice cream. This rage was felt at the site of the spoken subject as well. I first saw this film in a Berkeley theater where several of the spectators were Black. The whole theater held its breath during the parallel editing between Leticia finding the Lawrence's sketches of Hank and Sonny in Sonny's bedroom and Hank's buying chocolate ice cream, driving across town to "our" gas station to look at the sign, and now, driving home. Leticia's hands shake as she looks at the drawings and realizes that not only has this man put her husband to death but he has been sleeping with her all along knowing what she is only now finding out. She falls onto Sonny's bed and beats it violently. Presently, Hank comes in and mucks about in the kitchen. She walks through the threshold, dazed and perhaps a little crazed. At that moment a Black person in the theater said, "Aw shit, she's got a gun." The spoken subject (the spectator) intuited or, more precisely, was hailed by the modality of murder that constitutes the Master/Slave relation, and expected that modality to manifest itself narratively. So did the writers and the director, the speaking subjects of the apparatus. While watching this scene, Will Rokos, one of the screenwriters, comments, "This was the best ending that we ever came up with—that you [Marc Forster] finally got to shoot. But originally, this ending here, she comes down and she shoots him through the ice cream and the bullet goes into him and the blood dissolves with the ice cream as it comes out of him and he ends up calling 911. She runs out. Storms out and you hear the door slam and he smashes through this, this screen door grabs the phone and calls the police and says that he accidentally shot himself. And he did so [that] he would take the fall." Considerably more elaborate than "Aw shit, she's got a gun," but in the same spirit nonetheless.

> ROKOS: But this! [*Leticia and Hank are now coming onto the porch to eat ice cream and the tombstones are in the foreground of the frame.*] This is the—this is the one!
> FORSTER: That's why I cut the arms of her off in the shot, so that we don't see what she has in her hands.
> ADDICA: I know a lot of people commented to me that they thought she was going to shoot him.[1]

Seated on the steps, Hank hands Leticia a white plastic spoon. She takes it absent-mindedly. Slowly she turns to her left, in his direction. But instead of seeing him, her eyes land on an image in the depth of field beyond him. For two or three beats we are made to watch Leticia as her eyes focus on the images beyond Hank, as her expression manifests recognition. At this moment, we cut from Leticia's face sighting the image to the image itself. This time it is the tombstones which are composed at the end of a long shot. We see them from the front, from her perspective, as opposed to seeing them from the back and side, in shadow, when they first appeared in this scene. The lighting falling on them is radiant; they glow bright and white in the night. In the foreground of this shot is another familiar image, the pillars of a small structure that may have been an old bunkhouse. Leaning on one of the pillars is a lone wagon wheel from a covered wagon, a stagecoach, or a buggy. The light from the tombstones reaches all the way to the porch of this small house, backlighting the pillars and the wagon wheel, illuminating the clay pots on the porch, lending its spirituality and transcendence to a classical American mise-en-scène. We cut back to a tight shot of Hank (out of focus and severed by the right border of the frame) and Leticia (in focus and centered in the frame). Her look is still transfixed by the tombstones and light. Her eyes do not move but her lips begin to part and her expression reflects a quiet epiphany: She has seen what we first saw when she was just a tiny figure at the end of a long shot: but she has experienced it in full illumination. A wave of recognition passes slowly over her face: she is not the only one who has lost family members to the insipient violence of the prison-industrial complex, not the only one whose life has been subsumed by the dead temporality of prison time.

Slowly she turns away from the graves and looks straight ahead. *The executioner, my lover, has suffered as much as I have. Maybe more: for not only has he lost his life to the dead temporality of prison time, he has lost three loved ones to its structural violence and I have lost only two.* This compassionate calculus—or simple subtraction—continues to set in. Hank's face now comes into focus. Leticia's face is blurred and severed by the left border of the frame. Hank's face anchors the center of the frame. The music intensifies: "A huge grouping of . . . acoustic instruments that have been treated using long . . . reverbs and long echoes" rising, slowly and steadily, sharing the moment with the two of them as though it were

19   Hank feeding Leticia ice cream with a white spoon, in a scene from *Monster's Ball*

a third character.[2] Hank turns to her and feeds her a spoonful of chocolate ice cream (figure 19). Leticia does not speak, but her face is eloquent.
She takes the ice cream into her mouth, slowly. Then, once more, her
eyes look past him, to the tombstones (though we are not treated to this
image again); and again she looks at Hank, knowingly, compassionately,
and with love.

> HANK: I went by our station on the way home. I like the sign.
> [*He takes a spoonful of ice cream for himself. Leticia begins to look up
> to the heavens.*]
> HANK: I think we're going to be all right.

We cut to a medium frontal shot of the two of them on the porch. And
here the cinematography makes a curious lighting adjustment. In this
sequence, as the film makes its last statement on love and redemption,
redemption through love, the three-point blend of lighting technique has
fluctuated between Hank and Leticia, graced them both intermittently.
The close-up of Leticia's face has been bathed in this light at those moments when she looks at the tombstones, as her face reaches its pinnacle
of recognition and mutuality, as she looks at him, and when she begins
to look up to heaven. He has been graced with this lighting as he scoops
the ice cream preparing to feed her. But now that the medium shot has
framed them together and in focus (she looks all the way up to the stars,
smiling, as though thanking God), a significant shadow falls over Leticia.
If Hank, however, were lit any more emphatically, we would have to wonder if Billy Bob Thornton had inherited a phosphorescent gene.

In chapter 10, I reflected on the lighting strategies of Lawrence Musgrove's head-shaving ritual. They are curious, given Lawrence's and the guard's common location (the cartography of incarceration and their common subsumption by prison time) and given Lawrence's centrality to the ritual (he is the one who will die and the film meditates on civil society and the discontent of the commons at several different scales— from the body of the proletarian guard to the incarceration of hegemony behind the glass of the witness room—by staging this ritualistic execution). Why, then, is his Black face not graced with the three-point blend of transcendent light, while the White hands of his captor are? Here, the question rears its head again, at the end of the film, when prison time is redeemed through love.

If we think back to Michael Hardt's project of divine constitution inspired by Jean Genet, then we realize that in the last moments of *Monster's Ball* it is Leticia's "saintly" "self-abandonment" to "a trajectory of encounters, always open and unforeseeable, continuously susceptible to the intervention of the new events," which secures Hank's personal redemption and, more important, hails the spectator to a social dream in which prison time is redeemed as the time of the living.[3] Leticia's rapid transition from homicidal rage on first "receiving" Lawrence's "letter" to embracing a dream for new "common names,"[4] is essential to *Monster's Ball*'s dream for a new notion of the commons, for new political desires, and for a better future. And yet, the classical and unified three-point blend of light which most often bestows saintliness on White women and locates them in "a space of transcendence" has been, in the last shots of the film, the moments when the extradiegetic music overtakes the frame, bestowed on Hank and denied to Leticia.[5] In closing, the camera comes in from behind them, pulls up to the sky, and holds on the stars. Roll credits.

From viewing *Monster's Ball* one would think that two equally determined people could transcend the structural prohibition which forecloses on subject-to-object recognition and find true love. But such mutual resistance, such subjective recognition, between Hank and Leticia, requires the death of her Black husband and her Black son. Ontologically speaking, both Hank and Leticia must be positioned, structurally, at a place where the same ensemble of ethical dilemmas can be shared by both of them. For such ethical sharing to take place, Leticia must be rescued, cinematically, from Blackness: once she is not a "nigger," she and Hank can struggle—socially; reconcile—sexually; and love—transcendently. Which is to say they can become legible, sovereign, to one another.

In chapter 10, I said that whereas Tyrell is simply "a" nigger, Leticia is "our" nigger in the sense that to the "mulatta" accrues a certain pride of place in civil society. I went on to suggest that this pride of place does not transform the "mullata" into one of civil society's addressees, or into one of its organizers of hegemony. Finally, I observed that, whereas Tyrell's and Lawrence's deaths were momentous and spectacular, Leticia's was the stuff of a slow bleed over the life of the entire film, and thus difficult to see. The delirium of cinema's hallucinations with respect to the "mulatta" imagines the "mulatta" as a corpse with a pulse. While, in the case of Tyrell and Lawrence, or the Black female which the presence of the "mulatta" implies, cinema sees only the social death of Blackness, its "genealogical isolation" and, as I have said, sees it in spectacular fashion.

Leticia is narratively alive and formally dead. Her social relation to Hank does indeed have a pulse, but her structural relation to him is as dead as Lawrence's and Tyrell's. By Hank, of course, I mean something more than the character who falls in love, leaves the prison, opens up a gas station, and no longer threatens little Black boys with his shotgun. In *Monster's Ball*, Hank Grotowski is the bearer of civil society's discontents; he stages its ethical dilemmas. Everyone who is structurally alive in *Monster's Ball* is alive because their interlocution with Hank in some way struggles to either maintain the composition, or to catalyze a recomposition, of the ensemble of questions that scaffold civil society's ethical dilemmas; which is to say they are alive because they interact with Hank as entities in dramas of value. This would include the warden, Sonny, and Hank's father, Buck. Temporally and spatially, they embody the possibility for stasis and change. As such they are a community rather than a bunch or a collection. But minor White characters can be included here as well. Even the White dead are essential to the drama of ethical value, and therefore structurally alive in ways which Lawrence, Tyrell, and the Black neighbor boys and father cannot be. Note, for example, how Hank's wife and mother remain interlocutors, even from beyond the grave. After Hank resigns from the prison he burns his uniform and goes inside to face his father.

HANK: I quit the team.

BUCK: That was a mistake.

HANK: I can't do it anymore.

BUCK: You're reminding me of your mother.

HANK: I guess that's bad, right.

BUCK: Your mother wasn't shit. That woman failed me. I got more pussy after she killed herself than I did when she was living as my wife. Point is, she quit on me. You're doing the same.

What's noteworthy here is the way Hank's actions invoke not only the counterhegemonic discourse of the mother, but that of Sonny as well: both Sonny and Hank's mother struggled to find symbolic confirmation for their suffering in the throes of prison time. But the superegoic sinews of patriarchal discourse overwhelmed them to the point where they chose the immediacy of corporeal death (suicide) over the extended death sentence of prison time. But though they are physically dead, they are structurally, ontologically, alive because their aborted attempts to constitute themselves as "new figures of struggle and new subjectivities" actually contributed to "the continuous movement of constituent power."[6] The White dead continue to have their say; now there are four people instead of two in the room; and a loose collectivity begins to form a bloc: Hank, his mother, and Sonny, the slowly congealing "multitude," against the isolated, emasculated, and soon to be eliminated (Hank will place Buck in a retirement home) embodiment of prison time.

The Whites, each accompanied by sometimes complementary, at other times competing, ensembles of questions, move up and down a pole of ethical dilemmas. Even the warden, who was at the execution with Hank and Sonny, and Vera, the prostitute to whom Hank and Sonny say very little, in their almost absolute banality, are structurally alive in this essential way. Hank's last encounter with Vera starts off as just another banal and cynical transaction of respite from work and relief of sexual tension. She comes into the seedy motel room and, as is their custom, makes idle chit chat while taking off her clothes and assuming the position with both palms on the desk. But this routine event of proletarian reproduction is framed, lighted, and edited in such a way as to render it a pivotal moment in "the continuous movement of constituent power": right after this scene the film cuts to a montage leading to Hank's "showdown" with the warden.

VERA: [*As Hank comes up from behind her, places his hands on her hips and prepares to mount her.*] So, how's Sonny?

HANK: I can't do this tonight, Vera.

VERA: You sure, hon'?

HANK: No, not tonight. [*They both begin to pull their clothes back on.*] I'm sorry.

VERA: Ain't no need to be sorry. Just do it some other time.

HANK: [*Sitting on the edge of bed, in shadow, his head hung low.*] All right. You can keep that money.

VERA: [*Pulling on her shirt. She has had her back to him the whole time and continues not to look at him.*] Oh, I'm going to. [*She leaves without looking around.*] Adios.

We now see Hank in a reverse shot, still on the bed, his face still draped in shadow. He is breathing softly but heavily, trying to steady himself. From here we cut to a long shot of a ferry drifting across the Mississippi River. The weather is dark and overcast, matching the mood that Vera's "So, how's Sonny?" put Hank into in the last scene. The long platform of the ferry is deserted. But at the bow we see a tiny object. It is a single automobile. The editing from this moment on seeks to disturb our time sense, but not too dramatically, in that we cut back and forth from medium close-ups of Hank driving down a dusty road, to medium close-ups of Hank sitting inside the car while on the ferry drifting across the Mississippi (in these shots the camera is positioned just outside the car, and as rain cascades down the window; Hank eats chocolate ice cream with a plastic spoon).

The images of the montage capturing Hank on the dusty road are interesting in their composition. The camera is positioned in the backseat of the car. We see the back of Hank's head, the left side of his face, his hands on the steering wheel, the dashboard and the depth of field beyond the front window. But we also see his eyes in the rearview mirror. At one moment his eyes look right in the rearview mirror and we would be forgiven for thinking that Hank was looking back at the camera or at us. At this moment, a long flatbed truck bearing almost fifty inmates, all standing, drives across our field of vision on the road perpendicular to the one on which we are traveling with Hank. Hank's eyes narrow in the rearview window. He turns left at the junction and follows them. We cut back to the ferry. The camera is in the ferry control room, and in the foreground of the shot are the back and shoulders of the ferry operator in the tower above the deck. This frame gives us a long, high angle shot of Hank's lone car, below the control tower, at the end of the ferry. We cut to a medium close-up of the rain-draped car window. Hank has finished his cup of ice cream. Aimlessly, he turns it about in his hand, contemplative and depressed. The montage puts us back on the dusty road with the fields of shoulder-high sugar cane. Decked in blue and white prison uniforms, the forty-odd men are now walking down a side road to the sugar cane. Their hoes rest long and high on their shoulders (cruel substitutions for rifles). A White prison guard rides a horse to the left of their formation. A shotgun, not a hoe, rests long and high on his shoulder.

The montage continues back and forth between Hank's car and the ferry and the vision from Hank's car, on the dusty road. It does not follow the true chronology of sailing and driving. It splices the images together in tandem with the long reverbs and echoes of the acoustic instruments that rise higher and higher in dramatic intensity as the montage progresses. Toward the end of the montage, as we cut from the end of the ferry ride back to the field of prison workers and guards on horseback, the musical intensity and its cadence are reminiscent of scores from Westerns at moments when the hero is emerging from an ethical dilemma and preparing (donning his hat, tightening his gunbelt) for a showdown. In one of the images, the guard with the shotgun spurs his horse and for some unknown reason, rides swiftly away from the formation of prisoners he is charged with guarding. The camera follows him and the rhythm and cadence of the music match his gallop. We follow him for a moment and then, still propelled along with the increasing cadence of the score, we cut to a frontal shot of Hank in his car, cigarette clenched between his teeth. The ferry has docked and the Hank is driving off. The next image of this montage shamelessly, and without parody, quotes the Western. A door opens at the end of long, antiseptic corridor. The sound of the door opening has been enhanced by the technician so that it snaps as loud as the rising music. Hank enters the hallway. The cigarette is gone from his mouth. He walks toward us. No, he literally swaggers; his palms held open toward his hips, his hands open and moving from side to side as though he had a six gun on either hip, as though he were moving toward us about to draw. The following dialogue is layered over the music and the sound of Hank's boots striding across the floor.

> WARDEN: Have a seat, Hank.
> HANK: Thank you, sir. I appreciate you seeing me.
> WARDEN: What brings you here, Hank?

Here the montage ends. We cut to the warden's office. The warden (played by Will Rokos, one of the screenwriters) sits tight-faced and up-right in his high-backed, stuffed leather chair. On the other side of his big mahogany desk, Hank leans back in a smaller chair with his left elbow propped on its back.

> HANK: [*Moving his head slowly from side to side, as Gary Cooper might do when admonishing the unethical townsfolk of* High Noon.] Sir, I'm, uh, resignin'. And uh, I wanted to come by and tell you per-sonally, ya know.

Now, the confrontational stance is revealed as having an additional di-mension. With the "ya know," Hank begins to nod as though respectful of the warden's place and status in Hank's own social universe. Hank is a little nervous.

> WARDEN: I appreciate that, Hank.
> [*They are both silent and respectful for one or two beats. They nod their heads a little.*]
> WARDEN: Why don't we wait a few weeks before we—uh, submit the paperwork.
> HANK: [*Now, the image no longer frames them both. Instead we have a medium close-up of Hank alone.*] That wouldn't do anybody any good to wait on that. I've got my mind made up. [*He nods his head, repeatedly, determinedly.*]
> WARDEN: [*His face sad, perhaps a little disappointed, not quite resent-ful.*] Awright. We gonna miss you.

Hank nods in recognition, but stops short of saying *I'm going to miss y'all, too.* He reaches into his shirt pocket.

HANK: Um, I brought my badge in. [*Places it on the desk.*]
WARDEN: Why don't you keep it?
HANK: I ain't got no use for it.

The camera cuts back and forth between the two men, looking at each other; the sound of kindling burning is layered over the image of their faces. Suddenly, we cut to the close-up of a fire of small twigs. Then, with a thud Hank's prison uniform hits the fire and the "Department of Corrections" emblem begins to burn. Hank walks back to the house, away from the fire, with the same *High Noon* swagger he had walking into the warden's office. He goes into the house to tell his father, "I quit the team."

When Hank drives out to see the warden and tender his resignation, the *High Noon* tension in the encounter is interlaced with an affectionate tenor indicative of years, generations, of unspoken reciprocity. We understand that Hank is not simply quitting a job; he is tearing himself away from a social fabric of affiliation which, for his entire life, has calibrated his psychic coordinates in tandem with his patriarchal fabric of filiation. In fact, here filiation and affiliation are woven together in a single fabric. Intellectually, we might know the warden as an organizer of prison time and its discourse (*Keep the badge*; *Let's wait a few weeks to submit the paperwork*) but affectively we experience him as "family." As such, he is a subject of recognition and mutual resistance with whom, and through whom, Hank (and the spectator as she is recomposed by a new commons over the length of the film) must struggle in this "continuous movement of constituent power." Likewise, Hank's last encounter with Vera, the White prostitute—in all its banality and cold-cash cynicism—is rendered, both formally and narratively, pivotal in this struggle over the ethics of filiation and affiliation: Vera's "So, how's Sonny?" sparks Hank's "I can't do this tonight, Vera," which in turn precipitates the journey of montage—across the river, over the fields, down the hallway, the showdown with the warden, to the smoldering uniform, and finally the confrontation with the father. "I can't do it anymore," as we have seen, is not an isolated gesture, but a collective refusal (Hank, dead Sonny, dead mother, Vera the prostitute, and we might add, Hank's dead wife) of a crumbling and unethical order (Buck and the warden).

Hank's encounters with the Whites in *Monster's Ball* consistently implies the composition and recomposition of civil society's ethical dilemmas: *Will we submit to civil society's deterritorialization by the modalities of violence (living time subsumed by prison time), or will we join forces and constitute a new cartography?* In other words, these encounters are constituted by each subject's potential for both stasis and change. *Monster's Ball* renders this spatial and temporal dynamism in a number of ways: through image composition within the frame; through editing— the way images of Black prison workers in the fields cross-cut with the rain and the ferry, in the montage leading up to the warden, function as the spectacle for Hank's (and the spectator's) pessimism and strengthen his resolve on his way to resign—and through lighting. It is important to note that during his pivotal encounters with Vera, the warden, and his father, the lighting characteristic of Hank's face for the first forty-five minutes of the film begins to change dramatically. Up to this point the lighting on Hank's face has been harsh and garish: for example, when his portrait is being sketched in the moments before Lawrence's execution, when he discharges the shotgun against the Black neighbor boys, when he punches Sonny in the prison bathroom for vomiting and falling out of formation on the death walk, or when he and Sonny argue at gunpoint just before Sonny kills himself. So harsh and garish is the lighting that Hank often appears haggard and ugly. But as he sits on the bed and Vera leaves the room, though there is a shadow cast over his face, it is a soft shadow formed by backlighting the right side of his face, which has the added dimension of producing something akin to a halo along his hairline. By the time he is seated in front of the warden, and then seated beside his father, he has become the recipient of the three-point blend of unified light assuring, at this halfway point in the film, his saintliness, his transcendence, finally achieved in the last scene of the film.

In addition to its formal strategies of editing, lighting, image, and sound, *Monster's Ball* renders the dynamism of subjective stasis and change through dialogue: Hank's ideological repartees with Sonny, Buck, and the warden, and his last encounter with cynical Vera (who is recomposed as a prostitute-with-a-heart-of-gold when her unconscious reveals a bond with father and son that cannot be broken by the cash transaction). Along this vertically integrated pole of ethical dilemmas, Whites in *Monster's Ball* rise and fall as the film deploys them in such a way as to facilitate, or impede, Hank's desire to recompose and thereby liberate himself (and the spectator's desire that he do so). If, at the beginning of the film, we are shown a world in which Sonny, the prostitute, and the two dead White women can tender no hegemonic currency, then, by the time the lighting on Hank's face begins to turn, and a counterhegemony's ensemble of questions starts to emerge, these three figures, though dead and not to be "seen" again, are capable of accompanying Hank in his ethical ascension. (In this way even the "unseen" of Whiteness is converted, recomposed by the "scene" of Stephen Heath's cinematic frame.) Rigor mortis is no obstacle to the living ontology of Whiteness.

The diversity of Whiteness is so profound that there are no fixed, always already, positions within it, no a priori criminality, for example, and no permanent saintliness.[7] Spatial and temporal capacity is so immanent on the field of Whiteness that the effects and permutations of its ensemble of questions and the kinds of White bodies that can mobilize this universe of combinations are seemingly infinite as well: White prostitutes can catalyze a 180-degree ethical reversal (given that prostitution is cinema's role-of-choice for Black women, one would expect—if Blacks and Whites were both structurally alive—these catalytic moments to pop up in every other film!). Even the White dead can hold the White living to account. We are dealing here with a structure whose idiom of power is autodidactic and autoproductive: it generates its lessons, its ensemble of questions and their attendant ethical dilemmas, and its institutional capacity, internally, without recourse to bodies or questions beyond its own gene pool. What keeps it from replicating the decline in genetic health experienced when incest takes place in biology is the fact that it is not biological. Whiteness has an infinite ensemble of signified possibilities: The infinite possibilities themselves cannot be definitively named; their dramas of value cannot be predicted with anything approaching precision; nor can the reproduction of these possibilities be threatened with mortality, because Whiteness's internal mutation is limitless. But what can be named, predicted, and put to death is the coherence of the ensemble as an ensemble. And the same *thing* that guarantees the ensemble's coherence is the thing that threatens its coherence with destruction: the Black.

The diversity of Whiteness, its "recovery of difference in a hierarchical and vertical distribution of being," depends on the "laterality" of

Blackness to maintain its internal diversity. Hortense Spillers uses the term *laterality* to mean that whereas Whiteness exists on a vertical plane where the "recovery of difference" is not only guaranteed, but ethically mandated, Blackness exists on a lateral plane where "it [is] possible to rank human with animal."[8] In other words, the taxonomy of things would indeed be dismantled as a taxonomy if "White person" were added to the list; but it would merely be expanded if "Black person" were added to the list. Blacks, broadly speaking, connote a taxonomy of *things*. As Ronald Judy asks, in a question I used as an epigraph for chapter 10, "Can there be a 'community' of niggers, as opposed to a 'bunch' or a 'collection'?"[9] "In effect, the humanity of the African personality is placed in quotation marks under . . . signs" like *community*.[10]

Hank Grotowski is the protagonist of *Monster's Ball* for two reasons beyond the fact that he is given top billing: (1) White verticality, as performance, as a play of signs, performs its "recovery of difference" in relation to his spiritual transcendence; and (2) through Black folks' encounters with Hank, Black laterality is positioned so as to secure paradigmatic coherence of that vertical recovery of difference: in short, Black laterality is positioned outside the drama of value in order to secure it. Discursive processes dating as far back as slavery's galley "logs and bills of lading and of sales," namely, "the collapse of human identity adopted to the needs of commerce and economic profit,"[11] are reinvigorated and recomposed in the narrative and formal strategies of White socially engaged cinema such as *Monster's Ball*. Hank's encounters with Whites displace and rearrange the ethical verticality of the commons; but his encounters with Blacks are what prevent the ground of the commons from quaking.

He meets Whites as interlocutors. He meets Blacks as inert mass, differentiated only by the spectacle that their flesh places before him—obstructive, tantalizing, pleasurable, disturbing, or all of the above. These are not ethical encounters through which both parties struggle for recognition, a recognition underwritten by the same grammar of suffering. Black Lawrence must be calmed and quieted in his cell and then put to death. Black boys from across the way must be tamed with an errant shotgun blast. Black boys' father must be faced down. Black Tyrell must be dragged from the side of the road and, when they reach the hospital, dragged onto a gurney—then Black Tyrell dies. "The world according to captives and their captors strikes the imagination as a grid of identities running at perpendicular angles to each other: *things* in serial and lateral array, beings in hierarchical and vertical array. On the serial grid, the captive—chattel property—is the equivalent of inanimate and other things."[12] In other words, one could easily move laterally along the taxonomy of animals and things and replace Black Lawrence, Black boys, Black boys' father, and Black Tyrell, with any number of objects without rupturing the taxonomy's smooth laterality: Horse must be calmed and quieted and then put to death. Bull must be faced down. Possum must be dragged from the side of the road. (Granted, the possum does not, generally speaking, warrant hospitalization and a gurney.)

Historical Stillness

Frantz Fanon and Hortense Spillers approach the phenomenon of the "mulatta" from different vantage points. They arrive, however, at complementary ontological conclusions. Fanon is interested in the "mulatta" as a psychic entity, in how the neurotic complex of "hallucinatory whitening" manifests itself in someone who is socially liminal, considered to be neither Black nor White.[13] Though both Spillers and Fanon agree that the "mulatta" maintains the status of a thing in her relation to Human beings, for our purposes, we will lean more on the methodological insights of Spillers than Fanon when thinking the "mulatta" and *Monster's Ball* together. The film itself mandates this choice because *Monster's Ball* is not interested in either the unconscious or conscious register of Leticia's psychic life, whereas the primary objective of Fanon's commentary is to investigate the psychic condition of the person who has been converted into the scene of "mulatta" and who, in addition, sees herself through this conversion.

If Fanon turns his attention to the identity, or rather identifications, of hemispheric antagonisms qua the "mulatta," Spillers turns her attention to the structure of U.S. (hemispheric) antagonisms qua the "mulatta." Spillers asks, what is the essence of historical conjunctures when civil society needs the "mulatta" (or "mulatto") most and how does this work? "The mulatta mediates between dualities, which would suggest that at least mimetic movement, imitating successful historical movement, is upward, along the vertical scale of being"; as opposed to ahistorical movement, sideways along the lateral scale of stillness. In addition,

Spillers asserts, "the 'mulatto/a,' just as the 'nigger,' tells us little or nothing about the subject buried beneath the epithets, but quite a great deal more concerning the psychic and cultural reflexes that invent and invoke them."[14] In other words, if *mulatta* and *mulatto* are epithets connoting, like *nigger*, the temporal and spatial incapacity of Blackness, how is the mimesis of White movement mimicked by the "mulatta" or "mulatto"? How can the figure of Leticia experience "the conversion of seen into scene" within the frame of *Monster's Ball* when such conversion is impossible for Lawrence and Tyrell?[15] Why does civil society need her conversion? Spiller's account of the "mulatta"-function resists summary, but some of its highpoints can be extracted in order to illustrate its articulation with *Monster's Ball*.

First, she argues that the "mulatta" and the "mulatto" "heal" a wound in civil society. The wound has what appears to be two separate lacerations, one sexual, and the other political; but Spillers demonstrates that they form one and the same scar.

Second, she notes that civil society's production of this figure has consequences among Blacks. Spillers spends more than three hundred pages reflecting on how slavery, broadly speaking, and the Middle Passage in particular, destroy the prospect for interontological relations between Blacks and the species modernity refers to as "humanity" (and that I refer to as "Humanity"). But, from this obliteration of time and space, a significant and painfully ironic political gain accrues to Blackness. Blackness is vested with the potential for unflinching, uncompromising, and comprehensive political movement because Black subjects—if they can be called "subjects"—have the potential to act, politically, through a collectivity that has nothing to salvage and nothing to lose. But when civil society introduces the "mulatta" and the "mulatto" into the mass of Blackness, it produces "bodies" that *appear* to have something to salvage and lose in the midst of flesh and the latter's absolute dereliction.[16] Here Spillers amplifies and develops a point that Fanon hints at: "mulattos" and "mulattas" are neither self-naming as individuals nor autocolonizing as a group, but instead constitute what Spillers calls a "a mythical or reified property . . . a stage prop of the literary,"[17] introduced without the consent of the Black masses and without the consent of Blacks who are "staged" as "mulattas" or "mulattos."

This intervention bodes ill for the insurgent potential of Blackness, manifest most dramatically in those moments when it seeks to assume the comprehensive antagonism of its structural position. "Subsequent to the intrusion of the middle term [*mulatto* or *mulatta*], or middle ground—figuratively—between subjugated and dominant interests, public discourse gains, essentially, the advantages of a lie by orchestrating otherness through degrees of difference. The philosopher's 'great chain of being' ramifies now to disclose within American Africanity itself literal shades of human value so that the subject community refracts the oppressive mechanism just as certainly as the authoring forms put them in place. This fatalistic motion . . . turns the potentially insurgent community furiously back on itself."[18] Spiller's observation that Blackness ("the subject community") can refract the "oppressive mechanism" authored by civil society is chilling. Here she has unpacked the uncommon pain behind the painfully common common sense of such terms as *self-hatred* or *color-struck* (both of which are often used as a kind of lazy shorthand for Fanon's clinical term, *hallucinatory whitening*). Moreover, her structural analysis of "mulatta" and "mulatto" as function, not only deciphers this typical common-sense shorthand but reroutes its explanatory genesis away from "the subject community," Blacks, and back to civil society, Whites: "public discourse gains, essentially, the advantages of a lie by orchestrating otherness through degrees of difference." The lie that gets orchestrated is none other than the egoic monumentalization of the phallus, implied in my first summary point above. Again, there is a sexual, as well as a political, dimension to this egoic monumentalization and phallic aggrandizement "orchestrated" by civil society ("public discourse").

Spillers maintains that "lack of movement in the field of signification seems to be the origin of 'mulatto/a-ness.'" She goes on to say that civil society projects the "mulatta" onto its screen of dilemmas as a "wedge between the world of light and the step beyond"; the "beyond," of course, being Blackness, that "undifferentiated, unarticulated mass of moving and movable *things*. . . . Between these dualities, the 'shadow' of the 'mulatto/a' is interposed." The appearance of "mulattas" and "mulattos" is historically motivated, but their embodiment is historically barren because their appearance is overdetermined from without. The political dimension of civil society's egoic monumentalization calls on them as a "stage prop" at those moments in the drama when the mise-en-scène is in need. "The 'mulatto/a' appears, historically, when African female and male personality become hyphenated American political entities; at the moment when they enter public and political discourse in the codes of slavery, the rise of the fugitive, the advertisement of the runaway man/woman." "Apparently the 'runaway slave' was neither rare nor forgotten. The plentifulness of advertisements describing the *person* of the fugitive—the model, we might suppose, for the contemporary 'All Points Bulletin' of the Federal Bureau of Investigation and those mug shots that grace the otherwise uniform local post office—argue the absolute solidification of captivity—the major American social landscape, in my view, for two and a half centuries of human hurt on the scene of 'man's last best hope.'"[19] When Black women and men push against the coherence, the limits, of political economy and libidinal economy, civil society finds it increasingly difficult to reconcile the structural necessity of its gratuitous violence and its manifest rituals performed on Blacks with its "public discourse"—its monumentalizing—of its boundless diversity and its ethical posture.

Spillers thus gestures toward a significant moment in modernity's construction of Whiteness qua civil society, the period from 1800 to the Civil War. Furthermore, she marks the significance of that era in relation to the time of her own writing, the late 1980s and early 1990s, which we know also holds a special significance for Antonio Negri and Michael Hardt as a period of crumbling national economies and the solidification of postindustrial, or postcivil, civil society. There is a parallelism between these two periods which I am developing elsewhere.[20] For now, suffice it to say that Spillers's parallel between the runaway slave advertisement and the FBI All Points Bulletin indexes two periods that are more than one hundred years apart but whose effects on Blacks and Whites evince "a stunning mutuality."[21]

> By the close of the eighteenth century . . . settlers began pouring into the new states of Kentucky and Tennessee, where Revolutionary War veterans cashed in on land grants. Georgia, Alabama, Mississippi, and eventually Louisiana lured thousands onto their rich soils with a promise of extravagant fortunes, all to be made in the wake of slavery's widening sphere. . . . Cotton was not a cash crop in Maryland, but its plantations produced one of the most invaluable crops for the

southern antebellum market: slaves. The children of slaves quickly became a vital commodity and source of income for cash-poor planters
of the Chesapeake, and of increasing significance to the prosperity of
the lower South. . . . During the half century leading up to the Civil
War . . . approximately 10 percent of adolescent slaves in the upper
South were sold by owners; another 10 percent were sold off in their
twenties. Slave parents lived in abject terror of separation from their
children. . . . By the 1820s Maryland newspapers were filled with advertisements seeking slaves for sale; sometimes as many as two hundred were sought at a time.[22]

In Georgia, Alabama, Mississippi, and Louisiana, Blacks were deskilled
(i.e., turned from smithies and seamstresses into cotton pickers) and subjected to more intense and cruel forms of captivity and punishment than
they had previously known in the Revolutionary War period. All in all
more than 1 million Black youth were uprooted and re-enslaved within
a thirty-year period. In addition, 3 million Native Americans died during this period, massacred or sent on deadly forced marches (most infa-
mously, the Trail of Tears) to "clear" land that the White working class
(and its coffles of slaves) would inhabit for small family farms; and the
Indians lost more than 23 million hectares of land to this dramatic expansion of civil society.

In the 1980s and 1990s another 1 million Black youth were uprooted
from their "homes" and "families" and formally incarcerated in the prison-
industrial complex (PIC). This translates into an incarceration rate of one
in four Black youth. However, when one considers that another 5 million or so Blacks are captured by other forms of PIC modalities, proba-
tion, parole, halfway houses, electronic ankle bracelets, and so on, then
the percentage increases. That makes 6 million Black people, primarily
youth, who are somehow captured by the apparatus of roundup. Now, if
each of those 6 million people has, conservatively, four immediate family
members, then 24 million Black Americans in the late twentieth and early
twenty-first century are intimate with the apparatus of roundup. This
amounts to roughly 70 percent of all Black people in the United States.
What should be shocking and cause for public outcry is that the percentage of Black people intimate, through lockdown or relations, with the
PIC is significantly higher than the percentage of Black people intimate

in this way with nineteenth-century slavery. But ethical dilemmas arising from such intimacy do not enter the fabric of "public discourse." In this way, there is a structural mimesis between "the absolute solidification of captivity" in the first half of the nineteenth century and the last half of the twentieth.

There is a structural mimesis between dramatic expansion of civil society in the first thirty years of the nineteenth century (the Jacksonian movement) and in the last twenty years of the twentieth century (the antiglobalization movement). The rotation of that wheel which renews the solidification of Black captivity (captivity solidified by the runaway slave ad or by the All Points Bulletin), and the rotation of that wheel which renews the labor of White redemption (space and time redeemed either through the Jacksonian expansion of civil cartography or through the Negrian recomposition of the multitude) are stunningly calibrated. These moments of calibration engender a need for the "mulatta" and "mulatto" because civil society cannot come clean as to how and why dramas of White redemption require, for the coherence—rather than the outcome—of the drama, the most brutal reenactments of violence against Black flesh.

The calibration of these two wheels' rotation threatens to affect a political rupture. The figure of the "mulatto/a . . . heals the rupture at [these] points of wounding."[23] This does not mean that this figure becomes an interlocutor when made to administer the salve. Put another way: The fact of incarceration oozes out of every pore of *Monster's Ball*, and Blackness's synonymity with containment is confirmed by the image track as well. However, given the film's own admission of incarceration as the fact of Blackness, the screenwriters could imagine no exchange between Blacks (whether "mulatta" or "African") catalyzed by the ethical dilemmas of accumulation and fungibility. In *Monster's Ball*, and in so many other White socially engaged films where prison figures as a main character, where prison has a speaking role, prison is *seen* as Black captivity, but *scened* as White suffering.

An intra-Black articulation of ethical dilemmas finds no elaboration in the script; nor does the script appear particularly reflective of, or conversant with, a Black ensemble of questions or a Black grammar of suffering, when Blacks are speaking to Whites:

LETICIA: [*Seated on the couch, speaking to Hank.*] This here is my husband. He went and got hisself 'lectricuted over there in Jackson.

Or . . .

WARDEN: [*Holding a mike to Lawrence.*] Do you have any last words?
LAWRENCE: Push da button.

The political dimension of civil society's egoic monumentalization calls on the "mulatta" as a "stage prop" at those moments in the drama when the mise-en-scène is in need. There is the White, who is constructed as "woman." There is the Black, who is constructed as "female." "Woman" is vested with the qualities of both virginity and motherhood: White women, then, are "ladies. . . . whom gentlemen someday marry." The Black, or African, is "female"—and not "woman"—because she is constructed through the grammar of accumulation and fungibility. The slaveocracy, in a chain of metonymy from the Middle Passage, names the African "female" as a "condition of mindless fertility." The prohibition against not only being able to claim her own skin—hence the designation *flesh*, instead of *body*—but against being able to claim her own offspring, is what allows the very perpetrators of this gratuitous violence, "the authoring forms [that] put them in place," to name her fertility as "mindless." In this way, Black women are "known" to be so hypersexual as to be, ultimately, asexual. But without the structure of gratuitous violence, followed by the symbolic intervention of naming the victim as "mindless fertility," or "female," there would be no White woman in the imaginary of the White male, and motherhood would lose coherence as a social category. "Robbery" is the metaphor Spillers uses to epitomize this coherence: "The third caste [Black/female/slave] robs the first [White/woman/virgin] of a putative clitoral and vaginal pleasure, as the first purloins from the third a uterine functionality. Only the first caste gains here the right to the rites and claims of motherhood, blind to its potential female pleasure and reduced, paradoxically, in the scale of things to a transcendent and opaque Womanhood."[24] Spillers is clear that though White "women" and Black "females" are both thus named, written, by the phallic monumentalization of civil society's private and public discourse (respectively, the White male ego, on the one hand, and the requirements of family, private property, and the state, on the other), this common experience of misrecognition by way of phallic naming strategies does not translate into a common ontology, a common grammar of suffering. Still, after suggesting that clitoral and vaginal pleasure "are purloined" from White "women" by Black "females," she informs us that Black "females" are not constructed in such a way as to be able to keep, to hold onto, make something special and personal of, that pleasure. This is because the site of Black femininity is designated as being so hyperbolically sexual as to not allow clitoral and vaginal pleasure coherence in time and space: that which goes by the shorthand *sexuality*.

Civil society's phallic wound is a laceration between, on the one hand, the open access to Black women's "sexuality"—marked by their open vulnerability to the violence of the slaveocracy—a sexual access so open that it spreads across boundless space and endless time. This sexuality has no coordinates and as such it cannot provide the White male with the satisfaction of access: there is no woman's "body," thus there was no sexual "event." On the other hand, on the other side of the phallic wound's laceration is the White "woman," the antithesis of a sexual access so open it is meaningless: White "woman's" sexuality is so meaning*ful* as to be inaccessible, forbidden (until marriage).

Ultimately the uterine function must be preserved. "The African-American female . . . robbed of the benefits of the 'reproduction of mother,' is, consequently, the very negation of femaleness that accrues as the peculiar property of Anglo-American woman." The uterine function is a vector of spatial and temporal capacity: space cohered as place: the womb; time cohered as event: childbirth. As such, this conversion from *seen* into *scene* is what makes a White "woman" both a "woman" and White, which is to say, not a "female" and not Black. And, by metonymic extension, it makes a family a family. In fact, the coherence of both private property and the state also depends on the White "woman's" safeguarding the uterine function.[25]

But the attendant "sacrifice" of sexual pleasure which this safeguarding requires (the aura of virginity that must accompany the chronology which predates the uterine function) debilitates the egoic monumentalization of White masculinity at the same time as it enables civil society's more collective institutions (family, property, state). This is a point of wounding which the "mulatta" is called on to heal. The "mulatta" is "a site of cultural and political maneuver" between the White "virgin whom gentlemen someday married" and the Black slave on whom the White virgin rested and to whom she "doubtless owed her virginity."[26]

It would be safe to say that, when Halle Berry is made to appear on screen, she appears as a "mulatta." This assumption can be made on the basis of how Berry appears as an aspect of the cinematic apparatus: that is by taking into consideration the fascination of star magazines and the entertainment news industry with Berry's White mother and her "absent" Black father. The assumption can also be made by examining the "wedge" work Berry's diegetic figure performs in films where dark-skinned Black women are not merely implied by her presence but present on screen with her. In Warren Beatty's *Bulworth* (1999), for example, it becomes clear in the first twenty minutes that, though Berry's character is one of a female trio Senator Bulworth encounters in South Central Los Angeles, the two darker women are made to appear too loud, too "crude," and too sexually aggressive to stand any possibility of emerging as Bulworth's "love interest." This is not to suggest that her appearance is in any way announced as such, that the various scripts in some way take up the politics of biracial identity, but that the cinematic "pose" she is compelled to strike implies, as its condition of possibility, the presence of African females—women who (in other films, and in the world beyond the film) are made to appear, when they are even allowed to appear, as Black. "Unlike the African female personality implied in her presence, the 'mulatta' designates those notions of femaleness that would re-enforce the latter as an object of gazing—the dimensions of the spectacular that . . . [are] virtually the unique property of the 'mulatto/a.'"[27] This difference between Black female incapacity and the "mulatta's" presumed capacity is the sleight of hand *Monster's Ball* attempts to press into service of its social dream. In short, without the "mulatta," albeit understated in comparison to midcentury melodramas like Douglas Sirk's *Imitation of Life* (1959), the inspiration of *we* on which redemptive narratives rest would break apart.

If, as I have said, Leticia's "mulatta" stillness equals the Black stillness of Lawrence, Tyrell, the two boys, and their father, how do we account for her movement, socially, and how and why does *Monster's Ball*, as an example of what Spillers calls "public discourse," gain the "advantage of a lie by orchestrating otherness through degrees of difference"?[28] In other words, how does civil society deploy this movement to mask and disavow the antagonism between the vertical and the lateral? Diegetically, the "mulatta" and the "mulatto" appear as a subject position imbued with the Human capacity of temporal and spatial movement which is absent in the Black.

As a diegetic and public discourse stage prop, "mulattas" can be thought of as "the courtesans to whom [White men] went while on sabbaticals to the cities." "Allowing the male to have his cake and eat it too, or to rejoin the 'female' with the 'woman,' the mulatta has no name because there is not a locus, or strategy, for this Unitarian principle of the erotic."[29]

Spillers alerts us to the fact that the "mulatta" is barred from civil society, politically, by her status as chattel property: "'Mulatto' originates etymologically in notions of 'sterile mule[,]' . . . [which] is not a genetically transferable trait."[30] (The psychogenesis of *mulatto* and *mulatta* is not only a piece of chattel, but chattel with no capacity for filiation.) At the same time she is advanced, libidinally, by her status as an arbiter of chivalry. She "literally belongs to a class of masters, who protect their property by way of various devices that cluster in notions of 'honor.' It would not do, for instance, for [one White man] to call another [White man's] mistress a 'whore,' since he, or any other, male committing the *faux pas*, would be 'forced to purchase that privilege with some of [his] blood.'"[31] When Leticia pawns her wedding ring in order to buy Hank a ten-gallon cowboy hat, she meets Hank's father, Buck, who lures her into a conversation in which he holds all the cards: he is able to find out everything about her (that Lawrence Musgrove was her husband and that she and Hank are sleeping together) and not only is she unable to know anything about him but she is not wise to the complete significance of his fishing expedition. Finally, after she has lit his cigarette and spoken kindly to him, he says, "Yep, I had a taste for the nigger juice when I was Hank's age. He's jes' like his Daddy." Leticia storms out of the house, and, in her fury, even storms past Hank (who has just arrived in the yard). The next scene is of Hank committing Buck to a retirement home, signing the papers, setting him up with, no less, a Black roommate, and then leaving. Buck has called Hank's mistress a "whore" and thus paid for it with his blood. Eventually, Hank and Leticia reconcile, she moves in with him and, as the diegesis intends in the last scene, "the peace and order of the world [are] restored in [Leticia's] happiness."[32]

Still, the contrastive work which wedges the "mulatta" as a "shadow" between Blackness and Whiteness[33] does not transform Leticia from the object status of Blackness sufficiently to allow her to share Hank Grotowski's ethical dilemmas: Hank and Leticia are not elaborated, ontologically, by the same grammar of suffering simply because Buck called Hank's property "property." But the screenplay's insistence to the contrary haunts our assertion. After all, *Monster's Ball* is a love story, and love is enabled only by way of mutual recognition. I have said that such recognition is only possible when the parties that confront each other do so through "conflictual harmony" (found in the encounter between men and women, postcolonials and the motherland's subjects, and liminally, Settlers and "Savages"). A conflictual relation can find its way to the imaginative labor of love for the simple reason that recognition is already its constitutive element. Both parties are articulate and in general agreement that they both are indeed parties: they are sovereign to themselves and to one another. But for an antagonistic relation, the imaginative labor of love is a hallucination. Murder, rather than recognition, is *its* constitutive element. What, generically speaking, is the substance of this "mulatta" delirium? The fantasy of a corpse with a pulse. Through the intercourse of dreaming, a dead object is dreamed to life, dreamed of as alive (dreamed of as loved and in love) within the relationship, rather than seen as murdered by the relationship. The last lines of the film—Hank's "I went by our station on the way home. I like our sign" and "I think we're going to be all right"—locate their inspiration not in the irreconcilable duality between beings and things but in the promise of the personal pronoun *we*, and suggest that whatever problems the future may hold for Hank and Leticia, they will be civil problems, problems in common, and should violence erupt from them, that violence will be contingent—the outgrowth of some ethical and symbolically comprehended transgression. Here, at the end, the film would assure us that Leticia is somehow special: she is not the stuff of things that die meaninglessly on the side of a road, that can be executed in silence, run off with a shotgun blast, or faced down like a bull. But neither is she allowed to be illuminated by a three-point blend of light, or positioned by way of editing and camera angle, as a Human entity to whom the film's ethical dilemmas accrue, and for whom value functions as an arbiter—except in moments when illuminating her face transcendentally indexes Hank's, not her, recomposition and redemption. In this way Leticia, unlike the Black woman in cinema, takes on the property of light, while remaining, much like the Black woman in cinema, the quintessence of property.

Contemporary film reviews debate whether or not *Monster's Ball* succeeds in unmasking the social relations which the reviewers assume the category of Whiteness to mask. The debate itself is problematic because Whiteness as value-form is important but inessential.[34] Unmasking Whiteness's value-form is essential to demystifying what inhibits the play of identificatory hybridity; but such work is inessential to an explanation of how Whites are positioned, structurally, as White in relation to Black. It has social but not ontological explanatory power.

Kalpana Seshadri-Crooks's *Desiring Whiteness: A Lacanian Analysis of Race* labors rigorously to contradict my assessment by reading "black" and "white" through the same intellectual protocols through which Judith Butler reads gender, as the "unpacking of the category of women as subjects of representation." Butler "challenges the notion of gender as tendentious cultural inscription upon the natural sex of the person. Sex is not to nature and the 'raw' as gender is to culture and the 'cooked,' [Butler] contends." Like Butler, Seshadri-Crooks believes that "the assumption that gender identity follows from sex, which in turn entails the stabilizing of desire as heterosexual, is an effect of power." To drive home her point, that she might support her own intellectual protocol in which she does not "focus on the way . . . racial identity . . . is produced by ideology—its investments and its regulations—but rather on the way identity is marked and thought,"[35] Seshadri-Crooks quotes Butler at length:

> Gender is the repeated *stylization of the body*, a set of repeated acts within a highly rigid *regulatory frame that congeal over time* to produce *the appearance of substance*, of *a natural sort of being*. A political genealogy of *gender ontologies*, if it is successful, will deconstruct the substantive appearance of gender into its constitutive acts and locate and account for those acts within the compulsory frames set by the various forces that police the social appearance of gender. To expose the contingent acts that create the appearance of a naturalistic neces-

sity . . . is a task that now takes on the added burden of showing how
the very notion of the subject, intelligible only through its appearance
as gendered, admits of possibilities that have been forcibly foreclosed
by the various *reifications* of gender that have constituted its contingent ontologies.[36]

"Stylization of the body," "acts within a . . . regulatory frame that congeal
over time," "the appearance of substance," "a natural sort of being," "reifications"—such notions mark gender as the arbiter between disparate
entities: gender as a value-form. A value-form that masks and redacts.
Seshadri-Crooks applauds Butler's surgical strike because it can "unmask
the relations of necessity" posited by power and show them to be "purely
contingent." Borrowing Butler's protocol for her work on race, Seshadri-
Crooks then asks, "Is there any 'sense' to naming someone black or
white?" This is a rhetorical way of saying that "one's critical task . . . is
to eliminate the modality of necessity and install in its place the contingency of all relations."[37] But her transposition of Butler's protocols from
the unmasking of gendered relations to a project of unmasking relations
between Black and White runs aground both in theory and in practice.

Let me sum up my objections to this passage by starting at the end.
There is no such narrative as a political genealogy and there is no such
entity as a "gender[ed] ontology" unless the subject under discussion is
not Black. Furthermore, "gender ontology" is an oxymoron marked by
analytic imprecision because it collapses and confuses the social and performative with the structural and positional. In other words, it collapses
and confuses the important with the essential. Throughout this book I
insist on pressing the social and performative into analytic service of the
structural and positional; not vice versa, and certainly not back and forth
on some plane of horizontal significance. If the work of Afro-pessimists
like Saidiya Hartman can be read not only as cultural history but also as
"allegor[ies] of the present . . . narrative[s] for the slave,"[38] then the Afro-
pessimists' skepticism as regards the explanatory power of the analyses
bound to the social and performative functions as a spanner in the works
of Butler's "political genealogy of gender ontologies." Consider Hartman's
questions:

Is it possible to consider, let alone imagine, the agency of the performative when the black performative is inextricably linked with the

specter of contented subjection, the torturous display of the captive body, and the ravishing of the body that is the condition of the other's pleasure? As well, how does one explicate the conditions of slave agency when the very expression seems little more than an oxymoron that restates the paradox of the object status and pained subject constitution of the enslaved? How is it possible to think "agency" when the slave's very condition of being or social existence is defined as a state of determinate negation? In other words, what are the constituents of agency when one's social condition is defined by negation and personhood refigured in the fetishized and fungible terms of the object of property?[39]

Butler suggests that "a political genealogy of gender ontologies . . . will deconstruct the substantive appearance of gender." Here she demonstrates the same optimism for Human liberation found in Negri, Hardt, and film studies. Put crudely, but nonetheless to the point, she seems to be saying, *Free your mind and your ass will follow.* Unmasking, for Butler and Seshadri-Crooks, "the various forces that police the social appearance of gender" takes on the same emancipatory essence that the task of unmasking the social relations pressed into service of the commodity-form takes for Antonio Negri, Michael Hardt, and Lindon Barrett. But Hartman makes it clear that there remains an essential difference, a structural irreconcilability, which is to say an antagonism, between a position duped by "the appearance of a naturalistic necessity"[40] and a "captive body . . . [whose] condition of being . . . is defined as a state of determinate negation . . . [and whose] personhood [is] refigured in the fetishized and fungible terms of the object of property."[41] And this structural antagonism between the subject status of the body and the object status of the Slave hinges, ironically, on their polarized relationships to the performative.

For feminists such as Butler and Seshadri-Crooks, the performative involves a destylization and restylization of the body—an unmasking and subsequent reconfiguring of bodily reification, namely, gender. Hartman has no direct, Black critique or rejection of feminism's de-re-styling performance (whether that performance be analytic or aesthetic, which I will discuss in the next chapter in relation to nudity and Whiteness).

But her text maintains an unpersuaded and underwhelmed stance toward the explanatory, much less liberatory, power of the performative when asserted in conjunction with the Black. This is because it is impossible to divorce Blackness from captivity, mutilation, and the pleasure of non-Blacks. Butler and company assume a presence, masked and reified; Hartman assumes a negation, captive and fungible.

Above I suggested that Seshadri-Crooks, by way of Butler, contradicts my assessments. This is imprecise: in point of fact, she is simply mute in the face of my assessments. Again, the drama of value that Butler imagines is one in which gender stands in as a reified form that masks the hybridity of bodies. The body then, or rather disparate bodies, is a basic "always already" for Butler, Seshadri-Crooks, and most feminism (this includes the feminism of film theory). Granted, though it appears in her assessment as the smallest scale of cartographic coherence, it nonetheless appears as—and herein lies the rub!—a capacity for spatiality and temporality possessed universally by all. But surely Judith Butler, a White American, if not Kalpana Seshadri-Crooks, an East Indian, must recall that Africans went into the hold of ships as bodies and emerged from the holds of those ships as "flesh." "I . . . make a distinction . . . between 'body' and 'flesh' and impose that distinction as the central one between captive and liberated subject-positions. In that sense, before the 'body' there is the 'flesh,' that zero degree of social conceptualization that does not escape concealment under the brush of discourse or the reflexes of iconography."[42] For the body's reification of gender to constitute an essential grammar of suffering there must first be a body there. Feminism, Marxism, and film studies must provide and account for a corpus delicti, the corpse of a murder victim. One would think that true rigor demands some, however short, nod to that historical process through which Black flesh was recomposed as a body before one can write about a universal template called "the body" which can perform and contest gender in dramas of value. In other words, what "event" (what coherence of time) reinstated Black corporeal integrity (reinstated cartographic coherence) so that philosophers and film theorists (and Marxists, filmmakers, and White feminists) could imagine Blackness as possessing the capacity to be staged in dramas where bodily stylization is repeated—where value reifies as gender? This burden of proof is on the Master, not the Slave.

Lacan, Silverman, Negri, Hardt, Butler, Heath, Marc Forster and company must make that case to Fanon, Spillers, Patterson, Hartman, Marriott, Judy, and Mbembe.

> I . . . suggest that "gendering" takes place within the confines of the domestic, an essential metaphor that then spreads its tentacles for male and female subjects over a wide ground of human and social purposes [that ground being civil society]. Domesticity appears to gain its power by way of a common origin of cultural fictions that are grounded in the specificity of proper names, more exactly, a patronymic, which, in turn, situates those subjects that it covers in a particular place. Contrarily, the cargo of a ship might not be regarded as elements of the domestic, even though the vessel that carries the cargo is sometimes romantically personified as "she." The human cargo of a slave vessel—in the effacement and remission of African family and proper names—contravenes notions of the domestic. . . . Under these conditions, one is neither female, nor male, as both subjects are taken into account as *quantities*.[43]

Until one can demonstrate how the corporeal integrity of the Black has indeed been repaired, "a political genealogy of gender ontologies" which "blow[s] apart the sex-gender-desire nexus . . . [and thus] permits resignification of identity as contingency" is a political project the Slave can only laugh at, or weep at. But whether laughing or weeping (for the Slave's counterhegemonic responses are of no essential value and have no structural impact), the Slave is always sidelined by such "resignification of [Human] identity." Resignification of an identity which never signified— an identity void of semiotic play—is nothing to look forward to. Here, an unforgivable obscenity is performed twice over: first, through the typical White feminist gesture that assumes all women (and men) have bodies, ergo all bodies contest gender's drama of value; and, second, by way of the more recent, but no less common, assertions that the analysis of "relations" between White and Black has a handy analog in the analysis of gendered relations. Indeed, for such intellectual protocols to transpose themselves from obscenities to protocols truly meaningful to the Slave (in other words, for their explanatory power to be essential and not merely important), the operative verbs, attached to what Butler calls "the . . . forces that police," would have to be not *mask* and *redact* but *murder.* "Identity" may very well be "the investiture of name, and the marking of reference"[44]—and here is where the postcolonial subject and the White subject of empire can duke it out (if, in the process, they would leave us alone!)—but Blackness marks, references, names, and identifies a corpse. And a corpse is not relational because death is beyond representation, and relation always occurs within representation.

What is the "it" beyond representation that Whiteness murders? In other words, what "evidence" do we have that the violence that positions the Slave, is structurally different from the violence inflicted on the worker, the woman, the spectator, and the postcolonial? Again, as I demonstrated in part 1, the murdered "it" is capacity par excellence, spatial and temporal capacity. Marxism, film theory, and the political common sense of socially engaged White cinema think Human capacity as Butler and Seshadri-Crooks do, as universal phenomena. But Blacks experience Human capacity as a homicidal phenomenon. Fanon, Judy, Mbembe, Hartman, Marriott, Patterson, and Spillers have each, in his or her own way, shown us that the Black lost the coherence of space and time in the hold of the Middle Passage. The philosophy of Judith Butler, the film theory of Kaja Silverman, Mary Ann Doane, and Kalpana Seshadri-Crooks, the Marxism of Antonio Negri and Michael Hardt, the social optimism or pessimism of popular film reviews, and the auteurial intention of the director Marc Forster all leave the Slave unthought. They take as given that the Black has access to dramas of value. But each disparate entity in any drama of value must possess not only spatiality (for even a patch of grass exists in space), but the power to labor on space, the cartographic capacity to make place—if only at the scale of the body. Each disparate entity in any drama of value must possess not only temporality (for even a patch of grass begins-exists-and-is-no-more) but the power to labor over time: the historiographic capacity to narrate "events"—if only the "event" of sexuality. The terrain of the body and the event of sexuality were murdered when the African became a "genealogical isolate."[45] Thus, the explanatory power of the theorists, filmmaker, and film reviewers cited above, at its very best, is capable of thinking Blackness as identity or as identification, conceding, however, as the more rigorous among them do, that "black and white do not say much about *identity*, though they do establish group and personal *identifications* of the subjects involved."[46] But even this concession gets us nowhere. At best, it is a red herring investing our attention in a semiotic impossibility: that of the Slave as signifier. At worst, it puts the cart before the horse, which is to say that no Marxist theory of social change and proletarian recomposition, and no feminist theory of bodily resignification, has been able (or cared) to demonstrate how, when, and where Abraham Lincoln freed the slaves. Yet, they remain, if only by omission, steadfast in their conviction that slavery was abolished. At moments, however, the sensory excess of cinema lets ordinary White film say what extraordinary White folks will not.

TWELVE

Make Me Feel Good

> The story doesn't work if the child doesn't die.
> —MILOS ADDICA, coscreenwriter
> of *Monster's Ball*

THOUGH LITTLE of a scholarly nature has been written about *Monster's Ball*, its release unleashed a torrent of journalistic ink. Given the breadth of social issues the film engages (interracial sex, the burgeoning of the prison-industrial complex, capital punishment, the generative crises in filiation, and the ennui of White masculinity in the twenty-first century) and given the fact that Halle Berry became the second Black woman in history to win a Best Actress Oscar for her performance, no doubt two or three academic articles are at this moment being written or slated for publication. The wide spectrum of journalism about the film spans from the ephemeral "good film/bad film" impressionism of local newspapers' movie sections to more reflective articles in magazines and weekly tabloids such as *Currency* and the *Village Voice*. Taken broadly, the latter reviews are leading indicators of how issues will be framed and how concerns will be distributed once *Monster's Ball* finds its way into the journals of film studies. What the more engaged commentaries share with the short, pithy, newspaper pieces is a proclivity to pronounce the film as "good" or "bad" not as good or bad entertainment (this is left to the local newspaper's movie section) but as social art.

The headlines of the local newspaper reviews indicate a consensus of approval: "Poetic, Fragile 'Ball' "; "Hot and Heavy"; "A Beauty of a Role for Berry"; "Probing American Taboos."[1] Even Nicole Keeter's review in *Time* magazine, one of the few short pieces which lament the film's "symbolic heavy-handedness," nonetheless contends that this "might have resulted in an oppressive film had [Forster] not backed off to facilitate memorable lead performances" by Halle Berry and Billy Bob Thornton.[2] The enthusiasm of, and kudos from, local papers was almost too robust for their columns to contain. Witness Robert Koehler's genuflection to Thornton's portrayal of Hank Grotowski: "It's a measure of Thornton's extra-ordinary subtle performance that the changes in Hank arrive in barely perceptible movements. There's the sense, one that only comes in the most exciting screen acting works, of a thesp uncovering his character's layers in the moment it happens on camera." And to the film's acoustic minimalism Koehler's nod is just as approving: "In a year of dreadful overscoring, Asche and Spencer's synth and guitar underscore is in perfect moody tandem with the images."[3]

There is widespread consensus among the newspaper articles that the raw sex scene between Berry and Thornton is not a racist pornotroping of Black female sexuality but a sensitive and poignant plot point which elegantly facilitates the much anticipated transformation of Hank Grotowski. (In fact, the question of racist pornotroping only arose, as far as I am aware, in a radio discussion between several Black film critics and scholars on *Democracy Now!* the morning after the Oscars.)[4]

As we ascend out of the commonplace into the rare, that is, from local newspaper reviews to magazine articles, the consensus stands in stark contrast. Unlike daily newspaper journalists who applauded the ability of a Swiss director to shoot Southern gothic and get it right, Michael Atkinson of the *Village Voice* calls Marc Forster "a careerist dallying in the foothills of American crackerdom as if earning a Cub Scout badge."[5] Alex Fung demurs: "The pivotal sex scene, designed as the film's turning point, where the oppressive despair and hopelessness pervading the grim Southern gothic gradually gives way to a fragile optimism, fails to fulfill its transcendent ambitions, and becomes bogged down by ill-conceived directional flourishes."[6] Both Richard von Busack's "The Hot Squat" and

Jonathan Rosenbaum's "All Is Forgiven" bemoan what they consider to be the script's contrivance and the faux social consciousness of its narrative. "The key for scripting a *succès d'estime*," writes von Busack, is to "take a not very controversial subject [miscegenation] and treat it with the maximum amount of sordidness, to make it seem more vital. . . . The questions *Monster's Ball* raises get settled with risible ease—if we all just sat on a porch and ate ice cream together, we'd all get along." Rosenbaum, however, unlike von Busack, is willing to elevate the film to art-house status. He suggests that it does indeed interpellate the high-brow sensibilities of the same kind of progressive and college-educated spectator who left the theater reflecting on the atom bomb and the vulnerability of human intimacy thirty years ago after viewing *Hiroshima, Mon Amour*. Rosenbaum believes the script and narrative strategies to be "ridiculously contrived" and in service to an "outlandish absolution fantasy." He resuscitates Pauline Kael's early essay "Fantasies of the Art House Audience," along with Raymond Durgnat's rejoinder to Kael, "How Not to Enjoy the Movies," to contemplate why literati such as Rosenbaum himself find " 'wish fulfillment in the form of cheap and easy congratulation on their sensitivities and their liberalism.' " Rosenbaum's overarching sense that *Monster's Ball* provides White educated liberals absolution without guilt gives his essay the same negative orientation toward the film's socially transformative potential as Fung's, von Busack's, and Atkinson's. Toward the end of his essay he drives this point home: "*Monster's Ball* pointedly excludes as many traces of society as possible, ascribing racism to individuals and their own twisted orneriness . . . and assigning responsibility for capital punishment and even the desire for it mainly to the people being executed. We're never told what Leticia's husband's crime was, but no matter. He accepts the judgment that he's worthless and deserves to be exterminated, silencing any of our objections before we can raise them."[7]

I have no desire to settle the argument which the local reviews and the magazine and tabloid articles construct: Is the film entertaining or boring? Is it powerfully interpellative and socially transformative art, or is it naive and contrived agitprop? Even the question of whether the film slides into racist pornotroping or scales new cinematic heights in Black femininity needs to be set aside until we can return to it later on, armed with the proper intellectual protocols. At this point we have only the protocols of exploitation and alienation which, as we saw in part 1, are not only inadequate to an apprehension of the Black's grammar of suffering but are also the very protocols through which the Black's grammar of suffering is produced and compounded. (While giving her Oscar acceptance speech Halle Berry gasped—in horror or with gratitude, who could tell?—as she thanked Marc Forster for taking her places she had never been before. I want to demonstrate the fallacy of this sentiment: Forster, or more precisely the cinematic apparatus, did not "take" Berry anywhere but rather threw into relief the granite-like nature of her pained object status.)[8] For the Black female (or male, or child) body to be exploited there would have to be a Black female (or male, or child) body on screen. There was not. There has never been.

Still, the question of Halle Berry's femininity being exploited is one which I, like so many Black people, find hard to shake.[9] But in its very posing there is a trap. It snares us with the same structure of feeling out of which the local newspaper journalists and the magazine writers are snared by (as I predict the forthcoming White film theorizing on *Monster's Ball* will be): the dilemmas of a Human subject as engaged through the machinations of hegemony. Put another way, the snare is none other than the seduction of amnesia. We then begin to believe that we can be called, hailed by, a Gramscian historic bloc, and we forget that one cannot be Black and historic.

As I stated in part 1, I take the recent celebration of superstars Halle Berry and Denzel Washington in both the Black press and the mainstream critical establishment as symptomatic of a refusal or inability to countenance the long shadow of slavery insofar as it writes a history of the present. That is, the heralding of Black stardom, now disavowing its relation to long-standing cinematic stereotypes, is founded on a belief in not only the possibility of redress (or even reparation) in civil society but also its relative ease. Central to this belief is (1) a historical reduction of slavery to the relation of chattel and (2) a formulation of Black emancipation and enfranchisement limited to the most nominal dimensions of civil rights and liberties.

Embracing Black people's agency as subjects of civil society (i.e., as subjects of rights and liberties) and even their potential to act as or partner with enforcers of the law (in an ordinary cop show or as with Denzel Washington's military psychologist in *Antwone Fisher*) presents itself as an acting out of the historic paradox of Black nonexistence (i.e., the mutable continuity of social death). Here, Black "achievement," in films like *Antwone Fisher* (discussed in part 2) and *Monster's Ball*, for example, requires the bracketing out of that nonexistence in hopes of telling a tale of loss and recovery that is intelligible in the national imagination.[10] And cinema's insistence on Black personhood (rather than a radical questioning of the terror embedded in that very notion) operates most poignantly in *Monster's Ball*'s problematic coding of gender and domesticity—as well as in journalistic and theoretical responses to that cinematic coding.

Rosenbaum's "All Is Forgiven" resembles the concerns of Black writers on cinema who ask if the Black woman's (or man's) sexuality is exploited or instead lovingly portrayed when he declares *Monster's Ball* to be agitprop because, as he contends, the film ascribes "racism to individuals and their own twisted orneriness" and because it "excludes as many traces of society as possible." Again, I am not arguing for or against the content of Rosenbaum's claims (though my sentiments are with the content of those Black claims which suggest Berry's "body" has indeed been pornotroped). I am attempting something more essential than what Jared Sexton calls "an anthropology of sentiment" (even when those sentiments are my own). What I am saying is that—content of the concerns aside—the labor of being concerned is ethical work, essential to one's ontological status only to the degree one is not Black, because there is no Black ontology. Rosenbaum is, however (and however accidentally), on to something essential with respect to Blacks when he observes that Lawrence Musgrove "accepts the judgment that he's worthless and deserves to be exterminated, silencing any of our objections before we can raise them."[11] This is essential because an objection silenced before it can be raised has yet to become an objection: it is pre-ontological, or, perhaps more precisely, hyper-ontological. If, as in the case of Lawrence Musgrove, this objection not raised is indeed alive (can eat, shit, walk, fuck, speak, laugh, and cry), it is "a fatal way of being alive"; which is to say, "it" "'don't look human, does it?'"[12] We are back to the emergence of modernity discussed in part 1, back to the birth of civil society whose value-form is the "human" and whose "circuit of displacement, substitution, and signification" is hegemony—a drama of value staged between disparate entities, back to the articulation between Aztec and ecclesiastic, all of which brings us back to the Negro, those object(ions) silenced "before we can raise" them: "the beached whales of the sexual universe, unvoiced, misseen, not doing, awaiting *their* verb."[13]

Monster's Ball executes a mise-en-scène in which dramas are performed as struggles over filiation, masculinity, alienated labor-power, Whiteness, and the phallus, each one a value-form. Rosenbaum's film review stumbles, albeit symptomatically, on the realization that the value-form, regardless of its content—that is, the value-form as a generic arbiter—is not elastic enough to include the Black as one of its disparate entities.[14] And the film itself, both at the level of the diegesis and at the level of enunciation (that is, at the level of the cinematic apparatus) is unable to maintain the illusion of a Black articulation with, or within, the world. This breakdown of the illusion of Black articulation, which happens only symptomatically if at all in feminism, film theory, and metacentury-commentaries on suffering like the tomes of Antonio Negri and Michael Hardt, breaks through *Monster's Ball* with a vengeance. This eruption occurs, however, no thanks to the script or the intentionality of the film's director, but as a result of the sensory excess of its form, an excess which allows in (demands of?) an ordinary White film what is disavowed by extraordinary White folks.

We have seen how the execution sequence is a highly concentrated track of imagery through which this breakdown occurs, but so is the sequence of shots immediately preceding the infamous and controversial sex scene: chapter 16 of the DVD, titled, without irony, "Make Me Feel Good." Producer Lee Daniels (a Black American) wanted a director who was "not Black" and "not White" (not White American, he adds), "someone that had a completely naive view on racism, someone that was foreign, that would look at the interracial relationship from a child's eye, and not give a Black and White perspective on the film."[15] However, the White, foreign-child director hired by Daniels directed a sex scene ("my director," Daniels disclaims, "is responsible for that scene") with enough adult-like quotations from the extensive corpus of interracial pornography as to call into question Daniels's claims regarding Forster's sexual naiveté or interracial wonder. Both Daniels and Forster (and the screenwriters Milo Addica and Will Rokos) would no doubt counter this assessment of a naked and inebriated Black woman being thrown about the couch, coffee table, and floor with some assertion of Leticia's agency during this scene. (Berry makes this claim herself when she comments—in the DVD's special features voice-over commentary—how Leticia's looking back at Hank when they are fucking "doggie style," marks a significant intervention whereby Leticia is telling him not to treat her like he treats the White prostitute, leading him to stop, Berry claims, and change positions. But in this anxious and self-protecting assertion, Berry does not explain how Leticia knows what Hank does with a White prostitute or that he sees a prostitute at all: this is a moment of anxious conflation between the speaking subject and the subject of speech, between the apparatus and the screen.) And Forster, Addica, and Rokos would no doubt counter my assessment by drawing our attention to the montage that cross-cuts the violent sex with images of a caged bird and pair of White hands setting it free, images, Forster informs us, inspired by Maya Angelou's *I Know Why the Caged Bird Sings*.[16] Being drawn into such arguments would only lead us down the road of film theory and radical feminism (à la Butler and Seshadri-Crooks, above), questions of cinema, interpretations of the body, and their combined significance to a socially transformative aesthetic. Instead, I accept that both Halle Berry and Leticia Musgrove belong to everything and every*body* from the cinematic apparatus (Forster, Addica, Rokos, and Thornton—but not Daniels) to the cinematic screen (Hank, but not Lawrence), if by "accept" I am understood to mean that I leave questions of presence and performance to White women, Marxists, and the bulk of Black film theorists.

Nudity and sex are at issue here but exploitation is not. How so? The flaunting nudity of White people in cinema, and in civil society more broadly, manifests itself as one of femininity's many contested dramas. What this nudity means; who (gender-wise) is allowed, or even should, display it; what political gestures the contestation and performance of its codes generate (whether exploitative or liberatory)—these are some of the tiresome and aggravating questions through which White women (and men) structure their drama of value arbitrations. The rub, of course, is that everyone must contend with the force and fallout of this drama for the simple reason that the assumptive logics of a woman's body in fact index a shared historical and anthropological capacity between White women and White men, and then, secondarily, between all non-Blacks, joint and severally. The White woman is the most narrativized trope of this phenomenon, but there exists a democracy of ontological capacity

between White men and White women, just as there is a democracy of
ontological incapacity between Black men and Black women: suffering
experiences are gendered, aged, and classed but the grammar of suffering
is not. Robert Williams, the Black revolutionary, was struck by this as a
young boy when his father worked at a railroad house in North Carolina:
"Black women walking from Newtown crossed the railroad yard on their
way to work in the kitchens of white families. White [male] workers using
the washroom 'would walk all around the place and in the yard nude. They
would do that,' according to black workers, 'just so that the black women
would see them.' . . . White workers acted this way, African American
men felt, because 'the only thing they had was their white authority, the
power of their white skin.'"[17]

There are important social implications of this performance of power
and authority, but a discussion of them would enable only a feeble return back to the "Make Me Feel Good" chapter of *Monster's Ball*. Instead, I wish to mine the essential structural implications of nudity. The
social implications would lead us to an interpretation of nudity and the
grammar of exploitation and alienation; what we need is to be led to
the structural implications of nudity and the grammar of accumulation
and fungibility. White nude men outside the railroad house or White nude
women in civil society are essential not because of the varying ways they
play out as value-forms, but because they can (they have the capacity to)
play out as value-forms. Nudity, then, in its display and contestation as a
value-form (its disparate valency in civil society), is a universal phenomena for some and a homicidal phenomenon for Blacks. The semiotics of
nudity as drama of value (whether performed through the barbarism of
White feminist gestures or the barbarism of White masculinist gestures)
is an assertion of White capacity in contradistinction to Black "monstrosity."[18] White women's structural capacity to claim and contest this drama
(whether win, lose, or draw, through personal displays of nudity in the
public and private, or by negotiating the battle lines between the sexual
exploitation of pornotroping and sexual "liberation" in theory and the
aesthetic), their dramaturgical capacity, if you will, their status as "entities," however disparate and devalued in relation to White male performances of nudity—in other words, their possible locations in the semiotics of intra-Master dramas—is what sets them apart from Leticia on the
couch, Lawrence in the death chamber, and Tyrell on the side of the road.

This marks a range of seemingly infinite positions which neither Leticia nor Halle Berry (Lawrence nor Sean Combs, Tyrell nor Coronji Calhoun) can take. And so the question of pornotroping and exploitation is hobbled at best and anti-Black at worst. While the performance of nude "bodies" can be either hegemonic or counter-hegemonic—that is, can have a socially regressive or socially transformative impact on the machinations of civil society—the performance of nude "flesh" cannot. This is common, though uncommonly unspoken, knowledge: the grammar of suffering's discourse as opposed to the discourse of suffering itself. Without this grammar, the structure of White pleasure through communal nudity would crumble. And every White (and Black) person knows how necessary the Black is to even the most naked White pleasures. Halle Berry knows this as she is about to take off her clothes, and she knows that "exploitation" cannot even begin to explain what she knows.

The sequence of shots leading up to "Make Me Feel Good" indicate this. Here, the homeostasis of Black flesh ruptures the hubris implied by film theory and feminism's need for a Black performative body.[19] This rupture is an unforeseen and unscripted irruption through which the homeostatic object, Berry-as-flesh, breaks in on the screen of the subject, Leticia-as-body. Tyrell has died. Hank has driven Leticia back to her home. They are seated on the sofa (figure 20). From the commentary of Forster, Addica, and Rokos, we are led to understand that the script called for Hank and Leticia to be positioned on the couch, for them to have a few drinks, exchange a few brief words, and then for Leticia to say "Make me feel good," start to take off her clothes, and crawl on top of Hank, to move swiftly from being seated to drinking to sex, for her to waste no time in putting the moves on Hank. As Milo Addica recalls: "When we wrote this we really had this whole animalistic kind of—you know—two people kind of grabbing and touching, sweating and fucking the living shit out of each other. Doing whatever they need to do to extract some kind of good feeling from it. . . . It wasn't the typical lovemaking scene, it was more about two people getting it on."[20] Forster then tells the two writers that when they started shooting, Berry, rather than sticking to the script, went into a long improvisation; in short, Leticia says things Leticia was not meant to say. Leticia tells Hank how often she told Tyrell that life in America is impossible for a man who is both fat and Black.

20 Leticia trying to speak with Hank (both are on the couch),
    in a scene from *Monster's Ball*

LETICIA: [*to Hank*] He was so *fat*! [*She is crying, grimacing, laughing
hysterically.*] You saw how fat he was. I don't care what I brought
in this house, he just ate it up. I don't care what it was I brought
in here. I bring some Popeye's Chicken, that boy eat the WHOLE
thing 'fore I even get a chance for me to get me a bite of the
chicken. He just eat it all! He would eat his little ass off! You ain't
never seen nobody eat like that. He would eat candy; gumballs.
He make me take him up there, over to the Super K-Mart and he
put them quarters in that gumball machine. He had to wait till
he get the red gumball. He always had to get the red gumball.

On this score Hank has nothing to say to her; he sits forward on the
couch and looks at his hands. It is not that he agrees with her, for as citizen and prison guard, his commerce with, or trafficking in, Blacks is not
burdened with the imposition of Black ethical dilemmas. Nor does he
disagree with her. It is not that Hank sees Tyrell as being either deserv-
ing or undeserving of the perils of obesity and Blackness, but that Hank
has no framework through which to think questions of deservability together with the figure of a Black child. Tyrell, in the private and quotidian
of Hank Grotowski, is an objection silenced before it can be raised. In
anthropomorphic terms, and in concert with what actually takes place,
Tyrell is already dead on arrival.

HANK: He sounds like a character, I guess.

At this point Billy Bob Thornton may be wondering what all of this is about, what kind of improvising he is going to have to do in response—in other words, will Berry take her clothes off and move on him, or will he have to make up some lines to get them there, and when, exactly they are going to do it.

> LETICIA: [*crying more*] He get that red gumball and he just eat.
> [*Hank puts his arm around her as she cries.*]
> LETICIA: I did every single thing [*slapping her knee*] I could do! I was really good. I was really good. [*crying*] I didn't want him to be fat like that. I did not want my baby to be fat like that; 'cause I know a Black man in America—you can't be like that. I try to—[*crying, slapping her knee*]. I tried to tell him you can't be like that, you can't be like that in America and Black. I was just—[*now sobbing inaudibly*].
> HANK: I'm not sure what you want me to do.

Is this a question or a demand: the demand to stop the improv, the stream of consciousness flow of Blackness and flesh? Whatever the case, Hank's, or Billy Bob's "I'm not sure what you want me to do" has the effect of punctuation on Leticia's, or Berry's stream of consciousness, it snaps them both back into their roles (see figure 21).

> LETICIA: I want you to—[*lowering her halter top, climbing on to his lap*] I want you to make me feel good.

The symptomatic progression of Halle Berry's "improvisation" advances through a rubric of terror, a rubric in excess of fear. It moves from Tyrell's obesity to images of the boy devouring the world: "that boy eat the WHOLE thing." In point of fact, however, it is Tyrell who has just been devoured, eaten alive by the necessity of the (White) body's drama of value. The extent to which this necrophilic necessity has been devouring Leticia—slowly, for the length of the screenplay, rather than in one spectacular feast—breaks in on Halle Berry, who cannot keep the knowledge of this terror from breaking in on Leticia. (The Black is homeostatic at the level of speaking subject—or apparatus—which is Berry the actor, as well as at the level of the subject of speech, which is Leticia the character. To quote Fanon, "the Negro is a Negro everywhere.") Still, there is

21 Leticia about to take off her shirt (with Hank on the couch)

displacement in her words "You can't be like that in America and Black," displacement in an effort to hold on to that thread of agency that might mark some real distance between Tyrell-the-devoured and Leticia-the-exploited. But the thin logic of the sentences yields an even thinner alibi for such distinctions. As she speaks, she collapses the distance and renders exploitation an inessential grammar of suffering. There is, in her "improv," a devastating annihilation of any distance between (a) a world devoured and devouring, (b) Blackness, and (c) America. In other words, the imaginary collapse of complete consummation, all of the Africans in the country, and all of the territory of that country cannibalizes any scintilla of agency, which is the flip side, that often unspoken and unacknowledged performative gesture against exploitation: agency is cannibalized and distance (distinction) is annihilated when Berry's stream of consciousness breaks in on the script and marks her (and Leticia, Sean Combs/Lawrence, and Coronji Calhoun/Tyrell) "as both victim and spectator—spectator as victim—of [a] lynching." Put differently, accumulation and fungibility break in on exploitation and alienation as the Black is confronted with the essence of the structural "reduction which is precisely, your annihilation and their pleasure."[21] And in the realm of the structural, as Hartman points out, performative agency is hardly the fellow traveler of accumulation and fungibility.[22]

Toward the end of her "improv," the alibi of exploitation wears even thinner as her stream of consciousness confronts her not only with the impossibility of being Black in America but with the impossibility of being a Black parent in America. Her inability to parent Tyrell is not performative but structural, inextricably bound to her inability to protect herself. The vulnerability of both "parent" and "child" is open, gratuitous, complete.

Only Tyrell's "parents" (and here the quotation marks matter, for I use the word skeptically) relate to Tyrell as though he had or even could possibly rise to the level of an objection. This is due in part to the fact that they are delusional enough to think that they have risen to such a level themselves. During their last moments together in the prisoners' visiting room, Lawrence tells Tyrell that he is to be executed because, as he puts it, "I'm a bad man." With this sentence, Lawrence inserts himself as a subject into modernity's moral, jurisprudential, and anthropological discourses which, we know from Ronald Judy, would break apart were they to look up and find him there.[23] But if Lawrence Musgrove can explain his execution as being contingent on moral and jurisprudential transgression—*I'm bad because I broke the Sixth Commandment; I'm to be executed because I broke the law*—and as also being possible due to his sense of his own spatial and temporal (i.e., anthropological) capacity—*I am a man*—then his embrace of his "son," manifest in the fatherly wisdom *Do not grow up to be like me* or *Avoid my mistakes*, would have to be more meaningful than the embrace of two "genealogical isolate[s]"[24] because, by definition, a Slave father's filial embrace of a Slave son has all the markings of an oxymoron, a "father" and "son" who perform filiation against a mise-en-scène void of the paternal signifier.

Certainly, Leticia's sentiments are in accord with this, intuitively if not analytically. But this profundity is lost on Hank as he sits with her in the living room and lost as well on the narrative of the film itself. The insatiable appetite for delusion which both "parents" share as regards "their" "child" is shared by neither the film itself nor the world beyond the frame which the film apprehends as referent. In the *San Francisco Chronicle*, Berry speaks of the scene in which she beats and berates Coronji Calhoun (Tyrell) as being "a lot harder than even the love scene." Carla Meyer, the (White) writer who interviewed Berry, attributes Berry's worry to the fact that "Coronji Calhoun had been cast through an open call in Louisiana and had little acting experience." Meyer does not make a connection between violence, Blackness, sexuality, and the impossibility of Black filiation.[25] But this connection links the claim of the speaking subject (Berry as actor, as a component of the cinematic apparatus) that beating Tyrell was "a lot harder than even the love scene" with the lament of the subject of speech (Leticia) that a man can not be both Black and fat in America.

Surprisingly, it is Coronji Calhoun, the "child" himself, who, unlike the critic Carla Meyer, unlike the subjects of speech Lawrence and Leticia Musgrove, and unlike the speaking subject Halle Berry, makes a good faith attempt to say something about what the referent (the world beyond the frame) and film "know," even in the midst of such widespread bad faith and disavowal. Berry said, " 'I worried that I would somehow damage him emotionally, not just in doing the scene, but down the road.' " Here, Berry, as speaking subject, a component of, if not the level of enunciation, at least the cinematic apparatus, imagines herself as elevated to the level of an objection, if not beyond. She speaks as though the materiality of her words and actions can have the impact of a structural intervention, which is to say she is a Slave with the hubris of a Human: "So I talked to him a lot and hugged and kissed him a lot. He said [and this is key], ' "You don't have to worry about what you say; it can't be as bad as how they treat me at school," ' Berry says, her voice softening. 'But I hear now he's the most popular kid in his school. So I guess (the movie) helped.' "[26] The compensatory hopefulness lodged in the phrase "So I guess (the movie) helped" has much in common with Lawrence Musgrove's confession, "I'm a bad man," and with Leticia Musgrove's observation that a man can't be that fat and Black in America. What, in this latter compensatory gesture, is the essential combination signifying structural impossibility: fat in America or Black in America? If obesity were indeed a bar in the United States of what Fanon referred to as absolute dereliction, then Henry Kissinger's power in political economy and sex appeal in the libidinal economy would bear the mark of a revolutionary breakthrough.[27]

These three compensatory gestures (the assumption of Black manhood, the presumption that a woman could raise a Black child to manhood, which further assumes that Black women and Black mothers are ontologically possible, and the belief that circuits of hegemony, the materiality of the symbolic order—*the film helped*—can have a structural impact on Blackness) subtend each other in a kind of iron-clad triangulation ensuring the humanity of the Black, until, that is, the Black "child" himself speaks: "You don't have to worry about what you say." Coronji Calhoun probably shares the aspirations of Leticia, Lawrence, and Berry to subjectivity (i.e., he may be on record as saying, *I'm a child just like any other child*), but his words are symptomatic of an unconscious knowledge of the referent, of the world, as a place where he is ontologically impossible, where *Black* and *child* cannot be reconciled. "You don't have to worry about what you say." It is interesting to note that in this, the first clause of his sentence, Coronji Calhoun does not tell Halle Berry, "You don't have worry about what you say *to me*." The phrase is, albeit unconsciously, abbreviated, interrupted, as though "to me" is not only grammatically gratuitous but existentially unwarranted. The hubris (or hope) through which the three Black adults (Leticia, Lawrence, and Halle Berry) assume a "me" is too elaborate, too sophisticated for a child. Coronji leaves it to them.

Coronji, young as he is, cannot manipulate speech in a compensatory fashion; he cannot manufacture the tissue of illusion needed to defend himself against "the violence of the real." As such, he cannot generate the kind of alibis of "survival" through which Leticia, Lawrence, and Halle Berry remake themselves as bodies. "As a symbol of the . . . lacerating ground upon which phobia and fantasy meet, the black child, in taking up the burden of such imagery . . . has been fatally exposed to the glare of the phobic anxieties constructed upon his visual image."[28] So, too, have the Black "child's" "parents" "been exposed" even as they labor rigorously and convincingly, if only to themselves and their kind, to resist "the burden of such imagery." But Coronji Calhoun's missing "to me" ropes the adults back into their filial thanatology which their compensatory speech-gestures had hoped to evade: his syntax marks them as a family of death.

Lawrence's "I'm a bad man," as a compensatory gesture, comforts the "father," and it also comforts the viewer with the notion that, genealogically speaking, Lawrence once had a position in the symbolic order, a place that he transgressed. Lawrence sees his execution as contingent on that transgression. The execution is proof of a transgression; the transgression is proof of a position within the symbolic order. Guilt, and therefore agency, can be ascribed to Lawrence Musgrove—even under sentence of death. *My agency*, he seems to be telling his "son," *is not in dodging the electric chair; on the contrary, I accept it: the chair is a consequence. The consequence confirms my agency. My agency is in my being able to pass useful knowledge down to you, father to son, as though you and I both were positioned by discourse, by symbolic relationality and not by filial thanatology.* This homosocial bond between Black "fathers" and Black "sons" is mythical. It cannot be sustained, if for no other reason than because at some point it is confronted with the necrophilia that sustains the homosocial bond between White fathers and sons, White mothers and daughters.

David Marriott's *On Black Men* establishes the relationship between, on the one hand, the murder of Blacks, along with the mutilation of Black genitals, common to the ritual of lynching and, on the other hand, ordinary White people's capacity to "recognize" themselves with filial and affilial coherence, that is, as men, women, parents, children, lovers, and citizens. Marriott suggests that the lynching photograph is an imagistic memento that stands in for the corporeal memento of Black fingers, toes, and genitals. The photograph's shelf life may not be much longer than the shelf life of Black genitals (many people kept Black body parts fermented in preservative jars). However, like the framed cinematic image, the lynching photograph's circuit of exchange, and thus its surplus value, is greater than that of the body part. This is because the White person who poses beside the strung-up, mutilated corpse becomes "a figure in a public event" and acquires "a means to fashion the self through the image of a dead black man and the identification with fellow whites which can follow."[29]

Marriott presents the *image* of Black death as a moment in a metonymic chain that begins with, and so contains the residue of, "the stink of the real"—that mutilated body whose decomposition is preserved by the image.[30] Decomposition, then, is what happens to Black flesh as the Slave's "genealogical isolation," his or her "object status,"[31] is reenacted, first in a lynching, then in a lynching photograph—and then, once again, in the average film, like *Monster's Ball.* Subsequently, the capacity for composition and recomposition of White subjectivity is accomplished by the White body's insertion into, and exchange of, this "grotesque family album" of Black flesh. The lynching, and the scene of lynching preserved in photography and in cinema, is a gift which Whites exchange, libidinally and literally, among themselves. Blackness is what gives this gift its fungible quality—its gift-ness—because no other body in modernity is synonymous with accumulation. "Blackness is a vicarious, disfiguring, joyful pleasure, passionately enabling as well as substitutively dead."[32] As such,

Whites experience lynching, whether "live" on the tree, or fragmented through the prism of photography and cinema, as the gift of filiation, the capacity to have and inherit parental "legacies," and as the gift of affiliation, the capacity to be recognized, and act as a community ("The crowd screamed as the knife flashed, first up, then down, cutting the dreadful thing away and the blood came roaring down. Then the crowd rushed forward tearing at the body with their hands, with knives, with rocks, with stones, howling and cursing").[33]

The White subject's desire (desire reproduced in cinema, on the photograph, or at the lynching itself) to be the one holding the knife instead of the one being cut "shows a willingness to pay [one's] dues and belong to something greater than [oneself], to be one with the general will."[34] What is fundamental—structural, ontological—here pertains not so much to the horrific experience, the grotesqueness, of lynching generically. This would lead us to conclude that lynching is undesirable and should therefore be discontinued. This is probably as significant a sentiment as those against torture or starvation. The ontological significance, however, is that recognition of Blacks is overdetermined by their status "as abject representatives of death" and, most important, that Whites cannot recognize themselves in a world where it is impossible to recognize Blacks. Recognition is overdetermined by Blackness because Blackness is overdetermined by death; lynching, photography, and cinema are the institutional memory of an ontological necessity.

Filial and affilial recognition—subjectivity—is a question of composition: the composition of the body and the composition of the commons. Curiously enough, we have returned not only to Antonio Negri, Michael Hardt, and Judith Butler, but to Stephen Heath as well. "*Composition*," Heath informs us, "will organize the frame in function of the human figures in their actions." The Black cannot be filially or affilially composed or re-composed because filiation and affiliation are predicated—that is, they trade—on Black decomposition (the structural violence of genealogical isolation and its institutional memory) as the guarantor of Human coherence: value. Without coherence, or "narrative significance," the frame falls apart. The logic of movement that centers the frame would appear illogical, and space could not cohere as place—all of which bodes ill for the subject and his or her commons. "It is narrative significance that at any moment sets the space of the frame to be followed and 'read,' and that determines the development of the filmic cues in their contributions to the definition of space frame. . . . *Space becomes place—narrative as the taking place of film.* . . . What is crucial is the conversion of seen into scene, the holding signifier on signified: the frame, composed, centered, narrated, is the point of that conversion." [35] But if David Marriott, Frantz Fanon, Hortense Spillers, Orlando Patterson, Saidiya Hartman, Ronald Judy, and Achille Mbembe are correct, then "human figures in their actions" cannot have their Humanness guaranteed if those actions are not a priori imbricated in the mutilation, the genealogical isolation, of the Black. If this were not the case, then on what grounds could those "actions" be deemed and redeemed, composed and recomposed, as "Human"? If "what is crucial is the conversion of seen into scene," then modernity has made it impossible to convert the "seen" of one body (the White) into the "scene" of a Human figure without first converting the "seen" of another body (the Black) into the "scene" of absolute dereliction. This, and not labor-power, is the essential "gift" of the Middle Passage to modernity. Lynching, photography, and cinema are among the institutional memories of this gift. Hence their necessity to the legacy of Human endeavor writ large: to the logics of filiation, affiliation, and the frame. Legacy, then, that metonymy of "events" which cohere as "heritage," has in modernity a necrophilic structure. It feeds off strange fruit. Legacy is indeed "a gift from father to son." "That gift, the desire and power to castrate—to take and so to take on—sexuality of black men, brings them together and forges their futures as white men."[36]

If this is the case, then the logics of filiation, affiliation, and the frame are not universal: someone must always be outside the frame. The White child, "seeing himself through the enraptured eyes of his mother and father *and the doomed eyes of the black man* . . . knows that what he has seen [the spectacle of Black death] is a mirror in whose reflection his father had chosen to reveal 'to him a great secret which would be the key to his life forever.' "[37] The fact that Sonny Grotowski turns his eyes away from "the doomed eyes of the black man," Lawrence, may or may not have social significance. Marc Forster places great hope in this gesture because Sonny's suicide is an important plot point in Hank's character transformation. But its structural, ontological, significance is nil, for the simple reason that Lawrence and Tyrell cannot strap Hank Grotowski to a chair and burn his genitals with electricity as a means of suturing their filiation. Before Lawrence Musgrove can pass his legacy on to Tyrell, he must intervene structurally in Hank's relationship to Sonny, which is nothing short of a revolution against the Western Hemisphere's touchstones of cohesion. To think of the living filiation of White families feeding off of the dead filiation of Black "families" would leave Lawrence speechless. Like Tyrell, he would witness his "to me" being eaten alive.

Likewise, Halle Berry's intervention stems from the presumption of a living, rather than a dead, filiation. "So I talked to him a lot and hugged and kissed him a lot"—just as any mother would. And then she performed the beating, the berating, the "hard" sex, the scenes of subjection (as Hartman puts it)—just as every Slave must. The compensatory gesture of Halle Berry and Leticia and Lawrence Musgrove, this lying and self-deception, is a form of necessity so widely circulated among Blacks as a virtue as to warrant its own name: *mentoring*.[38]

Perhaps Coronji Calhoun was trying to mentor Halle Berry and she was too distracted to be mentored. Or maybe she knew all too well how his words implicated her in his nonpersonhood. Omitting the "to me" in his clause suggests: *I have no subjective presence to be addressed—one's address cannot interpellate me, for the capacity to interpellate, in and of itself, is defined in my absence* (like an objection silenced before it can be raised). Then there is that part of the clause which was not omitted, "You don't have to worry about what you say." Here again, Coronji is mentoring Berry, and mentoring her in good faith, unlike the bad faith mentoring she imparts to him, and the Musgroves impart to Tyrell: *"You don't have to worry about what you say" because* you, *Halle Berry, have no interlocutors who could hear what you say. You are without "contemporaries."*[39] In this, my "mother" and my "father," we are one and the same. But Black children rarely mentor Black adults, and Black adults rarely mentor in good faith. There are things Black parents dare not speak to Black children, and that "rather homeostatic thought: the Negro" is foremost among them.[40]

The coherence of man, woman, child, family, home, and frame—civil society, the commons—depends on cinematic rituals to reenact this homeostasis, to fortify and extend the interlocutory life of that spectator who can hold the knife to the genitals, rather than that spectator whose genitals are to be chilled by the steel. In this way, true cinema's addressees experience something greater than themselves: a concrete ontics, a sense that they are at one with the general will of civil society, and that bonds of kinship can be forged between themselves and their contemporaries in the commons.

IT IS CUSTOMARY for a book like this to end with a prescriptive gesture, at least the germ of a new beginning if not a new world, a seed to be nurtured and cultivated by Vladimir Lenin's question, *What is to be done?* Even when such seeds were not sown throughout the book, an author might be tempted to harvest a yield, however meager, in the conclusion. Not only have such seeds not been sown in this book, but I have argued that anti-Blackness is the genome of this horticultural template for Human renewal. Given the structural violence that it takes to produce and reproduce a Slave—violence as the structure of Black life, as opposed to violence as one of many lived Black experiences— a concluding consideration of Lenin's question would ring hollow.

Frantz Fanon came closest to the only image of sowing and harvesting that befits this book. Quoting Aimé Césaire, he urged his readers to start "the end of the world," the "only thing . . . worth the effort of starting," a shift from horticulture to pyrotechnics.[1] Rather than mime the restoration and reorganization dreams which conclusions often fall prey to, however unwittingly,

Fanon dreams of an undoing, however implausible, for its own sake. Still, there are moments when Fanon finds his own flames too incendiary. So much so that he momentarily backs away from the comprehensive emancipation he calls for. Which is why one can find the Fanon of the Slave on the same page as the Fanon of the postcolonial subject. Nonetheless, I am humbled by his efforts, and though I am freighted with enough hubris to extend his ensemble of questions beyond his unintentional containment strategies, I know better than to underrate their gravitas by offering—or even hinting at—a roadmap to freedom so extensive it would free us from the epistemic air we breathe. To say we *must* be free of air, while admitting to knowing no other source of breath, is what I have tried to do here.

In the preceding chapters I have critiqued Marxism, White feminism, and Indigenism by arguing that their approach to the question *What is to be thought?* and to its doppelgänger *What is to be done?* advances through misrecognition of the Slave, a sentient being that cannot *be*. The way Marxism, White feminism, and Indigenism approach the problem of the paradigm, in other words, their account of unethical power relations, emerges as a constituent element of those relations. Through their indisputably robust interventions, the world they seek to clarify and deconstruct is the world they ultimately mystify and renew.

Furthermore, I have argued that the same codes and conventions that reify the horticultural labor mobilized by Antonio Negri's restoration of the commons, by Indigenism's restoration of Turtle Island, and by White feminism's search for alternative or "negative" Oedipus (an Oedipus complex "which is culturally disavowed and organizes subjectivity in fundamentally 'perverse: and homosexual ways,'" in short, an Oedipus complex endowed with the capacity to be claimed for a revolutionary feminist agenda)[2] are codes and conventions shared by the narrative strategies of some of the most politically motivated films.

In the spirit of the metacommentaries on political ontology I have reviewed in this book, films like *Bush Mama* and *Skins* attempt to raise the bar of political aesthetics by deploying discursive strategies allied more to analysis than to empathy. As an antidote to empathetic mystification, politically motivated films such as *Bush Mama* and *Skins* subordinate biographical time to historical time—"the [dramatic] unfolding of events [staged as] the product of collective humanity." In their repudiation of the unified self and the self-made (or self-unmade) individual, such films interpellate spectators through codes and conventions properly suited to the dramatization of "sociohistorical heterogeneity."[3] Which is to say, they heighten social and political contradictions, rather than smooth them over or crowd them out.

In contrast, empathetic aesthetics, which films like *Antwone Fisher* and *Monster's Ball* are underwritten by, dissipate cinema's critical potential by hailing the spectator to an impoverished ensemble of questions, such as *Isn't it sad? Isn't it tragic? Why do some people behave badly and others don't?* These are moral assessments made at the expense of institutional analysis. Analytic film aesthetics, however, strive to repudiate moral assessments by privileging effect over cause,[4] thereby locating causal agency (the "because" principle of the drama) within institutional relations of power as opposed to interpersonal acts of behavior.

Throughout this book, I have rejected, a priori, Hollywood's embrace of the Aristotelian promise of empathy, while remaining skeptical of independent (analytically motivated) cinema's implicit and explicit political promise. This is because, disparate as these aesthetic orientations appear, their ontological suppositions assume relational capacity for all sentient beings. In other words, films underwritten by both of these aesthetic orientations are rarely narrated through the voice of someone for whom relationality is a condition of irrevocable rupture—whether filial and interpersonal, in the case of empathy, or affilial and institutional, in the case of analysis. The dispute between an empathetic aesthetic orientation and an analytic one is not over whether relationality itself is possible or impossible, but over the proper scale at which existing, though frayed, relations should be dramatized, and whether the drama should be set in biographical time or in historical time.

Historical time is the time of the worker, the time of the Indian, and the time of the woman—the time of analysis. But whereas historical time marks stasis and change *within* a paradigm, it does not mark the time *of* the paradigm, the time of time itself, the time by which the Slave's dramatic clock is set. For the Slave, historical time is no more viable a temporality of emancipation than biographical time—the time of empathy. Thus, neither the analytic aesthetic nor the empathetic aesthetic can accompany a theory of change that restores Black people to relationality. The social and political time of emancipation proclamations should not be confused with the ontological and epistemological time of modernity itself, in which Blackness and Slaveness are imbricated *ab initio*. Socially engaged cinema and politically inspired meditations on ontology are hobbled by their misrecognition of the former for the latter.

In films like *Antwone Fisher* and *Monster's Ball*, this displacement is often sentimentalized. In such films, an acknowledgment of structural violence as the condition of Black possibility is rendered visually. Here, that acknowledgment is a dreadful, omnipresent knowledge of the violence that separates ontological time (the time of the paradigm) from historical time (the time *in* the paradigm). In other words, it is knowledge of the violence that secures the essential stasis of Black "life" and in turn makes legible the essential capacity for transformation and mobility that characterizes Human life: in the images, editing, and camera work of even the most sentimental socially engaged films one finds confirmation of structural violence.

I have endeavored to illustrate the ways a film's narrative strategies tenaciously disavow this knowledge of the chasm between Human life and Black death, only to be disturbed and sometimes disrupted by equally tenacious cinematic strategies that insist on patrolling this divide. The narrative strategies labor like responsible citizens, razing social barriers of the "past" and democratizing the personal pronoun *we*. The cinematic strategies labor like watch commanders, sending the spectator out on patrol.

We are not living in the nineteenth century, when Humans were not ashamed to embrace their embodied capacity out in the open and, if need be, close their fists and forge their weapons to hold the line between the living and the dead themselves, rather than by proxy, the police. Given civil society's twentieth- and twenty-first-century libidinal investments in a presumed distance between its "democratic" present and its despotic past, civic "evolution" as an article of faith, film narratives are charged with the task of imposing an illusion of unity on repressed affirmations of relational logic that the images, editing, and camera work threaten to unleash.

Antwone Fisher begins the film as a genealogical isolate, someone who is known to and positioned by others as a thing with no relations. He ends the film at a feast, with those lost relations he dreamed of when the film began. We are asked to believe that his isolation from kinship, the effect of a violent extraction at the highest scale imaginable, has been overcome through inner fortitude catalyzed by three or four sessions of therapy, interventions at the lowest scale imaginable. Similarly, as Hank spoon-feeds Leticia chocolate ice cream, the narrative of *Monster's Ball* reminds us that love conquers all, and facilitates our forgetting of a violence that has always already conquered love.

In the face of an extensive corpus of sentimental apologies for structural violence, exemplified here by *Antwone Fisher* and *Monster's Ball*, films such as *Bush Mama* and *Skins* are oases of critical thinking. For in their effort to perform paradigmatic analyses, they attempt to reassert relational logic on the illusion of unity. But, as I have argued throughout this book, their efforts to reassert relational logic on the illusion of unity fail to reassert relational logic on relationality itself.

How does one deconstruct life? Who would benefit from such an undertaking? The coffle approaches with its answers in tow.

Introduction

1 Spillers, *Black, White and in Color*, 206.
2 For examples of pre-1980 Settler/Master films, see Wexler, *Medium Cool*; Cohen, *Bone*; Pakula, *Parallax View*; Ashby, *Coming Home*; and Bridges, *China Syndrome*. For examples of pre-1980 Slave films, see Burnett, *Killer of Sheep*; Robertson, *Melinda*; Campus, *Mack*; Dixon, *Spook Who Sat by the Door*; and Gerima, *Bush Mama*.
3 After the Watts Rebellion, Robert Kennedy observed: "There is no point in telling Negroes to observe the law. . . . It has almost always been used against them. . . . All these places—Harlem, Watts, South Side [of Chicago]—are riots waiting to happen." Quoted in Clark, "Wonder There Have Been So Few Riots."
4 "Slave estate" is a term borrowed from Spillers, *Black, White and in Color*.
5 See Benveniste, *Problems in General Linguistics*.
6 Fanon, *Black Skin, White Masks*, 110.
7 Charles S. Maier, *In Search of Stability*, 3–6.
8 Jared Sexton, from a handout he created for my Black Protest Tradition class, November 29, 2007. I am grateful to Sexton for his lectures, professional exchange, and correspondence, which helped me formulate this summary definition.
9 See the following chapters from Churchill, *Little Matter of Genocide*: "Genocide in the Americas: Landmarks from

North and South America, 1492–1992"; "'Nits Make Lice': The Extermination of North American Indians, 1607–1996"; and "Cold War Impacts on Native North America: The Political Economy of Radioactive Colonization."

10 Baldwin, "Black Boy Looks at the White Boy," 174, 175, 172.

11 Dorsey, "To 'Corroborate Our Claims,'" 354–59.

12 Baldwin, "Black Boy Looks at the White Boy," 172.

13 Dorsey, "To 'Corroborate Our Claims,'" 355.

14 Marx, *Capital*, 874, 1033; my emphasis.

15 Ibid., 1033.

16 Eltis, "Europeans and the Rise and Fall of African Slavery," 1404.

17 Ibid., 1407.

18 Orlando Patterson, *Slavery and Social Death*, 13; emphasis in original.

19 See "The Constituent Elements of Slavery" and "The Idiom of Power" in Orlando Patterson, *Slavery and Social Death*.

20 Hartman, *Scenes of Subjection*.

21 Eltis, "Europeans and the Rise and Fall of African Slavery," 1405, 1422.

22 Ibid., 1410.

23 Marx, *Capital*, 896–905.

24 Quoted in ibid., 897. Queen Elizabeth I (1572), King James I, and France's Louis XVI (1777) all passed ordinances similar to Edward VI's.

25 Spillers, *Black, White and in Color*, 210.

26 Orlando Patterson, 6.

27 Hartman, *Scenes of Subjection*, 22.

28 Paul Gilroy makes this argument in chapter 2 of *Black Atlantic*.

29 Benton, "The Superior Race and the Divine Command."

30 Eltis, "Europeans and the Rise and Fall of African Slavery," 1413, 1423.

31 Ibid., 1413.

32 Dorsey, "To 'Corroborate Our Claims,'" 359.

33 Ibid., 355.

34 Ibid., 354.

35 Ibid., 359. See also Bradley, "The *Boston Gazette* and Slavery as Revolutionary Propaganda," 591; and Bradley, *Slavery, Propaganda, and the American Revolution*, xxiv.

36 Eltis, "Europeans and the Rise and Fall of African Slavery," 1423.

37 Lee, *Jacques Lacan*, 33.

38 Dyer, *White*, 9, 11–12.

39 As I have argued, however, a non-Native, non-Black filmography could be substituted without corrupting the integrity of a paradigmatic analysis.

40 Sexton, "Consequences of Race Mixture"; Trask, *From a Native Daughter*.

41 See Cohen, *Housewife*; Wexler, *Medium Cool*; Hagmann, *Strawberry Statement*; and Kramer, *R.P.M.*

42   The 1530s mark, for Ronald Judy, *(Dis)Forming the American Canon*, the time
     of the Thomists, leading ecclesiastics of Salamanca; this decade saw the be-
     ginning of what I will describe below as ecclesiastic (or Settler) and Native
     American "conflictual harmony."

ONE The Ruse of Analogy

1   Agamben, *Remnants of Auschwitz*, 81, 82.
2   Fanon, *Black Skin, White Masks*, 115.
3   See Yancey, *Who Is White?*
4   Fanon, *Black Skin, White Masks*, 115–16.
5   Ibid., 116.
6   Gates and West, *Future of the Race*, 82.
7   Fanon, *Black Skin, White Masks*, 110.
8   Ibid.
9   It would be absurd to think of the academy as a safe haven where Black aca-
     demics' musings on structural antagonisms are routinely occasioned and al-
     lowed. Though the tactics the academy uses to marginalize and stigmatize
     such meditations as "seditious" are genteel when compared to those used
     against similar intellectual output in prisons, the operative word that charac-
     terizes this difference is *tactical*; and they are no less effective.
10   Jared Sexton, private conversation, November 22, 2007.
11   Judy, *(Dis)Forming the American Canon*, 88, 97.
12   Ibid., 89; my emphasis.
13   Ibid., 107.
14   Ibid., 19.
15   Judy, "On the Question of Nigga Authenticity," 225.
16   Judy, *(Dis)Forming the American Canon*, 19.
17   Ibid., 20, 20–21, 97.
18   Ibid., 19, 96, 88–89.
19   Hartman, *Scenes of Subjection*, 52.
20   Judy, *(Dis)Forming the American Canon*, 92.
21   Ibid., 97.
22   Fanon, *Black Skin, White Masks*, 139; my emphasis.
23   Judy, *(Dis)Forming the American Canon*, 97, 94.
24   The Subject does not exist there, at least, as a slave.
25   Dyer, *White*, 3.
26   Judy, *(Dis)Forming the American Canon*, 92, 93–94, 97.
27   Or that the warden is a swell woman, as in the case of many women's
     prisons.
28   Judy, *(Dis)Forming the American Canon*, 89, 84.

29 Spillers, *Black, White and in Color*, 206; Judy, *(Dis)Forming the American Canon*, 89.

30 Judy, *(Dis)Forming the American Canon*, 89.

31 "Ontology—once it is finally admitted as leaving existence by the wayside— does not permit us to understand the being of the black man. For not only must the black man be black; but he must be black in relation to the white man"; Fanon, *Black Skin, White Masks*, 110.

32 See Deloria, *God Is Red*, 217; and Deloria, *Metaphysics of Modern Existence*, ix–xiii, 14–18, 86–101, and 118–20.

33 Deloria, *God Is Red*, 75–89.

34 Judy, *(Dis)Forming the American Canon*, 80–81.

35 Ibid., 301, 81, 89.

36 Orlando Patterson, *Slavery and Social Death*, 10, 5.

37 Judy, *(Dis)Forming the American Canon*, 72–73; Deloria, *Documents of American Indian Diplomacy*; Deloria and Wilkins, *Tribes, Treaties, and Constitutional Tribulations*; Kidwell, "Choctaw Women and Cultural Persistence," 120–23, 125, 127; Deloria, *Metaphysics of Modern Existence*, ix–xiii, 14–18, 86–101, 118–20. This point I infer here simply from the fact that of all the metacommentators on "Savage" ontology, Ward Churchill is the only one who works persistently off of the modality of genocide. All of the others are obsessed with the ethical dilemmas of sovereignty. See Churchill, *Little Matter of Genocide*. I will return to this overriding proclivity for one modality and not the other in the way "Savage" positionality is imagined in my discussion of *Skins* in part 3.

38 Judy, *(Dis)Forming the American Canon*, 82–83.

39 Sassoon, *Approaches to Gramsci*, 13–14; Gramsci, *Selections from the Prison Notebooks*, 5–14, 178–90.

40 Judy, *(Dis)Forming the American Canon*, 82–83.

TWO The Narcissistic Slave

1 Lacan, *Ecrits*, 86; Marx, *Capital*, vol. 1, 203, 716.

2 Hartman, *Scenes of Subjection*.

3 Spillers, *Black, White and in Color*.

4 The other pillar is Gramscian Marxism.

5 Sexton, "Consequences of Race Mixture."

6 Fanon, *Black Skin, White Masks*, 109, 110.

7 Ibid., 110.

8 Fanon *Black Skin, White Masks*; Yancey, *Who Is White?*

9 Thanks to Saidiya Hartman, who suggested to me the moniker *Afro-pessimism*. The term has been used to describe the assumptive logic of international-relations journalists and scholars who view sub-Saharan Africa as a region too riddled with problems for good governance and economic development.

It gained currency in the 1980s, when many scholars and journalists in Western countries believed that there was no hope for bringing about democracy and achieving sustainable economic development in the region. My use of the word bears no resemblance to this definition.

10 Smith, *Representing Blackness*, 3.

11 Ibid. See also hooks, *Reel to Real*; Snead, *White Screen, Black Images*; and Diawara, *Black American Cinema*.

12 Bogle, *Toms, Coons, Mulattoes, Mammies, & Bucks*, 27.

13 Ibid., 42.

14 Snead, *White Screen, Black Images*, 1.

15 Yearwood, *Black Film as a Signifying Practice*, 5.

16 Ibid., 70.

17 Lott, "No-Theory Theory of Contemporary Black Cinema," 92.

18 Hartman, "Position of the Unthought," 187.

19 Judy, "On the Question of Nigga Authenticity," 212.

20 For an exposé of anti-Blackness as foundational to the libidinal economy of multiracial political formations, see Sexton, *Amalgamation Schemes*. For an analysis of anti-Blackness as manifest in the political and social economy of multicultural political formations, see Yancey, *Who Is White?*

21 Fanon, *The Wretched of the Earth*, 35–45.

22 Ibid.

23 For Spillers's notion of a Black embrace of absolute vulnerability, see *Black, White and in Color*, 229.

24 Spillers, *Black, White and in Color*, 206, emphasis in the original.

25 In Lacan, *Ecrits*.

26 Silverman, *World Spectators*, 65–66.

27 Ibid.

28 Ibid., 66.

29 Melanie Klein's emphasis on a normative progress of libidinal object choices ran counter to an emphasis on the analysand's speech, an emphasis which Lacan believed should guide the course of analysis. He took Klein to task for her promotion of a psychoanalytic cure which centralized the "interplay of reality and fantasy in the subject's choice of sexual objects," otherwise known as object relations theory. Secondly, new attention was being paid to the role of counter transference in the psychoanalytic encounter and thus to the importance, in training, of dealing with its typical manifestations (Lee, *Jacques Lacan*, 33–34). Through what Lacan considered to be a second theoretical "wrong turn" the ego (or imaginary) of the analyst ran the risk of becoming entangled with the ego (or imaginary) of the analysand, leading the psychoanalytic encounter through a perpetual hall of mirrors—empty or egoic reflections speaking to similarly empty, egoic, reflections, a process that could fortify and extend the interlocutory life of what Lacan called "empty speech." This is why, "Throughout the course of the analysis, on the sole condition that

the ego of the analyst does agree not to be there, on the sole condition that the analyst is not a living mirror, but an empty mirror, what happens happens between the ego of the subject . . . and the others" (Lacan, *Seminar*, 246). "The others" are what Lacan calls the analysand's "contemporaries" (Lacan, *Ecrits*, 47). For Lacan, the analytic encounter must bring analysands to a place where they are able to see what they are depositing at the place of the analyst. If the analyst's ego is present, if the analyst is not an empty mirror, then analysands will not come to understand where they are in relation to the analyst. The place of the analyst will not become what, for Lacan, it should become, the symbolic Other through which analysands can hear their own language. For this to happen, the analyst must become a "headless," or a*sephalic*, subject; a subject that mirrors nothing other than a void. In this way, and in this way only, will analysands come to understand themselves as a void papered over by language.

30 Lee, *Jacques Lacan*, 32–33.

31 Lacan, *Ecrits*, 36.

32 Ibid., 101.

33 Lacan, *Seminar*, 246.

34 Lee, *Jacques Lacan*, 33–34.

35 Lacan, *Ecrits*, 42, 106.

36 Ibid., 40.

37 Ibid., 42.

38 Ibid., 101.

39 Here I am thinking alienation as a grammar psychoanalytically, that is through the framework of libidinal economy. In the opening section of chapter 1, I think alienation through the framework of political economy.

40 Fanon, *Black Skin, White Masks*, 96, 100.

41 Fanon, *The Wretched of the Earth*, 36–37.

42 See Wacquant, "From Slavery to Mass Incarceration."

43 Silverman, *Male Subjectivity*, 63–65, 126–28; Lacan, *Ecrits*, 47. By "White or Human" I mean Whites and their junior partners in civil society.

44 Silverman, *World Specators*, 157.

45 Fanon, *Black Skin, White Masks*, 112.

46 For the notion of "species," see Fanon, *The Wretched of the Earth*; and Hartman, *Scenes of Subjection*. For absolute dereliction, see Fanon, *Black Skin, White Masks*, 33 and *The Wretched of the Earth*, 40, 41, 43, 93. For the hybrid of "person and property," see Hartman, *Scenes of Subjection*. See also Martinot and Sexton, "Avant-Garde of White Supremacy."

47 I am tweaking Fanon's notion of decolonization to meet the needs of the post-emancipation subject (the slave) as opposed to the post-colonial subject (the native). I think Fanon himself does this in *Black Skin, White Masks*. When he writes *The Wretched of the Earth*, I would argue that he is often times ventriloquizing on behalf of the post-colonial subject. His letters to his brother

seem to suggest how (if not why) he cannot be a "contemporary" of the Arab, even though they fight in the same guerrilla army against an enemy in common: France.

48 Hartman, *Scenes of Subjection*, 17–22.
49 Barrett, "The 'I' of the Beholder."
50 Fanon, *The Wretched of the Earth*, 39–40.
51 Fanon, *The Wretched of the Earth*; Martinot and Sexton, "Avant-garde of White Supremacy."
52 I thank Donovan Sherman for helping me clarify this; e-mail correspondence, March 13, 2008.
53 Fanon, *The Wretched of the Earth*, 38–39.
54 Martinot and Sexton, "Avant-garde of White Supremacy," 6; my emphasis.
55 Ibid., 8.
56 "Between the years 1882 and 1968, lynching claimed, on average, at least one life a week. Almost 5,000 black men were lynched. In addition, black women, Jews, White cattle rustlers and a few white women became its objects. The practice began long before the Civil War but peaked during the backlash to Reconstruction, particularly during the decade just prior to World War I. [According to Leon Litwack] . . . the violence inflicted . . . was often selective, aimed at educated and successful Blacks, those in positions of leadership, those determined to improve themselves, those who owned farms and stores, those suspected of having saved their earnings, those who had just made a crop—that is, black men and women perceived by whites as have stepped out of their place, *trying to be white*"; Williams, "Without Sanctuary," 6, 9. Lynchings ranged, geographically, from San Jose, California, to St. Paul, Minnesota, to Dixie.
57 Henry, "Police Control of the Slave," 28–29.
58 Martinot and Sexton, "Avant-garde of White Supremacy," 6.
59 Ibid., 6–7.
60 Ibid., 8.
61 Fanon, *The Wretched of the Earth*, 40.
62 Marriott, *On Black Men*, 16; Orlando Patterson, *Slavery and Social Death*; Fanon, *The Wretched of the Earth*.
63 Martinot and Sexton, "Avant-garde of White Supremacy," 7–9.
64 Ibid., 10.
65 Lacan, *Ecrits*, 101.
66 Fanon, *The Wretched of the Earth*, 41.
67 Donovan Sherman, e-mail correspondence, March 13, 2008.
68 In Lacan, *Ecrits*, 100–101.
69 Silverman, *Male Subjectivity*, 266, 275.
70 Ibid., 64; Fanon, *The Wretched of the Earth*, 44.
71 Fanon, *The Wretched of the Earth*, 40.
72 Silverman, *Acoustic Mirror*, 120.

73 Fanon, *The Wretched of the Earth*, 40–41.

74 Hartman, *Scenes of Subjection*, 19.

75 Ibid., 23–25.

76 Silverman, *Male Subjectivity at the Margins*, 266.

77 Hartman, *Scenes of Subjection*, 19.

78 Ibid.

79 Genovese, "Eugene Rivers's Challenge"; Hartman, *Scenes of Subjection*; Patterson, *Slavery and Social Death*.

80 Martinot and Sexton, "Avant-garde of White Supremacy."

81 Sherman, e-mail correspondence, March 13, 2008.

82 Hartman, 77 *Scenes of Subjection*.

THREE Fishing for Antwone

1 Mbembe, *On the Postcolony*, 183, 176, 173.

2 Hartman, *Scenes of Subjection*, 25.

3 As I implied in part 1, the revolutionary "good sense" of the Slave is going to have different rhetorical elements than the revolutionary "good sense" of the worker. The latter needs a "good sense" that throws exploitation and alienation into relief; the former needs a "good sense" that throws accumulation and fungibility into relief. In addition, "good sense" takes on different characteristics depending on whether it must explain structural violence that is gratuitous or contingent.

4 Kauffmann, "An American Informer."

5 Hartman, "Position of the Unthought," 185.

6 I thank Jared Sexton for this insight.

7 I thank Saidiya Hartman for her insight regarding *Antwone Fisher*'s juxtaposition of filial rejuvenation with a screen of Black women incapable of reproducing.

8 Hartman, "Position of the Unthought," 185.

9 Ibid.

10 Spillers, *Black, White and in Color*.

11 Ibid.

12 Hardy, "Antwone Fisher"; Fanon, *Black Skin, White Masks*, 112.

13 Jared Sexton, private conversation.

14 Spillers, *Black, White and in Color*, 206;

15 Fanon, *Black Skin, White Masks*, 146.

16 Hardy, "Antwone Fisher."

17 Wacquant, "From Slavery to Mass Incarceration."

18 Burrell, "Gang Evidence," 745.

19 California Penal Code 186.20–27.

20 Burrell, "Gang Evidence," 746–47.

21 Ibid., 775–76, 777.

22 Wacquant, "From Slavery to Mass Incarceration."

23 Gates and West, *Future of the Race*, 81.

24 Toni Morrison's *Beloved*; NWA's (in)famous rap song "Fuck the Police"; and Tom Feelings's harrowing collection of drawings, *Middle Passage* are just a few examples.

25 Judy, "On the Question of Nigga Authenticity," 225–26.

26 See Berlin, Favreau, and Miller, *Remembering Slavery*. In the introduction the editors have this to say about the world of Blacks at the turn of the eighteenth and nineteenth centuries, when they had grown to believe in the elasticity of accumulation and fungibility: "The movement of some million slaves from the seaboard to the Black Belt and the river bottoms of the interior deeply disrupted the civilization that black people had established in the aftermath of their forced exodus from Africa. During nearly two centuries of settlement along the seaboard, African and African-American slaves had created complex communities, linked by ties of kinship and friendship and resting on a foundation of shared values and beliefs. Those communities became increasing self-contained with the closing of the trans-Atlantic slave trade, which had ended in the Lower South by constitutional mandate in 1808 and a generation earlier in the Upper South. The westward movement of plantation culture—whether it was driven by individual owners who accompanied their slaves or by professional slave traders—tore that society asunder, exiling hundreds of thousands from their birthplace and traumatizing those who remained. Families and sometimes whole communities dissolved under the pressure of this Second Great Migration" (xxv). The essay goes on to say how more than 1 million slaves in their "reproductive" years were displaced in the first twenty years of the nineteenth century by this forced migration to new plantations. Between 1980 and 1999, the years of laws like STEP, another 1 million Blacks in their "reproductive" years were sent to the prison-industrial complex. This, I submit, is what has caused—however indirectly—a new generation of Afro-pessimists to reconsider the Black condition, structurally.

27 Hartman, "Position of the Unthought," 185.

28 Leo, "Chipping Away at Civil Liberties," 61.

29 California Penal Code 186.20–27 (West 1988 and Supp. 1990) (amended by ch. 1242, 1, 1988 stats.; amended by ch. 1256, 1, 1988 stat.), p. 474.

30 Internet Movie Data Base (IMDB), user comments on *Antwone Fisher*, December 30, 2002. http://www.imdb.com, accessed online December 20, 2003. Printout on file with the author.

31 "Commentary," *Antwone Fisher* DVD.

32 I went to see the film in a variety of neighborhoods.

33 Hardy, "Antwone Fisher."

34 Marriott, *On Black Men*, 6.

35 Fanon, *Black Skin, White Mask,* 49.

36 Political Film Society, "PFS Film Review: *Antwone Fisher.*" Accessed online April, 2004.

37 See IMDB user comments on *Antwone Fisher.*

FOUR Cinematic Unrest

1 *BAM/PFA Art & Film Notes,* March/April 2004.

2 Massood, *Black City Cinema,* 108–9.

3 Guerrero, *Framing Blackness,* 80.

4 Berry and Berry, *50 Most Influential Black Films,* 134.

5 Guerrero, *Framing Blackness,* 80.

6 Berry and Berry, *50 Most Influential Black Films,* 134.

7 Ivan Dixon, interviewed by S. Torriano Berry, June 7, 1998, in Berry and Berry, *50 Most Influential Black Films,* 137.

8 Guerrero, *Framing Blackness,* 71.

9 For more examples of the claims and assertions of this generally uncontested assumption, see David James, *Allegories of Cinema,* 177–99; Berry and Berry, *50 Most Influential Black Films,* 134; Masilela, "Los Angeles School," 107–9, 112; Massood, *Black City Cinema,* 97–98, 107–13; Guerrero, *Framing Blackness,* 69, 7, 76, 87–91; Taylor, "We Don't Need Another Hero," 81; Michener, "Black Movies," 235, 238–39; Hayward, *Cinema Studies,* 40–44; and Newton, "He Won't Bleed Me."

10 Masilela, "Los Angeles School," 107, 109.

11 Massood, *Black City Cinema,* 112–13.

12 Meyer Kantor, "This Spook Has No Respect for Human Life," *New York Times,* November 11, 1973; quoted in Berry and Berry, *50 Most Influential Black Films,* 135.

13 Berry and Berry, *50 Most Influential Black Films,* 140.

14 Marriott, *On Black Men.*

15 *Variety Reviews,* December 18, 1968.

16 Fanon, *The Wretched of the Earth,* 37, 39, 44; Fanon, *Black Skin, White Masks,* 96.

17 In the past five years, the scholarship of Achille Mbembe has recast the Angolan woman as a Slave. Because she stands as a Black (Slave) in relation to the world, prior to her standing as an Angolan (a postcolonial) in relation to the Settler (the Portuguese).

18 Fanon, *The Wretched of the Earth,* 37.

19 "Director's Commentary," DVD of *Medium Cool.*

20 Fanon, *Black Skin, White Masks.*

21 Quoted in Joy James, *Imprisoned Intellectuals,* 109.

22 Marks and Rudman, *David Gilbert.*

23 The preceding quotations from the Black Panther Party newspaper are collected in Heath, *Black Panther Leaders Speak*.

24 Marilyn Buck is a White political prisoner serving time in a federal prison
for her role in several alleged Black Liberation Army actions, including the
rescue of Assata Shakur from a maximum-security prison.

25 Quoted in Joy James, *Imprisoned Intellectuals*, 130.

26 Ibid.; emphasis in original.

27 Noam Chomsky talks about all these strategies, except affect, in the film
Manufacturing Consent.

28 Quoted in Joy James, *Imprisoned Intellectuals*, 132.

29 See the ex–New York policeman Robert Daley's controversial *Target Blue*, a
combination memoir, crime reporting, and right-wing political commentary
on New York Police Department investigations into the mafia and the Black
Liberation Army. A list of BLA actions compiled by the Justice Department
and reproduced from a Website sympathetic to the BLA, "The Talking Drum,"
accessed online December 19, 2003. Printout on file with the author.

30 For an extended exposition on Black feminism and a Black Liberation Army
soldier, see Shakur, *Assata*.

31 Spillers, *Black, White and in Color*, 80, 79; Fortunati, *The Arcane of Reproduction*, 8–9; emphasis in original.

32 Fanon, *Black Skin, White Masks*, 115.

33 Spillers, *Black, White and in Color*, 79, 80.

34 See Larry Cohen's *Housewife*, a.k.a. *Bone* (1972); Haskell Wexler's *Medium
Cool* (1969); Stuart Hagmann's *The Strawberry Statement* (1970); and Stanley
Kramer's *R.P.M.* (1970).

35 Fanon, *The Wretched of the Earth*, 36.

36 Hardt and Negri, *Empire*.

37 Jalil Muntaquim, in Joy James's *Imprisoned Intellectuals*, 109.

38 Fanon, *The Wretched of the Earth*, 58.

39 Marriott, *On Black Men*.

FIVE Absurd Mobility

1 This figure is cast in cop shows as the fat, balding chief of police, a first cousin
to the gangster.

2 Most demographers claim the number of indigenous people living in the
forty-eight contiguous states was between 12 and 19 million. By the end of
the nineteenth century the figure stood at 250,000. Today the population is
4,119,000.

3 Silverman, *Male Subjectivity at the Margins*, 63.

4 Whether Mogie Yellow Lodge or his brother Rudy is the main character is a
question central to my meditation on "Savage" ontology.

5 Eyre, "Director's Commentary," DVD of *Skins*.
6 Gardner, "Graham Greene."
7 Eyre, "Director's Commentary," DVD of *Skins*.
8 Compare Marriott, *On Black Men*, 19.

SIX The Ethics of Sovereignty

1 Trask, *From a Native Daughter*, 118.
2 Deloria, *God Is Red*, 222.
3 Deloria, *Metaphysics of Modern Existence*, xii.
4 Ibid., xii–xiii.
5 Ibid., vii.
6 Ibid., vii; Deloria, *God Is Red*, 249. Deloria is thinking specifically of people like Jung, as opposed to Freud, and of radical ecologists, as opposed to capitalist or, for that matter, Marxist industrialists.
7 See Silko, *Almanac of the Dead*; Churchill, *Marxism and Native Americans*; and Trask, *Notes from a Native Daughter*.
8 Trask, *Notes from a Native Daughter*, 1993; Silko, *Almanac of the Dead*, 760; Churchill, *Little Matter of Genocide*, 249.
9 Trask, *Notes from a Native Daughter*, 117. It is important to note that though the specificity of the political conflict between the United States and Hawaiians may bear greater similarities to those between White New Zealanders and that island's indigenous population, the structural relation is not altered by this.
10 Ibid., 117. Emphasis mine.
11 Alfred, *Peace, Power, Righteousness*, 60.
12 Trask, *Notes from a Native Daughter*, 117.
13 Ibid., 118.
14 Deloria, *God Is Red*, 249, 245, 255.
15 Ibid., 255, 260.
16 Ibid., 290.
17 White Shield, "Historical Trauma."
18 Deloria, *Metaphysics of Modern Existence*, 90–91, 118–20, 151–53, 205.
19 Ibid., 91, 118–20.
20 Deloria, *God Is Red*, 208.
21 Ibid., 222.
22 Ibid., 202, 204, 200–201, 198.
23 Ibid., 201.
24 Deloria, *Metaphysics of Modern Existence*, 151, 152.
25 Ibid., 152, 153.
26 Ibid., 153. Emphasis mine.
27 Trask, *Notes from a Native Daughter*, 132–33.
28 Alfred, *Peace, Power, Righteousness*, 60–61.
29 Churchill, *Marxism and Native Americans*, 185.

30 See Hardt and Negri, *Empire*. I will explore their dream of a restored "commons" in part 4, *Monster's Ball*.

31 Churchill, *Marxism and Native Americans*, 193.

32 Churchill, *Marxism and Native Americans*, 199–202. Foremost in the "body of anti-colonial theory" to which Churchill refers is Fanon's *The Wretched of the Earth*, a mainstay foundational to his own work and that of Haunani-Kay Trask.

33 This is also a foundation of Deloria's and Trask's arguments. See Deloria, *Metaphysics of Modern Existence*, 152; and Trask, *From a Native Daughter*, 116–21.

34 Miller and Rose, "On Therapeutic Authority," 31. Emphasis mine.

35 We began this exploration in parts 1 and 2 and will take it up again in our discussion of *Monster's Ball*.

36 Churchill, *Since Predator Came*, 6.

37 Deloria, *Metaphysics of Modern Existence*, 151.

38 Silko, *Almanac of the Dead*, 258.

39 Deloria, *Metaphysics of Modern Existence*, 151, quoting Jung, "Archaic Man," in *Civilization in Transition*, Collected Works, Vol. 10, 63.

40 Fanon, *The Wretched of the Earth*, 49, 44.

41 Alfred, *Peace, Power, Righteousness*, 56, 59.

42 Quoted in ibid., 65–66.

43 Quoted in ibid, 66.

44 Ibid., 66–69.

45 Churchill, *Little Matter of Genocide*, 312.

46 Hartman, *Scenes of Subjection*, 25.

47 It is important to bear in mind that whereas, in historical terms, the Settler and the Master may be different people, in ontological terms they are one and the same.

48 Slaves believed that, were they to get to Canada, oppression would be left behind them. Leonard Peltier fled to Canada, only to be extradited back to the United States. Malcolm X, in his speech "The Ballot or the Bullet," chastised Blacks to stop complaining about racist oppression in the South: "As long as you South of the Canadian border, you're South" (recording, Pacifica Radio Archives).

49 Quoted in Alfred, *Peace, Power, Righteousness*, 66.

SEVEN Excess Lack

1 Gardner, "Graham Greene."

2 Eyre, "Director's Commentary," on DVD of *Skins*.

3 Silverman, *Male Subjectivity at the Margins*, 86, 63, 64, 65, 53–65.

4 Eyre, "Director's Commentary," on DVD of *Skins*. In March 1997, Greene was hospitalized following a standoff with Toronto police that lasted for several

hours. One writer speculated that Greene was "armed and suicidal," while another wrote that "Greene was suicidal and according to the person who called the police, he had guns in his home, though no weapons were used during the encounter[,] which ended peacefully"; Killigaro, "Graham Greene Resume"; Brennan, article at www.allmovie.com. There seems to be a need to match the angst on screen with the angst in his real life; a need I would not object to were it not for the fact that none of these reporters attribute the angst to his status as an Indian in North America.

5   Gardner, "Graham Greene."

6   Eyre, "Director's Commentary," on DVD of *Skins*; Gardner, "Graham Greene."

7   Graham Greene was nominated for best supporting actor for his role as Kicking Bird in *Dances with Wolves*. He received a Screen Actors Guild Award for his work in *The Green Mile*.

8   Two Canadian films do allow Native actors to embrace the pathos of structural antagonism via drama: *Dance Me Outside*, and *Clearcut*. The U.S. film *Harold of Orange* also allowed for this embrace, but by way of comedy and satire rather than drama.

9   Churchill, *Little Matter of Genocide*.

10 Churchill, book tour speech, Berkeley, Calif., July 31, 2004.

EIGHT The Pleasures of Parity

1   The ontological and positional commonality between Whites, Latinos, and Asians does not, of course, rule out the plethora of conflicts that erupt between them.

2   I expand on this point in part 4, where I discuss Negri and Hardt's *Empire*, as well as Hardt's "Prison Time."

3   For these two positions, see, respectively, Silverman, *Male Subjectivity at the Margins*; and Hardt and Negri, *Empire*.

4   Compare Marriott, *On Black Men*, 19.

5   Between 1903 and 1995 roughly 20,000 Westerns were released in theaters or screened on television. Lentz's *Western and Frontier Film and Television Credits* contains 504 pages of film entries with an average of 20.1 entries per page, for an estimated total of 10,130.4 Western films. It contains 268 pages of television entries with an average of 36.4 entries per page, for an estimated 9,755 television Westerns. This adds up to 19,885.6 films and television programs all together. One must factor in the hundreds, perhaps thousands, of Westerns lost or destroyed; and factor in those Westerns released in the periods that Lentz does not cover: films released between 1894 and 1903, as well as those released between 1995 and 2004.

6   In John Ford's *Stagecoach*, a White child is born quite literally when its mother is trying to reach the clearing, a settled town, while being pursued across the desert by "Savages"—a word the film does not utter with scare quotes.

7 Simon, *Invention of the Western Film*, 6, 297n2.

8 Ibid., 6–7.

9 Quoted in Churchill, *Little Matter of Genocide*, 158.

10 Churchill, *Little Matter of Genocide*, 158.

11 Quoted in ibid.

12 Quoted in ibid., 244–25.

13 The fact that hegemony, rather than gratuitous violence, is essential to the idiom of power between the Asian and the White was established as far back as 1846, when Missouri Sen. Thomas Hart Benton, perhaps the most eloquent spokesman for Manifest Destiny, wrote, "The . . . Yellow race is there, four hundred million in number, spreading almost to Europe; a race once the foremost of the human family in the arts of civilization, but torpid and stationary for thousands of years. It is a race far above the . . . Black . . . and above the American Indian . . . but still far below the White. [Whites and Yellows] must talk together, and trade together, and marry together. Commerce is a great civilizer—social intercourse as great—and marriage greater"; *Congressional Globe*, May 28, 1846. Special thanks to Anita Wilkins for this citation.

14 Churchill, book tour speech, Berkeley, Calif., July 31, 2004.

15 Eltis, "Europeans and the Rise and Fall of African Slavery."

16 Judy, *(Dis)Forming the American Canon*, 81.

17 This and preceding quotations from Churchill's book tour speech, Berkeley, Calif., July 31, 2004.

18 When "Predator," as Churchill describes the Settler, arrived there were between 12.9 million and 19 million Native Americans in the 48 contiguous states.

19 Churchill, *Marxism and Native Americans*, 202.

20 Churchill, *On the Justice of Roosting Chickens*, 14.

21 Ibid., 14–15.

NINE "Savage" Negrophobia

1 My point throughout this book has been that there can be no such entity as Black culture. Culture emanates from a social formation of Human beings. As such they have the capacity to transform space into place and time into event, or chronology. Language and genealogical coherence are effects of the latter; homeland is an effect of the former. Such are the necessary currency for the "purchase" of culture. The Slave forfeits both forms of currency at the moment she or he is given social death (natal alienation) as a substitute for real death. This is not to say that many Blacks might "feel" as though Black culture exists, such is the bane of the assumptive logic of the Black film studies that I discussed in part 1. But they would be hard pressed to translate those cultural "feelings" into Culture, given the universality of the grammar of culture

that modernity reified in its relation to and dependence on, the African slave trade. "Style" is a far more fitting description.

2 Eyre, "Director's Commentary."

3 Scheckel, *Insistence of the Indian*, 129.

4 Ibid., 129–30.

5 Robinson, *Debt*, 3.

6 Ibid., 4–5.

7 Marriott, *On Black Men*, 19.

8 I would like to thank Jared Sexton for this insight on the fungibility of "nigger" under globalized hip-hop.

9 Fanon, *Black Skin, White Masks*, 115.

10 See Silko, *Almanac of the Dead*, 90–91, 309–26, 749.

11 Schweninger, "Writing Nature," 11.

12 Teale, "Silko Road from Chiapas," 165.

13 Silko, *Almanac of the Dead*, 404, 412–13.

14 Ibid., 413, 411–15, 427–28, 746, 742.

15 Ibid., 414–23, 741–46.

16 Ibid., 414–18.

17 Ibid., 742–47.

TEN A Crisis in the Commons

1 Barrett, *Blackness and Value*, 13, 12. Emphasis in original.

2 Ibid., 13.

3 Ibid.; my emphasis.

4 Dyer, *White*.

5 S/v = C is Marx's equation which describes the rate of surplus value, in which S = *surplus value* or profit derived of labor; v = *variable capital*, which translates into the labor power purchased by that capital; and C = *fixed capital*, or past, embodied labor and instruments of production. Marx offered this equation as a means of comprehending why capitalism is a paradigm that should be eradicated as opposed to a series of practices to be reformed. On its own, the equation tells us very little about relations of power between *types* of Humans (workers and bosses), but Marx demystified the equation's economic "innocence" by demonstrating the relationship between surplus value and the surplus part of the working day: "Since, on the one hand, the variable capital and the labour-power purchased by that capital (v) are equal in value, and the value of this labour-power determines the necessary part of the working day; and since, on the other hand, the surplus-value is determined by the surplus part of the working day, it follows that surplus-value is in the same ratio to variable capital as surplus labour is to necessary labour. In other words, the rate of surplus value, s/v = surplus labour/necessary labour. Both ratios, s/v and surplus labour/necessary labour, express the same thing in different

ways; in the one case in the form of objectified labour, in the other in the form of living, fluid labour" (Marx, *Capital*, Vo. 1, 326). The rate of surplus-value is therefore an exact expression for the degree of exploitation of labour-power by capital, or of the worker by the capitalist.

6 Gramsci believes that the socius is one entity, but he divides it into political society and civil society for methodological purposes—political society being the institutions of force: the police, the military, and prison.

7 Hardt, "Withering of Civil Society."

8 Silverman, *Acoustic Mirror*, 48–49, 51–54.

9 Wayne, *Theorising Video Practice*, 184.

10 Ibid., 184, 186.

11 "Anatomy of a Scene."

12 Hardt, "Withering of Civil Society," 80, 27.

13 See Silverman, *Male Subjectivity at the Margins*, 44–47.

14 Gramsci, *Selections from the Prison Notebooks*, 5–14, 388–90.

15 Hardt, "Withering of Civil Society," 40, 41.

16 That is, socially transformative optimism which often accrued to them prior to the anvil of a postindustrial world.

17 Examples of such films include Wexler, *Medium Cool*; Kramer, *R.P.M.*; Williams, *The Revolutionary*; Hagmann, *Strawberry Statement*; and Avildsen, *Joe*.

18 Negri and Hardt would agree with the postmodernists on this point.

19 Marriott, *On Black Men*, 34, 30, 40.

20 Doane, *Femmes Fatales*, 4.

21 Petro, *Aftershocks of the New*, 97, 148.

22 See Rodowick, *Crisis of Political Modernism*.

23 Spillers, *Black, White and in Color*.

24 Koehler, "Poetic Fragile 'Ball.'"

25 Barrett, *Blackness and Value*, 13.

26 Wayne, *Theorising Video Practice*, 97.

27 "Cast and Crew Interviews," on DVD of *Monster's Ball*.

28 Hartman, "Position of the Unthought," 191.

29 Silverman, *Subject of Semiotics*, 205.

30 "Anatomy of a Scene."

31 Fanon, *Black Skin, White Masks*, 177.

32 Dyer, *White*, 87, 88.

33 Hardt, "Prison Time," 66, 70.

34 Dyer, *White*, 87.

35 Fanon, *Black Skin, White Masks*, 177.

36 The United States never officially declared war on Vietnam or Iraq. In 1964 Congress passed the Gulf of Tonkin Resolution, which gave President Johnson the power to escalate war in Vietnam. Likewise, Congress passed the Iraq Resolution on October 10, 2002, which authorized President Bush to execute

an extended military engagement. Though war in Iraq was never formally declared, on March 19, 2003, Bush announced that the war in Iraq had begun.

37 Hardt, "Prison Time," 65–67.
38 Spillers, *Black, White and in Color*, 316.
39 Hardt, "Prison Time," 64.
40 Ibid., 78.
41 Hardt and Negri, *Empire*, 303.
42 Ibid., 61–62.
43 Ibid., 303, 61.
44 Hardt, "New Faces in Genoa."
45 Hardt, "Prison Time," 303, 72.
46 Hardt, "Prison Time," 73.
47 Genet, *Thief's Journal*, 10; quoted in Hardt, "Prison Time," 74.
48 Hardt, "Prison Time," 73–74.
49 Negri, *Macchina tempo*, 253; quoted in Hardt, "Prison Time," 78.
50 Marriott, *On Black Men*, 15.
51 Silverman, *Male Subjectivity at the Margins*, 264–70; Hardt and Negri, *Em-
    pire*, 61; Hardt, "Prison Time," 67; Forster in "Cast and Crew Interviews."
52 Silverman, *Male Subjectivity at the Margins*, 121.
53 Ibid., 126–27.
54 Hardt, "Prison Time," 73, 74.
55 Silverman, *Male Subjectivity at the Margins*, 121.
56 Hardt, "Prison Time," 64.
57 Judy, *(Dis)Forming the American Canon*.
58 Stephen Heath, *Questions of Cinema*.
59 Ibid., 36–37; my emphasis.
60 Fanon, *Black Skin, White Masks*, 177; Stephen Heath, *Questions of Cinema*, 37.
61 Sexton, email, November 27, 2007.
62 On the factory, see the early essays in Negri, *Revolution Retrieved*. On the
    socius at large, see essays in the same volume on the "social worker" as well as
    Negri, *Marx beyond Marx*.
63 See Negri, *Revolution Retrieved* and *Marx beyond Marx*.
64 Judy, *(Dis)Forming the American Canon*, 89. Emphasis mine.
65 Hardt, "Prison Time," 70.
66 Patterson, *Slavery and Social Death*, 5.
67 Hardt, "Prison Time," 70.
68 Ibid., 69, 70.

ELEVEN Half-White Healing

1 "Commentary by Forster, Addica, and Rokos," on DVD of *Monster's Ball*.
2 Composer Richard Werbowenko, in "*Anatomy of a Scene*."
3 Hardt, "Prison Time," 73–74.

4 Hardt and Negri, *Empire*, 303.

5 Dyer, *White*, 88.

6 Hardt and Negri, *Empire*, 61; Hardt, "Prison Time," 78.

7 For a quick and easy demonstration of this see John Ford's *Stagecoach* (1939). Here civil society is hermetically sealed within the tight, knee-knee confines of the stagecoach compartment, and atop, where the driver and the sheriff ride. As the film progresses we come to see the ethical dilemmas of civil society being rearticulated through the recomposition of its standard bearers: transcendence leaves the Southern lady and is embodied in the prostitute, leaves the banker to be embodied in the drunken Irish doctor, leaves the gentleman card shark to be re-embodied, jointly, in both the sheriff and the outlaw (John Wayne as the Ringo Kid). In this way, John Ford restages the drama of value surrounding the expansion of Whiteness as a category and access to the institutionality of civil society. A drama first staged during the Jacksonian period and continuously restaged with each historical episode of American migration and immigration (such as the time in which John Ford lived and worked). The dynamism and drama bode ill for any possibility of fixed ethicality within civil society; but what keeps this dynamic drama from becoming so expansive that it rends the very fabric of civil society's coherence qua civil society, what allows the internal chaos of shifting agents to be unthreatening to the structural coherence of the drama, is the fact that the stagecoach itself—in other words, the very possibility of this tumultuous drama—is always being threatened by "Savages"—the Apaches who "jumped the reservation" and now ride out to kill "innocent" Whites.

8 Spillers, *Black, White and in Color*, 315.

9 Judy, "On the Question of Nigga Authenticity," 222.

10 Spillers, *Black, White and in Color*, 315.

11 Ibid., 314.

12 Ibid.

13 Fanon, *Black Skin, White Masks*, 100.

14 Spillers, *Black, White and in Color*, 316, 302.

15 Stephen Heath, *Questions of Cinema*, 37.

16 See Fanon on absolute dereliction: *Black Skin, White Masks*, 33; *The Wretched of the Earth*, 40–41, 43, 93.

17 Spillers, *Black, White and in Color*, 27.

18 Ibid., 313.

19 Ibid., 315, 313, 505n18.

20 My *The Black Position: Civil Death in Civil Society* is a work in progress that will address this issue.

21 Spillers, *Black, White and in Color*, 316.

22 Clinton, *Harriet Tubman*, 8–10.

23 Spillers, *Black, White and in Color*, 308.

24 Ibid., 307.

25 Ibid., 305, 307–9.
26 Ibid., 307.
27 Ibid., 308.
28 Ibid., 313.
29 Ibid., 307, 308.
30 Ibid., 311.
31 Ibid., 309; quoting Faulkner, *Absalom, Absalom!*, 115.
32 Spillers, *Black, White and in Color*, 316.
33 Ibid., 315.
34 Whiteness as value-form is indeed essential to relations between White and Asian, White and Latino, and often White and Indigenous. But I am not talking about that. Postcolonial paradigms are often helpful analytic lenses for such conflicts, but they lose their explanatory power when cast on what Hortense Spillers calls "the slave estate."
35 Seshadri-Crooks, *Desiring Whiteness*, 135, 136, 136–37
36 Ibid., 136; quoting Butler, *Gender Trouble*, 33; my emphases.
37 Ibid., 136, 137, 136.
38 Hartman, "Position of the Unthought," 184, 190.
39 Hartman, *Scenes of Subjection*, 52.
40 Seshadri-Crooks, *Desiring Whiteness*, 136; quoting Butler, *Gender Trouble*, 33.
41 Hartman, *Scenes of Subjection*, 52.
42 Spillers, *Black, White and in Color*, 206.
43 Ibid., 214–15.
44 Seshadri-Crooks, *Desiring Whiteness*, 136, 137.
45 Orlando Patterson, *Slavery and Social Death*, 5.
46 Seshadri-Crooks, *Desiring Whiteness*, 133. Emphasis in original.

TWELVE Make Me Feel Good

1 Koehler, "Poetic, Fragile 'Ball'"; Guthman, "Hot and Heavy"; Meyer, "Beauty of a Role for Berry"; Graham, "Probing American Taboos."
2 Keeter, "*Monster's Ball*."
3 Koehler, "Poetic, Fragile 'Ball.'"
4 *Democracy Now!*, Pacifica Radio, March 26, 2002. Guests: Ruby Dee, Dr. Clara Rodriguez, Jack Shaheen, Anna Deveare Smith, Michelle Wallace, Richard Wesley, and Armond White.
5 Graham, "Probing American Taboos"; Atkinson, "Hate Worse than Death."
6 Fung, "*Monster's Ball*," 77.
7 Von Busack, "Hot Squat"; Rosenbaum, "All Is Forgiven." Kael, "Fantasies of the Art House Audience"; Durgnat, "How Not to Enjoy the Movies."
8 Hartman, *Scenes of Subjection*, 52.
9 A friend of mine, a middle-aged African American woman, saw *Monster's*

Ball during a matinee with single men dotting the seats all around. She told me she felt very uncomfortable, as though she were in a "porno" theater. Like Fanon's Black spectator in a French cinema where *Tarzan* is being screened, my friend waits for herself to appear and she appears in the sex scene and they, the men in the seats, appear with her. But does her discomfort (or terror!) suggest exploitation? Something more is at stake.

10 Hartman, "Position of the Unthought," 187.

11 Rosenbaum, "All Is Forgiven."

12 Marriott, *On Black Men*, 15, 9.

13 Barrett, *Blackness and Value*, 13; Spillers, *Black, White and in Color*, 153.

14 Not even in the cynical way in which the "Treaty" or reification of the idea of "Land" arbitrate dramas of value between the Settler and the "Savage." There are moments when genocide gives way to sovereignty and the Indian's humanity is once again in question. But the Slave's humanity is never in question.

15 "Behind the Scenes," on DVD of *Monster's Ball*.

16 "Cast and Crew Interviews," on DVD of *Monster's Ball*.

17 Quoted in Tyson, *Radio Free Dixie*, 19.

18 Spillers, *Black, White and in Color*, 229.

19 Ibid., 209; Judy, *(Dis)Forming the American Canon*, 97.

20 "Commentary by Forster, Addica, and Rokos."

21 Marriott, *On Black Men*, 4, 9.

22 Hartman, *Scenes of Subjection*, 4, 9.

23 Judy, *(Dis)Forming the American Canon*, 84–89, 94–97, 309.

24 Orlando Patterson, *Slavery and Social Death*, 5.

25 Meyer, "Beauty of a Role for Berry."

26 Ibid.

27 In 1976 Kissinger was displayed nude as a *Playgirl* centerfold. See Fanon on absolute dereliction: *Black Skin, White Masks*, 33; *The Wretched of the Earth*, 40–41, 43, 93.

28 Marriott, *On Black Men*, 13.

29 Ibid., 9.

30 Ibid.

31 Orlando Patterson, *Slavery and Scoial Death*, 5; Hartman, *Scenes of Subjection*, 52.

32 Marriott, *On Black Men*, 19.

33 Baldwin, *Going to Meet the Man*, 250–51; quoted in Marriott, *On Black Men*, 18.

34 Marriott, *On Black Men*, 19.

35 Heath, *Questions of Cinema*, 37, 36.

36 Marriott, *On Black Men*, 18.

37 Ibid., quoting Baldwin, *Going to the Meet the Man*, 251. Emphasis mine.

38 Judy, "On the Question of Nigga Authenticity."
39 Lacan, *Ecrits*, 46.
40 Judy, *(Dis)Forming the American Canon*, 97.

EPILOGUE

1 Fanon, *Black Skin, White Masks*, 96.
2 Silverman, *Acoustic Mirror*, 120.
3 Wayne, *Theorising Video Practice*, 164.
4 Ibid., 211.

Bibliography

Agamben, Giorgio. *Remnants of Auschwitz: The Witness and the Archive.* Trans. Daniel Heller-Roazen. New York: Zone, 1999.

Alfred, Taiaiake. *Peace, Power, Righteousness: An Indigenous Manifesto.* Don Mills, Ont.: Oxford University Press, 1999.

Angelou, Maya. *I Know Why the Caged Bird Sings.* New York: Bantam, 1971.

Atkinson, Michael. "A Hate Worse than Death: The Sorrow and the P. Diddy." *Village Voice,* January 1, 2002.

Baldwin, James. "The Black Boy Looks at the White Boy." *Nobody Knows My Name: More Notes of a Native Son.* New York: Dell, 1961.

———. *The Fire Next Time.* New York: Vintage, 1993 (1963).

———. *Going to Meet the Man.* London: Michael Joseph, 1965.

———. *Tell Me How Long the Train's Been Gone.* New York: Vintage, 1998 (1968).

BAM/PFA [Berkeley Art Museum and Pacific Film Archive]. *Art & Film Notes,* March/April 2004.

Barrett, Lindon. *Blackness and Value: Seeing Double.* Cambridge: Cambridge University Press, 1999.

———. "The 'I' of the Beholder: The Modern Subject and the African Diaspora." Paper presented at "Blackness in Global Contexts" conference, University of California, Davis, March 28–30, 2002.

Benton, Thomas Hart. "The Superior Race and the Divine Command." *Congressional Globe*, May 28, 1846.

Benveniste, Emile. *Problems in General Linguistics*. Trans. Mary Elizabeth Meek. Coral Gables, Fla.: University of Miami Press, 1971.

Berlin, Ira, Marc Favreau, and Steven F. Miller, eds. *Remembering Slavery: African Americans Talk about Their Personal Experiences of Slavery and Emancipation*. New York: New Press, 1998.

Berry, S. Torriano, and Venise T. Berry. *The 50 Most Influential Black Films: A Celebration of African-American Talent, Determination, and Creativity*. New York: Citadel, 2001.

Bogle, Donald. *Toms, Coons, Mulattoes, Mammies, & Bucks: An Interpretive History of Blacks in American Films*. New York: Continuum, 1989 (1973).

Bradley, Patricia. "The *Boston Gazette* and Slavery as Revolutionary Propaganda." *Journalism and Mass Communication Quarterly* 72 (autumn 1995): 581–96.

———. *Slavery, Propaganda, and the American Revolution*. Jackson: University Press of Mississippi, 1998.

Brennan, Sandra. Biographical article about Graham Greene at www.allmovie .com, accessed online March 30, 2003.

Burrell, Susan L. "Gang Evidence: Issues for Criminal Defense." *Santa Clara Law Review* 30.3 (1990): 739–83.

Butler, Judith. *Gender Trouble: Feminism and the Subversion of Identity*. New York: Routledge, 1990.

Churchill, Ward. *A Little Matter of Genocide*. San Francisco: City Lights, 1997.

———, ed. *Marxism and Native Americans*. Boston: South End, 1983.

———. *On the Justice of Roosting Chickens: Reflections on the Consequences of U.S. Imperialism, Arrogance, and Criminality*. Edinburgh: AK Press, 2003.

———. *Since Predator Came: Notes on the Struggle for American Indian Liberation*. Littleton, Colo.: Aigis, 1995.

Clark, Kenneth B. "The Wonder Is There Have Been So Few Riots." *New York Times Magazine*, September 5, 1965.

Clinton, Catherine. *Harriet Tubman: The Road to Freedom*. New York: Little, Brown, 2004.

Cripps, Thomas. *Black Film as Genre*. Bloomington: Indiana University Press, 1978.

Daley, Robert. *Target Blue: An Insider's View of the N.Y.P.D.* New York: Delacorte, 1973.

Deloria, Vine, Jr., comp. *Documents of American Indian Diplomacy: Treaties, Agreements, and Conventions, 1775–1979*. Norman: University of Oklahoma Press, 1999.

———. *God Is Red*. New York: Grosset and Dunlap, 1973.

———. *The Metaphysics of Modern Existence*. New York: Harper and Row, 1979.

————and David E. Wilkins. *Tribes, Treaties, and Constitutional Tribulations.* Austin: University of Texas Press, 1999.

Diawara, Manthia, ed. *Black American Cinema.* New York: Routledge, 1993.

Doane, Mary Ann. *Femmes Fatales: Feminism, Film Theory, Psychoanalysis.* New York: Routledge, 1991.

Dorsey, Peter A. "To 'Corroborate Our Claims': Public Positioning and the Slavery Metaphor in Revolutionary America." *American Quarterly* 55.3 (2003): 353–86.

Durgnat, Raymond. "How Not to Enjoy the Movies." In *Films and Feeling.* London: Faber, 1967.

Dyer, Richard. *White.* London: Routledge, 1997.

Eltis, David. "Europeans and the Rise and Fall of African Slavery in the Americas: An Interpretation." *American Historical Review* 98.5 (1993), 1399–1423.

Fanon, Frantz. *Black Skin, White Masks.* Trans. Charles Lam Markmann. New York: Grove, 1967.

————. *The Wretched of the Earth.* Trans. Constance Farrington. New York: Grove, 1963.

Faulkner, William. *Absalom, Absalom!* New York: Random House, 1936.

Feelings, Tom. *Middle Passage: White Ships, Black Cargo.* New York: Dial, 1995.

Fortunati, Leopoldina. *The Arcane of Reproduction: Housework, Prostitution, Labor and Capital.* Trans. Hillary Creek. Ed. Jim Fleming. Brooklyn, N.Y.: Autonomedia, 1995.

Fung, Alex. "*Monster's Ball*: Like Fathers, Like Sons." *Currency* 10 (2002), 77.

Gardner, Allen. "Graham Greene, the Spirit of *Skins*." Web page, accessed online March 28, 2003.

Gates, Henry Louis Jr., and Cornel West. *The Future of the Race.* New York: Alfred A. Knopf, 1996.

Genet, Jean. *The Thief's Journal.* Paris: Olympia, 1959.

Genovese, Eugene. "Eugene Rivers's Challenge: A Response," *Boston Review* (Oct/Nov 1993). Accessed online June 18, 2009. Printout on file with author.

Gilroy, Paul. *The Black Atlantic: Modernity and Double Consciousness.* Cambridge: Harvard University Press, 1993.

Graham, Bob. "Probing American Taboos: Swiss Director Takes on Race in 'Monster's Ball.'" *San Francisco Chronicle*, January 24, 2002.

Gramsci, Antonio. *Selections from the Prison Notebooks.* Ed. and trans. Quintin Hoare and Geoffrey Nowell Smith. New York: International, 1971.

Guerrero, Ed. *Framing Blackness: The African American Image in Film.* Philadelphia: Temple University Press, 1993.

Guthman, Edward. "Hot and Heavy." *San Francisco Chronicle*, January 25, 2002.

Hardt, Michael. "The New Faces in Genoa Want a Different Future." *New York Times*, July 25, 2001.

————. "Prison Time." In *Genet: In the Language of the Enemy.* Special issue, *Yale French Studies*, no. 91 (1997): 64–79.

———. "The Withering of Civil Society." *Social Text*, no. 45 (1995): 27–44.

———and Antonio Negri. *Empire.* Cambridge: Harvard University Press, 2000.

Hardy, Ernest. "Antwone Fisher." *L.A. Weekly*, December 20–26, 2002. Reprinted in *New York Times*, December 24, 2002.

Hartman, Saidiya V. "'The Position of the Unthought': An Interview with Saidiya V. Hartman." By Frank B. Wilderson III. *Qui Parle* 13.2 (2003), 183–201.

———. *Scenes of Subjection: Terror, Slavery, and Self-Making in Nineteenth-Century America.* New York: Oxford University Press, 1997.

Hayward, Susan. *Cinema Studies: The Key Concepts.* London: Routledge, 2000.

Heath, G. Louis, ed. *The Black Panther Leaders Speak: Huey P. Newton, Bobby Seale, Eldridge Cleaver and Company Speak Out through the Black Panther Party's Official Newspaper.* Metuchen, N.J.: Scarecrow, 1976.

Heath, Stephen. *Questions of Cinema.* London: Macmillan, 1981.

Henry, H. M. "The Police Control of the Slave in South Carolina." PhD diss., Vanderbilt University, 1914.

hooks, bell. *Reel to Real: Race, Sex, and Class at the Movies.* New York: Routledge, 1996.

James, David. *Allegories of Cinema: American Film in the Sixties.* Princeton, N.J.: Princeton University Press, 1988.

James, Joy, ed. *Imprisoned Intellectuals: America's Political Prisoners Write on Life, Liberation, and Rebellion.* Lanham, Md.: Rowman and Littlefield, 2003.

Judy, Ronald. *(Dis)Forming the American Canon: African-Arabic Slave Narratives and the Vernacular.* Minneapolis: University of Minnesota Press, 1993.

———. "On the Question of Nigga Authenticity." *boundary* 2 21.3 (1994): 211–30.

Kael, Pauline. "Fantasies of the Art House Audience." *I Lost It at the Movies.* Boston: Little, Brown, 1965.

Kauffmann, Stanley. "An American Informer: Stanley Kauffmann on Film." *New Republic*, December 21, 1968, 41–42.

Keeter, Nicole. "*Monster's Ball.*" *Time*, December 27, 2001–January 2, 2002.

Kidwell, Clara Sue. "Choctaw Women and Cultural Persistence in Mississippi." In *Negotiators of Change: Historical Perspectives on Native American Women*, edited by Nancy Shoemaker. New York: Routledge, 1995.

Killigaro, Wieland. "Graham Greene Resume." Accessed online March 11, 2003. Printout on file with author.

Koehler, Robert. "Poetic Fragile 'Ball.'" *Variety*, February 19–21, 2001.

Lacan, Jacques. *Ecrits: A Selection.* Trans. Alan Sheridan. New York: W. W. Norton, 1977.

———. *The Seminar of Jacques Lacan.* Book 2, *The Ego in Freud's Theory and in the Technique of Psychoanalysis, 1954–1955*, edited by Jacques-Alain Miller. Trans. Sylvana Tomaselli. New York: W. W. Norton, 1991.

Lee, Jonathan Scott. *Jacques Lacan.* Amherst: University of Massachusetts Press, 1990.

Lentz, Harris M., III. *Western and Frontier Film and Television Credits, 1903–1995*, Vol. 2. Jefferson, N.C.: McFarland, 1996.

Leo, John. "Chipping Away at Civil Liberties." *U.S. News and World Report*, June 26, 1989, 61.

Lott, Tommy. "A No-Theory Theory of Contemporary Black Cinema." In *Representing Blackness: Issues in Film and Video*, edited by Valerie Smith. New Brunswick, N.J.: Rutgers University Press, 1997.

Maier, Charles S. *In Search of Stability: Explorations in Historical Political Economy*. Cambridge: Cambridge University Press, 1987.

Marriott, David. *On Black Men*. New York: Columbia University Press, 2000.

Martinot, Steve, and Jared Sexton. "The Avant-Garde of White Supremacy." *Social Identities* 9.2 (2003): 169–81.

Marx, Karl. *Capital*. Vol. 1. Trans. Ben Fowkes. London: Penguin, 1976.

Masilela, Ntongela. "The Los Angeles School of Black Filmmakers." In *Black American Cinema*. Ed. Manthia Diawara. New York: Routledge, 1993.

Massood, Paula J. *Black City Cinema: African American Urban Experiences in Film*. Philadelphia: Temple University Press, 2003.

Mbembe, Achille. *On the Postcolony*. Berkeley: University of California Press, 2001.

Meyer, Carla. "A Beauty of a Role for Berry." *San Francisco Chronicle*, January 20, 2002.

Michener, Charles. "Black Movies." In *Black Films and Film-Makers: A Comprehensive Anthology from Stereotype to Superhero*. Ed. Lindsay Paterson. New York: Dodd, Mead, 1975.

Miller, Peter, and Nikolas Rose. "On Therapeutic Authority: Psychoanalytical Expertise under Advanced Liberalism." *History of Sciences* 7.3 (1994): 29–64.

Morrison, Toni. *Beloved*. New York: Random House, 1987.

Muntaquim, Jalil. "On the Black Liberation Army." In *Imprisoned Intellectuals: America's Political Prisoners Write on Life, Liberation, and Rebellion*. Ed. Joy James. Lanham, Md.: Rowman & Littlefield, 2003.

Negri, Antonio. *Macchina tempo*. Milan: Feltrinelli, 1982.

———. *Marx beyond Marx: Lessons on the Grundrisse*. Brooklyn, N.Y.: Autonomedia, 1991.

———. *Revolution Retrieved: Selected Writings on Marx, Keynes, Capitalist Crisis and New Social Subjects, 1967–1983*. Introductory notes by John Merrington. London: Red Notes, 1983.

Newton, Huey P. "He Won't Bleed Me: A Revolutionary Analysis of 'Sweet Sweetback's Baadasssss Song.'" *Black Panther*, June 19, 1971.

Noble, Peter. *The Negro in Films* London: Skelton Robinson, 1948.

NWA. "Fuck the Police." On *Straight outta Compton!* (Priority Records, 1988).

Patterson, Orlando. *Slavery and Social Death: A Comparative Study*. Cambridge: Harvard University Press, 1982.

Petro, Patrice. *Aftershocks of the New: Feminism and Film History.* New Brunswick, N.J.: Rutgers University Press, 2002.

Robinson, Randall. *The Debt: What America Owes to Blacks.* New York: Plume, 2000.

Rodowick, D. N. *The Crisis of Political Modernism: Criticism and Ideology in Contemporary Film Theory.* Berkeley: University of California Press, 1988.

Rosenbaum, Jonathan. "All Is Forgiven." *Chicago Reader,* February 22, 2002.

Sassoon, Anne Showstack. *Approaches to Gramsci.* London: Writers and Readers, 1982.

Scheckel, Susan. *The Insistence of the Indian: Race and Nationalism in Nineteenth-Century American Culture.* Princeton, N.J.: Princeton University Press, 1998.

Schweninger, Lee. "Writing Nature: Silko and Native Americans as Nature Writers." *MELUS* 18.2 (1993): 47–60.

Seshadri-Crooks, Kalpana. *Desiring Whiteness: A Lacanian Analysis of Race.* London: Routledge, 2000.

Sexton, Jared. *Amalgamation Schemes.* Minneapolis: University of Minnesota Press, 2008.

———. "The Consequences of Race Mixture: Racialised Barriers and the Politics of Desire." *Social Identities* 9.2 (2003): 241–75.

———. E-mail correspondence. November 27, 2007.

Shakur, Assata. *Assata: An Autobiography.* Chicago: Lawrence Hill, 1987.

Sherman, Donovan. E-mail correspondence. March 13, 2008.

Silko, Leslie. *Almanac of the Dead.* New York: Simon and Schuster, 1991.

Silverman, Kaja. *The Acoustic Mirror: The Female Voice in Psychoanalysis and Cinema.* Bloomington: Indiana University Press, 1988.

———. *Male Subjectivity at the Margins.* New York: Routledge, 1992.

———. *The Subject of Semiotics.* New York: Oxford University Press, 1983.

———. *World Spectators.* Palo Alto, Calif.: Stanford University Press, 2000.

Simon, Scott. *The Invention of the Western Film: A Cultural History of the Genre's First Half-Century.* Cambridge: Cambridge University Press, 2003.

Smith, Valerie, ed. *Representing Blackness: Issues in Film and Video.* New Brunswick, N.J.: Rutgers University Press, 1997.

Snead, James. *White Screen, Black Images: Hollywood from the Dark Side.* New York: Routledge, 1994.

Spillers, Hortense. *Black, White and in Color: Essays on American Literature and Culture.* Chicago: University of Chicago Press, 2003.

Spivak, Gayatri. *In Other Worlds: Essays in Cultural Politics.* New York: Methuen, 1987.

Taylor, Clyde. "We Don't Need Another Hero: Anti-theses on Aesthetics." In *Black Frames: Critical Perspectives on Black Independent Cinema,* edited by Mbye B. Cham and Claire Andrade-Watkins. Cambridge: MIT Press, 1988.

Teale, Tamara M. "The Silko Road from Chiapas, or Why Native Americans Cannot Be Marxists." *MELUS* 23.4 (1998): 157–66.

Trask, Haunani-Kay. *From a Native Daughter: Colonialism and Sovereignty in Hawai'i*. Monroe, Maine: Common Courage, 1993.

Tyson, Timothy B. *Radio Free Dixie: Robert F. Williams and the Roots of Black Power*. Chapel Hill: University of North Carolina Press, 1999.

von Busack, Richard. "The Hot Squat: Billy Bob Thornton Romances Halle Berry in the Deep South of *Monster's Ball*." *Oakland Urban View*, January 30, 2002.

Wacquant, Loïc. "From Slavery to Mass Incarceration: Rethinking the 'Race Question' in the US." *New Left Review*, no. 13 (2002): 41–60.

Wayne, Mike. *Theorising Video Practice*. London: Lawrence and Wishart, 1997.

White Shield, Rosemary. "Historical Trauma." *The Circle: Native American News and Arts*, January 2001.

Williams, Patricia J. "Without Sanctuary." *Nation*, February 14, 2000.

Yancey, George. *Who Is White? Latinos, Asians, and the New Black/Nonblack Divide*. Boulder, Colo.: Lynne Rienner, 2003.

Yearwood, Gladstone L. *Black Film as a Signifying Practice: Cinema, Narration and the African-American Aesthetic Tradition*. Trenton, N.J.: Africa World, 2000.

Filmography

Achbar, Mark, and Peter Wintonick, dirs. *Manufacturing Consent: Noam Chomsky and the Media*. 1992.

Alexie, Sherman, dir. *The Business of Fancydancing*. 2002. Starring Evan Adams, Michelle St. John, and Gene Tagaban.

"Anatomy of a Scene." Sundance Channel presentation on DVD version of *Monster's Ball*, directed by Marc Forster. Starring Halle Berry and Billy Bob Thornton. Lion's Gate, 2002.

Apted, Michael, dir. *Incident at Oglala*. 1992. Documentary starring Leonard Peltier and John Trudell. Narrated by Robert Redford.

Arthur, Robert Alan, dir. *The Lost Man*. 1969. Starring Sidney Poitier, Joanna Shimkus, Al Freeman Jr., and Michael Tolan.

Ashby, Hal, dir. *Coming Home*. 1978. Starring Jane Fonda, Jon Voight, and Bruce Dern.

Avildsen, John B., dir. *Joe*. 1970. Starring Peter Boyle, Dennis Patrick, Audrey Caire, and Susan Sarandon.

Beatty, Warren, dir. *Bullworth*. 1999. Starring Halle Berry and Warren Beatty.

"Behind the Scenes with Producer Lee Daniels." On DVD version of *Monster's Ball*, directed by Marc Forster. Starring Halle Berry and Billy Bob Thornton. Lion's Gate, 2002.

Bratt, Peter, dir. *Follow Me Home*. 1996. Starring Alfie Woodward, Jesse Borrego, and Benjamin Bratt.

Bridges, James, dir. *The China Syndrome*. 1979. Starring Jane Fonda, Jack Lemmon, and Michael Douglas.

Bugajski, Ryszard, dir. *Clearcut*. 1991. Starring Graham Greene, Floyd "Red Crow" Westerman, Ron Lea, and Michael Hogan.

Burnett, Charles, dir. *The Horse*. 1973. Starring Gordon Houston, Maury Wright, and Gary Morrin.

———. *Killer of Sheep*. 1972. Starring Henry G. Sanders, Kaycee Moore, Charles Bracy, and Angela Burnett.

Campus, Michael, dir. *The Mack*. 1973. Starring Max Julien, Don Gordon, Richard Pryor, and Carol Speed.

"Cast and Crew Interviews." On DVD version of *Monster's Ball*, directed by Marc Forster. Starring Halle Berry and Billy Bob Thornton. Lion's Gate, 2002.

Cohen, Larry, dir. *Housewife*, a.k.a. *Bone*. 1972. Starring Yaphet Kotto.

"Commentary by Director Denzel Washington and Producer Todd Black." 2002. On DVD version of *Antwone Fisher*, directed by Denzel Washington. Starring Denzel Washington, Derek Luke, and Salli Richardson.

"Commentary by Marc Forster and Academy Award–Nominated Writers Milo Addica and Will Rokos." On DVD version of *Monster's Ball*, directed by Marc Forster. Starring Halle Berry and Billy Bob Thornton. 2002.

Costner, Kevin, dir. *Dances with Wolves*. 1990. Starring Kevin Costner, Graham Greene, Mary McDonnell, Floyd "Red Crow" Westerman, and Tantoo Cardinal.

Darabont, Frank, dir. *The Green Mile*. 1999. Starring Tom Hanks, David Morse, Graham Greene, and Bonnie Hunt.

Dash, Julie, dir. *Daughters of the Dust*. 1991. Starring Cora Lee Day, Barbara-O (Jones), Cheryl Lynn Bruce, and Tommy Hicks.

Dassin, Jules, dir. *Up Tight!* 1968. Starring Raymond St. Jacques, Ruby Dee, Frank Silvera, Roscoe Lee Brown, and Max Julien.

"Director's Commentary." On DVD version of *Medium Cool*. 1969. Directed by Haskell Wexler. Starring Christine Bergstrom, Harold Blankenship, and Verna Bloom.

Dixon, Ivan, dir. *The Spook Who Sat by the Door*. 1973. Starring Lawrence Cook.

Ellington, Duke, dir. *Black and Tan*. 1929. Starring Duke Ellington.

Eyre, Chris. "Director's Commentary." On DVD version of *Skins*, directed by Chris Eyre, 2002. Starring Graham Greene, Eric Schweig, Gary Farmer, Noah Watts, Michelle Thrush, Lois Red Elk, and Tina Keeper.

———, dir. *Skins*. 2002. Starring Graham Greene, Eric Schweig, Gary Farmer, Noah Watts, Michelle Thrush, Lois Red Elk, and Tina Keeper.

———. *Smoke Signals*. 1998. Starring Adam Beach, Evan Adams, Irene Bedard, Gary Farmer, Tantoo Cardinal, and John Trudell.

Fanaka, Jamaa, dir. *Soul Vengeance*, a.k.a. *Welcome Home, Brother Charles*. 1975. Starring Marlo Monte, Reatha Grey, Stan Kamber, and Tiffany Peters.

Ford, John, dir. *Stagecoach*. 1939. Starring Claire Trevor, John Wayne, Andy Devine, John Carradine, and Louise Platt.

Forster, Marc, dir. *Monster's Ball*. 2001. Starring Halle Berry and Billy Bob Thornton.

Fugua, Antoine, dir. *Training Day*. 2001. Starring Denzel Washington.

Gerima, Haile, dir. *Bush Mama*. 1977. Starring Barbara O. Jones.

Gilliam, Terry, dir. *Fear and Loathing in Las Vegas*. 1998. Starring Johnny Depp, Ellen Barkin, and Benicio Del Toro.

Hagmann, Stuart, dir. *The Strawberry Statement*. 1970. Starring Bruce Davison, Kim Darby, Bud Cort, and Murray MacLeod.

Hill, Jack, dir. *Coffy*. 1973. Starring Pam Grier.

Hughes, Allen, and Albert Hughes, dirs. *Menace II Society*. 1993. Starring Tyrin Turner, Larenz Tate, Jada Pinkett Smith, and Samuel Jackson.

Jewison, Norman, dir. *In the Heat of the Night*. 1967. Starring Sidney Poitier and Rod Steiger. Internet Movie Data Base. "User Comments." Accessed online April 11, 2004.

Kramer, Stanley, dir. *Guess Who's Coming to Dinner?* 1967. Starring Sidney Poitier, Katherine Hepburn, Spencer Tracy, and Katherine Houghton.

———. *Home of the Brave*. 1949. Starring Jeff Corey, James Edwards, and Lloyd Bridges.

———. *R.P.M.* [Revolutions per Minute]. 1970. Starring Anthony Quinn, Ann Margret, Gary Lockwood, and Paul Winfield.

Marks, Claude, and Lisa Rudman, eds. *David Gilbert: A Lifetime of Struggle*. 2002. Filmed interview, 29 mins. Based on interview, July 1998, Great Meadows Prison, Comstock, N.Y., with Sam Green and Bill Siegel. Camera: Federico Salsano.

McDonald, Bruce, dir. *Dance Me Outside*. 1995. Starring Ryan Rajendra Black, Jennifer Podemski, Adam Beach, and Michael Greyeyes.

Pakula, Alan J., dir. *The Parallax View*. 1974. Starring Warren Beatty, Paula Prentiss, and William Daniels.

Parks, Gordon, dir. *The Learning Tree*. 1968. Starring Kyle Johnson, Alex Clarke, and Estelle Evans.

Phillips, Lou Diamond, dir. *Sioux City*. 1994. Starring Lou Diamond Phillips, Salli Richardson, Gary Farmer, and Tantoo Cardinal.

Pontecorvo, Gillo, dir. *Battle of Algiers*. 1966. Starring Brahim Haggiag, Jean Martin, Yacef Saadi, and Samia Kerbash.

Resnais, Alain, dir. *Hiroshima, Mon Amour*. 1959. Starring Emmanuelle Riva and Eiji Okada.

Robertson, Hugh, dir. *Melinda*. 1972. Starring Calvin Lockhart, Rosalind Cash, and Vonetta McGee.

Sayles, John, dir. *Lone Star*. 1996. Starring Stephen Mendillo, Stephen J. Lang, Chris Cooper, and Elizabeth Peña.

———. *Passion Fish*. 1992. Starring Mary McDonnell and Alfre Woodard.

Schulz, Michael, dir. *Cooley High*. 1975. Starring Glynn Thurman, Garrett Morris, and Lawrence Hilton-Jacobs.

Scott, Ridley, dir. *Thelma and Louise*. 1991. Starring Susan Sarandon, Geena Davis, Harvey Keitel, and Brad Pitt.

Shah, Krishna, dir. *The River Niger*. 1976. Starring Cicely Tyson, James Earl Jones, Glynn Thurman, and Louis Gossett Jr.

Sirk, Douglas, dir. *Imitation of Life*. 1959. Starring Lana Turner, John Gavin, and Juanita Moore.

Stevenson, Robert, dir. *Mary Poppins*. 1964. Starring Dick Van Dyke.

Van Peebles, Mario, dir. *New Jack City*. 1991. Starring Wesley Snipes, Ice-T, and Allen Payne.

———. *Sweet Sweetback's Baadasssss Song*. 1971. Starring Melvin Van Peebles and Brer Soul.

Van Sant, Gus, dir. *Good Will Hunting*. 1997. Starring Matt Damon, Robin Williams, and Ben Affleck.

Washington, Denzel, dir. *Antwone Fisher*. 2002. Starring Denzel Washington, Derek Luke, and Salli Richardson.

Weise, Richard, dir. *Harold of Orange*. 1984. Starring Charlie Hill.

Wexler, Haskell, dir. *Medium Cool*. 1969. Starring Christine Bergstrom, Harold Blankenship, and Verna Bloom.

Williams, Paul, dir. The Revolutionary. 1970. Starring Jon Voight, Seymour Cassel, and Robert Duvall.

X, Malcolm. "The Ballot or the Bullet." Speech delivered February 4, 1964. Detroit. Audiocassette: Pacifica Archives.

Zinnemann, Fred, dir. *High Noon*. 1952. Starring Gary Cooper, Katy Jurado, Grace Kelly, Thomas Mitchell, and Lloyd Bridges.

FRANK B. WILDERSON III is an associate professor of
African American studies and drama at the University
of California, Irvine. He is the author of *Incognegro: A
Memoir of Exile and Apartheid* (2008), winner of the
American Book Award.

Library of Congress Cataloging-in-Publication Data

Wilderson, Frank B.
Red, white & black : cinema and the structure of
U.S. antagonisms / Frank B. Wilderson III.
p. cm.
Includes bibliographical references and index.
ISBN 978-0-8223-4692-0 (cloth : alk. paper)
ISBN 978-0-8223-4701-9 (pbk. : alk. paper)
1. Minorities in motion pictures.
2. Race in motion pictures.
3. African Americans in motion pictures.
4. Indians in motion pictures.
5. Motion pictures—United States—History.
I. Title. II. Title: Red, white and black.
PN1995.9.M56W55 2010
791.43'6529—dc22   2009043380